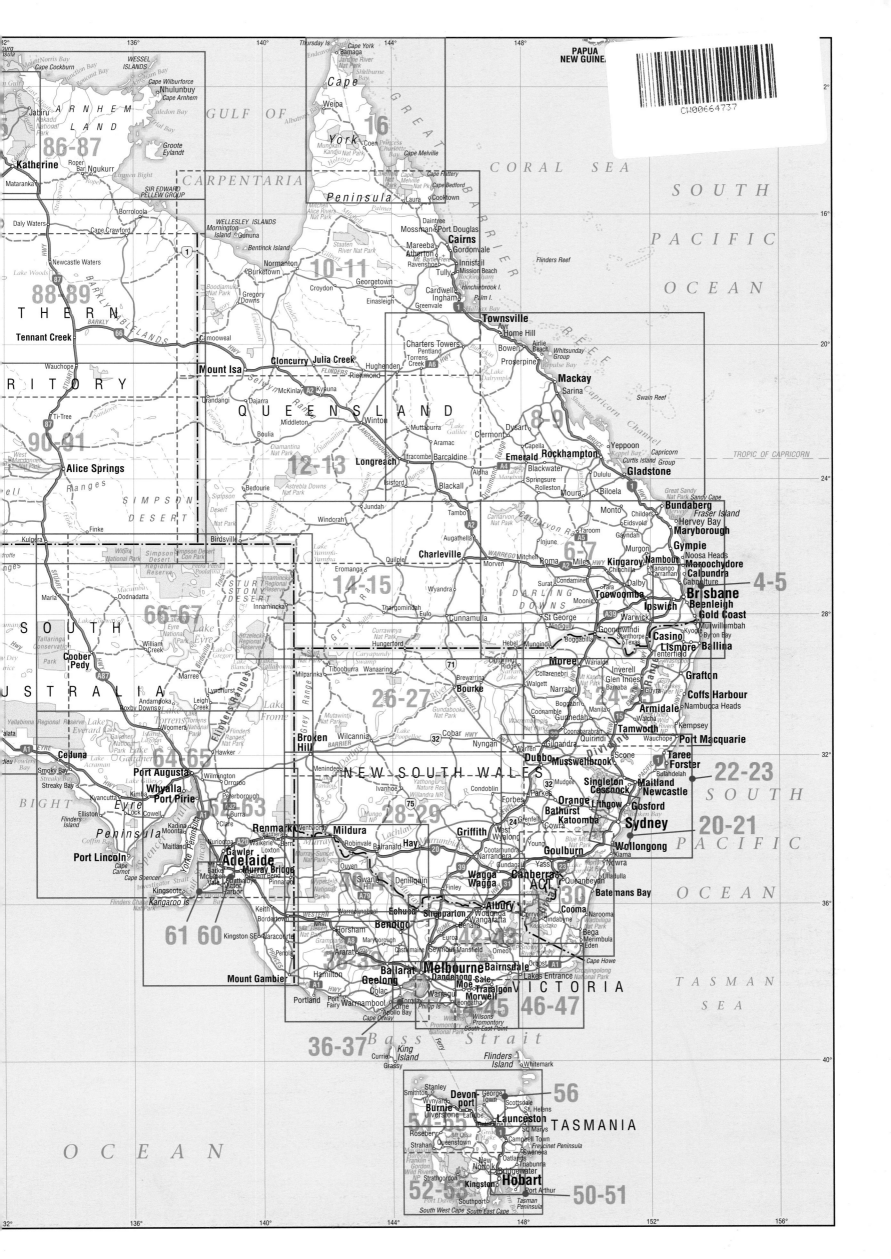

Contents

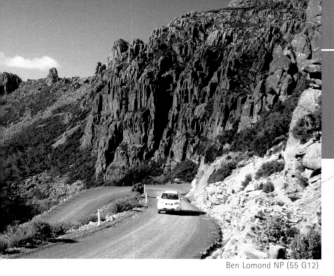

Ben Lomond NP (55 G12)

Legend

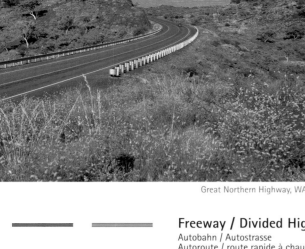

Great Northern Highway, WA

Freeway / Divided Highway – sealed
Autobahn / Autostrasse
Autoroute / route rapide à chaussées séparées
Autostrada / superstrada

Freeway – future
Autobahn – im Bau
Autoroute – en construction
Autostrada - in costruzione

Major Highway – sealed / unsealed
Durchgangsstrasse – befestigt / unbefestigt
Route principale – revêtue / non revêtue
Strada di grande comunicazione – pavimentata / non pavimentata

Metroad
Metroad

Main Road – sealed / unsealed
Hauptstrasse – befestigt / unbefestigt
Route de communication – revêtue / non revêtue
Strada principale – pavimentata / non pavimentata

Minor Road – sealed / unsealed
Sonstige Strasse – befestigt / unbefestigt
Autre route revêtue / non revêtue
Altra strada – pavimentata / non pavimentata

Track, four-wheel drive only
Piste, nur mit 4-Rad-Antrieb befahrbar
Piste, utilisable pour véhicule à 4 roues motrices
Pista, praticabile solo con trazione integrale

Walking Track / Trail
Fussweg / Pfad
Sentier
Sentiero / viottolo

Total Kilometres
Totaldistanz in km
Distance totale en km
Distanza totale in km

Intermediate Kilometres
Teildistanz
Distance partielle
Distanza parziale

**National Route Number /
National Highway Number**
Nationale Strassennummer / Nationale
Durchgangsstrassen-Nummer
Numéro de route nationale / de route rapide
Numero della strada nazionale / Numero della strada di grande comunicazione

State Route Number
Staats-Strassennummer
Numéro de route d'Etat
Nùmero della strada dello stato

Tourist Route
Touristenstrasse
Route touristique
Strada turistica

Railway – in use / disused
Eisenbahn – in Betrieb / stillgelegt
Chemin de fer – en service / abandonné
Ferrovia – in esercizio / interrotto

Lake or Reservoir
See oder Reservoir
Lac ou réservoir
Lago o lago artificiale

Intermittent or Salt Lake
Periodischer oder Salzwassersee
Lac périodique ou d'eau salée
Lago periodico o salato

National Park / Reserve
Nationalpark / Reservat
Parc national / réserve
Parco nazionale / riserva

Regional Reserve
Regionalreservat
Réserve régionale
Riserva regionale

Conservation / Protected Area
Schutzgebiet
Zone protégée
Regione protetta

Aboriginal Land
Aborigines-Gebiet
Région d'aborigènes
Regione d'aborigeni

Gawler ● City / Major Town
Gross-oder wichtige Stadt
Ville importante
Città grande o importante

Skipton ● Town / Community / Locality
Stadt oder Gemeinde
Ville ou commune
Città o comunità

'Plumbago' ■ Homestead
Gehöft
Ferme
Masseria

Lookout ● Tourist Point of Interest
Touristische Sehenswürdigkeit
Curiosité touristique
Curiosità turistica

+ Mt Brown Mountain / Hill
Berg / Hügel
Montagne / colline
Monte / colle

Camping Area (with facilities)
Camping (mit Einrichtungen)
Camping (avec équipement)
Campeggio (con equipaggiamento)

Rest Area (toilet/water tank in remote areas)
...and with overnight camping
Rastplatz (Toilette/Wassertank in der Nähe)
...und Camping (nur 1 Nacht)
Aire de repos (Toilettes/citerne d'eau à proximité)
...et camping (seulement 1 nuit)
Area di riposo (Gabinetto/serbatoio d'acqua a prossimità)
...e campeggio (solo 1 notte)

Outback Rest Area (no facilities)
Rastplatz (Outback; ohne Einrichtungen)
Aire de repos (Outback; sans équipement)
Area di riposo (Outback; senza equipaggiamento)

Picnic Area (city maps only)
Picknick-Platz (Stadtpläne)
Place pique-nique (Plans de villes)
Picnic (Piante di città)

Outback Fuel (diesel and unleaded available)
Tankstelle (Outback; Diesel und bleifreies Benzin erhältlich)
Station-service (Outback; diesel et carburant sans plomb disponible)
Stazione di servizio (Outback; diesel e benzina senza piombo disponibile)

Airport
Flughafen
Aéroport
Aeroporto

State Border
Staatsgrenze
Frontière d'Etat
Confine dello stato

National Parks

Legend:
- ⛺ Camping Area
- 🏕 Bush Camping
- ⛱ Picnic Area
- 🔥 Fireplace/Barbecue
- 🚻 Toilets
- 🚿 Showers
- 🚰 Drinking Water
- 🚶 Walking Trail
- 🧍 Ranger Station
- 🚙 Four Wheel Drive Advisable
- 🚐 Caravan Access

Bungle Bungle Range, Purnululu NP (81 G13)

Queensland

Info Ph (07) 3227 8185
www.env.qld.gov.au/parks_and_forests

Facility key: C = Camping Area, BC = Bush Camping, P = Picnic Area, F = Fireplace/Barbecue, T = Toilets, S = Showers, DW = Drinking Water, W = Walking Trail, R = Ranger Station, 4WD = Four Wheel Drive Advisable, CA = Caravan Access

Park	Ref	Notes	C	BC	P	F	T	S	DW	W	R	4WD	CA
Alton	6 H6												
Astrebla Downs	12 G5	No public access											
Auburn River	7 C9		●		●	●	●			●			●
Barnard Island Group*	11 E13			●	●								
Barron Gorge	11 D12		●		●	●	●	●		●	●		
Bendidee	7 H8												
Black Mountain	11 B12												
Blackbraes	11 H10											●	
Blackdown Tableland	9 H8		●		●	●	●			●			
Blackwood	8 D5												
Bladensburg	13 D9		●	●	●		●				●	●	●
Blue Lake	5 A8									●			
Boodjamulla	10 G2		●		●	●	●	●		●	●	●	●
Bowling Green Bay	8 A6		●	●	●	●	●	●		●	●		●
Brampton Islands	9 C8				●	●	●			●			
Bribie Island	4 E3		●	●	●	●	●			●	●	●	
Broad Sound Island	9 E9			●									
Brook Islands*	11 F13	No access											
Bulleringa	11 E10	No access											
Bunya Mountains	7 E10		●		●	●	●	●		●	●		
Burleigh Head	5 B13				●	●				●	●		
Burrum Coast	7 A12		●	●	●		●	●	●	●		●	
Byfield	9 G10											●	
Camooweal Caves	10 J1		●		●		●					●	●
Cania Gorge	9 K11				●	●	●		●	●			
Cape Hillsborough	9 C8		●		●	●	●			●			●
Cape Melville	16 H5			●								●	
Cape Palmerston	9 E9		●	●	●		●					●	
Cape Upstart	8 A6	Boat access only		●									
Capricorn Coast	9 G11				●	●	●	●		●			
Capricornia Cays	9 H13		●	●			●			●			
Carnarvon	6 A4		●	●	●	●	●	●	●	●	●	●	●
Castle Tower	9 J11	No access											
Cedar Bay	11 B12	Walk-in/boat access only		●						●			
Chesterton Range	6 D2	No access											
Chillagoe-Mungana Caves	11 D11												
Claremont Isles	16 G4			●									
Cliff Island*	16 H4												
Clump Mountain*	11 E13									●			
Coalstoun Lakes*	7 C11									●		●	
Conondale	4 J1												
Conway	9 C8		●		●	●	●		●	●	●		
Crater Lakes*	11 D12				●	●	●			●			
Crows Nest	7 F11		●		●	●	●	●		●			●
Cudmore	8 G4	No access											
Culgoa Floodplain	6 K1			●							●	●	
Currawinya	15 J10		●		●	●	●	●			●	●	●
Curtis Island	9 H11												
D'Aguilar	4 G6			●	●	●	●		●	●			
Daintree	11 C12		●		●		●	●	●	●	●		
Dalrymple	11 J13			●								●	
Davies Creek	11 D12		●				●			●			
Deepwater	9 J12		●	●	●		●	●					
Denham Group	16 C3												
Diamantina	12 F6		●		●	●	●				●	●	●
Dipperu	8 E7	Scientific – permit access only											
Dryander	8 B7	Boat access only	●				●						
Dularcha	4 F2											●	
Edmund Kennedy	11 F13				●		●			●			
Ella Bay	11 E13											●	
Endeavour River	11 A12												
Epping Forest	8 F4	Scientific – permit access only											
Erringibba	6 F7												
Eubenangee Swamp	11 E13				●					●			
Eudlo Creek	4 F1	No access											
Eungella	8 C7		●	●	●	●	●			●	●		
Eurimbula	9 J12		●	●	●		●			●		●	
Expedition	6 B5		●	●	●	●	●			●			
Fairlies Knob*	7 B11												
Family Islands	11 F13		●	●	●	●	●		●	●			
Ferntree Creek*	7 E13												
Finucane Island	10 E4												
Fitzroy Island	11 D13												
Flinders Group	16 H5		●		●		●			●			
Forbes Islands*	16 E4												
Forest Den	13 C12											●	
Fort Lytton	4 D7				●		●		●		●		
Forty Mile Scrub	11 F11				●		●			●			
Frankland Group*	11 D13		●	●	●		●			●			
Freshwater	4 F5												
Girraween	7 K11		●	●	●	●	●	●	●	●	●		●
Girringun	11 F13		●	●	●	●	●		●	●		●	
Glasshouse Mountains	4 F3				●	●	●			●			
Gloucester Island	8 B7		●	●			●						
Goneaway	13 F8	No access											
Goodedulla	9 G9											●	
Goodnight Scrub	7 B11				●								
Goold Island	11 F13		●		●	●	●			●			
Great Basalt Wall	11 J12	No access											
Great Sandy (Cooloola)	7 D13		●	●	●	●	●		●	●	●	●	
Great Sandy (Fraser)	7 B13		●	●	●	●	●	●	●	●	●	●	●
Green Island	11 D13				●		●			●			
Grey Peaks	11 D13	No access											
Halifax Bay Wetlands*	11 G13												
Hann Tableland	11 D12	No access											
Hasties Swamp*	11 E13						●						
Hell Hole Gorge	15 B10	No access											
Hinchinbrook Island	11 F13		●	●	●	●	●			●			
Holbourne Islands*	8 B7												

Queensland continued

Name	Map Ref	Notes
Homevale	8 D7	
Hope Islands*	11 B12	
Howick Group	16 H6	
Hull River*	11 F13	
Idalia	13 H11	
Iron Range	16 E3	
Isla Gorge	6 B7	
Japoon*	11 E13	
Jardine River	16 C2	
Junee	9 G8	
Keppel Bay Islands	9 G11	
Kinrara	11 F12	
Kondalilla	4 G1	
Kroombit Tops	9 J11	
Kurrimine Beach	11 E13	
Lake Bindegolly	15 H10	
Lakefield	16 J5	
Lamington	5 D14	
Lindeman Islands	9 C8	
Littabella	9 K12	
Lizard Island	16 J7	
Lochern	13 F9	
Magnetic Island	11 G14	
Main Range	5 K13	
Mapleton Falls*	7 E12	
Maria Creek*	11 E13	
Mariala	15 C11	Walk-in access only
Mazeppa	8 F5	
Michaelmas & Upolu Cays	11 C13	
Millstream Falls	11 E12	
Minerva Hills	8 J6	
Mitchell – Alice Rivers	16 K2	
Molle Islands*	9 B8	
Moogerah Peaks	5 J13	
Mooloolah River	4 E1	
Moorrinya	8 D2	
Moresby Range*	11 E13	
Moreton Island	4 B5	
Mount Aberdeen	8 B6	No access
Mount Archer	9 H10	
Mount Barney	7 J12	
Mount Bauple	7 C12	Scientific – permit access only
Mount Chinghee*	7 J12	
Mount Colosseum	9 J12	
Mount Cook	16 K6	
Mount Coolum*	7 E13	
Mount Etna Caves	9 G10	
Mount Hypipamee	11 E12	
Mount Jim Crow*	9 G10	
Mount Martin *	9 D8	
Mount O'Connell	9 G10	No access
Mount Ossa*	9 D8	
Mount Pinbarren*	7 D12	No access
Mount Walsh	7 C11	
Mount Webb	16 J6	
Mowbray*	11 C12	
Mungkan Kandju	16 G3	
Nairana	8 D5	No access
Narrien Range	8 G5	No access
Newry Islands	9 C8	
Nicoll Scrub	5 B14	No access
Noosa	7 D13	

Name	Map Ref	Notes
North East Island	9 E10	
Northumberland Islands	9 D9	
Nuga Nuga	6 A5	
Orpheus Island	11 G14	
Palmerston Rocks*	11 E13	
Palmgrove	6 A6	Scientific – permit access only
Paluma Range	11 G13	Walk-in access only
Peak Range	8 F6	
Percy Isles	9 E10	
Pioneer Peaks*	9 D8	
Pipeclay*	7 D13	
Piper Islands*	16 E3	
Poona	7 C12	
Porcupine Gorge	11 K11	
Possession Island	16 B2	
Precipice	6 B7	No access
Quoin Island*	16 E4	
Ravensbourne*	7 G11	
Reliance Creek*	9 D8	
Repulse Island*	9 C8	
Restoration Island*	16 E4	
Rundle Range	9 H11	
Russell River	11 D13	
Sandbanks*	16 G4	
Sarabah*	5 D13	No access
Saunders Islands*	16 D3	
Simpson Desert	12 J2	
Sir Charles Hardy Group*	16 D4	
Smith Islands	9 C8	
Snake Range	8 J6	No access
South Cumberland Islands	9 C9	
South Island	9 E10	
Southern Moreton Bay Islands	5 B11	
Southwood	6 G7	
Springbrook	5 C14	
St Helena Island	4 C7	
Staaten River	11 C8	
Starcke	16 J6	
Sundown	7 K10	
Swain Reefs	9 E13	
Tamborine	5 D11	
Tarong*	7 E10	
Taunton	9 H8	Scientific – permit access only
The Palms*	7 F11	
Three Islands*	16 J7	
Thrushton	6 G3	
Topaz Road*	11 E13	
Tregole	6 D2	
Triunia*	4 F1	
Tully Gorge	11 E13	
Turtle Group	16 J6	
Undara Volcanic (Undara Lodge)	11 F11	
Venman Bushland	3 J7	
Welford	13 H9	
West Hill	9 E9	
White Mountains	11 K12	
Whitsunday Islands	9 B8	
Wild Cattle Island*	9 J11	No access
Wondul Range	7 H9	
Wooroonooran	11 D13	
Yungaburra*	11 D11	

The National Park is not shown on the map

New South Wales

Info Ph 1300 361 967
www.npws.nsw.gov.au

Park	Ref		Notes
Abercrombie River	22 J6		
Arakwal	25 B14		
Bago Bluff	23 A13		
Bald Rock	25 C10		
Bangadilly	22 K7		
Barakee	23 A11		
Barool	25 E11		
Barrington Tops	23 C10		
Basket Swamp	25 C11		
Bellinger River	25 G12		
Ben Boyd	31 K11		
Ben Halls Gap	23 A9		No access
Benambra	29 K13		
Biamanga	31 H11		
Bimberamala	30 E6		
Bindarri	25 G12		
Biriwal Bulga	23 A12		
Blue Mountains	21 H9		
Bongil Bongil	25 G13		
Booderee (Comm. Terr.)	30 D7		
Boonoo Boonoo	25 B11		
Booti Booti	23 C13		
Border Ranges	25 A12		
Botany Bay	21 B10		
Bouddi	20 B5		
Bournda	30 J5		
Brindabella	30 D2		
Brisbane Water	20 C5		
Broadwater	25 C14		
Budawang	30 E5		
Budderoo	30 B7		
Bugong	30 C6		
Bundjalung	25 D13		
Bungawalbin	25 C13		
Butterleaf	25 D10		
Capoompeta	25 D10		
Carrai	25 H10		
Cascade	25 G12		
Cataract	25 B11		
Cathedral Rock	25 G10		
Cattai	20 F6		
Chaelundi	25 F11		
Clyde River	30 E5		
Cocoparra	29 F11		
Conimbla	22 H3		
Conjola	30 D7		
Coolah Tops	22 B7		
Coorabakh	23 B12		
Cotton-Bimbang	23 A12		
Crowdy Bay	23 B13		
Culgoa	27 C12		
Cunnawarra	25 H10		
Deua	30 F5		
Dharug	20 E4		
Dooragan	23 B13		
Dorrigo	25 G12		
Dunggir	25 H11		
Eurobodalla	30 F6		
Fortis Creek	25 D12		
Gardens of Stone	22 F7		
Garigal	19 C5		
Georges River	19 H2		
Ghin-Doo-Ee	23 C11		
Gibraltar Range	25 E11		
Goobang	22 E3		
Goonengerry	25 B14		
Goulburn River	22 C7		
Gourock	30 F4		
Gulaga	30 G5		
Gundabooka	27 F10		
Guy Fawkes River	25 F11		
Hat Head	25 J12		
Heathcote	21 D11		No vehicle access
Jerrawangala	30 C6		
Jervis Bay	30 C7		
Junuy Juluum	25 G11		
Kanangra-Boyd	22 H6		
Kinchega	26 K3		
Kings Plains	25 E9		
Kooraban	30 G5		
Koreelah	25 A11		
Kosciuszko	30 G1		
Kumbatine	25 J11		
Ku-ring-gai Chase	20 C6		
Kwiambal	25 C8		
Lane Cove	21 C8		
Livingstone	29 H13		
Macquarie Pass	30 B7		
Mallanganee	25 C12		
Mallee Cliffs	28 F4		No access
Maria	25 J12		
Marramarra	20 D5		
Maryland	25 A10		
Mebbin	25 A13		
Meroo	30 E6		
Middle Brother	23 B13		
Mimosa Rocks	30 H5		
Minjary	29 H14		
Monga	30 E5		
Mooball	25 A14		
Morton	30 C6		
Mount Clunie	25 A11		
Mount Imlay	30 K4		
Mount Jerusalem	25 B14		
Mount Kaputar	24 F6		
Mount Nothofagus	25 A12		
Mount Pikapene	25 C12		
Mount Royal	23 C10		
Mount Warning	25 A13		
Mummel Gulf	23 A11		
Mungo	28 E5		
Murramarang	30 E6		
Mutawintji	26 H4		
Myall Lakes	23 D12		
Nangar	22 F3		
Nattai	21 H13		
New England	25 G11		
Nightcap	25 B13		
Nowendoc	23 A10		
Nymboi-Binderay	25 F12		
Nymboida	25 E11		
Oolambeyan	29 G9		

New South Wales continued

Park	Ref
Oxley Wild Rivers	25 H10
Paroo-Darling	26 F6
Popran	20 D4
Ramornie	25 E12
Richmond Range	25 B12
Royal	21 C11
Saltwater	23 C13
Scheyville	20 F6
Seven Mile Beach	30 C7
Single	25 F9 No access
South East Forest	30 J4
Sturt	26 C1
Sydney Harbour	21 B8
Tallaganda	30 F4
Tapin Tops	23 B12
Tarlo River	30 B5
Thirlmere Lakes	21 G13
Timbarra	25 C11
Tomaree	23 E11
Tooloom	25 A11
Toonumbar	25 B12
Towarri	23 B8
Turon	22 F6
Ulidarra	25 G13
Wadbilliga	31 G10
Wallarah	23 F10
Wallingat	23 C12
Warra	25 F10
Warrabah	24 G7
Warrumbungle	24 J3
Washpool	25 D11
Watagans	23 E9
Weddin Mountains	22 H2
Werakata	23 E10
Werrikimbe	25 J10
Willandra	29 C8
Willi Willi	25 J11
Woko	23 B11
Wollemi	20 K4
Wollumbin	25 A13
Woomargama	29 K13
Wyrrabalong	20 A2
Yabbra	25 B11
Yanununbeyan	30 E4
Yarriabini	25 H12
Yengo	20 G1
Yuraygir	25 E13

Victoria
Info Ph 13 19 63
www.parkweb.vic.gov.au

Park	Ref
Alfred	47 C12
Alpine	43 E11
Baw Baw	44 B7
Brisbane Ranges	36 D2
Burrowa Pine Mountain	43 B12
Chiltern - Mt Pilot	43 B8
Churchill	37 E9
Coopracambra	47 B12
Croajingolong	47 D12
Dandenong Ranges	37 D10
Errinundra	47 B10
French Island	37 J10

Park	Ref
Grampians	38 C6
Greater Bendigo	39 A12
Hattah-Kulkyne	40 C5
Heathcote-Graytown	39 B13
Kinglake	37 A10
Lake Eildon	42 G5
Lind	47 C10
Little Desert	38 A3
Lower Glenelg	38 G3
Mitchell River	45 A12
Mornington Peninsula	36 K7
Morwell	45 F8
Mount Buffalo	43 E8
Mount Eccles	38 G4
Mount Richmond	38 H3
Murray – Sunset	40 D3
Organ Pipes	36 B6
Otway	39 K10
Port Campbell	39 J8
Snowy River	43 G14
St Arnaud Range	39 B9
Tarra Bulga	45 F8
Terrick Terrick	41 J11
The Lakes	45 D13
Wilsons Promontory	44 J7
Wyperfeld	40 G4
Yarra Ranges	37 B12

Tasmania
Info Ph 1300 135 513
www.parks.tas.gov.au

Park	Ref
Ben Lomond	55 G12
Cradle Mt - Lake St Clair	54 H5
Douglas-Apsley	55 H13
Franklin-Gordon	52 D5
Freycinet	55 K14
Hartz Mountains	53 H8
Kent Group*	
Maria Island	53 E13
Mole Creek Karst	54 G7
Mt Field	53 E8
Mt William	55 D14
Narawntapu	55 D8
Rocky Cape	54 C4
Savage River	54 E4
South Bruny	53 J10
Southwest	52 H6
Strzelecki	55 C9
Tasman	51 J13
Walls of Jerusalem	54 H6 (Walk-in access only)

*The National Park is not shown on the map

South Australia
Info Ph (08) 8204 1910
www.environment.sa.gov.au/parks

Park	Ref
Belair	60 H3
Canunda	63 C13
Coffin Bay	64 H5
Coorong	63 E9
Flinders Chase	63 K9
Flinders Ranges	65 B10
Gawler Ranges	64 D5
Great Australian Bight Marine	68 K3
Innes	62 J7

X

(South Australia continued)

Park	Ref
Lake Eyre	67 F8
Lake Gairdner	64 B6
Lake Torrens	65 A9
Lincoln	64 J6
Mount Remarkable	62 G2
Murray River	62 B6
Naracoorte Caves	38 C1
Nullarbor	68 J2
Onkaparinga River	61 D6
Vulkathuna-Gammon Ranges	67 K11
Witjira	66 B5

Western Australia
Info Ph (08) 9334 0333
www.calm.wa.gov.au/national_parks/

Park	Ref
Alexander Morrison	76 H4
Avon Valley	72 E2
Badgingarra	76 H4
Beedelup	73 F14
Boorabbin	75 B10
Brockman	74 J3
Cape Arid	83 J2
Cape Le Grand	75 G14
Cape Range	78 F1
Collier Range	82 K5
D'Entrecasteaux	74 J3
Drovers Cave	76 H3
Drysdale River	81 C11 (No vehicle access)
Eucla	83 G7
Fitzgerald River	75 H9
Francois Peron	76 B2
Frank Hann	75 E10
Geikie Gorge	81 H9
Gloucester	73 F14
Goldfields-Woodland	75 B11
Goongarrie	77 G11
Gooseberry Hill	72 F3
Greenmount	72 F3
Hassell	74 J7
John Forrest	72 F3
Kalamunda	72 F3
Kalbarri	76 D2
Karijini (Hamersley Range)	82 F4
Kennedy Range	78 H2
Leeuwin-Naturaliste	73 K12
Lesmurdie	72 F3
Lesueur	76 H3
Millstream-Chichester	82 D2
Mirima (Hidden Valley)	81 D14
Mitchell River	81 C9
Moore River	74 B2
Mount Augustus	82 J2
Mount Frankland	74 J5
Nambung	74 A1
Neerabup	72 G2
Peak Charles	75 E12
Porongurup	74 J6
Purnululu	81 G13
Rudall River	79 F9
Scott	73 J13
Serpentine	72 F5
Shannon	74 J4
Stirling Range	74 H6

Park	Ref
Stockyard Gully	76 H3
Stokes	75 G11
Tathra	76 G4
Torndirrup	74 K7
Tuart Forest	73 H10
Tunnel Creek	81 G8
Walpole-Nornalup	74 K4
Walyunga	72 F2
Warren	73 F14
Watheroo	76 H4
Waychinicup	74 J7
Wellington	73 F10
West Cape Howe	74 K6
William Bay	74 K5
Windjana Gorge	81 G8
Wolfe Creek Crater	79 C13
Yalgorup	72 H7
Yanchep	72 G1

Northern Territory
Info Ph Alice Springs (08) 8951 8250
Darwin (08) 8999 5511
Katherine (08) 8973 8888   www.nt.gov.au/ipe/pwcnt

Park	Ref
Barranyi (North Island)	87 J13
Charles Darwin	84 D3
Davenport Range	89 J10
Djukbinj	85 C3
Dulcie Ranges	91 D11
Elsey	86 H7
Finke Gorge	90 G7
Garig Gunak Barlu	86 B5
Gregory	88 B3
Kakadu (Comm. Terr.)	85 C6
Keep River	88 A1
Lawley River	81 B9
Limmen (Proposed)	87 J10
Litchfield	85 E1
Mary River	85 D4
Nitmiluk (Katherine Gorge)	85 H6
Uluru-Kata Tjuṯa (Comm. Terr.)	90 J4
Watarrka (Kings Canyon)	90 G5
West MacDonnell	90 F7

Australian Capital Territory
Info Ph (02) 6207 9777
www.environment.act.gov.au/bushparksandreserves/bushparksandreserves.html

Park	Ref
Namadgi	32 K1

The publisher gratefully acknowledges the assistance provided by Australia's rangers and parks office personnel in researching the park facilities.

The following publications offer more detailed information on parks, camps and rest areas around Australia. Some of these publications also refer to the Australia Road Atlas maps within their texts.

– Hema Maps' state-based Camping Atlas products

– Camps Australia Wide by Philip Procter (www.campsaustraliawide.com)

– Highway Guide Around Australia and Highway Guide Across Australia by Paul Smedley (www.highwaymanproductions.com)

– Boiling Billy Publications' assorted camping guides by Craig Lewis and Cathy Savage (www.boilingbilly.com.au)

Hinchinbrook Island, QLD (11 F13)

Queensland

Lindeman Island (9 C8)

Distances are shown in kilometres and follow the most direct major sealed route

	Brisbane	Bundaberg	Cairns	Charleville	Goondiwindi	Longreach	Mackay	Mount Isa	Rockhampton	Roma	Toowoomba	Townsville	Winton
Bamaga	2712	2374	1000	2618	2712	2106	1743	2239	2077	2353	2702	1349	1926
Brisbane		361	1712	742	350	1172	969	1826	635	477	128	1363	1352
Bundaberg			1374	916	591	970	656	1624	297	651	412	1025	1150
Cairns				1618	1712	1111	743	1259	1077	1353	1702	349	931
Charleville					588	511	1039	1165	833	265	614	1269	691
Goondiwindi						1054	981	1708	647	359	222	1363	1234
Longreach							788	654	673	695	1044	762	180
Mackay								1289	334	774	971	394	968
Mount Isa									1327	1349	1694	895	474
Rockhampton										568	637	728	853
Roma											349	1004	875
Toowoomba												1353	1224
Townsville													582
Winton													

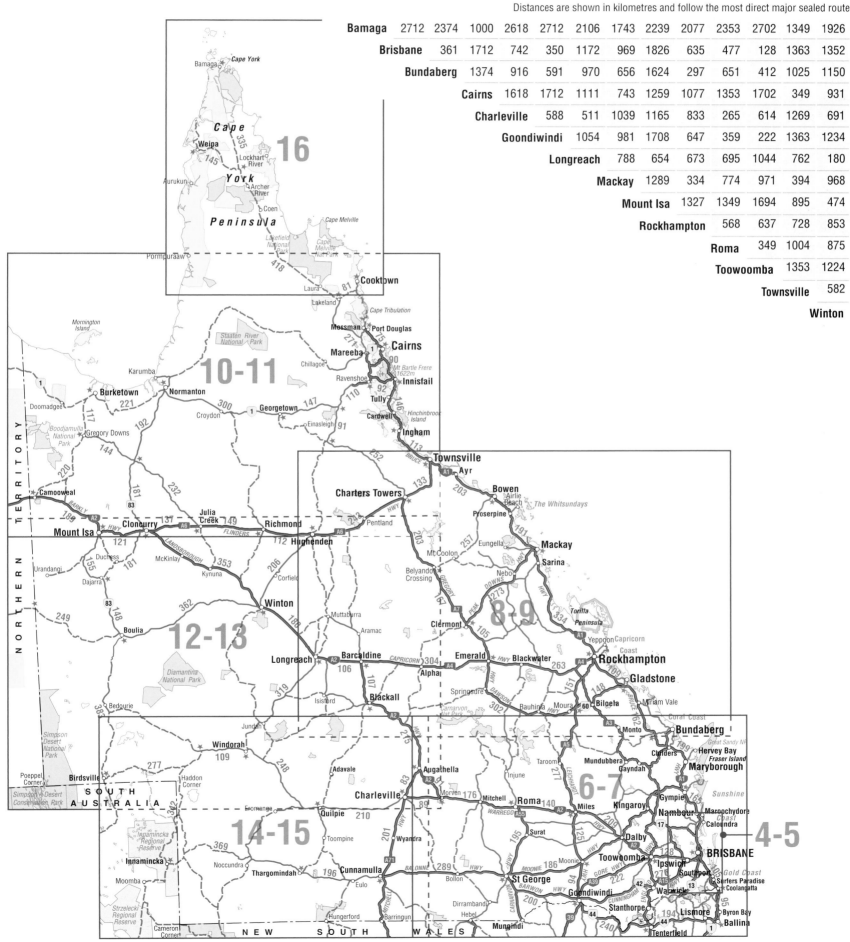

Map of Brisbane CBD

Places of Interest

1 Anzac Memorial B3
2 Botanic Gardens C3
3 Brisbane Convention & Exhib Ctr C2
4 City Hall B2
5 Conrad Treasury Casino C2
6 Customs House B3
7 King George Square B2
8 Old Government House C3
9 Old Windmill Observatory B2
10 Performing Arts Complex C2
11 Queen Street Mall B2
12 Queensland Art Gallery C2
13 Queensland Cultural Centre C2
14 Queensland Museum C2
15 Queensland University of Tech C3
16 South Bank C2
17 St Johns Cathedral B3
18 St Stephens Cathedral B3
19 State Library of Queensland C2
20 Suncorp Entertainment Piazza C2
21 Victoria Army Barracks B1

Accommodation

30 Albert Park Hotel A2
31 Bridgewater Quest Apts B4
32 Brisbane Marriott B3
33 Carlton Crest Hotel B2
34 Centrepoint Apartments B2
35 City Backpackers B1
36 Dockside Apartment Hotel C4
37 Goodearth Hotel B2
38 Hilton Brisbane B3
39 Holiday Inn Hotel Brisbane B2
40 Hotel Conrad C2
41 Hotel George Williams Bris B2
42 Hotel Grand Chancellor B2
43 Hotel Ibis Brisbane B2
44 Medina Executive Brisbane B3
45 Mercure Hotel Brisbane C2
46 Metro Inn Tower Mill B2
47 Novotel Brisbane B3
48 Pacific International Apartments B3
49 Palace Embassy Backpackers B2
50 Quay West Suites Brisbane C3
51 Oaks North Quay B1
52 Rendezvous Hotel B2
53 Riverside Hotel C1
54 Rothbury on Ann Hotel B3
55 Royal Albert Hotel C3
56 Royal on the Park C3
57 Rydges South Bank Hotel C2
58 Sofitel Brisbane Hotel B3
59 Stamford Plaza Brisbane C3
60 Summit Central Apartments B2
61 The Astor Apartments B2
62 The Astor Metropole Motel B2
63 The Chifley on George C2
64 The Chifley on Lennons C2
65 The Manor Apartment Hotel B3
66 The Point Brisbane C4
67 The Sebel Suites Brisbane C3

LEGEND

Freeway	Major Building
Metroad	Govt Building
Highway	Accommodation
Major Road	Theatre/Cinema
Minor Road	Shopping
Lane / Path	Church
Railway, Station	Hospital
Busway, Station	Ferry Route

0 100 200 300 400 500 600 700 800m

© Hema Maps Pty Ltd

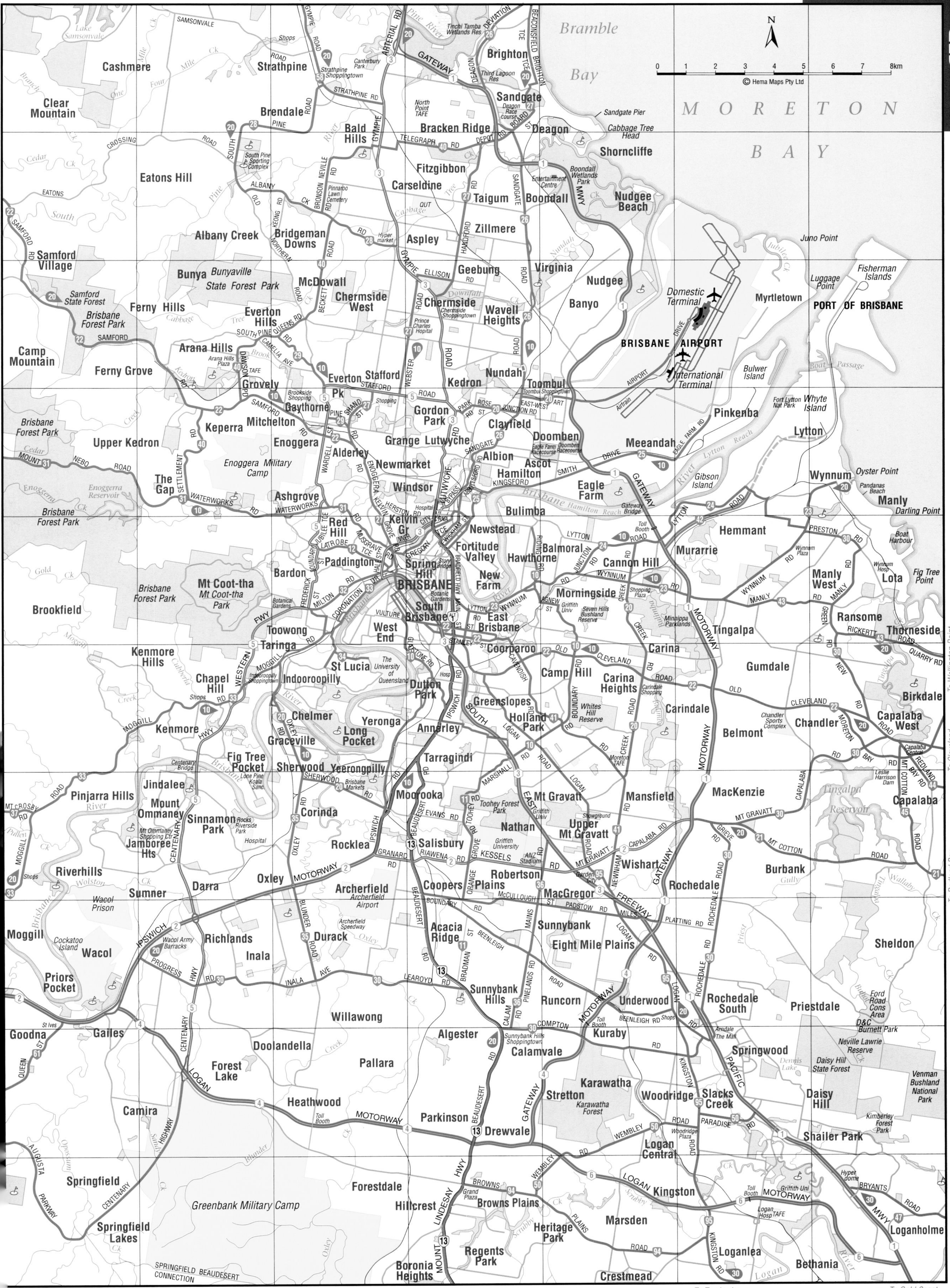
To Dayboro
To Sunshine Coast
To Redcliffe
To Beaudesert
To Tamborine
To Gold Coast
To Wellington Point
To Cleveland
To Redland Bay
© Hema Maps Pty Ltd
0 1 2 3 4 5 6 7 8km
Bramble Bay
MORETON BAY
Lake Samsonvale
Cashmere
Strathpine
Clear Mountain
Brendale
Bald Hills
Bracken Ridge
Brighton
Sandgate
Deagon
Sandgate Pier
Cabbage Tree Head
Shorncliffe
Eatons Hill
Fitzgibbon
Carseldine
Taigum
Boondall
Nudgee Beach
Boondall Wetlands Park
Albany Creek
Bridgeman Downs
Aspley
Zillmere
Juno Point
Samford Village
Bunya
Bunyaville State Forest Park
McDowall
Geebung
Virginia
Nudgee
Fisherman Islands
Luggage Point
Myrtletown
PORT OF BRISBANE
Domestic Terminal
Samford State Forest
Brisbane Forest Park
Ferny Hills
Everton Hills
Chermside West
Chermside
Wavell Heights
Banyo
BRISBANE AIRPORT
Camp Mountain
Ferny Grove
Arana Hills
International Terminal
Bulwer Island
Grovely
Everton Pk
Stafford
Kedron
Nundah
Toombul
Gaythorne
Gordon Park
Whyte Island
Fort Lytton Nat Park
Mitchelton
Keperra
Clayfield
Pinkenba
Brisbane Forest Park
Upper Kedron
Enoggera
Grange
Lutwyche
Doomben
Meeandah
Lytton
Alderley
Newmarket
Albion
Ascot
Enoggera Military Camp
Hamilton
Gibson Island
Wynnum
Oyster Point
The Gap
Ashgrove
Windsor
Eagle Farm
Manly
Darling Point
Enoggera Reservoir
Brisbane Forest Park
Red Hill
Kelvin Gr
Bulimba
Newstead
Hemmant
Boat Harbour
Paddington
Fortitude Valley
Balmoral
Cannon Hill
Murarrie
Spring Hill
BRISBANE
New Farm
Hawthorne
Bardon
Manly West
Lota
Fig Tree Point
Brookfield
Brisbane Forest Park
Mt Coot-tha
Mt Coot-tha Park
Morningside
South Brisbane
East Brisbane
Toowong
West End
Tingalpa
Ransome
Thorneside
Taringa
Coorparoo
Carina
Kenmore Hills
St Lucia
The University of Queensland
Camp Hill
Carina Heights
Gumdale
Chapel Hill
Indooroopilly
Dutton Park
Greenslopes
Carindale
Birkdale
Chelmer
Long Pocket
Holland Park
Yeronga
Chandler
Capalaba West
Kenmore
Graceville
Annerley
Belmont
Fig Tree Pocket
Tarragindi
Sherwood
Yeerongpilly
Jindalee
Pinjarra Hills
Moorooka
Mt Gravatt
Mansfield
MacKenzie
Capalaba
Mount Ommaney
Sinnamon Park
Corinda
Nathan
Upper Mt Gravatt
Jamboree Hts
Rocklea
Salisbury
Riverhills
Oxley
Wishart
Burbank
Darra
Archerfield
Coopers Plains
Robertson
Rochedale
Sumner
Wacol Prison
MacGregor
Moggill
Cockatoo Island
Wacol
Richlands
Inala
Durack
Acacia Ridge
Sunnybank
Eight Mile Plains
Sheldon
Priors Pocket
Sunnybank Hills
Runcorn
Underwood
Rochedale South
Priestdale
Willawong
Ford Road Cons Area
Goodna
Gailes
Algester
Kuraby
D&C Burnett Park
Neville Lawrie Reserve
Doolandella
Calamvale
Springwood
Daisy Hill State Forest
Forest Lake
Pallara
Karawatha
Venman Bushland National Park
Camira
Heathwood
Stretton
Karawatha Forest
Woodridge
Slacks Creek
Daisy Hill
Parkinson
Drewvale
Logan Central
Shailer Park
Kimberley Forest Park
Springfield
Forestdale
Kingston
Hillcrest
Browns Plains
Greenbank Military Camp
Heritage Park
Marsden
Loganholme
Springfield Lakes
Regents Park
Loganlea
Bethania
Boronia Heights
Crestmead
GATEWAY MOTORWAY
LOGAN MOTORWAY
IPSWICH MOTORWAY
PACIFIC MOTORWAY
SOUTH EAST FREEWAY
WESTERN FWY
GYMPIE ROAD
SANDGATE ROAD
CENTENARY HWY
IPSWICH HWY
MOUNT LINDESAY HWY
BEAUDESERT RD
LOGAN RD
OLD CLEVELAND RD
WYNNUM RD
MT COTTON ROAD
SPRINGFIELD BEAUDESERT CONNECTION
A B C D E F G H J K
1 2 3 4 5 6 7

N

© Hema Maps Pty Ltd

15 km
10
5
0

153°30'
153°00'
152°30'
27°00'

SOUTH PACIFIC OCEAN

MORETON BAY

Cape Moreton
North Pt
Comboyuro Pt
Bulwer
Cowan Cowan
Moreton Island National Park
Moreton Island
Tangalooma
Tangalooma Pt
Kooringal
Campbell Pt
Reeders Pt
Amity Pt
Amity
Mud Island
St Helena Island
St Helena Island Nat Pk
Fisherman Islands

Sunshine Coast

Maroochydore
Alexandra Headland
Underwater World
Mooloolaba
Buddina
Warana
Bokarina
Wurtulla
Currimundi
Dicky Beach
Shelley Beach
Caloundra

For more detail on this area, see Hema's Sunshine Coast Map

Buderim
Mountain Creek
Kawana Waters
Palmview
Mooloolah River National Park
Sunshine Coast Turf Club
Golden Beach
Pelican Waters
Coochin Creek
Campbellville

Bribie Island
Bribie Island National Park
Banksia Beach
Bellara
Bongaree
Woorim
Skirmish Pt
Woody Bay
Bald Pt
Sandstone Point
South Pt
Ningi
Godwin Beach
Toorbul
Meldale
Donnybrook
Long Is
Thoolebra Is
Wild Horse Mountain Lookout

Pumicestone Channel

Woombye
Palmwoods
Flaxton
Eudlo
Mooloolah
Montville
Lake Baroon
Kondalilla Nat Park
Maleny
Witta
Wootha
Candle Mtn
Peachester
Landsborough
Bald Knob
Mt Mellum
Beerwah
Australia Zoo
Mt Coochin
Glass House
Mt Beerwah
Glass House Mountains
Glass House Mountains National Park
Coonowrin Nat Park
Mt Ngungun
Beerburrum
Elimbah
Beerburrum State Forest
Caboolture Aerodrome

Caboolture
Morayfield
Upper Caboolture
Bellmere
Moodlu
Wamuran
Wamuran Basin
Rocksberg
Bracalba
Woodford
D'Aguilar
Durundur
Delaneys Creek
Neurum
Neurum Mtn
Mt Delaney
Mt Mee
Ocean View
Mount Mee
Mt Pleasant

Deception Bay
Beachmere
Rothwell
Deception Bay
Scarborough Pt
Osborne Pt
Redcliffe
Redcliffe Pt
Margate Beach
Woody Point
Clontarf
Woody Pt
Oyster Pt
Scarborough

Bramble Bay
Brighton
Shorncliffe
Sandgate
Nudgee Beach
Cabbage Tree Head
Boondall
Nudgee
BRISBANE AIRPORT
Juno Pt
Whyte

Griffin
Bracken Ridge
Kallangur
Petrie
Strathpine
Lawnton
Dakabin
Cashmere
Albany Creek
Mount Samson
Samsonvale
Kurwongbah
Dayboro
Mt Kobble
Kurwongbah
Samford Valley
Camp Mountain
Ferny Grove
Mt Nebo
Mt Glorious
D'Aguilar Range Nat Park
Brisbane Forest Park
D'AGUILAR
Cedar Creek

Aspley
Chermside
Everton Park
Eatons Hill
Carseldine
Zillmere

Conondale
Conondale Nat Park
Borobin
Cedarton
Stanmore
Villeneuve
Mt Archer
Winya
Glenfern
Kilcoy
Mt Kilcoy
Lake Somerset
Somerset Dam
Crossdale
Bryden
Mombra
Dundas
Wivenhoe Dam
Lake Wivenhoe

Jimna
Yednia
Monsildale
Gregors Creek
Lower Cresswell
Caboonbah
Mt Beppo
Mt Brisbane
Fulham Vale
Mt Beppo
Esk
Coominya

RANGE
CONONDALE RANGE
D'AGUILAR RANGE
D'AGUILAR

BRUCE HWY
BRUCE HWY
D'AGUILAR HWY
BRISBANE VALLEY HWY

To Noosa Heads
To Gympie
To Yarraman
To Toogoolawah

NSW

North Stradbroke Island

South Stradbroke Island

Gold Coast

Coolangatta
Tweed Heads
Pt Danger
Bilinga
Tugun
Currumbin
Currumbin Waters
Palm Beach
Burleigh Heads
Burleigh Head National Park
Miami
Mermaid Beach
Broadbeach
Surfers Paradise
Main Beach
The Spit
Southport
Labrador
Sea World

Tallebudgera
Tallebudgera Valley
Upper Tallebudgera
Reedy Creek
Robina
Clear Island Waters
Stephens
Andrews
Bonogin
Austinville
Mudgeeraba
Tallai
Worongary
Gilston
Benowa
Ashmore
Bundall
Carrara
Merrimac

Springbrook
Springbrook National Park
Natural Bridge
Numinbah
Numinbah Valley
Advancetown
Mount Nathan
Beechmont
Lower Beechmont
Binna Burra
Green Mountains
Lamington National Park
DARLINGTON RANGE

Nerang
Gaven
Maudsland
Wongawallan
Guanaba
Mount Tamborine
North Tamborine
Eagle Heights
Tamborine
Tamborine National Park
Coomera
Upper Coomera
Oxenford
Helensvale
Pimpama
Yatala
Ormeau
Woongoolba
Luscombe
Jacobs Well

Redland Bay
Cleveland
Ormiston
Wellington Point
Birkdale
Thornlands
Victoria Point
Point Halloran
Redland Bay
Coochiemudlo Island
Peel Island
Dunwich
Blue Lake Nat Park

Russell Island
Lamb Is
Macleay Is
Karragarra Is
Coochiemudlo
Stradbroke
Moreton Bay Islands National Park
Jumpinpin

Springwood
Daisy Hill
Shailer Park
Loganholme
Loganlea
Beenleigh
Eagleby
Carbrook
Cornubia
Alberton
Stapylton
Woodridge
Kingston
Marsden
Crestmead
Browns Plains
Calamvale
Park Ridge
Forestdale
Greenbank
New Beith
Chambers Flat
Stockleigh

Mt Gravatt
Mansfield
MacGregor
Eight Mile Plains
Rochedale
Kuraby
Acacia Ridge
Archerfield
Rocklea
Oxley
Inala
Durack
Forest Lake
Richlands
Heathwood

Kenmore
Chapel Hill
Jindalee
Middle Park
Mount Ommaney
Jamboree Heights
Sinnamon Park
Seventeen Mile Rocks
Wacol
Gailes
Goodna
Bellbird Park
Springfield
Camira
Redbank Plains
Redbank
Collingwood Park
Dinmore
Riverview
Karana Downs
Mount Crosby
Chuwar

Brookfield
Pullenvale
Moggill
Bellbowrie
Kholo

Ipswich
North Ipswich
Amberley
RAAF Base
Yamanto
Purga
Loamside
Ripley
Willowbank
Walloon
Rosewood
Marburg
Haigslea
Minden
Glamorgan Vale
Tallegalla
Lowood
Brightview

Hatton Vale
Laidley
Plainland
Grandchester
Calvert
Lower Mount Walker
Mount Mort
Rosevale
Franklin Vale
Hidden Vale

Jimboomba
North Maclean
South Maclean
Cedar Grove
Veresdale
Woodhill
Kagaru
Brooklands
Gleneagle

Logan Village

Canungra
Biddaddaba
Boyland
Ferny Glen
Kerry
Darlington

Beaudesert
Bromelton
Josephville
Laravale
Mt Mahomet
Innisplain
Hillview
Christmas Creek
Tamrookum
Rathdowney
Mt Lindesay
Kooralbyn Resort
Cannon Creek

Boonah
Milford
Coulson
Teviotville
Templin
Kalbar
Roadvale
Bunjurgen
Mount Alford
Charlwood
Aratula
Fassifern
Silverdale
Warrill View
Coleyville
Merryvale
Lower Mount Walker
Tarome
Moogerah
Moogerah Park
Lake Moogerah
Maroon
Lake Maroon
Bunburra
Croftby

CUNNINGHAM HWY

Flinders Peak
Mt Goolman
Mt Walker
Mt Walker
Harrisville
Mutdapilly
Peak Crossing
Willowbank Raceway

WARREGO HWY
IPSWICH MWY
GATEWAY MWY
LOGAN MWY
PACIFIC MWY
PACIFIC HWY
MT LINDESAY HWY

Main Range National Park
Cunninghams Gap
Spicers Gap
Mt Mitchell
Mt Cordeaux
Mt Huntley
Mt Superbus
Mt Asplenium
Mt May
Mt French
Mt Maroon
Mt Greville
Mt Moon
Mt Moogerah
Mt Edwards

27°30'
28°00'
27°30'
28°00'
152°30'
152°00'

For more detail on this area, see Hema's North Stradbroke Island Map
For more detail of this area, see Hema's Gold Coast Map

To Toowoomba
To Warwick
To Woodenbong
To Murwillumbah
To Ballina

A B C D E F G H J K
8 9 10 11 12 13 14

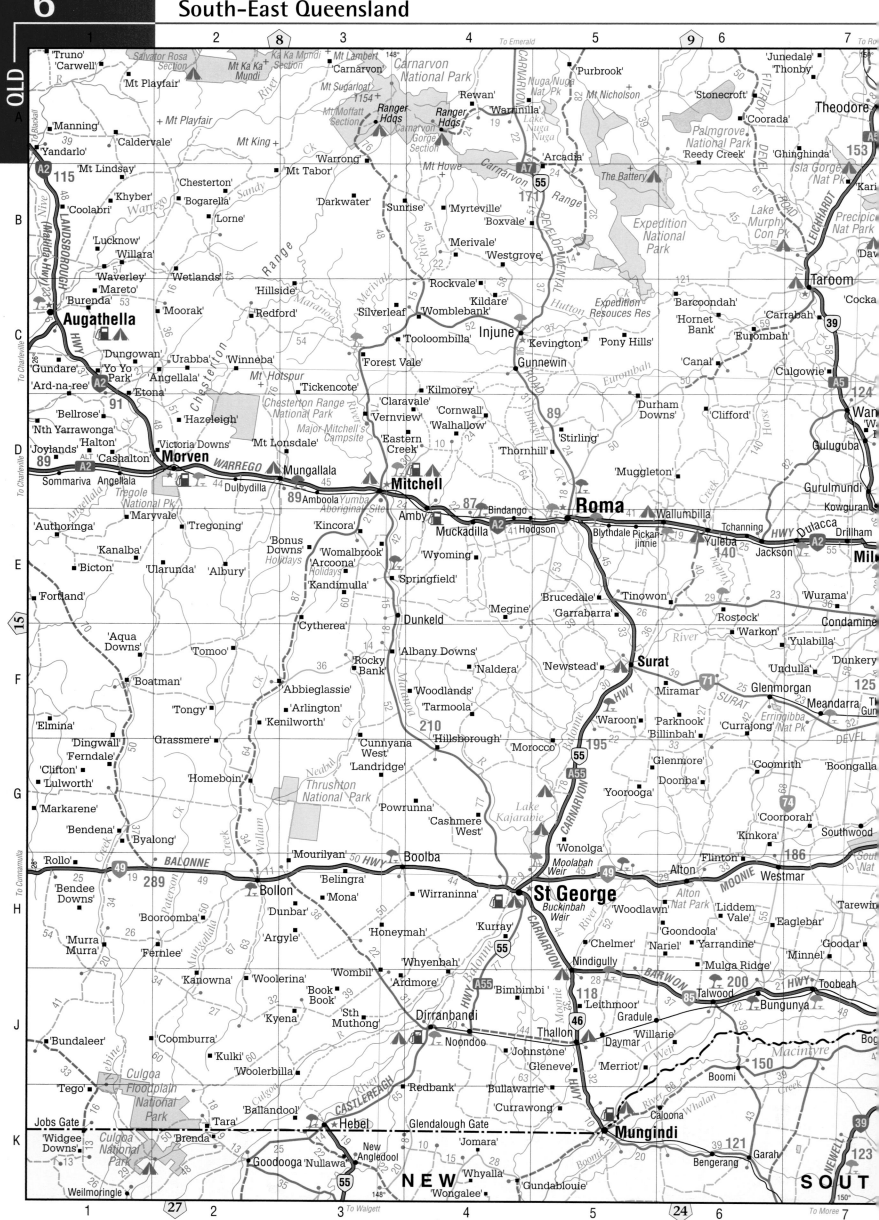

To Rockhampton

8 9 10 To Gladstone & Rockhampton 11 12 13 14

9

© Hema Maps Pty Ltd
0 50km
N

A

rajong' Cania Gorge NP Kalpowar Kolan River Miara Moore Park Burnett Heads Coral
dore' Moonford Mungungo Bancroft Yandaran Avondale Bargara Sandy Cape
19 20 33 Three Moon **Monto** Mulgildie Bundaberg Burnett Heads South Kolan Bullyard Rum Distillery **Bundaberg** HERVEY BAY Rooney Pt Marloo Bay
Camboon Rawbelle 17 Burnett River Gin Gin Wallaville Bruce HWY Elliott Heads MARINE PARK Platypus Bay Waddy Point
'Barram' Abercorn A3 Mount Perry Booyal Elliott Burrum Coast Hervey Orchid Beach

B

'Glencoe' 'Tireen' Cynthia 113 'Rosslyn' Cordalba Isis Junction Woodgate National Park Burrum Heads Whale Watching Great Sandy
ow Ceratodus Eidsvold 'Kerwee' Goodwood Buxtonville Hervey Bay Woody Is Cathedral Beach National Park
yland' 'Calrossie' 42 'Widbury' Binjour Byrnestown Childers Howard Torbanlea Hervey Bay Happy Valley Fraser Island
'Redbank' 'Yerilla' Dallarnil Howard Colton River Heads Kingfisher Bay For more detail on this area,
Mundubbera Coalstoun Biggenden 52 Bruce Lenthalls Dam Eurong Five see Hema's Fraser Island and
Dykehead 45 Lakes Brooweena 86 Wide Bay - Burnett Maps
Gayndah Ban Ban Mt Walsh Aramara Mungar **Maryborough** Maaroom Mile SOUTH

C

'Hawkwood' Springs Nat Park 147 Teebar Mungar Boonooroo
Auburn River Boogooramunya Poona Nat Pk Tiaro Tuan Poona
National Park Mt Bauple Theebine Bauple
Mt Misery 'Auburn' Mt Saul Nat Park 81 Military Training Hook Point
Brovinia Boondoora Woolooga Glenwood Area Inskip Point
Monogorilby 75 Windera Tansey Kilkivan Gunalda Wide Bay Tin Can Bay Rainbow Beach
'Pinedale' 'Lismore' Lake Proston Goomeri 20 Noosa River Double Island Point
'Durah' Allies Durong Hivesville Byee Manyung WIDE BAY 75 HWY Great Sandy 26°

D

rowan' Barakula Creek Murgon Wondai Cherbourg Glastonbury Wolvi National Park PACIFIC
Durong South Boondooma Tingoora Manumbar Kin Kin Gympie Boreen Pt
'Fairyland' Memerambi Wooroolin Lake Barambah Amamoor Cooran Pomona Lake Cootharaba
mboola Baking Board Kingaroy Elgin Kandanga Cooroy Tewantin Laguna Bay
inchilla Canaga Kumbia 173 Goodger Vale Brooloo A1 Noosa Nat Park Noosa Heads

E

mbi' Boonarga 82 Nanango Jimna Kenilworth Yandina Eumundi Coolum Beach
Brigalow Warra 126 Cooranga North Conondale Mapleton Nambour Sunshine
Kogan Macalister Yarraman Bunya Mtns Nat Pk NP Montville Maroochydore
Daandine Bell Linville Yednia Maleny Landsborough Buderim Mooloolaba
Jimbour Pirrinuan Kaimkillenbun Cononondale Beerwah Caloundra Alexandra Headland Coast

F

Tara Goranba Weranga Gulera A2 Blackbutt Moore Kilcoy Woodford Glass Hs Bribie Is Nat Park OCEAN
Tullagrie Kumbarilla Quinalow Cooyar Harlin Somerset Dam Wamuran Beerburrum Bribie Island Cape Moreton
Bowenville Wutul Toogoolawah L.Somerset Dayboro Bongaree Moreton Island Nat Park
112 Jondaryan Meringandan Esk Somervale Deception Bay Moreton Island
49 Oakey Hampton Coominya Caboolture Petrie Deception Bay Tangalooma
'Halliford' Cecil Plains Aubigny Murphys Ck Helidon Lowood Marburg Strathpine see Hema's South East

G

Moonie 'Waar Waar' Brookstead **TOOWOOMBA** Gatton Laidley Rosewood Samford **BRISBANE** Amity
'New Dunmore' Cambooya 128 Ipswich Capalaba Point Lookout
'Allawah' Pittsworth Greenmount Logan Dunwich North Stradbroke
222 Millmerran Nobby Clifton 42 Beenleigh Redland Bay Island

H

Trevanna 85 Leyburn 84 Aratula Jimboomba Tamborine Coomera South Stradbroke
Downs' Hendon Allora Boonah 13 Nerang Southport Island
'Wyaga' Karara Main Range Rathdowney Beaudesert Surfers Paradise Gold
Bendiee Nat Park Nat Park 283 Canungra Broadbeach 28°
A39 GORE Inglewood Killarney Mudgeeraba Burleigh Heads Coast

J

ondiwindi Whetstone 42 200 Cobba-da-mana Woodenbong Binna Burra Coolangatta
Gibinbell Yelarbon Coolmunda Dam Urbenville Springbrook Tweed Heads
Kurumbil Pikedale 114 Wiangaree Tyalgum Uki Murwillumbah
Limevale Bonalbo Kunghur Mooball 95

K

rth Star Texas Stanthorpe Ettrick Kyogle Bangalow Byron Bay
Yallaroi Silver Spur 240 44 Wallangarra Mummulgum 127 44 Casino Lismore Lennox Head
Bonshaw Mole River **WALES** **Tenterfield** Alice Coraki Ballina Evans Head

152° 154°

8 9 10 To Glen Innes & Armidale 25 11 12 To Grafton & Coffs Harbour 13 14

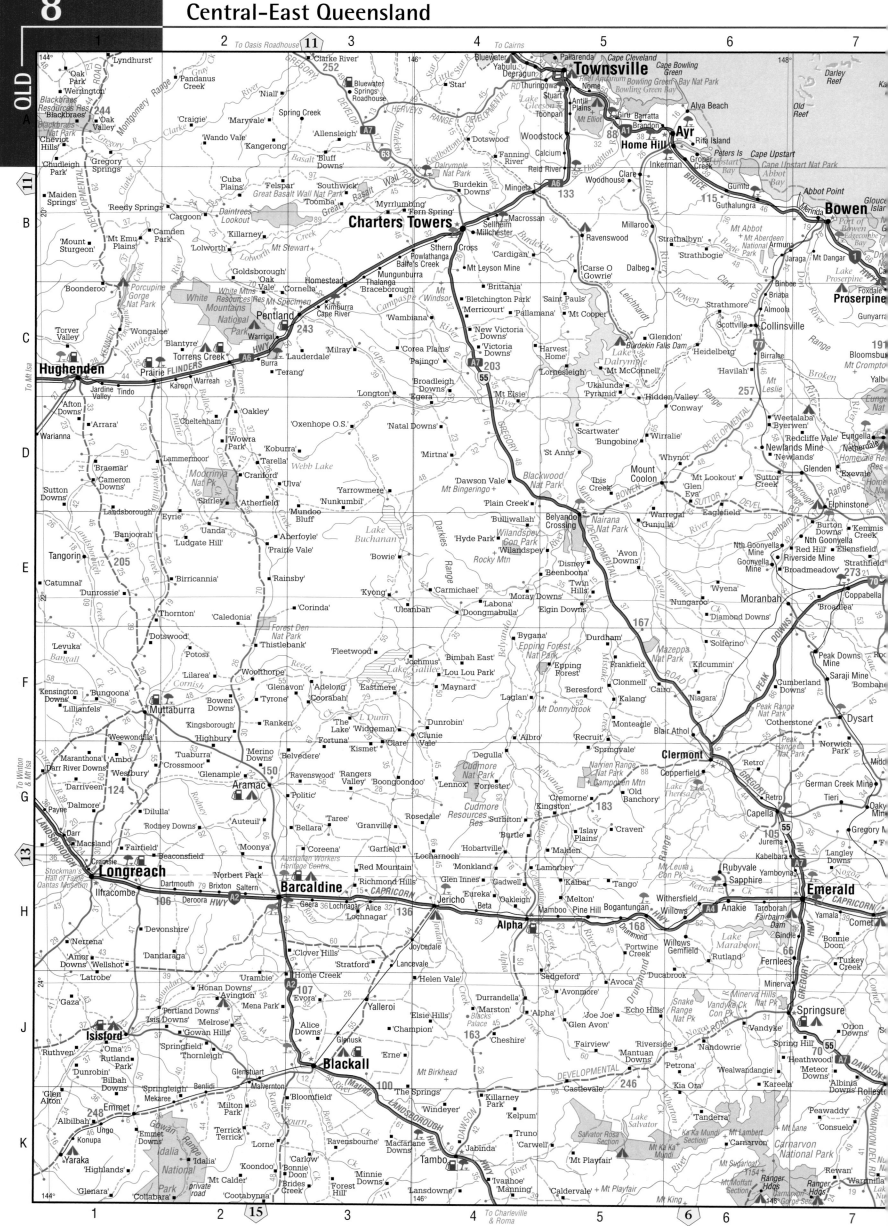

N

0   50   100km
© Hema Maps Pty Ltd

A

150°   152°   Marion Reef

B
20°

Great ...

Hardy Reef
Black Reef East
Hook Reef

Cayman Island
Hook Island
WHITSUNDAY GROUP
th Molle Is
Daydream Is   Border Island
Sth Molle Is   Whitsunday Island
Harbour   Whitsunday Islands Nat Park
Hazelwood Island
Long   Hamilton Island
Island   Lindeman Island
Beach   Lindeman Islands Nat Park
Bay   Shaw Island
Point   Blacksmith Is
lays   Goldsmith Is   Linne Island
Wigton Island
Rabbit Is   Carlisle Is
Newry Is   Cockermouth
NP   Is   Sth Cumberland Islands Nat Park
Seaforth   Brampton Is
C Hillsborough NP   Scawfell Is
Sand Bay   St Bees Is
Bucasia
Eimeo
Marian   Slade Point
Mackay   Sandringham Bay
Walkerston   Bakers Creek
on   Hay Point
Homebush   Grasstree   Prudhoe Is
Campwin Beach   NORTHUMBERLAND
Shinfield   **Sarina**   Knight Is   ISLANDS Nat Park
oulston Park   Llewellyn Bay   Digby Is   Hotspur Island
ndee'   Yukan   Ince Bay   Pine Peak Island
Koumala   Cape Palmerston   Middle
Koumala   Cape Palmerston Nat Park   Island   Percy Isles NP
South Ibilbie   Temple Is   Curlew Is   North East Island
Greenhill   PERCY ISLES
West Hill   Yarrawonga Point   South Island
West Hill Is   Poynter
Orkabie   Island
Nat Park   Bamborough
Carmila   Carmila Beach   Is   DUKE   ISLANDS
Aquila Is   Wild Duck   Is   High Peak Island
Flaggy Rock   North Pt   Marble Is
Elalie   Broad   Quail Is   Hexham Is   Cheviot Island
'Collaroy'   Clairview   Kalarka   Long   Sound Nat Park   Arthur Pt
'Cardowan'   Island   Sound Channel
229   Clairview Bluff   Stanage   Shoalwater Broad
St Lawrence   Collins I   Cape Townshend
Croydon'   Torilla   Broad   Con Pk   Townshend Island
neaston'   Wumalgi   Sound   Leicester Is   Reef Point
Rosewood Is   Shoalwater
River   **Peninsula**   Warginburra   Bay
Ogmore   Peninsula   Perforated Point
'Junee'   Bowman   Double Mtn   Mt Clinton
Junee   Koolandra   SHOALWATER BAY   Cape Clinton
Nat Park   A1   Tooloombah   MILITARY TRAINING AREA   Freshwater Bay
Marlborough   Cliff Point
'Apis Creek'   Princhester   Cape Manifold
'Royles'   Kunawarara   Byfield   Stockyard Point
'Eden Garry'   Byfield National Park
Goodedulla   Water Park Point
Nat Park   River   Orio Bay
'Kaiuroo'   105   Capricorn
'Burkan'   Mt Etna Caves   North Keppel Island
Yaamba   Nat Park   Keppel Bay Islands Nat Park
Ridgelands   The Caves   Roslyn   Great Keppel Island
Dalma   Cawarral   Capricorn Coast Nat Park
Foleyvale   Parkhurst   Emu Park   Coast
Gracemere   **Rockhampton**   Keppel Sands
lackwater   Stanwell   Kabra   Cape Keppel
Parnabal   Wycarbah   Broadmont   Cape Capricorn
Bluff'   Boulbercombe   Port Alma
263   Westwood   Mount   Bajool   Curtis Island
Dingo   Duaringa   Morgan   Marmor   Black Head
Blackdown Tableland   Gogango   17   Raglan   A1
Nat Park   109   Ambrose   Southend
'Eastbrook'   Dululu   Bindawalla'   Yarwun
Wowan   145   Mount Larcom   **Gladstone**
'Wooronah'   Deeford   'Lancefield'   Mt Alma   Boyne Island
'Perch Ck'   Rannes   Tannum Sands
Woorabinda   Gbovigen   Calliope   Benaraby   Richards Point
Baralaba   Kukotungo   60   102   Taragoola   Bustard Point
'Mimosa Park'   Jambin   Barmundu   Rodds   Turkey Beach
'Goomally'   Callide   Iveragh   Bay   Bustard Bay
'Barranga'   39   Callide Coalfields   Boynedale   Bororen   Round Hill Head
Downs'   Banana   Weitalaba   Castle   Miriam Vale   Seventeen Seventy
Moura   46   **Biloela**   Tower   Nagoorin   Agnes Water
Bauhinia   Thangool   Nat Park   Ubobo   Deepwater Nat Park
'Bauhinia   166   Kroombit Tops   Littlemore   Makowata   Rules Beach
Downs'   Kianga   National Park   Builyan   Lowmead   Wartburg
'Stonecroft'   Kurrajong   Many Peaks   162   Winfield
Palmgrove   97   Mt Molangul   Kalpawar   Berajondo   Norval Park
National Park   Cania Gorge   A1   Rosedale
Nat Park   16   Moore Park
'Glandore'   Lake   Mungungo   Bargara   Burnett Heads
Theodore   Cania   Bancroft   Avondale   Coral
Coorada'   17   **Monto**   Mulgildie   South   Rum Distillery   Coast
Camboon   Three Moon   Kolan   **Bundaberg**
Rawbelle   Gin Gin   Elliott Heads
cholson   150°   Bullyard   Elliott

SOUTH   CORAL   SEA

Barrier   Reef

POMPEY   COMPLEX

Ripetide   Elusive
Cay   Reef

Thomas   Cay

PACIFIC

SWAIN   REEFS
National Park

Gannet   Cay

GREAT BARRIER REEF MARINE PARK

Mackay / Capricorn Section

Capricorn

For more detail on this area, see
Hema's Central Queensland Map

Channel

North Reef

Tryon Is   Wilson Is
North West Is   Wreck Island   Scientific
CAPRICORN
Heron Island

Capricornia Cays

One Tree Island
National Park

TROPIC OF CAPRICORN

Erskine Is   GROUP
Masthead Is

Fitzroy Reef
Llewellyn Reef

Hoskyn Islands
Scientific

BUNKER   GROUP
Fairfax Islands   Lady Musgrave
Scientific   Island

Round Hill Head   Lady Elliot Island
Joseph Banks (Round Hill Head)

OCEAN

Sandy Cape
HERVEY BAY   Rooney Pt   Marloo
MARINE PARK   Bay
Platypus Bay   Fraser Island
Coast   Orchid   Beach
Waddy Point

1 2 3 4 5 6 16 7

A

GULF OF CARPENTARIA

N

0 50 100km

© Hema Maps Pty Ltd

B

Pormpuraaw

Wallaby Island

Kowanyama
Kowanyama

'Lochnagar OS'
'Rutland Plains'

'Inkerman'

C

For more detail on this area,
see Hema's Top End and Western
Gulf Map and Cairns to Broome

Manowar Island
Rocky Island
Birri Lodge
Thabugan Point
Halls Point
Bilmgun Point
Mornington Island
Lingnoonganee Is
Cape Van Diemen
WELLESLEY ISLANDS

'Galbraith'
'Dorunda'
'Macaroni O/S'
private road

D

Gee Wee Pt
Gununa
Denham Island
Midbagar Pt
Pains Is
Bayley Is
Ngawalgeah Pt
Sydney Island
Woolgunjin Pt
Tulburrerr Is
Forsyth Island
FORSYTH ISLANDS
Bentinck Island
SOUTH WELLESLEY ISLANDS
Sweers Island
Bountiful Is
Pt Parker
Allen Is

Van Diemen Inlet
Point Burrows
Point Austin
Fitzmaurice Point

'Myra Vale'
'Delta Downs'
'Lotus Vale'
'Stirling'
'Double Lagoon'
'Glencoe'
'Miranda Downs'
'Vanrook'

E

'Wollogorang'
'Westmoreland'
Hells Gate Roadhouse
Doomadgee
Tarrant Point
Pascoe Inlet
Finuncane Is
Kangaroo Point
Gore Point
Middle Point
Disaster Inlet
'Escott'
Burketown

Karumba
Alligator Point
'Maggieville'

Normanton
'Magowra'
Clarina
Glenore
Timora
151 Blackbull
GULFLANDER

89

F

Waanyi Garawa
'Bowthorn'
Nicholson
Kingfisher Camp
'Corinda' (ruins)
Doomadgee
225
'Beames Brook'
'Brookdale'
'Punjaub'
'Brinawa'
117
'Almora'
'Armraynald'
'Wernadinga'
'New Armraynald'
'Floraville'
Leichhardt Falls
WAY
221
'Inverleigh'
'Macalister'
'Milgarra'
'Warren Vale'
192
East Haydon
'Gum Ck'
'Ellavale'
'Guildford'
'Coralie' (ruins)
Crov

G

'Highland Plains'
Lawn Hill (Stockyard Creek) Resources Reserve
Boodjamulla (Lawn Hill) National Park
Adels Grove
Pasminco Century Mine
Lawn Hill Gorge
'Mt Oscar OS'
'Lawn Hill'
'Kunkulla'
'Planet Downs'
'Kamarga'
Gregory Downs
'Nardoo'
144
'Augustus Downs'
'Talawanta'
'Neumayer Valley'
'Bang Bang'
'Wondoola'
'Cowan Downs'
'Donors Hill'
83
'Iffley'
'Beach'
'Vena Park'
'Claraville'

H

'Old Herbert Vale'
'Riversleigh'
'Norfolk'
'Mellish Park'
'Lorraine'
'Alhambra'
Waggabundi
Mt Oxide Mines
'White Hills OS'
'Gleeson'
'Aisace'
'Kamileroi'
'Boomarra'
DEVELOPMENTAL
'Wurung'
Burke & Wills Roadhouse
Wurung OS
'Myola'
'Taldora'
'Lyrian'
'Doravale'
'Arizona'
'Canobe'

J

'Rocklands'
Camooweal
'Morstone'
220
Thorntonia
'Undilla'
Gunpowder
Mammoth Mines
Lady Annie Mine
Waggaboonya Lake
'Split Rock'
Mt Kelly Mine
Dobbyn
'Coolullah'
'Yarabungan'
'Alcala'
'Melinda Downs'
'Kingfield'
Mount Cuthbert Mine
Kajabbi
83
'Rose Green'
'The Nobbies'
'Illistrin' (Abandoned)
'Bellman'
'Granada'
'Lady Wallace'
'Clonagh'
181
'Alva Downs'
232
'Baloothara'
Violet Vale'
'Monstraven'
'Numil Downs'
'Etta Plains'
'Milungera'
'Euroka Springs'
'Lindfield'
Sedan Dip
'Lara Downs'
Haddington Downs'
'Dalgonally'

K

'Austral Downs'
'Old Wooroona'
'Wooroona'
'Barkly Downs'
A2
Camooweal Caves National Park of Caves
'Flora'
'Yelvertoft'
189
'Old May Downs' (Ruins)
George Fisher Mine
Hilton Mine
BARKLY
Lake Julius
'Calton Hills'
Mt Remarkable
Mammoth
Koolamarra
'Jessievale'
'Glen Isla'
Quamby
'Fort Constantine'
Ernest Henry Mine
121
A6
'Zingari'
'Manfred Downs'
'Ernestina Plains'
'Eddington'
'Longford Plains'
137
Julia Creek

Mount Isa
Fossil Centre
Lake Moondarra
Mary Kathleen (ruins)
HWY
Cloncurry
Marimo
Bookin
Undina
Oorindi
Tibarri
Gilliat
Eddington
'Wynberg'

To Tennant Creek & Darwin
To Boulia
12
To Winton & Rockhampton

1 2 3 4 5 6 7

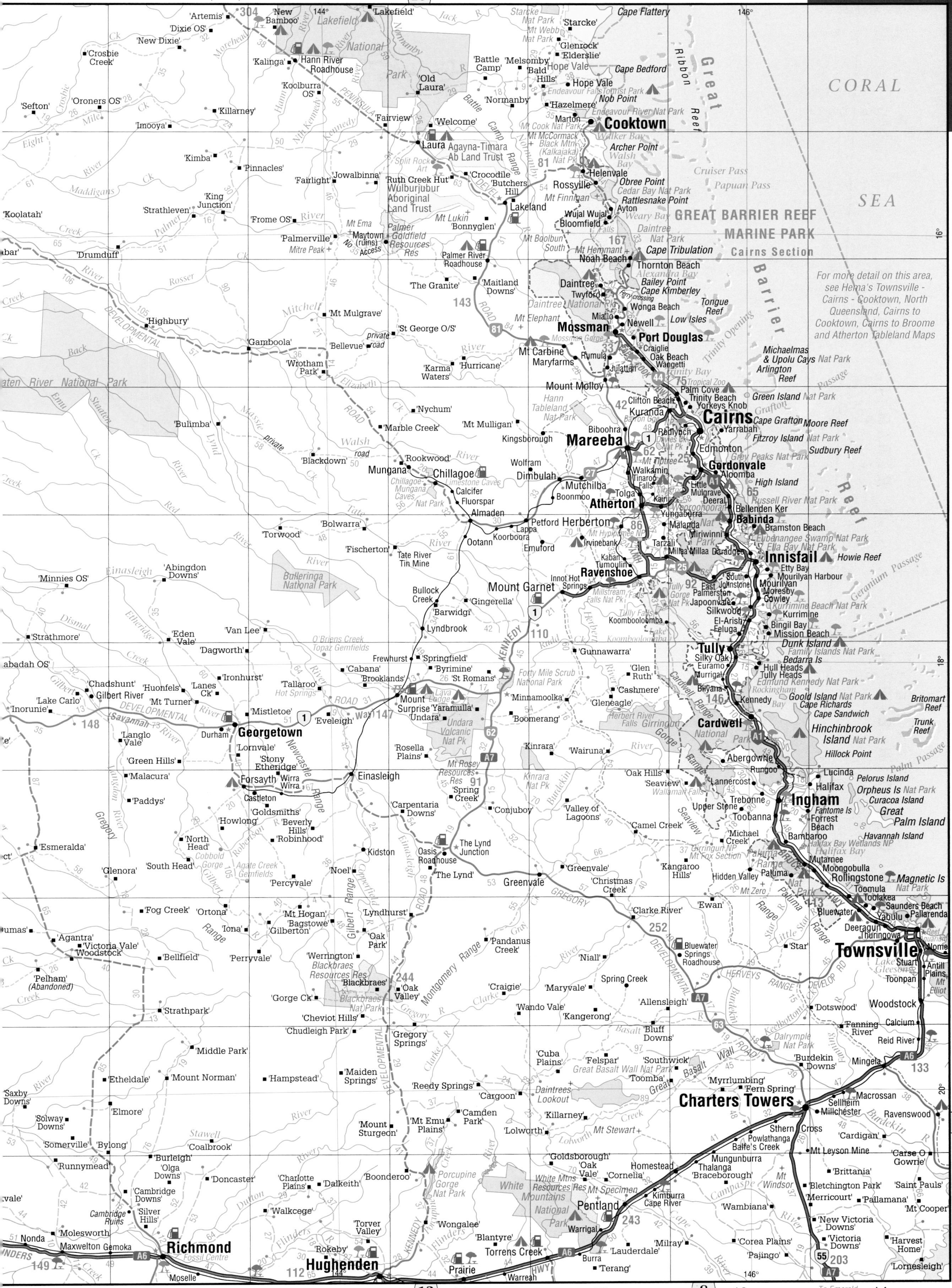

To Weipa & Cape York

CORAL

SEA

GREAT BARRIER REEF
MARINE PARK
Cairns Section

For more detail on this area,
see Hema's Townsville -
Cairns - Cooktown, North
Queensland, Cairns to
Cooktown, Cairns to Broome
and Atherton Tableland Maps

Cooktown

Mossman
Port Douglas

Cairns
Mareeba

Gordonvale

Atherton
Herberton

Babinda

Innisfail

Ravenshoe
Mount Garnet

Tully

Cardwell

Hinchinbrook
Island Nat Park

Ingham

Great
Palm Island

Magnetic Is

Georgetown

Townsville

Greenvale

Woodstock

Charters Towers

Richmond

Hughenden

To Winton

To Mackay

To Emerald

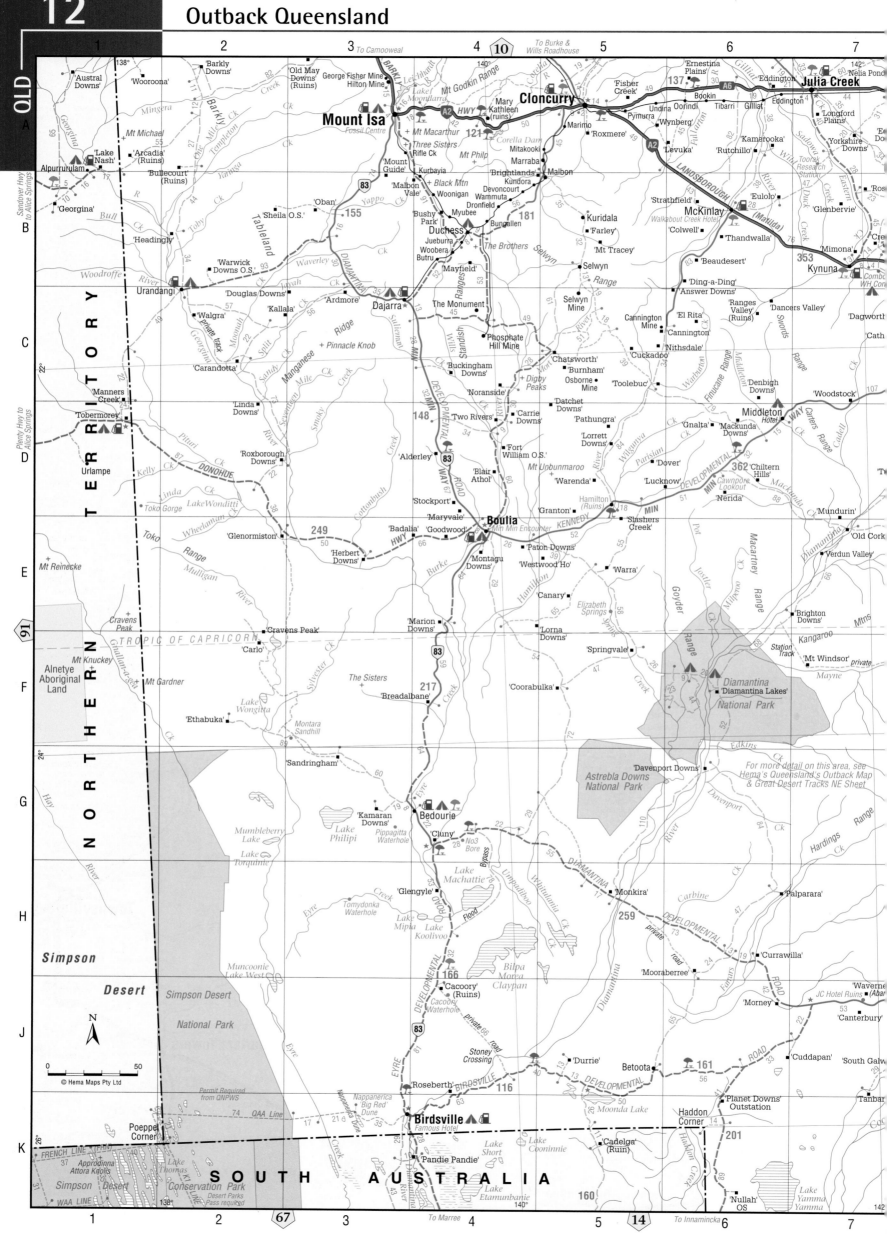

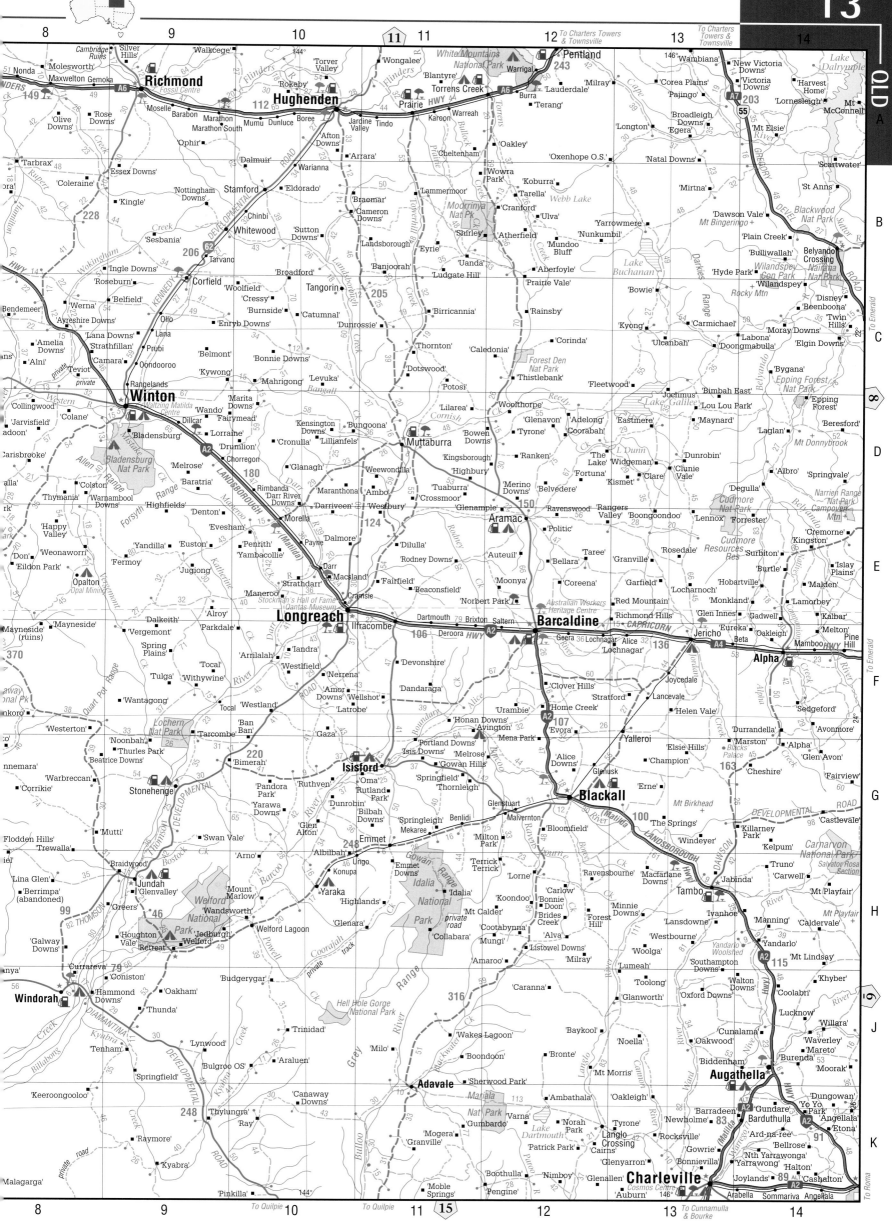

OLD

1 2 3 4 12 5 6 7

'Glengyle'
To Bedourie & Boulia
'Monkira'
'Palparara'
'Lina Glen'
'Braid'
'Berrimpa' (abandoned)

Lake Mipia
Lake Koolivoo
Flood Bypass
Lake Machattie
Umpadiboo Ck
Whitilama Ck
DIAMANTINA
Carbine Ck
CK
140°
142°
THOMSON
99
82 DEVEL
'G

259
DEVEL
private road
'Currawilla'
'Galway Downs'
'Hou

166
DEVELOPMENTAL ROAD
Diamantina
73
'Mooraberree'
Fenars
'Waverney' (Abandoned)
'Carranya'
'Currareva'
'Conis

EYRE
81
32
'Cacoory' (Ruins)
Cacoory Waterhole
Bilpa Morea Claypan
private road
42
'Morney'
JC Hotel Ruins
109
Windorah
Ham
D

83
Stoney Crossing
Diamantina
'Canterbury'
22
53
34
56
6

'Roseberth'
BIRDSVILLE
63
116
13
40
13
DEVELOPMENTAL
Betoota
161
56
33
'Cuddapan'
29
'South Galway'
'Ten

Birdsville
Famous Hotel
Moonda Lake
50
26
Haddon Corner
14
'Planet Downs' Outstation
41
'Tanbar'
'Keeroongooloo'

'Pandie Pandie'
10
Lake Cooninnie
'Cadelga' (Ruin)
ROAD
201
89
'Nullah' OS
Lake Yamma Yamma
'Malagarga'
'Co

Diamantina
Lake Short
Lake Etamunbanie
160
87
Providence Creek
'Mount Howitt'
'Plevna Downs'
15
36

'Alton Downs'
Andrewilla Waterhole
Lake Uloowarinie
Strzelecki
Desert
Lake Marrapootanie
'Cordillo Downs'
Australia's Largest Shearing Shed
36
'Arrabury'
Numerous mining tracks in this area
Coonaberry
Range
38
stock route
41
10

Goyder Lagoon
BIRDSVILLE TRACK
L. Apunburra
Lake Goyder
Coongie Lake
Lake Toontoowaranie
Monkelearn Ck
Cindradelka Ck
Lake Pure
'Lake Pure'
'Durham Downs'
16
Windulla Ck

To Marree
92
Innamincka
DOWNS
141
31
68
129
130
Gas Centre
34
'Karmona' (ruins)
63
'Bundeena'
'Bell
'Kihee'

Sturt Stony Desert
67
Cooper
COONGIE TRACK
Patchawarra Bore
Regional
Desert Parks Pass required
Reserve
Innamincka No 1 Bore
ADVENTURE
19
200
68
Naccowlah Oil Field
WAY
34

Walkers Crossing
Tirrawarra Oil & Gas Field
CORDILLO (CDR) ROAD
57
Burke & Wills Dig Tree
Gullymurra Waterhole
'Nappa Merrie'
15
14
Jackson Oil Field
19
36
Noccundra
7
'Nockatu

'Gidgealpa'
106
'Innamincka'
18
28
87
46

Innamincka
Lake Andree
21
63
TRACK 46 4WD
48
52
'Tennappera'
68

SOUTH
AUSTRALIA
28°
Lake Perigundi
Cooper Ck
24
Moomba Oil and Gas Field
155
41
16
Innamincka No 3 Bore
23
Dullingari Oil & Gas Field
27
'Orientos'
175
Watson Oil Field
150
86

Lake Warrakalanna
STRZELECKI CREEK
Della Gas Field
32
'Santos'
28
15
'Bransby'
63

Lake Hope
Strzelecki
50
Big Lake
Lake Moonba
Lake Moonba
'Epsilon'
Tickalara Oil Field
44
45

Strzelecki
Regional
Reserve
GAS TRACK (STR)
70
Lake Merteree
'Merty Merty'
Desert
BORE TRACK (BRT)
111
60
62
'Naryilco'
12
'Tickalara'
30
95
Bulloo Lakes

44
Strzelecki Crossing
95
119
Bollards Lagoon
'Omicron'
111
21 16
36
40
40

123
53
'Bollards Lagoon'
14
'The Corner Store'
Fortville Gate
Toona Gate
Warri Gate
Wompah Gate
Caryapundy
Adelaide Gate
Bull

Lake Blanche
140°
Cameron Corner
'Lindon'
Dog Fence
22
39
Fort Grey
STURT NATIONAL PARK
'Olive Downs'
46
'Onepah'
'Wompah' Swamp
NEW

To Lyndhurst
67
To Tibooburra
26
To Tibooburra & Broken Hill
142°

1 2 67 3 4 5 26 6 7

8 9 10 13 11 12 13 14

A

To Blackall · To Blackall · To Blackall

'Mount Marlow' · Konupa · 'Lorne' · 'Ravensbourne' · 'Macfarlane Downs' · 'Jabinda' · 'Truno'
Yaraka · 'Idalia' · 'Carlow' · 'Koondoo' · 'Bonnie Doon' · Tambo · 'Ivanhoe' · 'Manning'
'Highlands' · Idalia National Park · 'Mt Calder' · 'Brides Creek' · 'Minnie Downs' · 'Lansdowne' · 'Yandarlo'
'Wandsworth' · 'Glenara' · private road · 'Cootabynna' · 'Alva' · 'Forest Hill' · 'Westbourne' · 'Southampton Downs' · 'Walton Downs' · 'Coolabri'
Welford National Park · 'Jedburgh' · 'Welford' · Welford Lagoon · 'Collabara' · 'Mungi' · 'Listowel Downs' · 'Milray' · 'Woolga' · 'Oxford Downs'

B

'Budgerygar' · 'Amaroo' · 'Caranna' · 'Lumeah' · 'Toolong' · 'Glanworth'
'Oakham' · 'Thunda' · Hell Hole Gorge National Park · 'Baykool' · 'Noella' · 'Cunalama' · 'Oakwood'
'Trinidad' · 'Wakes Lagoon' · 'Bronte' · 'Biddenham' · Augathella

C

'Lynwood' · 'Milo' · 'Boondoon' · 'Mt Morris' · 'Barradeen' · 'Gundare' · Barduthulla
'Bulgroo OS' · 'Araluen' · 'Sherwood Park' · Adavale · Mariala Nat Park · 'Ambathala' · 'Oakleigh' · 'Newholme' · 'Ard-na-ree'
'Canaway Downs' · 'Varna' · 'Norah Park' · 'Tyrone' · 'Rocksville' · 'Gowrie' · 'Nth Yarrawonga'
'Thylungra' · 'Ray' · 'Gumbardo' · Langlo Crossing · 'Bonnievilla' · 'Yarrawong'

D

'Kyabra' · 'Mogera' · 'Patrick Park' · 'Cairns' · 'Glenyarron' · 'Joylands'
'Pinkilla' · 'Granville' · 'Boothulla' · 'Nimboy' · Charleville · Cosmos Centre
'Pengine' · 'Glenallen' · 'Auburn' · Arabella · Sommariva
'Moble Springs' · 'Arranfield' · Nimaru · Westgate

E

'Naretha' · Quilpie · Winbin · Cheepie · Yalamurra · Coothalla · Loddon · Wanko · Wallal
'Belombrie' · 'Whynot' · 'Tebin' · 'Coolbinga' · 'Dempsey' · 'Bierbank' · Cooladdi · 'Merigol' · Mangalore · 'Colombo'
'Congie' · 'Boolbanna' · 'Woolbunna' · 'Yarronvale' · 'Blackburn' · Dillalah Ridge · 'Verona'
'Margaret' · 'Moble' · 'Gooyana' · 'Coolabah' · 'Guestling' · 'Yallara' · Yanna Ridge · 'Fortland' · 'Bicton'
'Nerrigundah' · 'Cowley' · 'Fairlie' · Murweh · 'Wheatleigh'

F

'Tobermory' · Piastre · 'Bowalli' · 'Boran' · 'Beechal' · 'Mt Alfred' · 'Kynnersley' · Quilberry · 'Alpha' · 'Bankshire'
'Tinderry' · Toompine · 'Wareo' · 'Aldville' · 'Rosevale' · Wyandra · 'Yarramanbar'
'Humeburn' · 'Elverston'
'Tirga' · Claverton · 'Woodlands' · 'Elmina'

G

'Prairie' · 'Boobera' · Mirrabooka · 'Ardgour' · 'Yarmouth'
'Kiandra' · 'Dundoo' · 'Yerrel Creek' · Offham · Coongoola · 'Clifton' · 'Lulworth'
'Norley' · Soonah Crossing · 'Jandell' · 'Tilbooroo' · 'Glendilla' · 'Coongoola South' · Nardoo · 'Nara' · 'Markarene'
'Alroy' · 'Mayvale'

H

Thargomindah · 'Autumn Vale' · Lake Bindegolly Nat Park · 'Bundoona' · Phillott · Cunnamulla · 'Rollo'
'Nooyeah Downs' · Yowah · 'Penaroo' · 'Moonjaree' · 'Charlotte Plains' · 'Bendee Downs'
'Thyangra' · 'Dynevor Downs' · 'Carpet Springs' · Eulo · Burrenbilla · 'Weelamurra'
'Wombula' · Mud Springs · Leopardwood Mines (fossicking)

J

'Yakara' · Lake Bindegolly · 'Werewilka' · 'Tarko' · 'Mooning' · 'Gumahah' · 'Westlea'
'Yenloora' · 'Turn Turn' · 'Pitherty' · 'Thurulgoona' · 'Noorama' · 'Bundaleer'
'Zenonie' · 'Boodgherree' · 'Boorara' · 'Werai Park'
'Kilcowera' · Lake Wyara · L. Numalla · 'Caiwarro' (ruins) · 'Neverfail' · 'Tinnenburra'

K

'Moombidary' · 'Karto' · Currawinya National Park · Currawinya Ranger Stn · 'Rockwell' · Barringun · 'Eureka' · 'Morton Plains'
Hamilton Gate · Waverley Gate · Hungerford · 'Ningaling' · Wambah Lake · private track follows dog fence · Jobs Gate · 'Widgee Downs' · 'Waratah'
'Margalah' · 'Hillside' · 'Waverley Downs' · 'Gumbo' · 'Brindingabba' · 'Nahweenah' · 'Turra' · 'Sharoon' · 'Ellerslie'
SOUTH · WALES · 'Yarrallee' · 'Berawinnia Downs' · Willara Crossing · 'Warroo' · 'Wancobra' · 'Naree' · 'Gerara' · 'Fairfield'
'Glenhope' · 'Willara' · 'Thoura' · Terramia · 'Comeroo' · 'Milanda'

To Morven & Brisbane · To Bolton · To St George · To Bourke · To Wanaaring

Landsborough Hwy · Matilda Hwy · Mitchell Hwy · Balonne Hwy · Warrego Hwy · Adventure Way · Bulloo Way · Kidman Way

© Hema Maps Pty Ltd

0 50km

N

TORRES STRAIT

ARAFURA SEA

SOUTH PACIFIC OCEAN

Cape York Peninsula

© Hema Maps Pty Ltd

0   50   100km

Alcohol Restrictions
Be aware that alcohol restrictions apply in some of Cape York's indigenous communities. For more information contact the Alcohol Management Program information line on ph 1300 789 000 or look at the Queensland Government Liquor Licensing Division's website (www.liquor.qld.gov.au)

GREAT BARRIER REEF MARINE PARK
Far Northern Section
For more detail on this area, see Hema's Cape York Map

Quarantine
When travelling south from the Cape, present all animal and plant material for inspection at the Coen Quarantine Station. Ph 1800 084 881 for information

Selected place names: Cape York, Somerset (ruins), Albany Island, Seisia, Umagico, Bamaga, Injinoo, Thursday Island, Horn Island, Prince of Wales, Mabuiag Island, Moa Island, Badu Island, Captain Billy Landing, Heathlands, Bramwell Junction, Bramwell, Mapoon, Napranum, Weipa, Myerfield, Moreton Telegraph Station, Batavia Downs, Bromley, Wattle Hill, Portland Roads, Lockhart River, Iron Range, Cape Weymouth, Chilli Beach, Aurukun, Wutan, Kendall River, Rokeby, Merapah, Archer River Roadhouse, Coen, Mt White, Silver Plains, Moojeeba, Port Stewart, Ebagoola, Yaraden, Running Creek, Marina Plains, Musgrave, Glen Garland, Artemis, Mary Valley, Lakefield, Kalpowar, Bizant, Hann Crossing, Hann River Roadhouse, Pormpuraaw, Kowanyama, Laura, Cooktown, Hope Vale, Helenvale, Lizard Island, Cape Flattery, Cape Melville, Bathurst Bay

Iron Range Nat Park, Jardine River National Park, Mungkan Kandju National Park, Lakefield National Park, Mitchell-Alice Rivers National Park

New South Wales

Katoomba Falls, Blue Mountains National Park (22 G7)

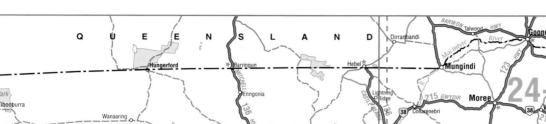

Albury															
1007	**Armidale**														
458	549	**Bathurst**													
849	1120	962	**Broken Hill**												
333	818	301	1096	**Canberra**											
548	432	202	760	403	**Dubbo**										
352	726	320	1115	92	422	**Goulburn**									
1184	194	743	1314	1044	626	797	**Grafton**								
1283	345	842	1413	1143	725	896	99	**Lismore**							
549	1244	823	300	882	812	901	1566	1665	**Mildura**						
709	329	322	1104	450	344	372	468	567	1192	**Newcastle**					
938	243	537	1313	665	547	572	237	336	1427	243	**Port Macquarie**				
545	465	205	1167	285	407	193	604	703	1028	164	379	**Sydney**			
902	105	444	1015	713	327	621	299	398	1139	277	276	413	**Tamworth**		
136	871	322	860	236	412	255	1065	1164	560	644	859	448	766	**Wagga Wagga**	
486	545	251	1218	226	458	134	684	783	949	244	473	80	440	389	**Wollongong**

Distances are shown in kilometres and assume the most direct major sealed route

LEGEND

Freeway	Major Building
Through Route	Govt Building
Major Road	Accommodation
Street	Theatre/Cinema
Lane/Walkway	Shopping
Railway — Underground	Church ✝
Railway Station Wynyard	Hospital ✚

0 100 200 300 400 500 600 700 800m

© Hema Maps Pty Ltd

Travel

- 90 Central Station D1
- 91 Circular Quay Station B2
- 92 Kings Cross Station C3
- 93 Martin Place Station C2
- 94 Museum Station D2
- 95 Town Hall Station C1
- 96 Wynyard Station B1

For more information on the ferry from Sydney to Devonport Ph 1800 634 906 www.spiritoftasmania.com.au

Places of Interest

1 Anzac War Memorial D2
2 Art Gallery of NSW C3
3 Australian Motor Museum C1
4 Australian Museum C2
5 Australian Nat. Maritime Museum C1
6 Cadmans Cottage A2
7 Chinatown D1
8 Conservatorium of Music B2
9 Darling Harbour C1
10 Government House B2
11 Harbour Bridge Arch Walk A2
12 Harbourside Festival Marketplace C1
13 Hyde Park Barracks C2
14 Mrs Macquarie's Chair B3
15 Museum of Contemporary Art B2
16 Panasonic IMAX Theatre C1
17 Parliament House B2
18 Powerhouse Museum D1
19 Royal Botanic Gardens B3
20 St Andrews Cathedral C1
21 St Marys Cathedral C2
22 St Stephens Church B2
23 Star City Casino C1
24 State Library of NSW B2
25 Sydney Aquarium C1
26 Sydney Convention Centre D1
27 Sydney Exhibition Centre D1
28 Sydney Entertainment Centre D1
29 Sydney Opera House A3
30 Sydney Tower C2
31 Sydney Town Hall C1
32 The Mint C2
33 The Rocks A2
34 Wharf Theatre A1

Accommodation

35 Aarons Hotel Sydney D1
36 Avillion Hotel Sydney D2
37 Carlton Crest Hotel Sydney D1
38 Castlereagh Boutique Hotel C2
39 Comfort Inn Cambridge D2
41 Crowne Plaza Darling Harbour C1
42 Four Points by Sheraton DH Sydney C1
43 Four Seasons Hotel Sydney B2
44 Grace Hotel Sydney (The) C1
45 Harbour Rocks Hotel (The) B2
46 Hotel Ibis Darling Harbour C1
47 Hotel Ibis World Square C2
48 Hyde Park Inn D2
49 Intercontinental Sydney B2
50 Leisure Inns Park Regis C2
51 Maestri Towers C1
52 Medina Grand Harbourside C1
53 Medina Grand Sydney C1
54 Menzies Sydney (The) B2
55 Mercure Sydney on Broadway D1
56 Millennium Hotel Sydney C3
57 Napoleon on Kent B1
58 Novotel Sydney on Darling Harbour C1
60 Observatory Hotel B1
60 Old Sydney Holiday Inn A2
61 Pacific Internatnl Suites Sydney D1
62 Park Hyatt Hotel Sydney A2
63 Quay Grand Suites Sydney B2
64 Quay West Suites Sydney B2
65 Quest on Dixon D2
66 Radisson Hotel & Suites Sydney C1
67 Radisson Plaza Hotel Sydney B2
69 Rendezvous Stafford Hotel B2
69 Royal Garden Hotel D2
70 Russell Hotel B1
71 Rydges Jamison Hotel B2
72 Saville 2 Bond Street B2
73 Sebel Pier One Sydney (The) A2
74 Shangri-La Hotel Sydney B1
75 Sheraton on the Park C2
76 Sir Stamford at Circular Quay B2
77 Sofitel Wentworth Sydney B2
78 Somerset Darling Harbour C1
79 Sullivans Hotel D3
80 Swissotel Sydney on Market Street C2
81 Sydney Boulevard Hotel (The) C3
82 Syd Harbour Marriott at Circ Quay B2
83 Sydney Marriott Hotel D2
84 The Oaks Hyde Park Plaza D2
85 W Sydney C3
86 Waldorf Apartment Sydney D1
87 Westin Sydney (The) C2
88 Woolloomooloo Waters Aparts Hotel C3
89 York Apartment Hotel (The) B1

Walsh Bay, Dawes Point, Millers Point, The Rocks, Sydney Cove, Circular Quay, PORT JACKSON, Sydney Opera House, Bennelong Point, Government House, Farm Cove, Royal Botanic Gardens, The Domain, Mrs Macquaries Point, Mrs Macquaries Chair, Woolloomooloo Bay, Garden Island, Captain Cook Dock, Potts Point, Darling Harbour, Cockle Bay, Sydney, Hyde Park, Cook Park, The Domain, Art Gallery of NSW, Woolloomooloo, Kings Cross, Fitzroy Gardens, Ultimo, Chinatown, Belmore Park, Central, Darlinghurst, Paddington

To North Sydney, To Pyrmont, To Bondi, To Airport

NSW

To Wisemans Ferry • To Newcastle, Raymond Tce • To Windsor • To Penrith, Katoomba • To Campbelltown, Goulburn • To Wollongong

SCALE
0 1 2 3 4 5 6 7 8km

© Hema Maps Pty Ltd

(Map of Sydney throughroads showing suburbs including Glenorie, Arcadia, Berowra Heights, Middle Dural, Galston, Kenthurst, Mt Kuring-gai, Ku-ring-gai Chase National Park, Lovett Bay, Scotland Is, Church Point, Newport, Mona Vale, Bayview, Ingleside, Terrey Hills, Elanora Heights, Narrabeen, Kellyville, Round Corner, Dural, Hornsby Heights, Mt Colah, Bobbin Head, Akuna Bay, Duffys Forest, Garigal National Park, Oxford Falls, Collaroy, Dee Why, Narraweena, Brookvale, Curl Curl, Castle Hill, Cherrybrook, Thornleigh, Wahroonga, Turramurra, St Ives, Davidson, Frenchs Forest, Killarney Heights, Allambie, Manly Vale, Queenscliff Beach, Manly, Blacktown, Baulkham Hills, West Pennant Hills, Pennant Hills, Cheltenham, Pymble, Gordon, Killara, Lindfield, Roseville, Chatswood, Castlecrag, Clontarf, Balgowlah, Seven Lane Cove, Ryde, Eastwood, Parramatta, Westmead, Prospect, Fairfield, Liverpool, Bankstown, Hurstville, Sutherland, Cronulla, Bundeena) and many more.

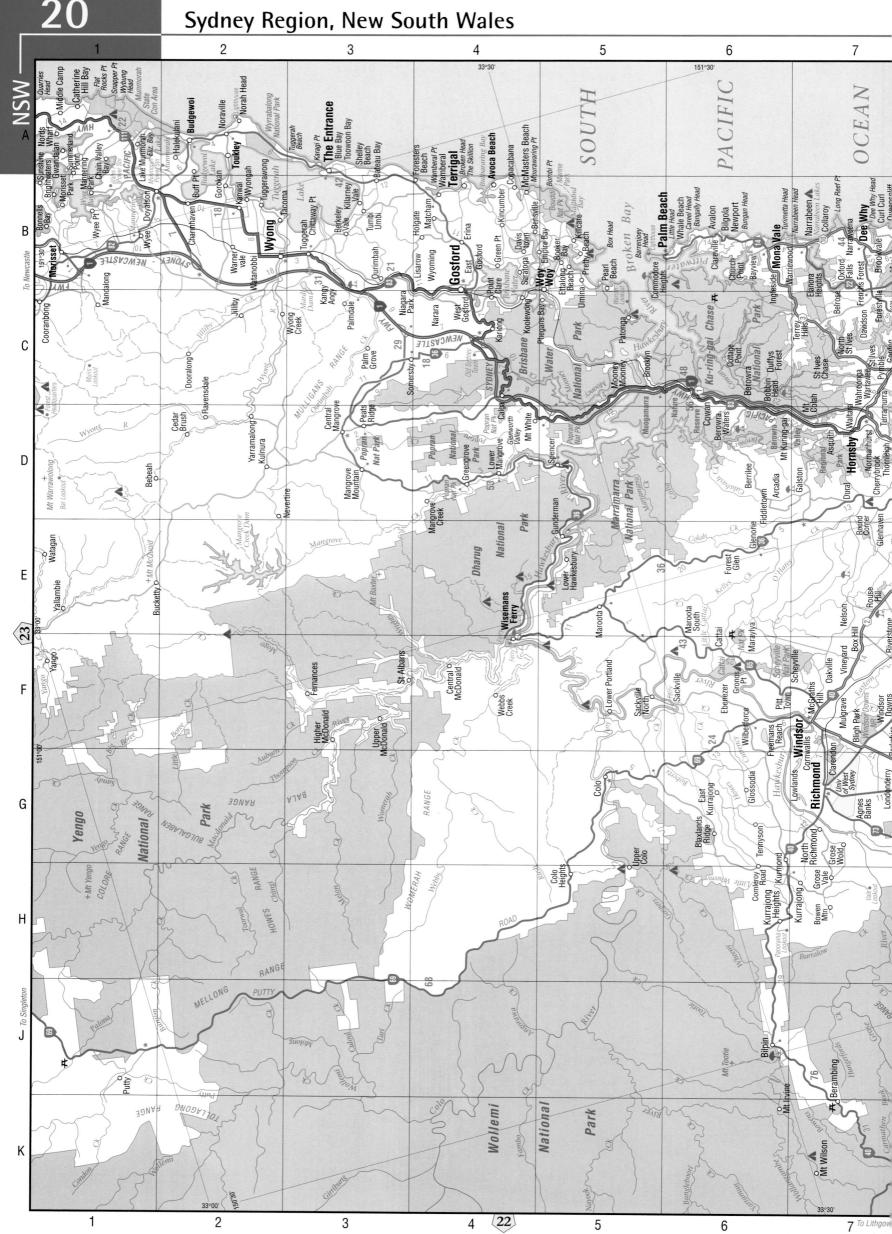

TASMAN SEA

SYDNEY
Bondi
Maroubra
Cronulla
Royal National Park
Sutherland
Parramatta
Ryde
Strathfield
Burwood
Hurstville
Bankstown
Fairfield
Liverpool
Blacktown
Penrith
St Marys
Mt Druid
Campbelltown
Camden
Picton
Tahmoor
Bargo
WOLLONGONG
Port Kembla
Bulli
Springwood
Blaxland
Glenbrook
Katoomba
Blackheath
Leppington
Bringelly
Luddenham
Warragamba
Thirlmere

Blue Mountains National Park
Nattai National Park
Burragorang State Conservation Area
Nattai State Conservation Area
Bargo State Con Area
Lake Burragorang
Yarranderie State Conservation Area

© Hema Maps Pty Ltd

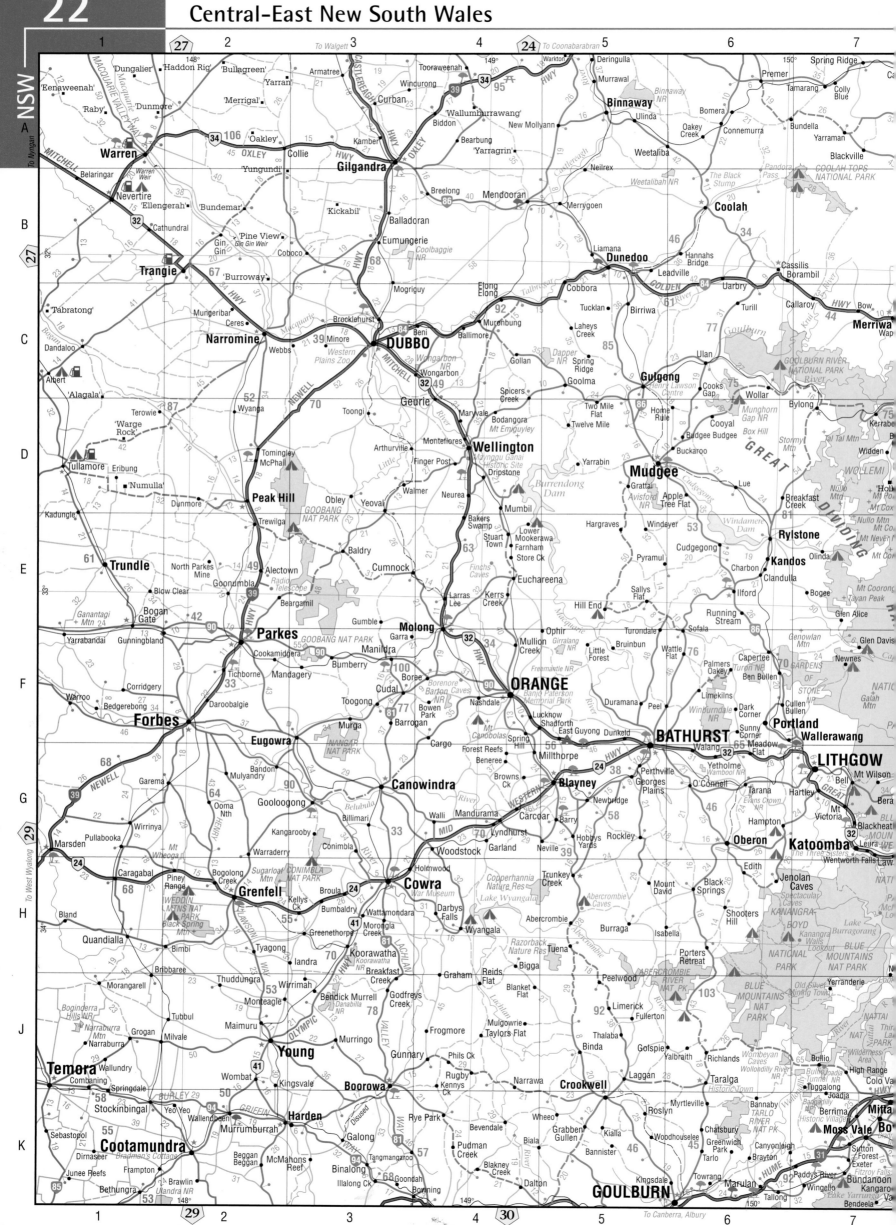

To Tamworth

8 9 10 25 11 To Walcha 12 13 To Kempsey 14

Port Macquarie

Quipolly
Quirindi
Bowling Alley Point
Hanging Rock
Nundle
Myrtle Scrub
Mt Seaview
Birdwood
Pappinbarra
Pembroke
Rollands Plains
Telegraph Point
Point Plomer
Limeburners Creek Nature Reserve

"The Ranch"
Wallabadah
Mt Seaview
Yarras
Ellenborough
Long Flat
Beechwood
Wauchope
Tacking Point

Braefield
Willow Tree
Nowendoc
Glenwarrin
Byabarra
Combyne
Comboyne
Lorne
Kendall
Laurieton
North Haven

Warrah
Murrurundi
Timor
Ellerston
Tomalla
Number One
Caparra
Bobin
Killabakh
Kinbee
Kew
Bonny Hills

Owens Gap
Kars Springs
Burning Mountain NR
Moonan Flat
Cootera Hill
'Hunter Springs'
Bretti NR
Knorrit Flat
Wherrol Flat
Killawarra
Landsdowne
Coopernook
CROWDY BAY NATIONAL PARK

Scone
Blandford
Wingen
Parkville
Gundy
Belltrees
Woolooma
Cobark
Rookhurst
Barrington
Bundook
Kimbriki
Tinonee
TAREE
Purfleet
Old Bar
Harrington
Crowdy Head

Aberdeen
Dangarfield
Rouchel Brook
Barrington Tops 1585m
BARRINGTON TOPS NAT PARK
Gloucester
Faulkland
Belbora
Krambach
Hallidays Point
Khappinghat NR

Muswellbrook
McCullys Gap
Davis Ck
Mt Royal
'Barrington House' 1433m
Stratford
Nabiac
Failford
Tuncurry

Castle Rock
Carrow Brook
Salisbury
Chichester
Craven
Running Creek NR
Warranulla
Bunya
Coolongolook
Forster
Cape Hawke

Denman
Dawsons Hill
Eccleston
Killarney
Main Ck
Wards River
Weismantels
Upper Myall
BOOTI BOOTI NAT PARK
Elizabeth Bay

Hebden
Lostock
Halton
Bandon Grove
Fosterton
Monkerai NR
Ghin-Doo-Ee Nat Park
Wootton
Wallingat NR

Liddell
St Clair
Mt Olive
Mirannie
Gresford
Dungog
Stroud Road
Bulahdelah
Stroud
Bungwahl
Pacific Palms

Ravensworth
Camberwell
Trevallyn
Marshdale
Booral
Girvan
Seal Rocks
Sugarloaf Bay
MYALL LAKES NATIONAL PARK

Jerrys Plains
Warkworth
Glendon Brook
Brookfield
Allworth
Karuah NR
Myall Lakes
SOUTH

Glen Gallic
Appleton Aboriginal Area
Vacy
Paterson
Clarence Town
Ferry
Mungo Brush
Tamboy
Broughton Island

Singleton
Branxton
Greta
Woodville
Lochinvar
Seaham
Tea Gardens

Belford
PACIFIC
Karuah
Lemon Tree Passage
Hawks Nest

Broke
MAITLAND
Raymond Terrace
Port Stephens

Wineries
Pokolbin
Kurri Kurri
Beresfield
Williamtown
Nelson Bay
TOMAREE NAT PARK

CESSNOCK
Bellbird
Hexham Swamp
Kooragang NR
Anna Bay
Morna Point

Paynes Crossing
Finchley Aboriginal Area
Millfield
Paxton
Mulbring
Wallsend
Stockton
Port Hunter

Wollombi
Watagans NP
Freemans Waterhole
NEWCASTLE

Toronto
Belmont
Swansea
Lake Macquarie
WALLARAH NAT PARK

Cooranbong
Morisset
Wyee
Bucketty
MUNMORAH STATE CON AREA
PACIFIC

Doyalson
Lake Munmorah
WYRRABALONG NAT PARK

Kulnura
Mangrove Mtn
Peats Ridge
Budgewoi
Norah Head

St Albans
Ourimbah
Wyong
Tuggerah Lake

Colo Heights
Wisemans Ferry
The Entrance

Kurrajong
Gosford
Terrigal
Wamberal Lagoon NR

Windsor
Kilcare
Marie Byles Lookout
BOUDDI NAT PARK

Penrith
Palm Beach
Broken Bay

Hornsby
Mona Vale

Parramatta
Long Reef
Manly
SYDNEY HARBOUR NP

Liverpool
SYDNEY
Opera House, Powerhouse Museum, Sydney Aquarium, Beautiful Harbour, Taronga Zoo, Sydney Tower, The Rocks, Australia's Wonderland, Darling Harbour.
OCEAN

Sutherland
Airport
Botany Bay
BOTANY BAY NP
Port Hacking

Campbelltown
Heathcote
Bundeena
ROYAL NATIONAL PARK

Waterfall
Garie

Appin
Helensburgh
Stanwell Park
Scarborough
TASMAN

Coledale
Thirroul
Bulli
Corrimal

WOLLONGONG
Red Point
Port Kembla
Shellharbour
Bass Point Marine Res

Kiama
Blowhole
Lighthouse
Minnamurra
Bombo

Gerringong
SEA

GREAT DIVIDING RANGE

N

0 10 20 30 40 50 60km

© Hema Maps Pty Ltd

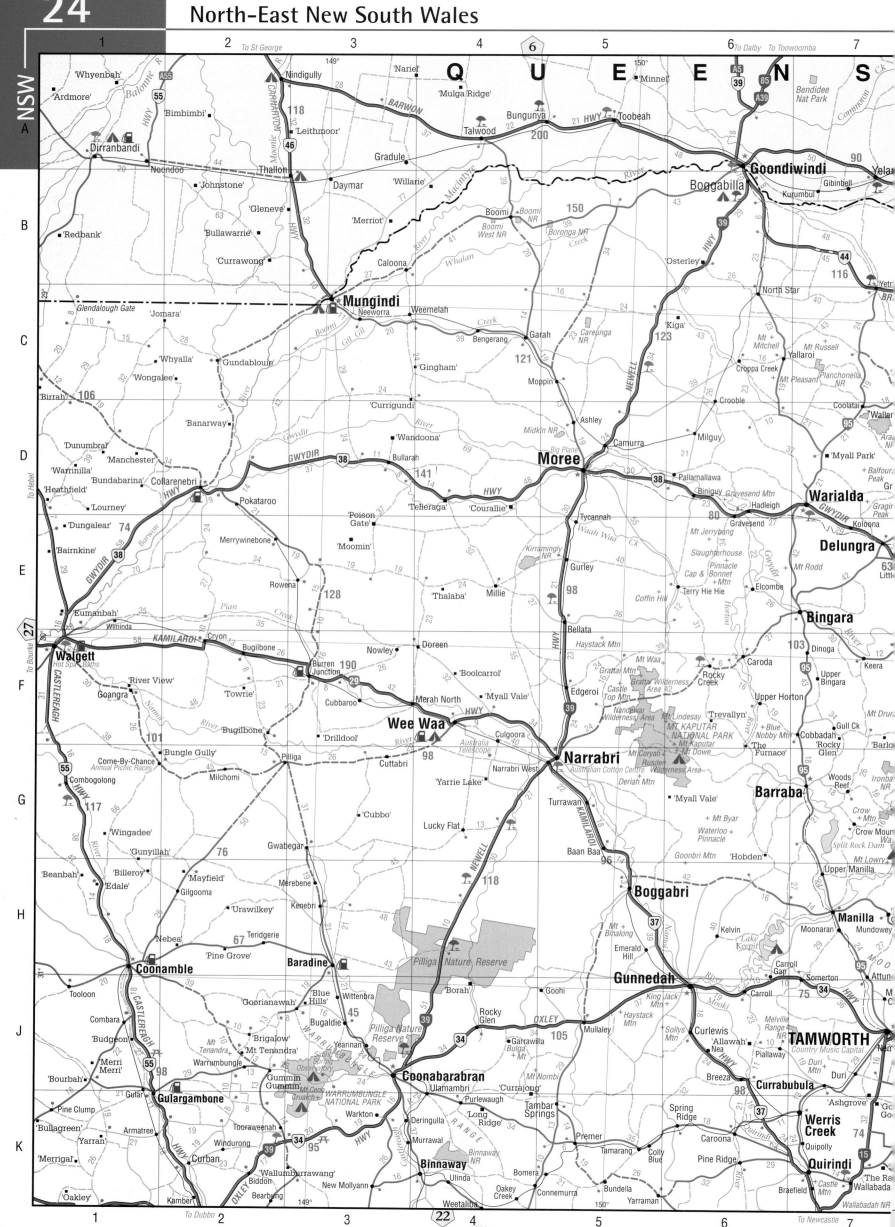

8 9 [7] 10 To Toowoomba, Brisbane 11 12 [5] To Brisbane 13 To Brisbane, Surfers Paradise 14

A N D

Coolangatta
Tweed Heads

Karara
108
Springbrook
Binna Burra
Rathdowney
Lamington Nat Park
O'Reillys
Springbrook
Bilambil
Terranora
Tumbulgum
Chinderah
Kingscliff
Cudgen
Bogangar

Warwick
Killarney
Legume
Woodenbong
Mt Barney Nat Park
Urbenville
Grevillia
BORDER RANGES
Chillingham
Condong
Uki
Burringbar
Mooball
Murwillumbah
Hastings Pt
Pottsville

Messines
Wylie Creek
Tooloom
Urbenville
The Risk
Kunghur
Nimbin
Billinudgel
Ocean Shores

Pikedale
Liston
Amosfield
Wilsons Downfall
Old Bonalbo
RICHMOND
Afterlee
Toonumbar Dam
Kyogle
Georgica
The Channon
Dunoon
Roseback
Mullumbimby
Brunswick Heads

Stanthorpe
Ballandean
Bonalbo
Fairy Hill
Bentley
Bexhill
Byron Bay
Cape Byron

Texas
Silver Spur
Girraween NP
Boonoo Boonoo Nat Park
Tabulam
Mummulgum
LISMORE
Clunes
Bangalow
Newrybar
Lennox Head

Limevale
Sundown Nat Park
Pretty Gully
123
Mallanganee
Casino
29
Alstonville
Wyrallah
Tevan
Ballina
Ballina NR

Bonshaw
Mingoola
Mole River
Tenterfield
Black Swamp
Alice
Wyan
Rappville
Coraki
46
Wardell
Broadwater

134
Wallangarra
Sunnyside
Bungulla
Mt Pikapene Nat Park
Busbys Flat
Yorklea
Tatham
30
BROADWATER NAT PARK
Evans Head

'The Gulf'
Torrington
Stannum
Bolivia
Baryulgil
Burnt-Down Scrub NR
Camira Ck
New Italy
Woodburn
Tabbimobile Swamp NR

Ashford
Stannifer
Tent Hill
Deepwater
WASHPOOL NATIONAL PARK
Fine Flower
Coaldale
99
Bundjalung
93
BUNDJALUNG NATIONAL PARK

Bukkulla
Emmaville
Dundee
Glen Elgin
157
Cangai
GIBRALTAR RANGE NAT PK
Copmanhurst
Maclean
Iluka
Yamba
For more details on this area, see Hema's North East New South Wales Map

Oakwood
Wellingrove
Bald Knob
Cooraldooral WA
Jackadgery
38 HWY
Ulmarra
Tyndale
Cowper
Angourie
Brooms Head

Sapphire
Matheson
Shannon Vale
Mann NR
NYMBOIDA NAT PARK
South Grafton
GRAFTON
Tucabia
Sandon
YURAYGIR NAT PARK

Glen Innes
Stonehenge
Red Range
Newton Boyd
Buccarumbi
Dalmorton
Coutts Crossing
Pillar Valley
Minnie Water
SOUTH

Tingha
Glencoe
Ben Lomond
Mt Mitchell
GUY FAWKES RIVER NAT PARK
Nymboida
Halfway Creek
Wooli
North Solitary Island NR

Bundarra
Wandsworth
Llangothlin
Backwater
Oban
Wards Mistake
Clouds Creek
Glenreagh
79
Red Rock
Corindi Beach
30°

Guyra
Wongwibinda
Rockvale
CATHEDRAL ROCK NAT PARK
Hernani
Billys Creek
Dundurrabin
Ulong
Coramba
Mullaway
Woolgoolga
Sandy Beach
Emerald Beach
Moonee Beach
Korora

Baldersleigh
124
Duval NR
Tilbuster
Wollomombi
Jeogla
Bostobrick
Megan
Upper Orara
Coffs Harbour
Big Banana

ARMIDALE
78
Dangarsleigh
Hillgrove
Oxley Wild Rivers
OXLEY WILD RIVERS NATIONAL PARK
Ebor
Dorrigo Falls
Dorrigo
Darkwood
Brineville
Thora
Bellingen
Raleigh
Sawtell
BONGIL BONGIL NATIONAL PARK

Uralla
Gostwyck
Kentucky
Enmore
Georges Junction
Comara
Burrapine
Bowraville
Missabotti
Argents Hill
Urunga
Mylestom
PACIFIC

Wollun
Woolbrook
'East Lake'
Lower Creek
Bellbrook
Taylors Arm
Warrell Ck
Macksville
Scotts Head
Grassy Head
Stuarts Point
Nambucca Heads

Walcha
34
Moona Plains
OXLEY WILD RIVERS NATIONAL PARK
Willawarrin
Millbank
Eungai
109
YARRIAHINI NATIONAL PARK
South West Rocks
Arakoon
Smoky Cape

Limbri
Niangala
Brackendale
Yarrowitch
WERRIKIMBE NAT PARK
Kookaburra
Sherwood
Burnt Bridge
Kempsey
Gladstone
Hat Head
HAT HEAD NATIONAL PARK
Crescent Head
OCEAN

Weabonga
Tia
Myrtle Scrub
Mt Seaview
Birdwood
Rollands Plains
Kundabung
Point Plomer

GREAT DIVIDING RANGE
Nowendoc
173
Yarras
34
Ellenborough
Long Flat
Beechwood
Telegraph Point
Pembrooke
Limeburners Creek Nature Reserve

To Gloucester [23] To Taree **Port Macquarie**
Wauchope
Byabarra
Tacking Point
Lake Innes Nature Res

© Hema Maps Pty Ltd

N

0 10 20 30 40 50km

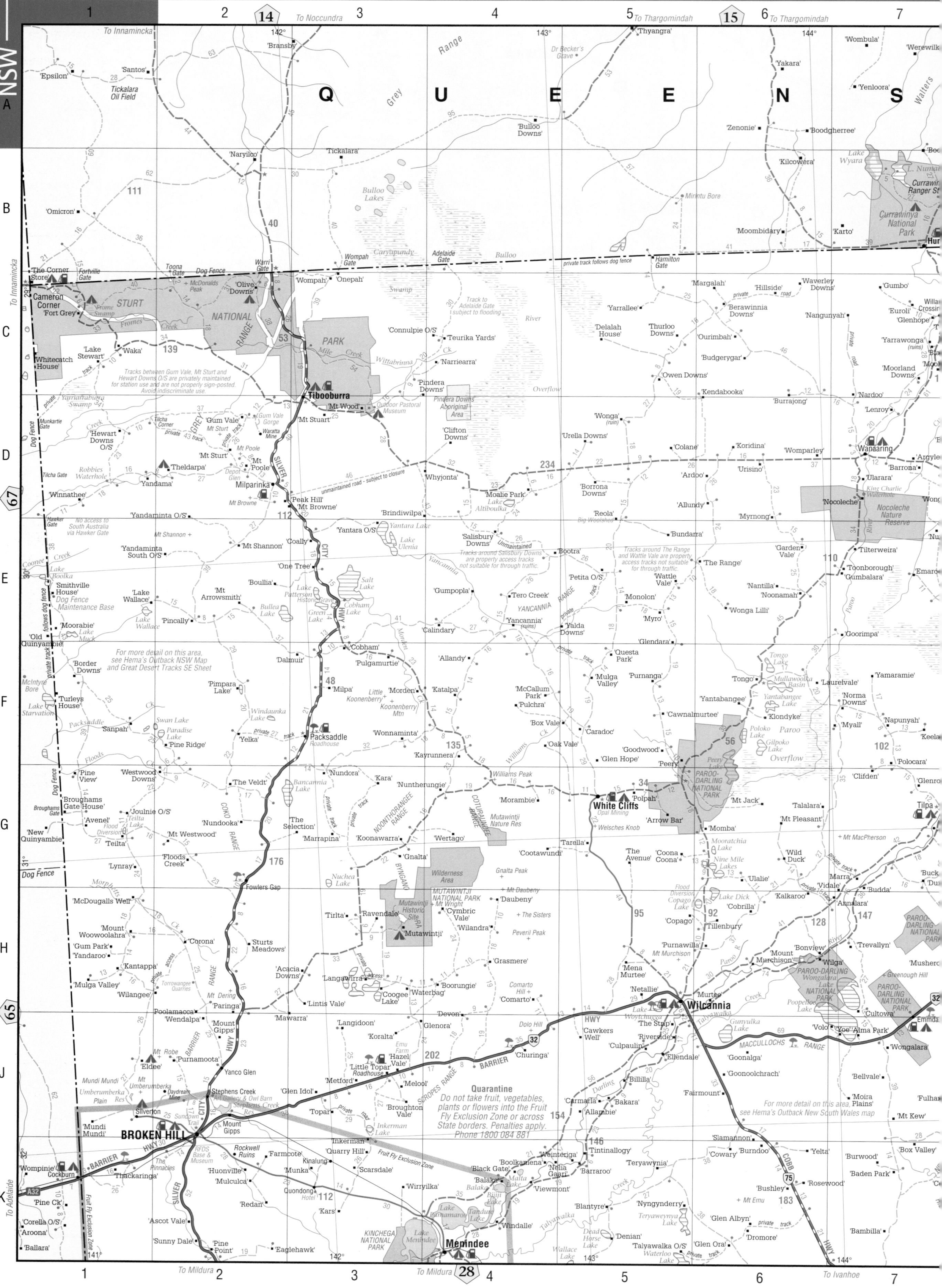
To Innamincka
To Noccundra
To Thargomindah
QUEENSLAND
Grey Range
Tickalara Oil Field
'Santos'
'Epsilon'
'Bransby'
'Thyangra'
Dr Becker's Grave
'Bulloo Downs'
'Zenonie'
'Boodgherree'
'Kilcowera'
'Yakara'
'Yenloora'
'Wombula'
'Naryilco'
'Tickalara'
Bulloo Lakes
'Omicron'
Mirintu Bore
'Moombidary'
'Karto'
Lake Wyara
Currawinya National Park
The Corner Store
Cameron Corner
'Fort Grey'
STURT NATIONAL PARK
Dog Fence
Warri Gate
'Olive Downs'
'Wompah'
'Onepah'
Wompah Gate
Adelaide Gate
Bulloo
Hamilton Gate
private track follows dog fence
Frome Swamp
Fromes Creek
'Lake Stewart'
'Waka'
Whitecatch House
Tracks between Gum Vale, Mt Sturt and Hewart Downs O/S are privately maintained for station use and are not properly sign-posted. Avoid indiscriminate use.
Tibooburra
'Mt Wood'
Outdoor Pastoral Museum
'Connulpie O/S'
'Teurika Yards'
'Narriearra'
'Pindera Downs'
Pindera Downs Aboriginal Area
Track to Adelaide Gate subject to flooding
'Yarrallee'
'Delalah House'
'Thurloo Downs'
'Margalah'
'Hillside'
'Berawinnia Downs'
'Waverley Downs'
'Ourimbah'
'Budgerygar'
'Owen Downs'
'Kendabooka'
'Gumbo'
'Nangunyah'
'Euroli'
'Glenhope'
'Yarrawonga'
'Moorland Downs'
'Nardoo'
'Burrajong'
'Lenroy'
Wanaaring
'Wompah'
'Gum Vale'
Gum Vale Gorge
'Mt Stuart'
'Hewart Downs O/S'
Tilcha Corner
'Mt Sturt'
Mt Poole
'Mt Poole'
'Theldarpa'
Robbies Waterhole
'Yandama'
Depot Glen
Milparinka
Mt Browne
'Peak Hill'
'Mt Browne'
'Winnathee'
Tilcha Gate
Hawker Gate
No access to South Australia via Hawker Gate
'Yandaminta O/S'
Mt Shannon
'Mt Shannon'
'Yandaminta South O/S'
'Clifton Downs'
'Whyjonta'
unmaintained road - subject to closure
'Brindiwilpa'
'Moalie Park'
Lake Altiboulka
'Urella Downs'
'Wonga'
'Colane'
'Ardoo'
'Borrona Downs'
'Reola'
'Allundy'
'Koridina'
'Urisino'
'Wompareley'
'Barrona'
'Ularara'
King Charlie Waterhole
'Nocoleche'
Nocoleche Nature Reserve
'Myrnong'
'Yantara O/S'
Yantara Lake
Lake Ulenia
'Coally'
'Salisbury Downs'
Tracks around Salisbury Downs are property access tracks not suitable for through traffic.
'Bootra'
'Bundarra'
Tracks around The Range and Wattle Vale are property access tracks not suitable for through traffic.
'The Range'
'Garden Vale'
'Tilterweira'
'Toonborough'
'Gumbalara'
'One Tree'
'Smithville House'
Dog Fence Maintenance Base
Lake Boolka
'Boullia'
'Mt Arrowsmith'
'Lake Wallace'
Salt Lake
Lake Patterson
Historic Grave
Green Lake
Cobham Lake
Bullea Lake
'Pincally'
'Gumpopla'
'Tero Creek'
YANCANNIA RANGE
'Yancannia'
'Yalda Downs'
'Petita O/S'
'Monolon'
'Wattle Vale'
'Nantilla'
'Noonamah'
'Wonga Lilli'
'Myro'
'Moorabie'
Lake Muck
'Old Quinyambie'
'Calindary'
'Glendara'
'Goorimpa'
For more detail on this area, see Hema's Outback NSW Map and Great Desert Tracks SE Sheet
'Border Downs'
'Dalmuir'
'Cobham'
'Pulgamurtie'
'Allandy'
'Questa Park'
'Mulga Valley'
'Purnanga'
Tongo Lake
'Tongo'
Mullawoolka Basin
'Laurelvale'
'Yamaramie'
McIntyre Bore
Lake Starvation
'Turleys House'
'Pimpara Lake'
'Milpa'
Little Koonenberry
Koonenberry Mtn
'Morden'
'Katalpa'
'McCallum Park'
'Pulchra'
'Yantabangee'
Yantabangee Lake
'Norma Downs'
'Napunyah'
'Myall'
'Sanpah'
Swan Lake
Paradise Lake
'Pine Ridge'
Windaunka Lake
'Yelka'
Packsaddle
Roadhouse
'Wonnaminta'
'Kayrunnera'
'Box Vale'
'Oak Vale'
'Caradoc'
'Cawnalmurtee'
'Klondyke'
Poloko Lake
Paroo
Gilpoko Lake
Overflow
'Goodwood'
'Glen Hope'
'Peery'
Peery Lake
'Polocara'
'Clifden'
'Pine View'
'Westwood Downs'
'The Veldt'
'Nundora'
Bancannia Lake
'Kara'
'Nuntherungie'
Williams Peak
NOONTHORANGEE RANGE
COTURAUNDEE RANGE
'Morambie'
White Cliffs
Opal Mining
'Polpah'
PAROO-DARLING NATIONAL PARK
'Mt Jack'
'Talalara'
Tilpa
'Broughams Gate House'
Broughams Gate
'Joulnie O/S'
'Avenel'
Teilta Lake
Flood Diversion
'Teilta'
'New Quinyambie'
'Nundooka'
COKO RANGE
'Mt Westwood'
'The Selection'
'Marrapina'
'Koonawarra'
'Wertago'
Mutawintji Nature Res
Welsches Knob
'Arrow Bar'
'Momba'
'Mt Pleasant'
Mt MacPherson
'Lynray'
'Floods Creek'
'Gnalta'
'Cootawundi'
'Tarella'
'The Avenue'
'Coona Coona'
Mooratchia Lake
Nine Mile Lakes
'Wild Duck'
'Marra'
Dog Fence
Fowlers Gap
Nuchea Lake
Gnalta Peak
Wilderness Area
MUTAWINTJI NATIONAL PARK
Mt Daubeny
'Daubeny'
Mt Wright
'Cymbric Vale'
'Ulalie'
'Vidale'
'Budda'
'McDougalls Well'
'Tirlta'
'Ravendale'
Mutawintji Historic Site
'Mutawintji'
The Sisters
Flood Diversion
Copago Lake
'Copago'
Lake Dick
'Cobrilla'
'Tillenbury'
'Kalkaroo'
'Annalara'
'Mount Woowoolahra'
'Corona'
'Sturts Meadows'
'Wilandra'
Peveril Peak
'Purnawilla'
Mt Murchison
'Bonview'
'Trevallyn'
'Gum Park'
'Yandaroo'
'Kantappa'
'Acacia Downs'
'Langawirra'
'Grasmere'
'Mena Murtee'
'Mount Murchison'
'Wilga'
PAROO-DARLING NATIONAL PARK
Greenough Hill
'Musheroo'
'Mulga Valley'
'Wilangee'
Torrowangee Quarries
Mt Dering
'Paringa'
'Coogee Lake'
'Waterbag'
'Boorungie'
Comarto Hill
'Comarto'
'Netallie'
Wilcannia
'Murtee'
Poopelloe Lake
'Cultowa'
'Lintis Vale'
'Poolamacca'
'Wendalpa'
'Mawarra'
'Devon'
'Mount Gipps'
'Langidoon'
'Glenora'
Dolo Hill
'Cawkers Well'
Lake Wytchugga
'The Strip'
'Riverside'
'Culpaulin'
Gunyulka Lake
MACCULLOCHS RANGE
'Volo'
'Zoe'
'Alma Park'
'Wongalara'
Emmdale
Mt Robe
'Eldee'
'Purnamoota'
BARRIER RANGE
'Koralta'
Emu Farm
'Hazel Vale'
'Little Topar'
Roadhouse
'Churinga'
'Ellendale'
'Goonalga'
'Goonoolchrach'
Yanco Glen
Mundi Mundi
Mt Umberumberka
Umberumberka Res
Daydream Mine
Plain
Stephens Creek
Art Gallery & Owl Barn
Stephens Creek Res
'Glen Idol'
'Metford'
'Melool'
SCROPES RANGE
Quarantine
Do not take fruit, vegetables, plants or flowers into the Fruit Fly Exclusion Zone or across State borders. Penalties apply. Phone 1800 084 881
'Billilla'
'Carmarla'
'Bakara'
'Allambie'
'Fairmount'
For more detail on this area, see Hema's Outback New South Wales map
'Bellvale'
'Moira Plains'
'Mt Kew'
'Mundi Mundi'
Silverton
Sundown Hill
BROKEN HILL
'Mount Gipps'
'Topar'
'Broughton Vale'
Inkerman Lake
'Slamannon'
'Burndoo'
'Yelta'
'Burwood'
'Box Valley'
'Wompinie'
Cockburn
BARRIER HWY
The Pinnacles
RFDS Base & Museum
Rockwell Ruins
'Farmcote'
'Inkerman'
'Quarry Hill'
Fruit Fly Exclusion Zone
'Bookkamena'
'Weinteriga'
'Nelia Gaari'
'Tintinallogy'
'Teryawynia'
'Cowary'
'Baden Park'
'Thackaringa'
'Huonville'
'Mulculca'
'Munka'
Kinalung
'Scarsdale'
'Black Gate'
'Balaka'
Balaka Lake
Malta Lake
Bijijie Lake
'Barraroo'
'Viewmont'
'Rosewood'
To Adelaide
'Pine Ck'
Quondong Hotel
'Wirryilka'
'Nyngynderry'
'Bushley'
Mt Emu
'Corella O/S'
'Aroona'
Fruit Fly Exclusion Zone
'Redan'
'Kars'
Lake Pamamaroo
Lake Tandure
'Blantyre'
Teryaweynya Lake
'Glen Albyn'
'Dromore'
'Windalle'
Talyawalka
Dead Horse Lake
'Denian'
'Bambilla'
'Ascot Vale'
'Sunny Dale'
'Pine Point'
'Eaglehawk'
KINCHEGA NATIONAL PARK
Lake Menindee
Menindee
Wallace Lake
'Talyawalka O/S'
Waterloo Lake
'Glen Ora'
'Ballara'
SILVER CITY HWY
COBB HWY
To Mildura
To Ivanhoe

To Eulo

8 9 15 To Cunnamulla 10 11 6 12 13 14

145° 146° N 147° 148°

'Murra Murra' 'Fernlee' 'Wombil' 'Ardmore'
'Tarko' 'Mooning' 'Kanowna' 'Woolerina' 'Book Book' 'Kyena' 'Sth Muthong'
rn Turn' 'Gumahah' 118 'Westlea' 'Noorama' CK 'Bundaleer' 'Coomburra' 'Kulki' 'Woolerbilla' Redbank
L A N D 'Pitherty' 'Werai Park' Thurulgoona 'Tego' 'Woolerbilla'
122 'Caiwarro' (ruins) 'Neverfail' Tinnenburra 'Noorama' Culgoa Floodplain National Park 'Ballandool' Hebel
Ningaling Wambah Lake 'Rockwell' Barringun Jobs Gate Toulby Gate 'Tara' New Angledool
private track follows dog fence Tuon 'Widgee Downs' Toulhy 'Brenda' 'Coobionda' 29°
'Brindingabba' 'Nahweenah' Turra 'Sharoon' 'Winrae' 'Morton Plains' 'Brooksville' Memnong 'Brenda' Goodooga 'Nullawa' 55
'Wancobra' 'Naree' Burrawantie 'Belaile' 'Eureka' 'Karalee' Ellerslie 'Kahmoo' 'Kulkyne Burbar' Kookaburra 'Gnomery' 'Birrah'
'Comeroo' 'Wirrawarra' 'Goolaring' Thurmylae Fairfield 'Dunsandle' 'Glenora' Weilmoringle Dunvegan 'Julie Vale' 'Muckerawa' 'Wirrawa'
'Thoura' 'Killowen' 'Clifton Downs' Tarwoona 'The Cato' Enngonia Ledknapper Nature Reserve 'Beulah' 'Nooroma' Baringa Woolahra 'Leander' Opal Mines Lightning Ridge
'Maureen Joy' Yantabulla 'Lochnagar' 'Wandella' 'Dalwood' 'Bora' 'Maylands' Taralba 'Bomali' 158 'Weetalibah'
'Stratheane' 'Ella Vale' 'Multagoona' 'Lila Springs' Lednapper Crossing 'Culgoa Downs' Talawanta 'Natran Plains' Grawin Opal Fields 'Heathfield' 136
'Wampra' 'Yulcarley' 'Pirillie' 'Bellfields' 'Corella' 'Mundiwa' 'Yarkeita' 'Mourabilla' 'Narran Park' Narran Lake Nature Reserve 'Llanillo' 'Strathmore'
'Minetta' 'South Kerribree' Lower Lila Tuncoona Grass Hut 'Bullaroon' Collerina 'Allambie' Narran Lake Cumborah 'Guisley' 'Bairnkine'
'Merita' 'Curragh' Fords Bridge 'Garlands' 'Lilyfield' Glandore 'Coola' 'Tungra' 'Gingie'
'Myroolia' 'Belvedere' 'Glengeera' 'Prairie' 'Wirracanna' Tungra 'Eumanbah'
'Wangamana' 'Pine View' 'Romani' Gumbalie Warrawenna Mt Druid 'Beemery' Brewarrina Aboriginal Cultural Museum KAMILAROI 'Coonong' Walgett
Hopelands 192 Pera Bore 'Rossmore' 98 'Yambacoona' The Cedars 121 'Cara Mia'
'Janina' 'Barrakee' Goonery 'Yandaroo' 'Delta' North Bourke 'Mooculta' Bourke Coolaburra 'Waratah' 'Booroma'
'Glenora' 'Lake Mere' Ballycastle Willeroo Lake 'Nulty' Fort Bourke Stockade Jandra 'Greenvale' 'Hastings' 'Toorang' 'Carramar' 'Brewon' 69
'Pelora' Lake 'Dara' 'Myndetta' Latoka 'Mt Oxley' Oakleigh 'Charlton' 'Boonery' 'Yarrawin' 'Wilgavale' 'Polly Brewan'
'Bellsgrove' 93 'Toorale' 121 Nine Mile Weir Prattenville 'Bendemeer' 'Sainsbury Park' Tarcoon 'Cuddy' Gongolgon 102 'Gilgoin' 'Warrawing' 'Wangrawally'
'Carney' Campamooka Mtn 91 Westmere Hamilton Park 99 'Ben Lomond' Boorindal Dwyers 'North Compton Downs' Compton Downs 'Billybingbone' 'Yamba' 'Ingalala' 'Nedgera'
'Idalia' 'Minley' Mt Deerina 'Rose Isle' Kinchela 78 'Wave Hill' 'Cowga' 'Ben Avon' 'Killarney' 'Ellimeek'
Arthur Lake Trilby 'Winbar' 'Deerina' 'Myrtle Vale' Toorale East 'Mulgowan' 'Knightvale' 'Wyuna Downs' NEW YEARS RA 'Mulgawarrina' 'Kimbriki' 'Womboin' 'Meranda' Macquarie Marshes Nature Reserve 'Peronne' 159
'Wee Toura' GUNDABOOKA NAT PARK 'Belah' Kenilworth Byrock 'Byrock' 'Glenariff' 'Pendiana' 'Tubbavilla' 'Mundadoo' Louth
'Wongawal' 'Mulya' The Three Sisters Aboriginal Rock Hole 'Wilga Downs' 'Glenariff' 'Fairlight' 'Marra' 'The Mote' 'Thurn' 'Muttama'
'Tundulya' 'Narwarre' 'Curraweena' 161 87 Curraweena Hill 'Wallangarra' Dijou Mtn Bahloo Glenariff 'Glen Idyll' 'Colossal' GIBSON WAY Viewing Platform 'Sandy Camp' Quambone
'Gambolalley' 130 'Wilgaroon' 'Yandilla' Mt Merrere Coronga Peak 'Runnymede' Buckeroo Mtn 'Boorara' 'Willie' Macquarie Marshes Nature Res 'Ringorah'
'Karoo' 'Darling Downs' Mookalimbirria Hill 'Tara' Coolabah 'Liskeard' 'Innisvale' 'Buckiinguy' VALLEY 'Emby'
'Mt Booroorra 'Wuttagoona' 'Booroondarra Downs' Tindarey 'Cooneybar' 'Balgillo' 126 'Pine Ridge' Mt Foster Gradgery
'Gidgee' 'Pulpulla' Mt Buckwaroon Elura Mine Copper 'Mount Drysdale' 'Carline' 'Berwick' Girilambone 'Carlton' 110
'Cable Downs' 'Yimkin' 'Elmore' 'Glenhope' 71 'Moonagee' Canonba 'Buttabone' Marebone Weir 'Bealbah'
'Mt Gap' Mt Grenfell Historic Site Aboriginal Rock Art 'Maryvale' 'Anna Vale' 'Bonnie View' 'Fairview' 'Inglegar' Pine Clump
'Tiltagoonah' 'Mt Grenfell' 'Buckwaroon' CSA Mine 'Booroomagga' 'Wilgalong' 'Birrimbol' Railway Fairview 'Dungalier' 'Bullagreen' 'Haddon Rig'
'Pinchinara' 'Windara' Tambua 'Cubba' Cobar 'Sussex' 'Glenace' 'Wilga Downs' 'Wilga' Nyngan 'Eenaweenah' Warren 34
BARRIER 'Lilyvale' Beaumont Hill 32 Amphitheatre 'Florida' 131 BARRIER 32 HWY Hermidale Miandetta 'Whitewood' 'Raby' 'Dunmore'
262 'Nullogoola' The Peak Goldmine Boppy Mount Canbelego 'Mangalore' 'Canonbar' Muffengudgerie Warren Weir Nevertire 22
'Barnato' 'Meadow Glen' 'Narri' 'Meryula' 'Restdown' 'Wirrena' 59 Belaringar 'Ellengerah'
'Boulkra' Broadmeadows 'Kia Ora' 'Double Gates' Lerida 'Hill View' 87 Mt Nurri The Rookery 'Fairview' 'Wylgalea' 'Kopyje' 'Elmsley' 'Poplar Grove' 32 'Bundemar'
'Bulla Bulla' 'Noona' The Meadows 'Bulgoo' 'Koree' 'Mount Lewis' Qoanda Nature Reserve Buddabaddah Cathundral
'Tiltagara' 'Everdale' Kaleno 'Pine Ridge' 'Linera' 'Rosevale' Rainbow Ridge The Ranch 'Panjee' 87 Trangie 67
'Beechworth' Buckambool Mtn 'Killala' 'Yarrama' Nymagee Old Mining Town 'Yarran Downs' Five Ways Tabratong
Mt Belarabon 'Bloomfield' 'Belford' 161 'Hartwood' Trigoona Tottenham
'Belarabon' BELARABON RIDGE Kulwin 'Paddington' 'Bindi' Yarranvale Norma Vale 'Shuttleton' 'Balowra' 'Niloc' 'Mogal Plain' Bobadah Dandaloo
233 'Keewong' Farm Holidays 4WD Tours 'Wiralong' Taringo Downs 'Ettawanda' 'Glenwood' Balemund The Bald Hills The Yellow Mtn Albert 53 Alagala
'Berangabah' 'Yallock' 'Red Tank' 'Karwarn' Gilgunnia Ashleigh Downs Yathong Nature Reserve Wirchilleba 'Burthong' 'Eremaran' 'Moothumbil' 'Walkers Hill' Tarran Hills Minnalong Terowie Wyanga Mungeribar

To Ivanhoe 8 To Hillston 9 10 29 To Trundle 11 12 To Trundle 13 14

© Hema Maps Pty Ltd
0 10 20 30 40 50 60km

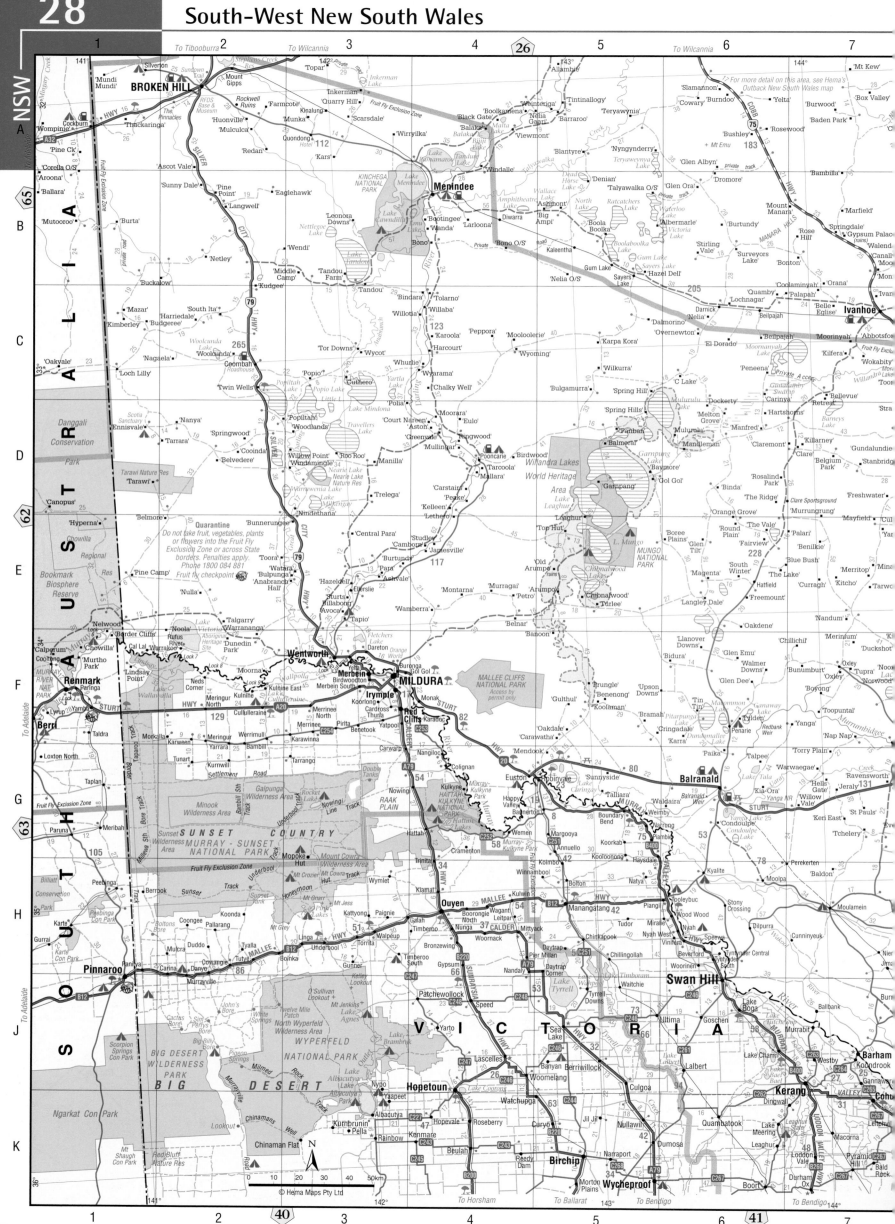

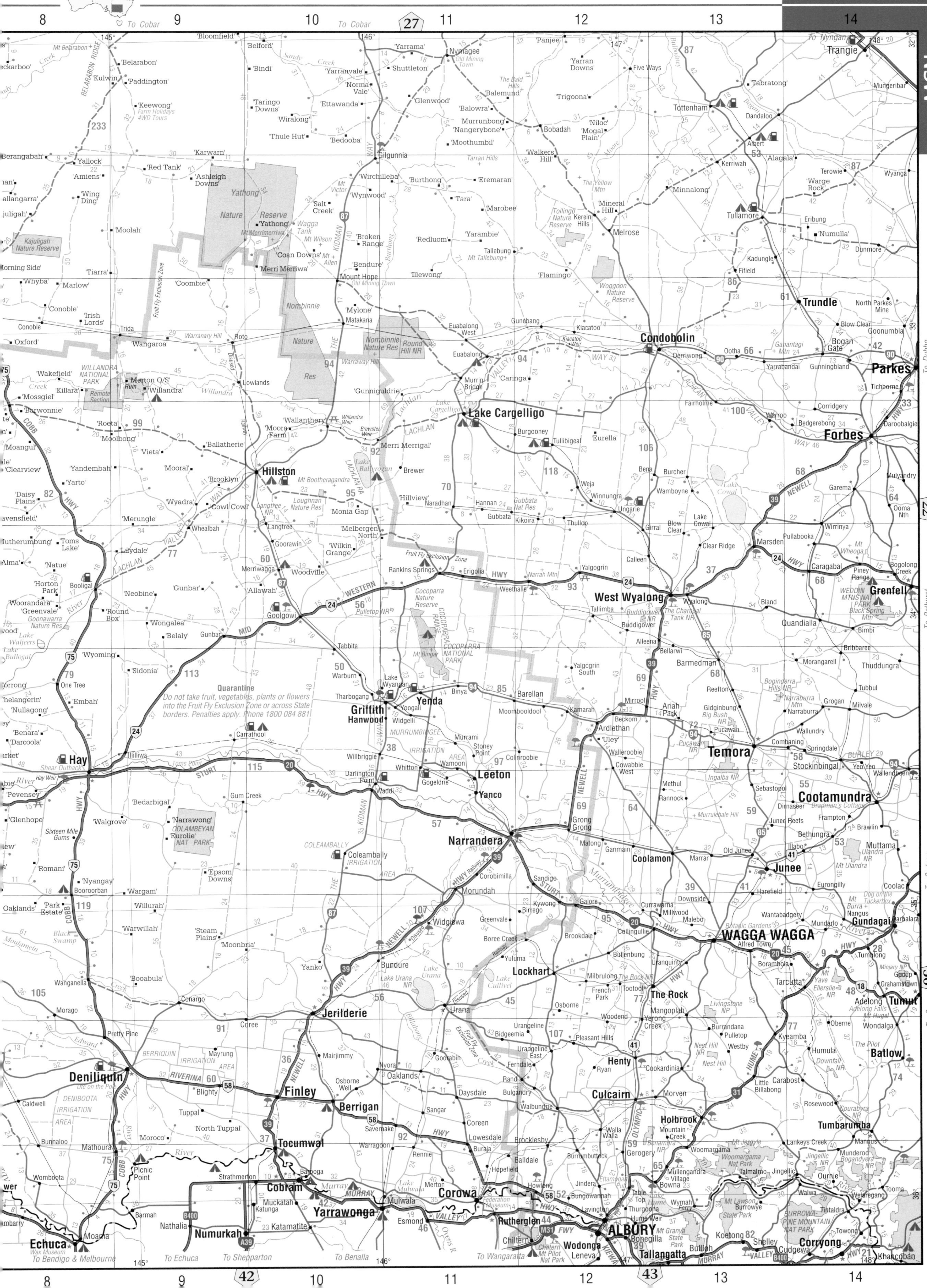
8
9
10
11
12
13
14
A
B
C
D
E
F
G
H
J
K
To Cobar
To Cobar
To Nyngan
Trangie
Nymagee
'Bloomfield'
'Belford'
'Belarabon'
'Kulwin'
'Paddington'
'Keewong'
'Yarrama'
'Shuttleton'
'Yarranvale'
'Norma Vale'
'Glenwood'
'Ettawanda'
'Taringo Downs'
'Wiralong'
'Thule Hut'
'Bedooba'
'Panjee'
'Yarran Downs'
Five Ways
'Balemund'
'Trigoona'
'Balowra'
'Murrunbong'
'Nangerybone'
'Moothumbil'
Bobadah
'Niloc'
'Mogal Plain'
Tottenham
'Tabratong'
Mungeribar
Dandaloo
Albert
'Alagala'
Kerriwah
Terowie
'Warge Rock'
Wyanga
'Minnalong'
'Mineral Hill'
Melrose
Tullamore
Eribung
'Numulla'
Dunmore
Kadungle
Fifield
Gilgunnia
'Wirchilleba'
'Burthong'
'Eremaran'
'Wynwood'
'Tara'
'Marobee'
'Salt Creek'
'Broken Range'
'Redluom'
'Yarambie'
Tallebung
'Bendure'
Mount Hope
'Illewong'
'Flamingo'
Yathong Nature Reserve
'Yathong'
'Coan Downs'
Merri Merriwa'
Nombinnie Nature Res
Woggoon Nature Reserve
Trundle
North Parkes Mine
Blow Clear
Goonumbla
Bogan Gate
Ootha
Condobolin
Derriwong
Kiacatoo
Gunebang
Euabalong West
Euabalong
'Mylone'
Matakana
'Yallock'
'Amiens'
'Red Tank'
'Ashleigh Downs'
'Wing Ding'
'Moolah'
'Tiarra'
'Whyba'
'Marlow'
'Coombie'
'Conoble'
'Irish Lords'
Conoble
Trida
Roto
'Wangaroa'
'Oxford'
Kajuligah Nature Reserve
Willandra National Park
'Wakefield'
'Killara'
'Mossgiel'
'Willandra'
Lowlands
'Burwonnie'
'Roeta'
'Moolbong'
'Vieta'
'Ballatherie'
'Moora Farm'
'Wallanthery'
'Gunniguldrie'
Murrin Bridge
'Caringa'
Lake Cargelligo
Burgooney
Tullibigeal
'Eurella'
Fairholme
Parkes
Yarrabandai
Gunningbland
Tichborne
Corridgery
Bedgerebong
Forbes
Daroobalgie
Warroo
Merri Merrigal'
Brewer
Hillston
'Moangul'
'Clearview'
'Yandembah'
'Yarto'
'Mooral'
'Brooklyn'
'Wyadra'
Cowl Cowl
'Daisy Plains'
'Merungle'
Whealbah
Langtree
'Monia Gap'
'Hillview'
Naradhan
Hannan
Gubbata
Kikoira
Thulloo
Weja
Winnungra
Ungarie
Bena
Burcher
Wamboyne
Girral
Blow Clear
Lake Cowal
Garema
Mulyandry
Ooma Nth
'Toms Lake'
'Lilydale'
Goorawin
'Melbergen North'
'Wilkin Grange'
Rankins Springs
Erigolia
Yalgogrin
Weethalle
West Wyalong
Wyalong
Calleen
Clear Ridge
Marsden
Pullabooka
Wirrinya
Caragabal
Bogolong Creek
Piney Range
Grenfell
'Natue'
'Horton Park'
Booligal
Merriwagga
'Woodville'
'Allawah'
'Gunbar'
'Neobine'
'Woorandara'
'Greenvale'
'Round Box'
Goolgowi
Cocoparra Nature Reserve
Tallimba
Buddigower
Alleena
Bland
Quandialla
Bimbi
'Wongalea'
'Belaly'
Gunbar
Tabbita
Cocoparra National Park
Bellarwi
Barmedman
Bribbaree
'Wyoming'
'Sidonia'
One Tree
'Embah'
Warburn
Lake Wyangan
Yenda
Binya
Barellan
Yalgogrin South
Morangarell
Thuddungra
Quarantine
Do not take fruit, vegetables, plants or flowers into the Fruit Fly Exclusion Zone or across State borders. Penalties apply. Phone 1800 084 881
Tharbogang
Griffith
Hanwood
Yoogali
Widgelli
Moombooldool
Kamarah
Mirrool
Ariah Park
Beckom
Ardlethan
Reefton
Gidginbung
Tubbul
Grogan
Milvale
'Nullagong'
'Benara'
'Darcoola'
Carrathool
Murrami
Stoney Point
Willbriggie
Wamoon
Colinroobie
'Uley'
Walleroobie
Cowabbie West
Pucawan
Temora
Wallundry
Narraburra
Combaning
Springdale
Stockinbingal
Yeo Yeo
Wallendbeen
Hay
Illilliwa
Whitton
Darlington Point
Gogeldrie
Leeton
Yanco
Methul
Rannock
Sebastopol
Dirnaseer
Cootamundra
Hay Weir
'Pevensey'
'Bedarbigal'
Gum Creek
'Glenhope'
'Walgrove'
'Narrawong'
'Eurolie'
Oolambeyan Nat Park
Narrandera
Grong Grong
Matong
Ganmain
Coolamon
Marrar
Old Junee
Junee
Junee Reefs
Frampton
Bethungra
Brawlin
Illabo
Muttama
Eurongilly
Coolac
'Romani'
Coleambally
Corobimilla
Morundah
Sandigo
Galore
Kywong
Birrego
Currawarna
Millwood
Downside
Harefield
Wantabadgery
Mundarlo
Gundagai
Bongongolong
Booroorban
'Nyangay'
'Wargam'
'Epsom Downs'
Oaklands
'Park Estate'
'Willurah'
Widgiewa
Greenvale
Boree Creek
Brookdale
Collingullie
Malebo
Wagga Wagga
Alfred Town
Borambola
Tumblong
Nangus
'Warwillah'
'Steam Plains'
'Moonbria'
Black Swamp
Yuluma
Lockhart
Bullenbung
Uranquinty
Tarcutta
Gobarralong
Grahamstown
Tumut
'Yanko'
Bundure
Lake Urana
Wanganella
'Booabula'
Milbrulong
Tootool
French Park
The Rock
Mangoplah
Yerong Creek
Adelong
105
Morago
Conargo
Jerilderie
Urana
Osborne
Woodend
Livingstone NP
Burrandana
Pulletop
Westby
Kyeamba
Oberne
Wondalga
Pretty Pine
Coree
Bidgeemia
Urangeline
Pleasant Hills
Humula
Batlow
Mayrung
Mairjimmy
Goombargana
Urangeline East
Ferndale
Henty
Cookardinia
Ryan
Deniliquin
Caldwell
Blighty
Finley
Oaklands
Nyora
Osborne Well
Daysdale
Rand
Bulgandry
Culcairn
Morven
Little Billabong
Carabost
Rosewood
Tumbarumba
Tuppal
Berrigan
Sangar
Savernake
Coreen
Walbundrie
Holbrook
Mountain Creek
'North Tuppal'
'Moroco'
Bunnaloo
Mathoura
Tocumwal
Warragoon
Rennie
Lowesdale
Buraja
Brocklesby
Walla Walla
Gerogery
Woomargama
Lankeys Creek
Mannus
Wombboota
Picnic Point
Strathmerton
Cobram
Barooga
Hopefield
Balldale
Burrumbuttock
Mullengandra Village
Bowna
Talmalmo
Jingellic
Ournie
Walwa
Welaregang
Tooma
Barmah
Nathalia
Katunga
Muckatah
Yarrawonga
Mulwala
Esmond
Corowa
Howlong
Jindera
Bungowannah
Table Top
Thurgoona
Hume Weir
Wymah
Tintaldra
Moama
Echuca
Wax Museum
To Bendigo & Melbourne
Numurkah
Katamatite
To Echuca
To Shepparton
To Benalla
Rutherglen
Chiltern
Wodonga
Leneva
Lavington
Albury
Bonegilla
Tallangatta
Bullioh
Koetong
Shelley
Cudgewa
Corryong
Towong
Khancoban
To Wangaratta
To Dubbo
To Bathurst
To Sydney
To Cooma

A B C D E F G H J K

VICTORIA

TASMAN SEA

Sapphire Coast

Eurobodalla Coast

Shoalhaven Coast

Major towns/cities: Young, Boorowa, Harden, Cootamundra, Murrumburrah, Crookwell, GOULBURN, WOLLONGONG, Bowral, Moss Vale, Mittagong, Port Kembla, Shellharbour, Kiama, Gerringong, Bomaderry, Nowra, Culburra, Gundagai, Yass, CANBERRA, QUEANBEYAN, Braidwood, Ulladulla, Tumut, Batlow, Tumbarumba, Captains Flat, Batemans Bay, Moruya, Cabramurra, Khancoban, Jindabyne, Thredbo, Cooma, Berridale, Narooma, Bermagui, Bega, Tathra, Merimbula, Bombala, Delegate, Eden

Canberra detail: Parliament House, National Gallery, Science & Technology Centre, Mint, War Memorial, National Aquarium

Australian Capital Territory

KOSCIUSZKO NATIONAL PARK, NAMADGI NATIONAL PARK, BRINDABELLA NAT PARK, MORTON NATIONAL PARK, BUDAWANG NATIONAL PARK, DEUA NATIONAL PARK, WADBILLIGA NATIONAL PARK, SOUTH EAST FORESTS NAT PK, BEN BOYD NATIONAL PARK, ALPINE NATIONAL PARK, SNOWY RIVER NATIONAL PARK, ERRINUNDRA NATIONAL PARK, COOPRACAMBRA NATIONAL PARK

Mt Kosciuszko 2229m+ Australia's Highest

SNOWY MOUNTAINS

GREAT DIVIDING RANGE

For more details on this area, see Hema's South East New South Wales Map

© Hema Maps Pty Ltd

0 10 20 30 40 50km

N

To Cowra · To Sydney · To Wagga Wagga, Albury · To Albury · To Orbost · To Cann River · To Cann River

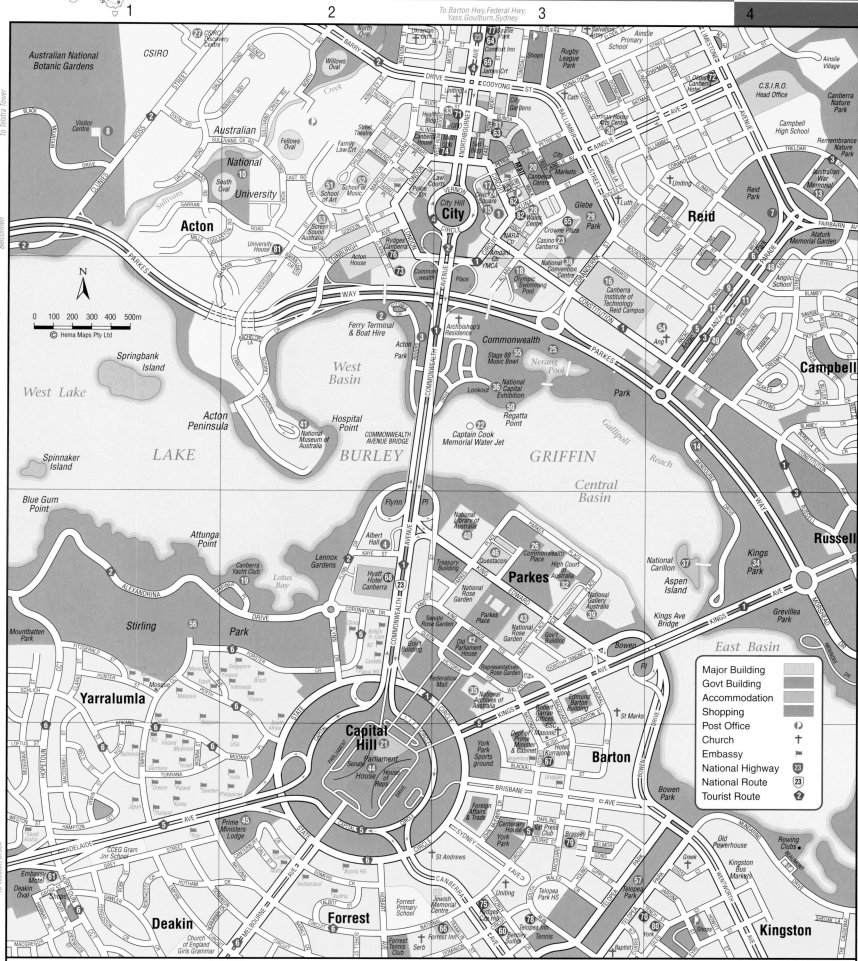

To Barton Hwy, Federal Hwy, Yass, Goulburn, Sydney

To Telstra Tower

To Weston Creek, Belconnen

To Red Hill

To Cooma, Queanbeyan

To Canberra Airport, Queanbeyan

0 100 200 300 400 500m
© Hema Maps Pty Ltd

Legend:
- Major Building
- Govt Building
- Accommodation
- Shopping
- Post Office
- Church
- Embassy
- National Highway (23)
- National Route (23)
- Tourist Route (2)

Places of Interest

1. ACT Legislative Assembly A3
2. Acton Ferry Terminal B2
3. Acton Park B2
4. Albert Hall C2
5. Aust and New Zealand Memorial B4
6. Aust Army National Memorial A4
7. Aust Hellenic Memorial A4
8. Aust National Botanic Gardens A1
9. Aust National Korean War Mem B4
10. Aust National University A2
11. Aust Service Nurses National Mem B4
12. Aust Vietnam Forces National Mem B4
13. Aust War Memorial A4
14. Blundell's Cottage B4
15. Canberra Centre A3

16. Canberra Institute of Technology B3
17. Canberra Museum & Gallery A3
18. Canberra Olympic Pool B3
19. Canberra Sthn Cross Yacht Club C2
20. Canberra Theatre Centre A3
21. Capital Hill D2
22. Captain Cook Memorial Jet B3
23. Casino Canberra A3
24. Civic Square A3
25. Commonwealth Park B3
26. Commonwealth Place C3
27. CSIRO Discovery Centre A1
28. Electric Shadows Cinema A3
29. Glebe Park A3
30. Gorman House Arts Centre A3
31. Greater Union Cinemas - City A3
32. High Court of Australia C3

33. Jolimont Centre A3
34. Kings Park C4
35. National Archives of Australia C3
36. National Capital Exhibition B3
37. National Carillon C4
38. National Convention Centre B3
39. National Gallery of Australia C3
40. National Library of Australia C3
41. National Museum of Australia B2
42. National Portrait Gallery C3
43. National Rose Garden C3
44. Old Parliament House C3
45. Parliament House D2
46. Questacon-Nat Science & Tech Ctr C3
47. RAAF Memorial B4
48. RAN Memorial B4

49. Rats of Tobruk Memorial B4
50. Regatta Point Jetty B3
51. School of Art A2
52. School of Music A2
53. ScreenSound Australia A2
54. St John's Schoolhouse Museum B4
55. Stage 88 B3
56. Stirling Park C1
57. Telopea Park D3
58. Telstra Tower A1

Accommodation

60. Bentley Suites Canberra D3
61. Best Western Embassy Motel D1
62. Canberra City Accommodation A3
63. City Walk Hotel A3
64. Comfort Inn Downtown A3

65. Crowne Plaza Canberra A3
66. Forrest Inn & Apartments D3
67. Hotel Kurrajong D3
68. Hyatt Hotel Canberra C2
69. James Court Apartment Hotel A3
70. Kingston Court Serviced Apartmts D4
71. Novotel Canberra A3
72. Olims Canberra Hotel A4
73. Pacific Intl Apartments-Capital Tower B2
74. Quest Hotel Canberra A3
75. Rydges Capital Hill Hotel D3
76. Rydges Lakeside Canberra A2
77. Saville Park Suites A3
78. Telopea Inn on the Park D3
79. The Brassey of Canberra D3
80. The York Canberra D4
81. University House at ANU A2
82. Waldorf Apartments Canberra A3

NSW NSW

To Yass, Young, Gundagai · To Gundaroo · To Goulburn, Moss Vale

GUNGAHLIN

Taylor · Moncrieff · Casey · Kinlyside · Ngunnawal · Amaroo · Forde · Canberra Nature Park · Throsby
Wallaroo · Fraser · Dunlop · Charnwood · Flynn · Spence · Nicholls · Palmerston · Harrison · Crace · Franklin · Mulanggari
Macgregor · Melba · Evatt · Giralang · Kenny
Latham · Florey · McKellar · Baldwin · Lawson · Kaleen · Mitchell · Watson · Majura
Holt · Higgins · Scullin · Page · BELCONNEN · University of Canberra · Federal Police · Bruce · Downer · Hackett · Canberra Nature Park
Hawker · Macquarie · Weetangera · Jamison Centre · Aranda · Lyneham · Dickson · O'Connor · Ainslie
Cook · Black Mtn 812m · Acton · Australian National University · Turner · Braddon · Mt Ainslie 843m
CITY · Reid · Campbell · Russell · Duntroon Royal Military College
Yarralumla · Parkes · Barton · Canberra International Airport
Deakin · Forrest · Manuka · Griffith · Kingston · Fyshwick · Pialligo
Curtin · Hughes · Red Hill · Narrabundah · Harman
WESTON CREEK · Holder · Weston · Lyons · Garran · Symonston · Oaks Estate · Crestwood
Duffy · Rivett · Stirling · Chifley · Phillip · O'Malley · Harman · Letchworth · Karabar · QUEANBEYAN
Waramanga · WODEN VALLEY · De Salis
Chapman · Fisher · Pearce · Mawson · Isaacs · Jerrabomberra · Gale
Torrens · Farrer · Hume
Kambah · Wanniassa · Fadden · Macarthur
Oxley · Monash · Gowrie
Greenway · TUGGERANONG · Chisholm · Richardson
Bonython · Isabella Plains · Calwell · Theodore
Gordon · Conder · Banks

Namadgi National Park

To Cotter Dam · To Tharwa · To Tharwa · To Cooma · To Bundendore

To Tidbinbilla Nature Reserve

© Hema Maps Pty Ltd

0 1 2 3 4 5km

N

Victoria

Sunrise, Port Phillip Bay (36 F6, 39 G13, 44 D1)

Distances are shown in kilometres and follow the most direct major sealed route

Albury	423	330	302	237	617	395	579	504	321	613	180	391	485	72	582
Ballarat		394	121	214	681	87	174	187	112	486	243	309	276	346	186
Bairnsdale			430	492	287	356	398	581	282	840	694	618	118	304	543
Bendigo				93	717	208	277	207	148	410	122	188	312	225	307
Echuca					751	284	370	300	210	376	71	154	374	160	400
Eden (NSW)						643	791	868	569	1127	694	905	405	591	830
Geelong							236	274	74	573	258	393	238	316	187
Hamilton								132	286	431	399	383	450	502	100
Horsham									299	299	329	251	463	432	232
Melbourne										558	184	336	164	242	261
Mildura											433	222	722	536	531
Shepparton												211	348	103	429
Swan Hill													500	314	385
Traralgon														406	425
Wangaratta															503
Warrnambool															

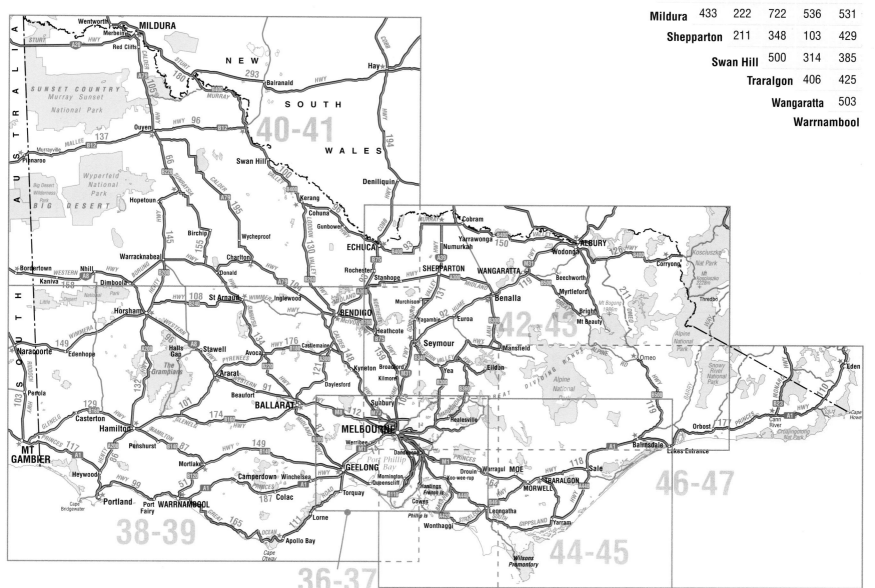

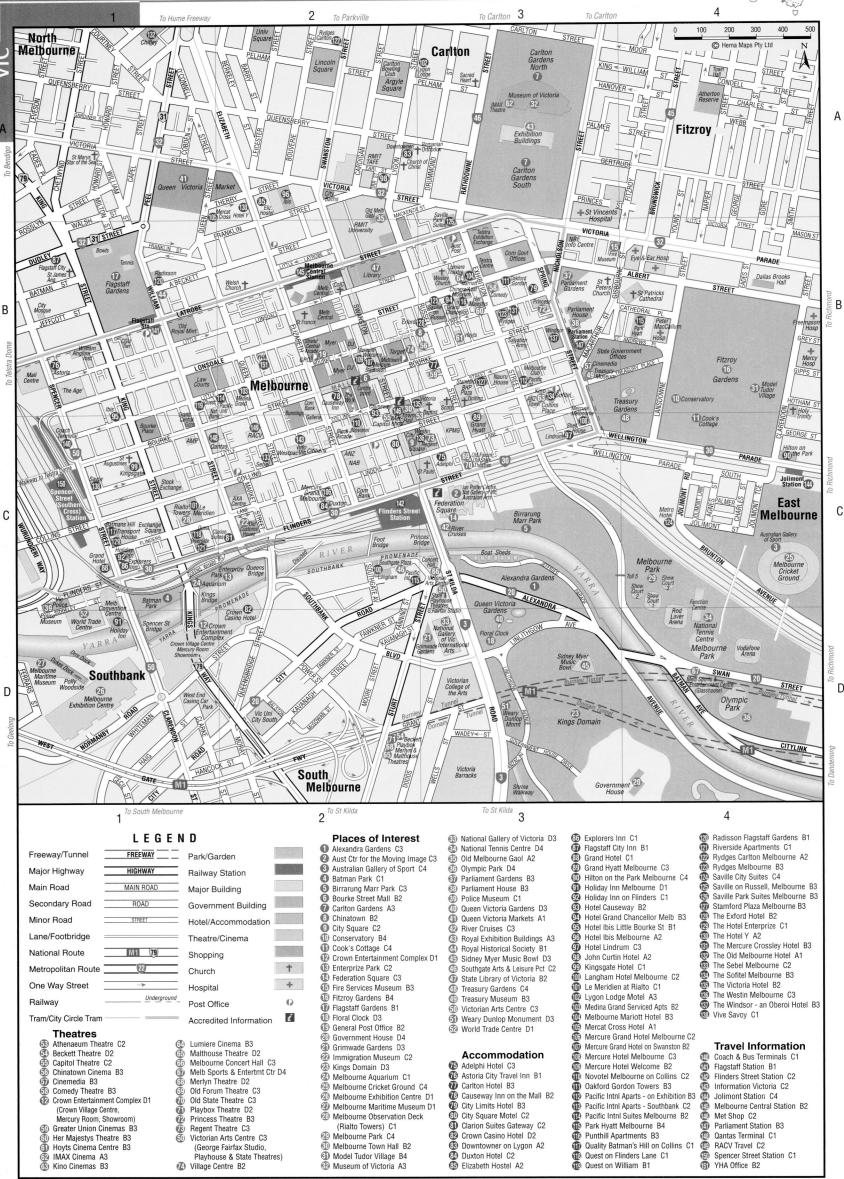

To Sunbury · To Seymour · To Kinglake

MELBOURNE

AIRPORT

Melbourne Airport Terminal

Greenvale · Bulla · Woodlands · Somerton · Hurstbridge
Coolaroo · Westmeadows · Epping · Plenty · Diamond Creek
Keilor North · Broadmeadows · Campbellfield · Thomastown · Mill Park · Kangaroo Ground
Tullamarine · Keilor · Bundoora · Greensborough · Watsonia · Research · Eltham
ESSENDON AIRPORT · Fawkner · Kingsbury · Macleod · Warrandyte
St Albans · Reservoir · Preston · Heidelberg · Templestowe
Essendon · Coburg · Thornbury · Doncaster · Park Orchards
Braybrook · Brunswick · Northcote · Balwyn · Mitcham
Sunshine · Highpoint · Kensington · Carlton · Kew · Box Hill · Blackburn · Ringwood
Ardeer · Brooklyn · Footscray · Fitzroy · Collingwood · Camberwell · Bayswater
Docklands · **MELBOURNE** · Richmond · Hawthorn · Burwood · Knox City
Newport · Port Melbourne · South Melbourne · Toorak · Burwood East
Altona · Williamstown · Prahran · Armadale · Mt Waverley · Glen Waverley · Scoresby
Altona Meadows · St Kilda · Caulfield · Chadstone · Wheelers Hill
Elwood · Oakleigh · Clayton · Springvale · Dandenong North · Doveton
Brighton · McKinnon · Moorabbin · Dandenong
Sandringham · Cheltenham · Dingley Village · Noble Park · Dandenong South · Lyndhurst
Black Rock · Mentone · Braeside · Keysborough · Bangholme
Mordialloc · Edithvale · Chelsea · Carrum · Carrum Downs · Cranbourne · Skye
Seaford · **Frankston**

PORT PHILLIP BAY

Hobsons Bay · Altona Bay · Point Cook · Point Ormond · Picnic Point · Beaumaris Bay · Ricketts Point

To Kynton · To Ballarat · To Geelong · To Mornington · To Emerald · To Lilydale · To Warragul · To Koo-wee-rup

CityLink Tollway
For information on CityLink Tollway day passes and e-TAGs phone 13 26 29 anytime.

Spirit of Tasmania
For more information on the ferry from Melbourne to Devonport
Ph 1800 634 906
www.spiritoftasmania.com.au

SCALE
0 1 2 3 4 5 6 7 8 9 10km

© Hema Maps Pty Ltd

VIC

Whittlesea · Humevale · Masons Falls · Kinglake West · Kinglake Central · Kinglake · Castella · Forest Discovery Centre · Toolangi · Marysville · Jaggerty R · Lake Mountain · Keppel Falls · Lookout · Nordic Ski Fields · Koala

Woodstock · Mt Sugarloaf · Kinglake National Park · Kinglake East · Mt Tanglefoot · Rainforest Walk · Granton · C512 · Mt Arnold · C512

Yan Yean Res · Strathewen · Mt St Leonard · St Fillans · Narbethong · Mt Kitchener · Mt Stinton · Cambarville · C513 · Walker

Yan Yean · Arthurs Creek · St Andrews · One Tree Hill · Steels Creek · Myers Creek Scenic Res · Lookout Tower · Mt Strickland · Mt Observation · Yarra · Historic Site

Wollert · Mernda · Doreen · Nutfield · Dixons Creek · Long Gully · Chum Creek · Maroondah Res · Fernshaw · Graceburn Weir · The Blacks' Spur · Deep · Yarra Ranges

Epping · South Morang · Hurstbridge · Yarrambat · Panton Hill · Christmas Hills · Yarra Glen · Tarrawarra · Healesville · Mt Riddell · Badger · Acheron Gap · National · Reefton · Upper Yarra Dam

Plenty · Diamond Creek · Watsons Creek · Yering · Maroondah · Aboriginal Cemetery · Mt Toole-be-wong · Mt Donna Buang · Lookout Tower · Cement Creek · Skywalk · McMahons Creek

Bundoora · Greensborough · Eltham · Kangaroo Ground · Wonga Park · Coldstream · Gruyere · Warramate Hills Wildlife Reserve · Ben Cairn · Warburton East · Park

Rosanna · Heidelberg · Templestowe · Warrandyte · State Park · Killara · Launching Place · Don Valley · Wesburn · Millgrove · Warburton · Big Pats Ck · Flowerpot Hill

Bulleen · Doncaster · Lilydale · Seville · Woori Yallock · Old Warburton · Britannia Creek · Starling Hill · Hyde Hill · Ada Tree

Balwyn · Box Hill · Croydon · Ringwood · Wandin North · Yellingbo · Yarra Junction · Gladysdale · Starling Gap · Marney Hill

Camberwell · Burwood · Vermont · Bayswater · Kalorama · Silvan · Hoddles Creek · Three Bridges · Gilderoy · Powelltown · The Bump

Glen Waverley · Scoresby · Boronia · Ferntree Gully · Mt Dandenong · Olinda · Burleigh · Macclesfield · Nangana · Kurth Kiln Park · Mt Beenak · Piedmont

Oakleigh · Clayton · Knoxfield · Sassafras · Monbulk · Kallista · Upper Ferntree Gully · Belgrave · Estcourt · Spion Kopje · Nayook

Moorabbin · Mulgrave · Springvale · Rowville · Narre Warren East · Menzies Ck · Clematis · Avonsleigh · Emerald · Lakeside · Cockatoo · Gembrook · Gentle Annie · Neerim

Dandenong · Narre Warren North · Narre Warren · Mt Burnett · Gembrook · Bunyip State Park · Tarago Res

Mordialloc · Braeside · Keysborough · Berwick · Beaconsfield Upper · Pakenham Upper · Nar Nar Goon North · Cornucopia · Tonimbuk · Jindivick North

Aspendale · Edithvale · Chelsea · Bonbeach · Lyndhurst · Beaconsfield · Officer · Maryknoll · Garfield North · Labertouche · Jindivick · Tarago

Carrum · Patterson Lakes · Carrum Downs · Pakenham · Nar Nar Goon · Tynong · Garfield · Bunyip · Longwarry North · Robin Hood · Drouin West · Buln Buln

Seaford · Skye · Cranbourne · Clyde · Cardinia · Pakenham South · Cora Lynn · Vervale · Iona · Longwarry · Drouin · Brandy Creek

Frankston · Langwarrin · Baxter · Fiyeways · Devon Meadows · Koo-Wee-Rup North · Bayles · Catani · Modella · Drouin Sth · Warragul

Mt Eliza · Somerville · Pearcedale · Dalmore · Tooradin · Koo-wee-rup · Yallock · Monomeith · Yannathan · Ripplebrook · Lardner · Bull Swamp

Mornington · Moorooduc · Tyabb · Warneet · Cannons Ck · Caldermeade · Lang Lang · Heath Hill · Athlone · Hallora · Ellinbank

Hastings · Old Tyabb · Western Port · Quail Island Wildlife Reserve · Chinaman Island · Pelican Point · Scrub Pt · Mountain View · Tetoora Road · Sea View

Bittern · Fairhaven · French Island National Park · Jam Jerrup · Nyora · Poowong North · Poowong East · Ferndale

Merricks North · Crib Pt · Crib Point · French Island · Stockyard Point · The Gurdies · Loch · Poowong · Strzelecki

Balnarring · HMAS Cerberus · Stony Point · Tankerton · McLeod Historic Prison · Blue Gum Point · St Helier · Jeetho · Ranceby · Arawata

Merricks · Somers · Hanns Inlet · French Island · Freeman Point · Pioneer Bay · Tenby Pt · Grantville · Woodleigh · Bena · Kardella · Fairbank

Merricks Beach · Pt Leo · Shoreham · Sandy Pt · Tortoise Head · Settlement Pt · Corinella · Queensferry · Kernot · Krowera · Korumburra · Kardella Tourist

Cowes · McHaffies Pt · Rhyll · Stony Pt · Coronet Bay · Cobb Pt · Almurta · Kilcunda Road · Jumbunna · Korumburra South · Ruby

Flinders · West Head · Ventnor · Phillip Island · Reid Bight · Churchill Island · Bass · Glen Forbes · Blackwood Forest · Glen Alvie · Burndale · Moyarra · Leongatha

Western Port · Summerland · Bass Landing · Wonthaggi

VIC

To Bordertown **To Warracknabeal**

40

Grid columns: 1 2 3 4 5 6 7
Grid rows: A B C D E F G H J K

Pooginagoric, Western Flat, Bangham, Bangham Con Park, Wallabrook, Frances, Minimay, Neuarpur, Morea (Carpolac), Booroopki, Binnum, Kybybolite, Tallageira, Bringalbert, Kangawall, Ozenkadnook, Benaye, Ullswater, Apsley, L. Ratzcastle, L. Koynock, L. Karnak, Pine Hut Lake, Miga Lake, Lillimur South, Miram South, Broughtons Waterhole, Little Desert, National Park, Goroke, Gymbowen, Duffholme, Mitre, Mt Arapiles, Arapiles, Mt Arapiles State Pk, Tooan, Tooan East, Tooan State Pk, Dimboola, Wail, Picnic Bend, Lake Duchembegarra, Grass Flat, Lake Wyn Wyn, Lake Natimuk, Mitre Rock, Quantong, Vectus, Natimuk, Haven, Horsham, Dooen, Dahlen, Pimpinio, Kalkee, Kewell, Juno, Murtoa, Longerenong, Drung Drung, Marma, Lubeck, Minyip, Rupanyup North, Coromby, Rupanyup, Banyena, Burrum, Raluana, Rapanyup South, Rich Avon, Campbells Bridge, Callawadda, Glenorchy, Dadswells Bridge, Green Lake, Roses Gap, Wartook, Lah-Arum, Brimpaen, Zumsteins, Cherrypool, Halls Gap, Fyans Ck, Mokepilly, Stawell, Deep Lead

Naracoorte, Naracoorte Caves Nat Park, Bool Lagoon, Straun, Joanna, Hynam, Langkoop, Edenhope, Charam, Douglas, Wombelano, Brooksby, Harrow, Kadnook, Powers Creek, Connewirrecoo, Mooree, Chetwynd, Balmoral, Englefield, Vasey, Coojar, Nareen, Tarrayoukyan, Brimboal, Dergholm, Dergholm State Park, Glenroy, Comaum, Coonawarra, Dorodong, Poolaijelo, Lake Mundi, Tullich, Dunrobin, Carapook, Konongwootong, Casterton, Sandford, Hilgay, Coleraine, Tahara, Henty, Merino, Strathdownie, Digby, Grassdale, Branxholme, Wannon, Hamilton, Tarrington, Penshurst, Macarthur, Heywood, Portland, Warrnambool, Port Fairy, Koroit, Mortlake

Mt Gambier, Nelson, Port MacDonnell, Dartmoor, Winnap, Greenwald, Lyons, Milltown, Mount Eckersley, Drumborg, Tyrendarra, Narrawong, Allestree, Cape Bridgewater, Cape Nelson, Discovery Bay, Southern Ocean, Lower Glenelg Nat Park

The Grampians, Grampians National Park, Mt William, Moyston, Barton, Mafeking, Mirranatwa, Victoria Valley, Glenthompson, Dunkeld, Wickliffe, Stavely, Willaura, Chatsworth, Hexham, Woolsthorpe, Framlingham, Purnim, Allansford, Dennington

VIC

To Donald 8 | 9 | To Charlton 10 | To Kerang 11 | 12 | To Echuca 13 | To Shepparton 14

To Wangaratta
To Yea
To Moe & Wonthaggi

Major towns:

St Arnaud, Inglewood, Bridgewater, Eaglehawk, **BENDIGO**, Elmore, Rushworth, Nagambie

Maryborough, Maldon, Castlemaine, Heathcote, Seymour, Broadford

Avoca, Clunes, Daylesford, Kyneton, Woodend, Kilmore

Beaufort, Creswick, **BALLARAT**, Ballan, Bacchus Marsh, Sunbury, Melton, **MELBOURNE**, Whittlesea

Werribee, Geelong, Portarlington, Frankston, Queenscliff, Mornington, Hastings

Camperdown, Winchelsea, Barwon Heads, Ocean Grove, Torquay, Sorrento, Rye

Cobden, Colac, Lorne, Anglesea, Apollo Bay

Bodies of water: Port Phillip Bay, Corio Bay, Bass Strait, Lake Corangamite, Lake Bolac

Features: GREAT DIVIDING RANGE, GREATER BENDIGO NAT PARK, ST ARNAUD RANGE NP, BRISBANE RANGES NATIONAL PARK, MORNINGTON PENINSULA NATIONAL PARK, OTWAY NATIONAL PARK, PORT CAMPBELL NAT PK, PHILLIP ISLAND

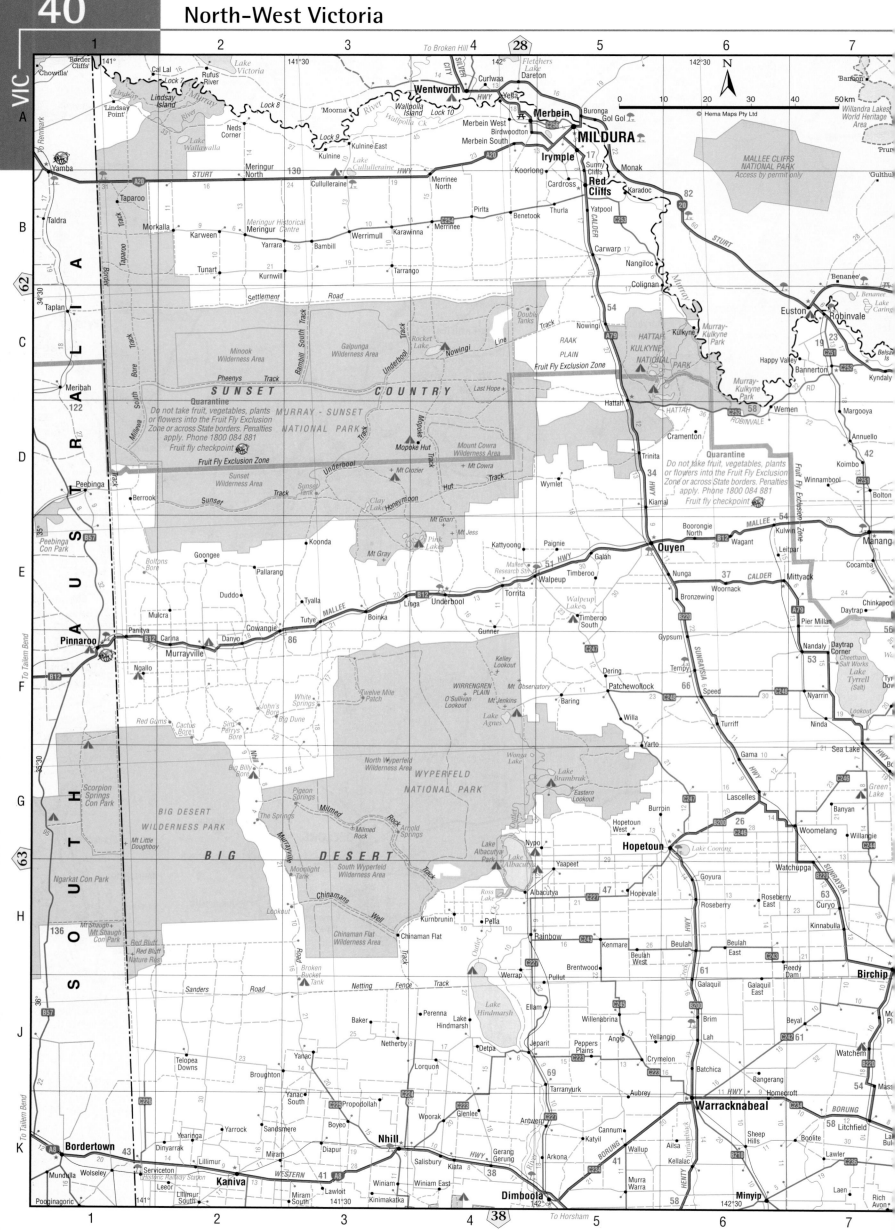

To Ivanhoe 28
To Wilcannia
To West Wyalong
To Wagga Wagga

N E W   S O U T H   W A L E S

'Wyoming'
'Sidonia'
'Corrong'
'Thelangerin'
One Tree
'Llanover Downs'
'Bidura'
'The Oaks'
'Bunumburt'
'Oxley Downs'
Oxley
'Norwood'
'Nullagong'
Illiliwa
'Upson Downs'
Tin Tin
'Benara'
'Darcoola'
'Bramah'
Tylden
Penarie
'Yanga'
'Toopuntal'
'Kempsey'
'Cringadale'
'Nap Nap'
Maude
Hay
'Paika'
Hay Weir

Balranald
'Hells Gate'
'Jeraly'
STURT
131
'Bedarbigal'
'Glenhope'
'Walgrove'
'Narrawong'
'St Pauls'
'Keri East'
'Clearview'
'Eurolie'
'Willow Vale'
'Tchelery'
'Everslee'
'Romani'
'Thalaka'
Weimby
Boundary Bend
Windomal Landing
'Condoulpe'
Yanga NR
'Miranda'
'Nyangay'
'Wargam'
Yungera
Narrung
Piambie
'Oaklands'
Booroorban
Koorkab
Kenley
Perekerten
'Willurah'
Kooloonong
Haysdale
'Warwillah'
Natya
Goodnight
Kyalite
Moolpa

Tooleybuc
Moulamein
Wanganella
'Booabula'
Piangil West
Piangil
Stony Crossing
Tudor
Miralie
Wood Wood
Dilpurra
Cunninyeuk
Nyah
Speewa
Niemur
Conargo
Chillingollah
Vinifera
Beverford
Jimaringle
Morago
Nyah West
Tyntynder Central
Woorinen Nth
Tyntynder South
Burraboi
Pretty Pine
Swan Hill
Pioneer Settlement
Waitchie
Pental Island
Ballbank
Wakool
Deniliquin
Gowanford
Lake Boga
Fish Point
Ultima
Goschen
Tresco
Benjeroop
Murrabit
DENIBOOTA IRRIGATION AREA
Lalbert Road
Kunat
Mystic Park
Myall
Caldwell
Meatian
Lake Charm
Capels Crossing
Beachamp
Barham
Koondrook
Westby
Bunnaloo
Moroco
Lalbert
Korrak Korrak
Fairley
Koroop
Gannawarra
Mathoura
Culgoa
Cokum
Tittybong
Cannie
Kerang
Kerang East
Cohuna
Gunbower Island
Picnic Point
Top Is
Budgerum
Budgerum East
Dingwall
Kerang South
Mead
Barmah State Park
Towaninnin
Quambatook
Lake Meering
Tragowel
McMillans
Wee-Wee-Rup
Womboota
Barmah
Appin
Macorna
Horfield
Leitchville
Torrumbarry Weir
Nullawil
Oakvale
Appin South
Patho
Moama
Picola
Narraport
Gredgwin
Leaghur
Mt Hope
Gunbower
Torrumbarry
Narioka
Nathalia
Wharparilla
Roslynmead
Dumosa
Barraport
Loddon Vale
Mincha
Catumnal
Gladfield
Bald Rock
Kotupna
Wycheproof
Bunguluke
Pyramid Hill
Echuca
Kyabram
Boort
Durham Ox
Ky Valley
Kotta
Koyuga
Simmie
Tongala
St Germains
Thalia
Narrewillock
Lake Marmal
Mitiamo
Bamawm Extension
Bamawm
Lancaster
Teddywaddy West
Teddywaddy
Wychitella
Mysia
Fernihurst
Jarklin
Prairie
Lockington
Merrigum
Banyenong
Wooloonook
Buckrabanyule
Calivil
Milloo
Tennyson
Ballendella
Girgarre
Cooma
Charlton
Jeffcott Nth
Woosang
Borung
Pompapiel
Yallook
Dingee
Warragamba
Rochester
Byrneside
Donald
Dooboobetic
Korong Vale
Fiery Flat
Serpentine
Tandarra
Hunter
Stanhope
Cope Cope
Coonooer Bridge
Wedderburn
Wedderburn Junction
Powlett Plains
Kamarooka
Elmore
Corop

To Bendigo & Melbourne
To Shepparton
To Cobram
To Albury

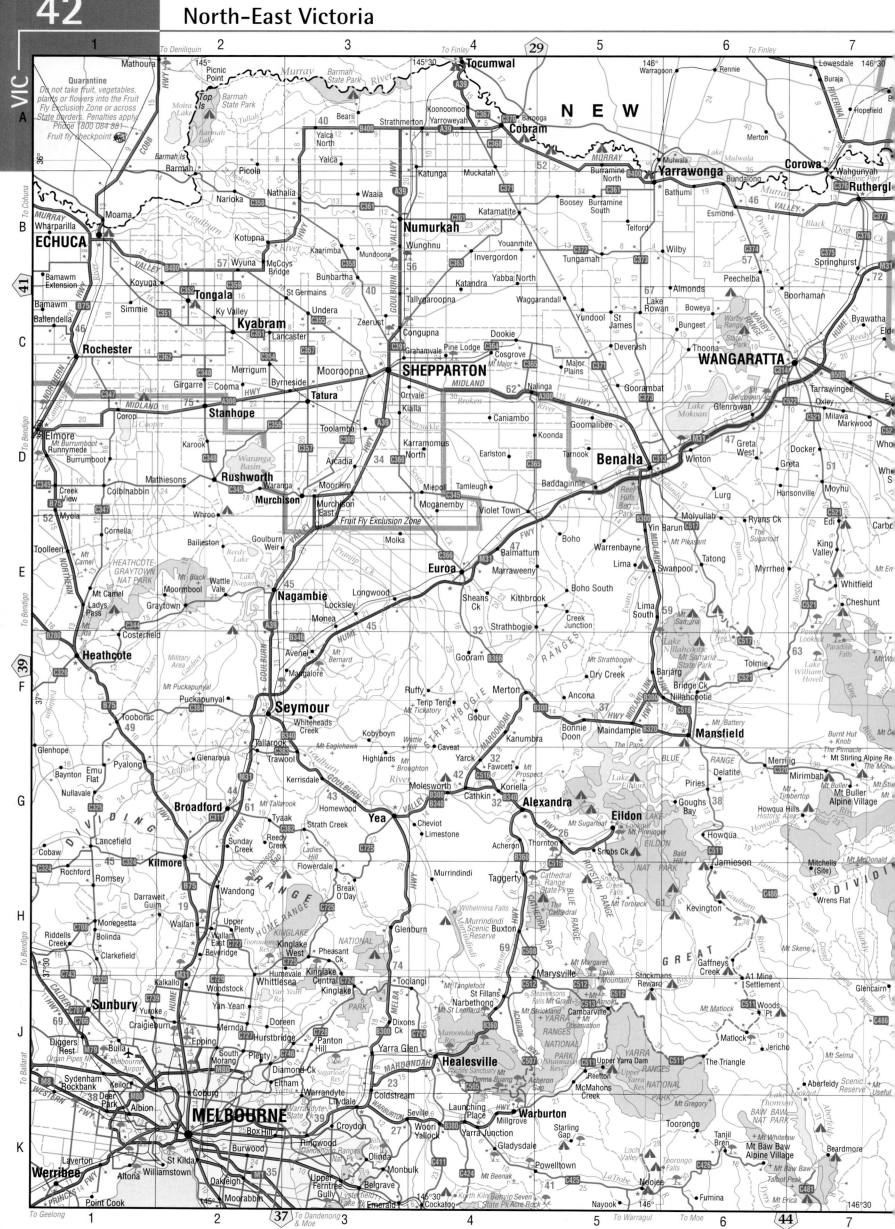

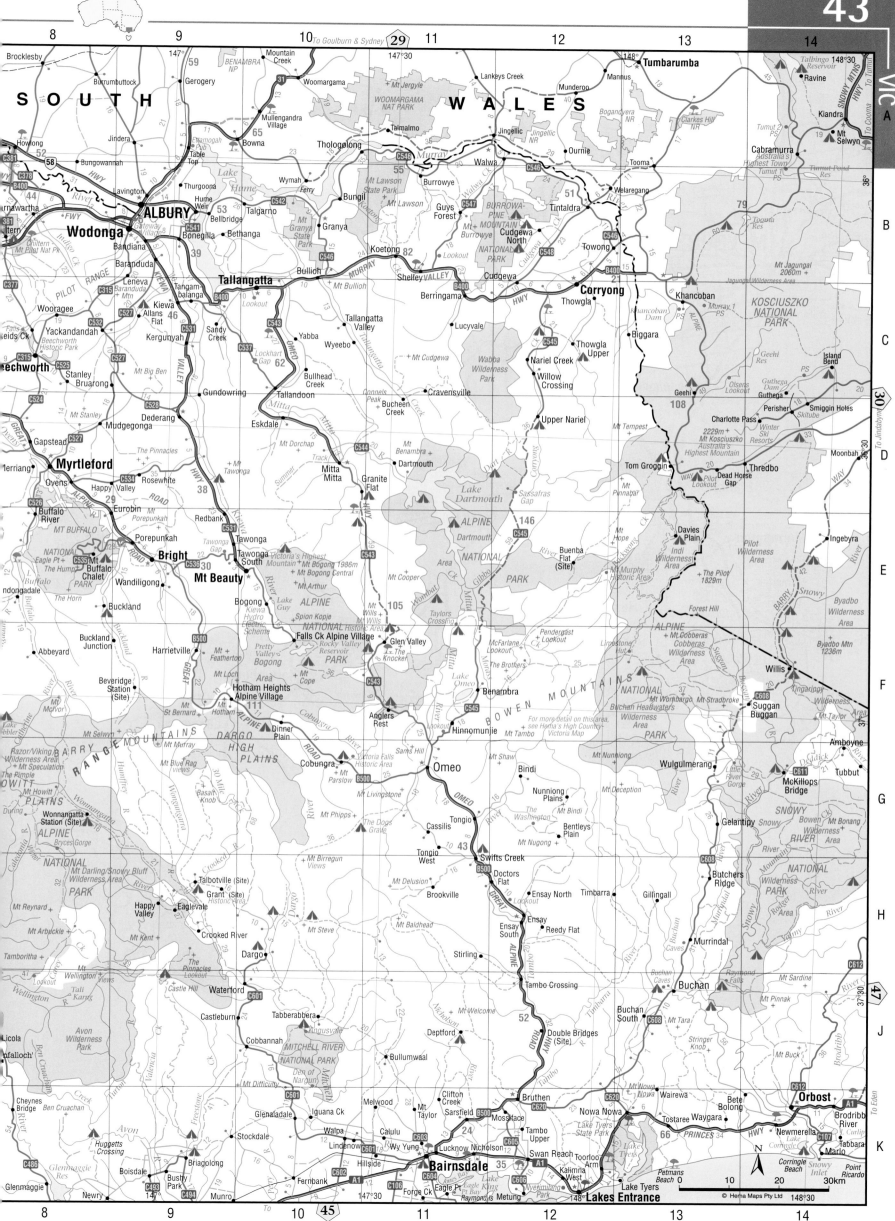

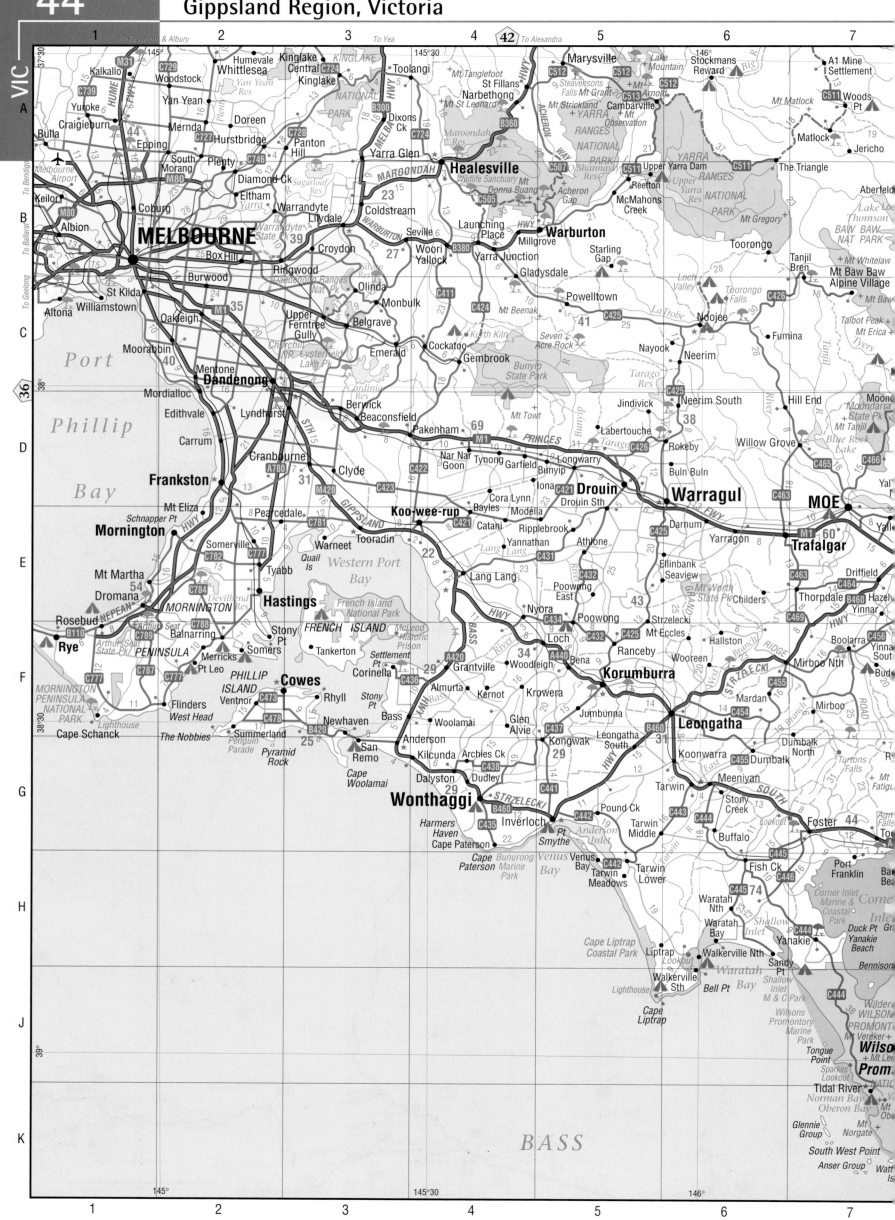

VIC

To Omeo

8 9 10 43 11 To Dargo 12 13 14

146°30' 147° 147°30'

A

Mt Tamboritha Lookout

Glencairn

Mt Wellington Views

Castle Hill

The Pinnacles Lookout

Waterford C601

Tambo Crossing

Mt Welcome

Deptford

Double Bridges (Site)

52

37°30'

47

Closed Winter Road During

Macalister

Wellington

Tali Karng

Castleburn

24

Tabberabbera

Cobbannah

Angusvale

MITCHELL RIVER NATIONAL PARK

Mt Difficulty

Den of Nargun

20

22

Bullumwaal

16

C601

GREAT ALPINE HWY

Licola

Mt Selma

'Glenfalloch'

Avon Wilderness Park

Ben Cruachan

Mt Useful

Scenic Reserve

Carey Ck

Glenaladale

Iguana Ck

Melwood

28

Mt Taylor

Clifton Creek

Sarsfield

Bruthen

C620

B

Nicholson

Beardmore

Cheynes Bridge

Ben Cruachan

41

Stockdale

Walpa

Calulu

Lindenow

12

C603

Wy Yung

Mossiface

Tambo Upper

B500

24

Glenmaggie River

Avon

55

Huggetts Crossing

Freestone Ck

16

C601

18

Hillside

Lucknow Nicholson

Bairnsdale

Swan Reach

A1

35

C605

C

wson

Walhalla

C461

Historic Area

Coopers Creek

Thomson

Glenmaggie Res

C486

Boisdale

Newry

Briagolong

C493

Bushy Park

C494

Munro

Fernbank

C602

A1 HWY 69

24

Ferry

14

27

Eagle Pt

Jones Bay

Eagle King Pt Bay

Forge Ck C106

Raymond Is

Paynesville

Metung

Bunga Arm

Nyerimilang Park

Kalimna West

Lakes Entrance

Heyfield

Maffra

Stratford

Tinamba

C105

8

C105

10

Goon Nure

Bengworden

Meerlieu

Wattle Pt

Lake Victoria

THE LAKES NATIONAL PARK

38°

D

Toongabbie

Glengarry

Tyers

C105

Cowwarr

C488

Nambrok

C487

Bundalaguah

C491

Kilmany

Wurruk

Sale

Longford

Airlie

Clydebank

Cobains

The Heart

Marlay Point

Lake Wellington

Holland Landing

Seacombe

Lake Coleman

Loch Sport

Lake Reeve

Ninety Mile

Gippsland Lakes Coastal Park

E

RARALGON

NORWELL

Churchill

PRINCES A1

Rosedale

HYLAND

Loy Yang

Traralgon Sth

C482

Willung

Gormandale

Powers Hill Lookout

Merriman

Holey Plains State Park

C485

Stradbroke West

Stradbroke

C485

C496

Paradise Beach

Golden Beach

The

26

38°30'

F

Mt Tassie Lookout

Balook

TARRA-BULGA NAT PARK

Carrajung

C484

C453

Won Wron

Darriman

A440

HWY 72

31

Giffard

Lake Denison

Jack Smith Lake

Seaspray

G

Hiawatha Falls

Jack River

Devon

Greenmount

C482

C484

Tarra

onyip

Binginwarri

GIPPSLAND

Yarram

Woodside

C453

C459

Woodside Beach

Reeves Beach

Alberton

Tarraville

C452

St Margaret Is

Manns Beach

McLaughlins Beach

H

Welshpool

Port Welshpool

Sunday Is

Port Albert

Clonmel Is

Nooramunga Marine & Coastal Park

ittle ake Is

Snake Is

J

Mt Hunter

Mt argaret

Mt undback rea

Johnny Souey Pt

Wilsons Promontory Marine Park

K

Sealers Cove

Horn Pt

Brown Head

Cape Wellington

Waterloo th Peak Boulder

ghthouse h Point

STRAIT

N

0 10 20 30km

© Hema Maps Pty Ltd

146°30' 147° 147°30' 148°

8 9 10 11 12 13 14

39°

Mansfield
Merrijig
Mirimbah
Delatite
Piries
Howqua
Jamieson
Kevington
Gaffneys Creek
Matlock
Jericho
Woods Pt
A1 Mine Settlement
The Triangle
Toorongo
Tanjil Bren
Beardmore
Aberfeldy
Glencairn
Licola
Mt Buller Alpine Village
Howqua Hills Historic Area
Mt Stirling Alpine Resort

GREAT DIVIDING RANGE
BARRY MOUNTAINS
ALPINE NATIONAL PARK
DARGO HIGH PLAINS
Dinner Plain
Cobungra
Omeo
Hinnomunjie
Bindi
Nunniong Plains
Tongio
Cassilis
Swifts Creek
Doctors Flat
Ensay
Ensay North
Timbarra
Reedy Flat
Stirling
Tambo Crossing
Double Bridges

Talbotville (Site)
Grant (Site)
Happy Valley
Eaglevale
Crooked River
Dargo
Waterford
Castleburn
Cobbannah
Tabberabbera
Deptford
Bullumwaal
Bruthen
Nowa Nowa
Lakes Entrance

Licola
Cheynes Bridge
Glenfalloch
Glenmaggie
Seaton
Heyfield
Maffra
Stratford
Boisdale
Briagolong
Newry
Bushy Park
Fernbank
Lindenow
Walpa
Calulu
Wy Yung
Bairnsdale
Lucknow
Nicholson
Swan Reach
Kalimna West
Metung
Paynesville
Raymond Is
Eagle Pt

Heyfield
Tinamba
Cowwarr
Toongabbie
Nambrok
Bundalaguah
Cobains
Airlie
Clydebank
Longford
Sale
Wurruk
Kilmany
Rosedale
The Heart
Bengworden
Goon Nure
Meerlieu
Loch Sport
Seacombe
Holland Landing
Marlay Point
Lake Wellington

MOE
TRARALGON
MORWELL
Churchill
Trafalgar
Yallourn
Driffield
Hazelwood
Yinnar
Boolarra
Mirboo Nth
Thorpdale
Childers
Gormandale
Willung
Loy Yang
Traralgon Sth
Stradbroke
Stradbroke West
Seaspray
Paradise Beach
Golden Beach

Balook
Carrajung
Giffard
Darriman
Woodside
Won Wron
Jack River
Devon
Greenmount
Yarram
Alberton
Tarraville
Port Albert
Welshpool
Toora
Foster
Port Welshpool
Port Franklin
Barrys Beach
Snake Is
Yanakie
Sandy Pt
Corner Inlet
Wilsons Promontory
Tidal River
Mt Oberon
South Point
WILSONS PROMONTORY NATIONAL PARK

Mirboo
Mardan
Dumbalk
Binginwarri

8 To Willis 43 9 10 11 To Cooma & Canberra 12 30 13 14

148°30 148°30 149° 149°30 150°

NEW SOUTH WALES

Coolumbooka NR
Maharatta

Mt Taylor
Mt Tingaringy
Amboyne
Tubbut
Delegate River
Delegate 73
Burragate
Egan Peaks NR
Lochiel
Greigs Flat
Haycock Point
Pambula
Pambula Beach

A

Wulgulmerang
McKillops Bridge
Dellicknora
Cabanandra
Haydens Bog
Craigie
Mila
Bondi Gulf NR
Platts
Mt Delegate
Bendoc North
Lower Bendoc
Rockton
Pericoe
Towamba
Boydtown
Kiah
Mt Imlay
BEN BOYD
Eden
Twofold Bay
Boyds Tower
Edrom
Nethercote

SNOWY
RIVER
NATIONAL
PARK
Gelantipy
Butchers Ridge
Murrindal
Buchan
Buchan South
Mt Tara

Bonang
Mt Bonang
Mt Bendoc
Bendoc

SOUTH EAST FORESTS NAT PK
Nungatta
Buldah
Genoa
Mt Merragunegin
COOPRACAMBRA NATIONAL PARK Wilderness Area
Nungatta South
Wroxham
Wangarabell
Timbillica
Narrabarba
Wonboyn Lake
Saltwater Creek PARK
Bittangabee Bay Lighthouse
Disaster Bay
Green Cape

B

ERRINUNDRA NATIONAL PARK
Goongerah
Mt Jersey
Errinundra
Combienbar
Chandlers Creek
Noorinbee North
Mt Buckle
NADGEE NATURE RESERVE
Newtons Beach

C

Raymond Falls
Mt Sardine
Mt Pinnak
Mt Ellery
Mt Jack
Mt Kuark
Club Terrace
LIND NATIONAL PARK
Tonghi Ck
Noorinbee
Cann River
ALFRED NATIONAL PARK
Genoa
Gipsy Pt
Fairhaven
Cape Howe Wilderness Area
Mallacoota Lookout
Cape Howe

Buchan Caves
Wairewa
Bete Bolong
Tostaree Waygara
Stringer Knob
Mt Buck
Murrungowar
Bellbird Creek
Manorina
Bemm River Rainforest
Mt Bemm
Rainforest Walk
Mallacoota Inlet
Mallacoota
Bastion Point
Gabo Island Lighthouse

D

Orbost
Brodribb River
Curlip
Cabbage Tree Creek
Cabbage Tree Palms Reserve
Newmerella
Tabbara
Mario
Bemm River
Lake Furnell
Swan Lake
Tamboon
Mt Everard
CROAJINGOLONG NATIONAL PARK
Sandpatch Wilderness Area
Little Rame Head
Sandpatch Pt
Wingan Inlet

Corringle Beach
Snowy Inlet
Point Ricardo
Cape Conran
Cape Conran Coastal Park
Pearl Point
Sydenham Inlet
Tamboon Inlet
Point Hicks
Lighthouse
Petrel Pt
Rame Head
Petmans Beach

Wilderness

E

TASMAN   SEA

G

N

0 10 20 30 40 50 km

© Hema Maps Pty Ltd

Tasmania

Wineglass Bay (53 C14)

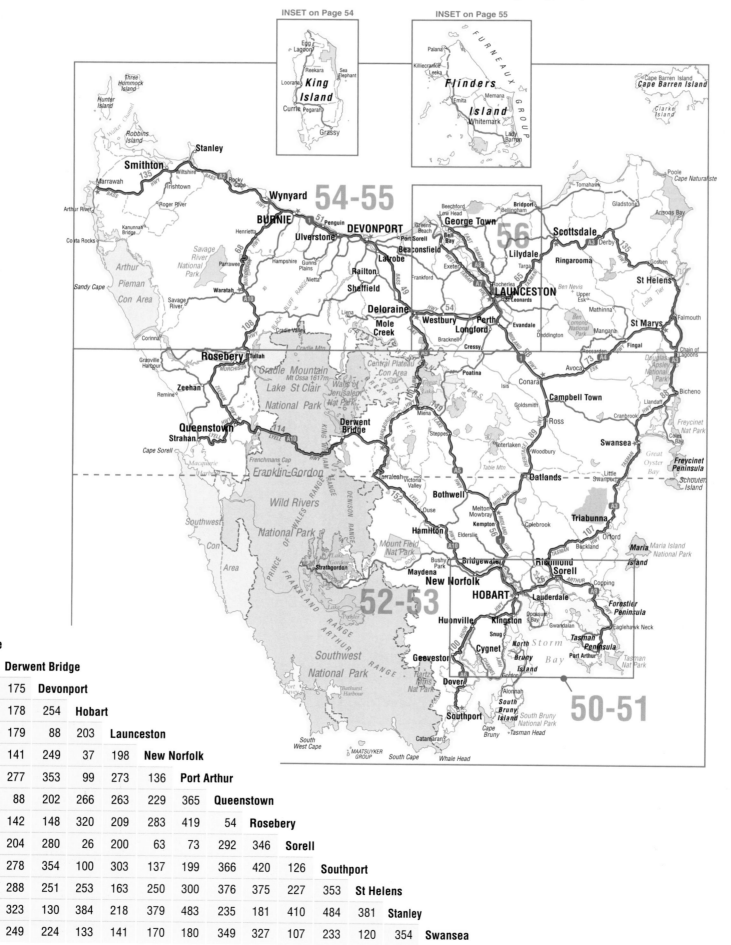

INSET on Page 54

King Island

INSET on Page 55

Flinders Island

54-55

56

52-53

50-51

Burnie												
226	**Derwent Bridge**											
51	175	**Devonport**										
305	178	254	**Hobart**									
139	179	88	203	**Launceston**								
300	141	249	37	198	**New Norfolk**							
404	277	353	99	273	136	**Port Arthur**						
163	88	202	266	263	229	365	**Queenstown**					
109	142	148	320	209	283	419	54	**Rosebery**				
331	204	280	26	200	63	73	292	346	**Sorell**			
405	278	354	100	303	137	199	366	420	126	**Southport**		
302	288	251	253	163	250	300	376	375	227	353	**St Helens**	
79	323	130	384	218	379	483	235	181	410	484	381	**Stanley**
275	249	224	133	141	170	180	349	327	107	233	120	354	**Swansea**

Distances are shown in kilometres and follow the most direct major sealed route

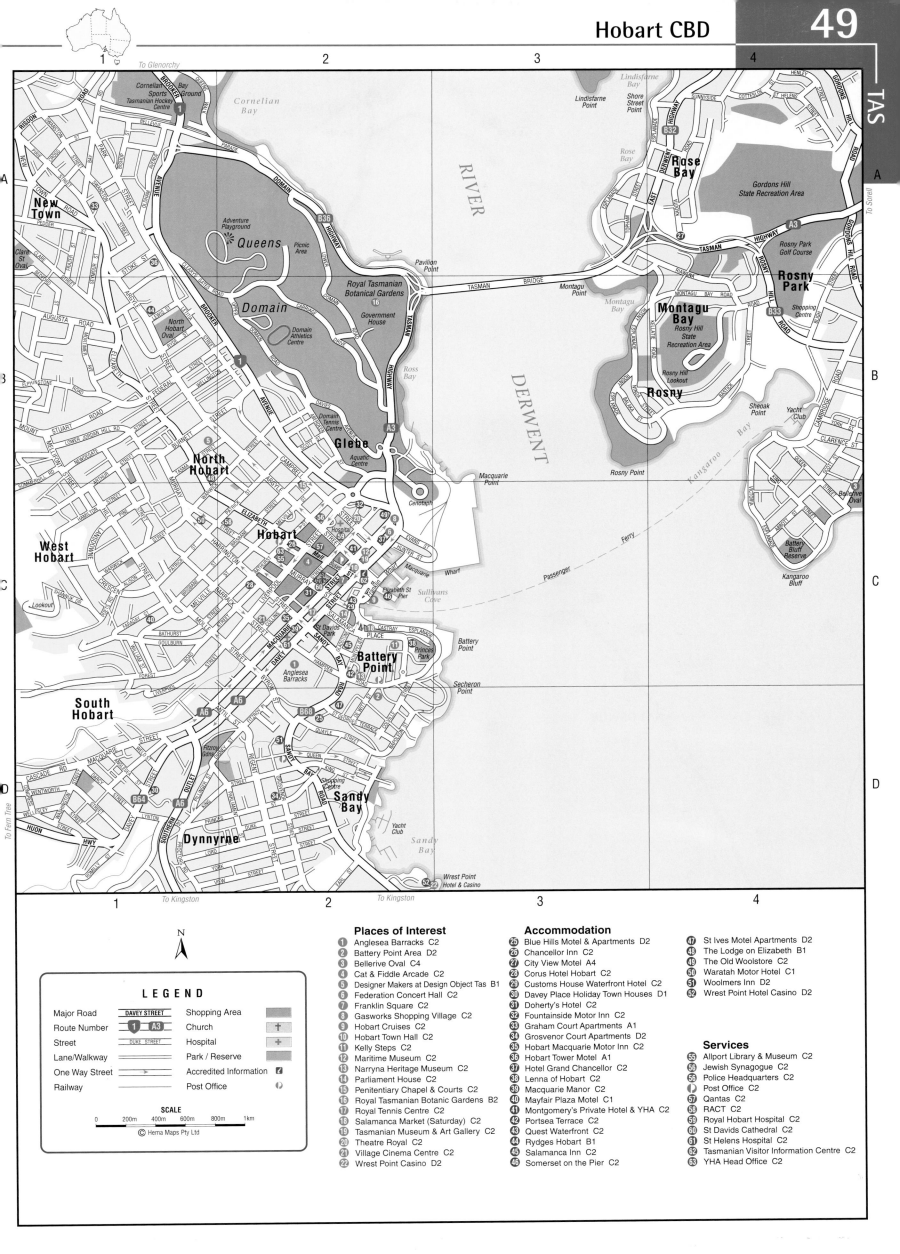

L E G E N D

Major Road	DAVEY STREET	Shopping Area	
Route Number	1 A3	Church	†
Street	DUKE STREET	Hospital	+
Lane/Walkway		Park / Reserve	
One Way Street		Accredited Information	i
Railway		Post Office	◯

SCALE
0   200m   400m   600m   800m   1km

© Hema Maps Pty Ltd

Places of Interest
1 Anglesea Barracks C2
2 Battery Point Area D2
3 Bellerive Oval C4
4 Cat & Fiddle Arcade C2
5 Designer Makers at Design Object Tas B1
6 Federation Concert Hall C2
7 Franklin Square C2
8 Gasworks Shopping Village C2
9 Hobart Cruises C2
10 Hobart Town Hall C2
11 Kelly Steps C2
12 Maritime Museum C2
13 Narryna Heritage Museum C2
14 Parliament House C2
15 Penitentiary Chapel & Courts C2
16 Royal Tasmanian Botanic Gardens B2
17 Royal Tennis Centre C2
18 Salamanca Market (Saturday) C2
19 Tasmanian Museum & Art Gallery C2
20 Theatre Royal C2
21 Village Cinema Centre C2
22 Wrest Point Casino D2

Accommodation
25 Blue Hills Motel & Apartments D2
26 Chancellor Inn C2
27 City View Motel A4
28 Corus Hotel Hobart C2
29 Customs House Waterfront Hotel C2
30 Davey Place Holiday Town Houses D1
31 Doherty's Hotel C2
32 Fountainside Motor Inn C2
33 Graham Court Apartments A1
34 Grosvenor Court Apartments D2
35 Hobart Macquarie Motor Inn C2
36 Hobart Tower Motel A1
37 Hotel Grand Chancellor C2
38 Lenna of Hobart C2
39 Macquarie Manor C2
40 Mayfair Plaza Motel C1
41 Montgomery's Private Hotel & YHA C2
42 Portsea Terrace C2
43 Quest Waterfront C2
44 Rydges Hobart B1
45 Salamanca Inn C2
46 Somerset on the Pier C2

47 St Ives Motel Apartments D2
48 The Lodge on Elizabeth B1
49 The Old Woolstore C2
50 Waratah Motor Hotel C1
51 Woolmers Inn D2
52 Wrest Point Hotel Casino D2

Services
55 Allport Library & Museum C2
56 Jewish Synagogue C2
56 Police Headquarters C2
◯ Post Office C2
57 Qantas C2
58 RACT C2
59 Royal Hobart Hospital C2
60 St Davids Cathedral C2
61 St Helens Hospital C2
62 Tasmanian Visitor Information Centre C2
63 YHA Head Office C2

TAS

53 To Kempton
To Oatlands
To Hamilton

1 2 3 4 53 5 6 7

A

Black Hills
Plenty
B62
Salmon Ponds
Oldest trout hatchery in
the Southern Hemisphere
Hayes
Magra
Pulpit Rock
Lookout
Boyer
ANM
Paper Tour
Dromedary
River
B10
WAY
Granite
Historic Watch House,
Winery
A10
12
11
Bridgewater
One of the earliest convict
built causeways in Tasmania
Historic Site
Cove Hill
Gagebrook
Baskerville
Raceway
C327
C326
Richmond
Historic Bridge
Historic Town
Palmara Vineyard
C323

Feilton
C610
C184
Historic Site
New Norfolk
Historic Town
32 5 WILD
Winery
Malbina
Molesworth
C615
Mt Faulkner
Alpenrail
Old Beach
Claremont
Cadbury
B32
Mt Direction
Otago
Grass Tree Hill
C324
B31
Duck
Hole
14

B
Plenty R
Glenfern
C613
Lachlan
Sorell Rvt
Glenlusk
Berriedale
Moorilla Estate
Vineyard
Elwick
Racetrack
B35
Bowen
Bridge
Risdon Cove
Historic Site
Risdon Vale
Richmond
Golf Club
Winery
Cambridge
26
A3
C328

C
Mt Lloyd
Mount R
Lachlan
Collins Cap
Collinsvale
Myrtle Forest
Tolosa Park
Collins Cap
Derwent Entertainment Centre
21
Glenorchy
Winery
Tasmanian
Transport
Museum
1
Royal Tasmanian
Botanic Gardens
Lady Franklin
Museum
Queens Domain
HOBART
Tasman
Bridge
Rosny Hill
Lookout
Bellerive
Historic
Sites
Lindisfarne
14
C329
B33
Roke
Lookout
Run

D
Collins
Bonnet
WELLINGTON RANGE
Lookout
Mt Wellington
Organ Pipes
C616
12
Mt Montagu
Wellington
Falls
Walking
Track
Fern Tree
Silver Falls
Cascade Brewery
& Gardens
O'Gradys
Falls
Waterworks
Res
Ridgeway
Museums, Casino, Markets,
University, Theatres, Ant-
arctic Science Centre
Historic
Site
11
A6
Mt Nelson
Signal
Station
13
15
Sandy
Bay
Truganini Reserve
Tudor Court
Droughty Pt
B68

E
Mt Misery
Judbury
Crabtree
C617
C618
Lower
Longley
Grove
Huon Valley Apple
& Heritage Museum
Lucaston
C645
Doran's
Jam Factory
6
Mountain
River
36
Longley
SOUTHERN
Sandfly
4
2
3
Leslie
Vale
HWY
9
12
Shot
Tower
Taroona
Historic Site
Crayfish Pt
Gellibrand Pt
Kingston
Ralphs Bay
Opossum
Bay

F
Glen
Huon
C619
Huon R
15
5
Ranelagh
A6
2
4
Huonville
HUON
Kaoota
C621
Nierinna
Margate
Pelverata
C622
35
Antarctic
Hdqrs
Blow
Hole
Blackmans
Bay
Howden
South
Arm

G
Franklin
Woodstock
Grey Mtn
Pelverata
Falls
Snug Falls
Kiernans
Falls
Electrona
Snug
Snug
Pt
Coningham
North
West
Bay
Tinderbox
Piersons Pt
Tinderbox
Marine Res
Dennes
Point
Cape Direction
Iron Pot
(Lighthouse)
Cape de la Sortie

H
Castle Forbes
Bay
South Franklin
Cradoc
Winery
Area
B68
Nicholls
Falls
C626
Oyster
Cove
Historic Site
Oyster
Cove
Kettering
Winery
Area
Passenger &
Vehicular
Ferry
Barnes
Bay
Roberts Pt
Lowes
Hill
C625
North
One Tree Pt
Barnes Bay
Yellow Bluff

J
Port Huon
Geeveston
Glaziers Bay
C641
Wattle
Grove
Cygnet
C627
Nicholls
Rivulet
Winery
Area
10
Hartziew Wine
Centre
Talune
Wildlife
Park
Woodbridge
Birchs Bay
Winery
Area
Roberts
Hill
B66
Bruny
Trumpeter
Bay
Trumpeter Pt

K
Cairns Bay
C639
Petcheys
Bay
C646
Lymington
Nicholls Rvt
60
Gardners
Bay
Winery
Area
Flowerpot
Domeney's
Fruit Farm
Green Is
Roberts
Hill
Island
Church
Hill
Waterloo
Surges Bay
C638
Glendevie
Police
Point
Garden Is
Creek
Garden
Is
Mt Grosse
Gordon
Middleton
Simpsons
Pt
Great
Bay
Variety
Bay
Isthmus
Bay
Penguin
Rookery
Adventure
Bay
Cape Queen
Elizabeth
A6
C637
To Southport

IAS

A

B

C

D

E

F

G

H

J

K

To Triabunna

Orielton
Pawleena
Orielton Rvr
A3
Mt Lord
Penna
Sorell
C332
Wattle Hill
Midway Pt
A3
Orani Vineyard
Forcett
A9
Lewisham
ARTHUR
Nugent
C331
Corbetts Lookout
Gordon SL
Kellevie
Ragged Tier
C335
Bream Creek
Winery
Copping
Museum
Convict & Colonial Collection
Cape Bernier
Point du Ressac
Bream Ck
Marion Bay

Pitt Water
Tasmania Golf Club
Oyster Farm
Hobart Airport
Llanherne Golf Club
Royal Hobart Golf Club
Seven Mile Beach Equestrian Centre
Seven Mile Beach
Sandy Pt
Tiger Head
Dodges Ferry
Carlton
C349
Carlton
Roches Beach
Carlton Bluff
C349
Primrose Sands
Primrose Pt
Tasman Monument
Dunalley
C334
Denison Canal
Blackman Bay
Cape Paul Lamanon
North Bay
Cape Frederick Hendrick

Lauderdale
Frederick Henry
Bay
Green Head
Lime Bay Nature Res
Smooth Is
Fulham Is
Dunalley Bay
Mt Forestier
Forestier
73
A9 HWY
Wellard Bridge
Murdunna
Tasman National Park
Cape Surville

Sandford
Cremorne
Mt Augustus
Pipe Clay Lagoon
B33
Cape Deslacs
Clifton Beach
Mutton Bird Viewing (Summer)
Sandford Equestrian Centre
Cape Contrariety
North West Head
Gwandalan
Whitehouse Pt
Mt Stewart
Coal Mines Historic Site
Convict Settlement Ruins
King George Is
Chronicle Pt
Norfolk Bay
Flinders Bay
Flinders
Macgregor Peak
Peninsula
Lookout
Tessellated Pavement
Eaglehawk Neck
Officers Quarters & Dogline
Cape

Iron Pot Lookout
Betsey Is
Garnetts Bridge
Deer Pt
Saltwater River
Hurdle Bridge
Halfway Bluff
C341
Premaydena
Mt Communication
Outer North Head
Auk Pt
Sand Dunes
B37
C343
9
Koonya
Taranna
Tasmanian Devil Centre
A9
Eaglehawk Bay
Pirates Bay
Cashs Lookout
Penzance
Doo Town
Tasman Blowhole
Tasman Arch
Devils Kitchen
Waterfall Bay
Camp Falls
O'Hara Bluff
Tasman National Park

Nubeena
Parsons Bridge
Wedge Bay
White Beach
Wedge Is
Highcroft
Storm Bay
Two Island Bay
Tasman Peninsula
Oakwood
Bush Mill Railway
Port Arthur
Convict Ruins Historic Ghost Tours Ocean Kayaking Tours
Stormlea
Isle of the Dead Historic Site
Palmers Lookout
Remarkable Cave
Curio Bay
Maingon Blowhole
Cape Raoul
Tasman National Park
Raoul Bay
West Arthur Head
Port Arthur
C347
C344
Mimosa Falls
Thumb Pt
Fortescue Bay
Cape Hauy
The Lanterns
Munro Bight
Tasman National Park
Black Head
Cape Pillar
Chasm Lookout
Tasman Is
Lighthouse
Maingon Bay

N

SCALE
0   5   10 km
© Hema Maps Pty Ltd

8   9   10   53   11   12   13   14

TAS

1 2 3 4 54 5 6 7

To Burnie

Ahrberg Bay
145°
Duck Ck
Stanley R
Lake Pieman
C252
145°30
Tullah
C252
Bastyan PS, Dam
High Tor
GRANITE TOR CON AREA
Barn Bluff +
Overland
Rowallan PS
Clumner Bluff +
Howells Bluff
Forty Lake
GREAT

A

Granville Harbour
C249
Renison Bell
MURCHISON
Rosebery
A10
Mt Murchison +
Murchison Dam
Granite Tor +
Victoria Peak
Mt Pelion West +
Mt Jerusalem
Pillans
Lake Ada
CEN GON
Lake Au

Granville Harbour
Mine
Mt Read +
Anthony PS
Mt Pelion East +
Cathedral Mtn +
WALLS OF JERUSALEM
Lake Meston
Williamsford
Montezuma Falls
Mt Ossa +
CRADLE MOUNTAIN
NATIONAL PARK
Lake Louisa

Mt Agnew
Museum
Dundas
Selina
Lake Plimsoll
Chalice L
Mt Myrtle
LAKE ST CLAIR
Norman
Lake
Mallees

A

Zeehan
C248
Mt Zeehan
Mt Dundas +
Lake Margaret
DU CANE RANGE
Mt Gould +
Lake Sappho
Mt Olympus +
Lake

Trial Harbour
C27
Little
Henty
L. Rolleston
PART OF WORLD HERITAGE AREA
Orion
Mt Hugel +

B
42°
Badger
Lookout
48
Henty Glacial Moraine
Mt Sedgwick + Lake Beatrice
High Dome
Eldon Bluff
Eldon
Eldon Peak +
NATIONAL PARK
Pyramid Mtn +

Henty
Beach
Dunes
Tully
Mt Lyell + Copper Mines
Linda
Burbury
Nelson Valley
LYELL
82
Mt Rufus +
Cheyne Range
Visitor Centre

Chairlift, Museum
Queenstown
B24
Mt Owen +
Victoria Pass
Nelson Falls
Mt Alma +
Mt Gell +
A10

C
Wharf Centre
Strahan
Regatta Pt
Lowana
41
38
Lynchford
Mt Huxley +
Crotty Dam
114
Mt Arrowsmith +
Mt King William I +
Derwent Bridge
HWY
A10
Bronte Park

Cruise
John Butters PS
Mt Jukes +
Donaghys Hill
Franklin River Nature Trail
Mt King William II +
King
Lake
Bronte
Lgn

Lighthouse
Cape Sorell
Macquarie Hds
King River Gorge
Darwin Dam
Franklin
Frenchmans Cap +
Mt King William III +
Guelph Basin
C501
25
Lake Binney

D
Sophia Pt
Macquarie
Mt Sorell +
Mt Darwin +
FRANKLIN - GORDON
WILD RIVERS
Mt King +
Mt Hobhouse +
Tarral

Liberty Pt
Gordon
Farm Cove
Jane
Erebus
Gordon
Mt Humboldt +
Wylds Craig +
Wayatina

Sloop Pt
George Pt
Harbour
River
Bird River Bridge
Pillinger
permit required
NATIONAL PARK
PART OF WORLD HERITAGE AREA

Gould Pt
Kelly Basin
Mt McCall +
Reeds Peak +
DENISON RANGE

E
Birthday Bay
Sarah Is Convict Ruins
Birches Inlet
Heritage Landing
Goodwins Peak +
Clear Hill +

Varna Bay
Modder
Mt Lee +
SOUTHWEST
Jane
Maxwell
Gordon

Hibbs Bay
Point Hibbs
Hibbs
Innes Pk +
CONSERVATION
Denison
Lake Gordon
Adamsfield
Tim Shea

F
Spero Bay
Spero
Wanderer
AREA
River
Olga
Gordon Dam
Strathgordon
Old Mine Permit Reqd
ROAD

Endeavour Bay
Christmas Cove
Mt Lewis +
Hales
B61
Serpentine Dam
Teds Beach
C61
Mt Mueller +
Frodshams Pass

High Rocky Pt
River
Mt Sprent +
74
Creepy Crawly Walk
Forest Res
Mt Wedge +

G
SOUTHERN
Lewis
McPartlan Pass
Mt Anne +
Mt Eliza +
Lake Judd

43°
Lighthouse
Low Rocky Pt
Elliott Bay
FRANKLAND RANGE
Lake Pedder
Mt Solitary +
Scotts Peak Dam
Edgar Dam

H
Nye Bay
Dodds
Lookout
C507

Elliott Pt
Mulcahy Bay
Castle Hill +
Crossing
Mt Hesperus +
Arthur Plains
West Portal +

Brier Holme Head
Mt Hean +
SOUTHWEST NATIONAL PARK
PART OF WORLD HERITAGE AREA
ARTHUR RANGE

Svenor Pt
Wreck Bay
Mt Norold +
Ripple Mtn +
Federation Peak +

J
OCEAN
James Kelly Basin
Payne Bay
Mt Rugby +
Bathurst Harbour
Moulters Inlet

North Head
Pt St Vincent
Breaksea Is
Port Davey
Mt Louisa +

Hilliard Head
Stephens Ba
Melaleuca Ranger Office & Bird Observatory
Mt Counsel +

K
43°30
N
Mutton Bird Is
Mt Karamu +
Cox Bight
Red Pt +
Cox Bluff
Havelock Bluff
Ile du Gol

0 10 20 30 40 km
© Hema Maps Pty Ltd
South West Cape
Telopea Pt
De Witt Is
Flat Witch Is
Walker Is
MAATSUYKER GROUP
Lighthouse
Maatsuyker Is

145°
145°30
146°

1 2 3 4 5 6 7

Grid columns: 8, 9, 10, 55, 11, 12, 13, 14
Grid rows: A, B, C, D, E, F, G, H, J, K

To Devonport, Launceston — To Launceston — To St Marys

WESTERN

Wild Dog Tier
Blackwood Creek
Breona
Poatina
GREAT WESTERN TIERS CONSERVATION AREA
Epping Forest
Cleveland
Avoca
St Pauls Dome
Mt Puzzler Forest Res
Piccaninny Pt
Long Pt
Seymour
Douglas River
DOUGLAS-APSLEY NATIONAL PARK
Maclean Bay
Bernacchi
Reynolds Neck
Mother Lords Plains
Mt Blackwood
Brazendale Is
Bradys Lookout
Cramps
CENTRAL PLATEAU CON AREA
Conara
St Pauls
Mt Henry
Royal George
St John
Harding Falls Forest Res
Birdlife & Animal Park
Waubs Harbour
Sealife Centre, Marine Res
Bicheno
Cape Lodi
Double Lagoon
Reynolds Is
Great Lake
Miena
Tods
Millers Bluff
Campbell Town
Historic Town
Mt Augusta
Goldsmith
Snow Hill
Weekend
Meetus Falls Forest Res
Meetus Falls
Llandaff
Apslawn
Courland Bay
Butlers Pt
Shannon
Flintstone
Waddaman
Wilburville
Steppes
Lagoon of Islands
Woods Lake
Ross
Historic Town
Glen Morriston
Lake Leake
Hobgoblin
Rawlinna Hill
Lost Falls Forest Res
Cranbrook
Wineries
FREYCINET NATIONAL PARK
Lake Echo
Lake Sorell
Mona Vale
Mt Connection
Nine Mile Beach
Pt Bagot
Bluestone Bay
Coles Bay
Cape Tourville Lighthouse
Freycinet Lodge
Sleepy Bay
Waterloo Pt
Hepburn Pt
Swansea
Bark Mill, Wine & Wool Centre, Winery
Interlaken
Tunbridge
Woodbury
Antill Ponds
Webber Pt
Great Oyster Bay
Cape Forestier
The Hazards
Wineglass Bay
Victoria Valley
Osterley
Strickland
St Peters Pass
York Plains
Nala
Pawtella
Lemont
Mayfield Bay Con Area
Mayfield Bay
Buxton Pt
Cape Freycinet
FREYCINET NATIONAL PARK
Cape Degerando
Dee Lagoon
Oatlands
Georgian Architecture
Parattah
Andover
Mt Seymour
Stonehenge
Little Swanport
Schouten Island
Cape Baudin
Cape Sonnerat
Taillefer Rocks
Bothwell
Historic Town
Lower Marshes
Jericho
Stonor
Baden
Tunnack
Whitefoord
Woodsdale
Little Swanport
Museum
Seaford Pt
Cape Faure
Sarah Ann Bay
Ile des Phoques
Hamilton
Kempton
Colebrook
Rhyndaston
Eldon
Mt Hobbs
Buckland Military Training Area
Mt Douglas
Boltons Beach Con Area
Grindstone Bay
Bluestone Tier
Cape Bougainville
Lords Bluff
Dunrobin Bridge
Lawrenny
Ouse
Melton Mowbray
Black Tier
Bagdad
Lowdina
Runnymede
Triabunna
Louisville
Cape Boullanger
Ellendale
Fentonbury
Westerway
Karania
Gretna
Rosegarland
Broadmarsh
Mangalore
Pontville
Campania
Brown Mtn
Orford
Spring Beach
Johnsons Pt
Rheban
Darlington
Bishop and Clerk
MARIA ISLAND NATIONAL PARK
Mt Maria
Mistaken Cape
National Park
Glenora
Bushy Park
Plenty
Hayes
Magra
Brighton
Gagebrook
Tea Tree
Wildlife Park
Richmond
Historic Town
Pawleena
Nugent
Sandspit Forest Res
Maria Island
Maydena
Tyenna
Fitzgerald
New Norfolk
Black Hills
Dromedary
Bridgewater
Old Beach
Sorell
Wattle Hill
Forcett
Kellevie
Cape Bernier
Cape Peron
Cape Maurouard
Glenfern
Mt Lloyd
Collins Cap
Collinsvale
Glenorchy
Lindisfarne
Midway Pt
Cambridge
Copping
Dunalley
Cape Paul Lamanon
Molesworth
Glenlusk
Bellerive
Seven Mile Beach Protected Area
Seven Mile Beach
Carlton
Cape Monument
Cape Frederick Hendrick
HOBART
Rokeby
Lauderdale
Primrose Sands
Primrose Pt
Murdunna
Forestier Peninsula
Cape Surville
TASMAN NAT PARK
Mt Wellington Lookout
Fern Tree
Taroona
Sandford
Cremorne
Sloping Is
Green Head
Smooth Is
Lime Bay Nature Res
Cape Paul Lamanon
Cape Forestier
Crabtree
Longley
Leslie Vale
Kingston
Opossum Bay
Cape Deslacs
Clifton Beach
Gwandalan
Coal Mines Historic Site
Norfolk Bay
Deer Pt
Eaglehawk Neck
Tessellated Pavement
Tasman Blowhole
Tasman Arch
Devils Kitchen
Judbury
Lucaston
Ranelagh
Grove
Sandfly
Kaoota
Margate
Blackmans Bay
Howden
South Arm
Saltwater River
Premaydena
Koonya
Taranna
Waterfall Bay
O'Hara Bluff
Huonville
Glen Huon
Nierinna
Electrona
Tinderbox
Cape Direction
Iron Pot
Cape de la Sortie
Auk Pt
Mt Communication
Highcroft
Tasman
Nubeena
Oakwood
Peninsula
Port Arthur
Thumb Pt
Hippolyte Rocks
Cape Hauy
Franklin
Woodstock
Grey Mtn
Cradoc
Snug
Oyster Cove
North Bruny
One Tree Pt
Barnes Bay
The Yellow Bluff
Wedge Bay
White Beach
Stormlea
Palmers Lookout
Remarkable Cave
TASMAN NAT PARK
South Franklin
Castle Forbes Bay
Port Huon
Cygnet
Woodbridge
Nicholls Rvt
Birchs Bay
Gardners Bay
Flowerpot
Kettering
Ferry
Trumpeter Bay
Trumpeter Pt
Bruny
Auk Bay
Wedge Is
Curio Bay
TASMAN NAT PARK
Cathedral Rock
Cape Pillar
Geeveston
Cairns Bay
Petcheys Bay
Lymington
Police Pt
Waterloo
Surges Bay
Glendevie
Glaziers Bay
Wattle Grove
Middleton
Garden Island Creek
Gordon
Variety Bay
Island
Great Bay
Simpsons Bay
Isthmus Bay
Cape Queen Elizabeth
Raoul Bay
Maingon Bay
Tasman Is
Cape Raoul
Lighthouse
HARTZ MTNS NAT PARK
Waratah Lookout
Arve Falls
Hartz Peak
Surveyors Bay
Verona Sands
Marine Res
Simpsons Bay
Adventure Bay
South Bruny
Lunawanna
Alonnah
Ventenat Pt
Fluted Cape
Captain Cook Monument
Munro Bight
Mt Bobs
Dover
Raminea
Strathblane
Esperance Pt
MtMangana
Cape Connella
Bruny Island
Cape Bruny Historic Lighthouse
TASMAN SEA
Hastings Caves
Thermal Springs
Lune River
Ida Bay Railway
Hastings
Southport
Partridge Is
Lady Bay
Hopwood Pt
Great Taylors Bay
Labillardiere Peninsula
Mangana Bluff
SOUTH BRUNY NATIONAL PARK
Precipitous Bluff
Mt La Perouse
Pindars Peak
Southport Lagoon
Leprena
Actaeon Is
Eliza Pt
Recherche Bay
Fishers Pt
Cloudy Bay
Boreel Head
Tasman Head
The Friars
Cecil
Vivian
Prettys Pt
surprise Bay
Shoemaker Pt
Catamaran
Cockle Creek
Whale Sculpture
Second Lookout Pt
South Cape
South East Cape
Whale Head
South Cape Bay

Storm Bay
Frederick Henry Bay
Pitt Water
Marion Bay
Riedle Bay

TASMAN SEA

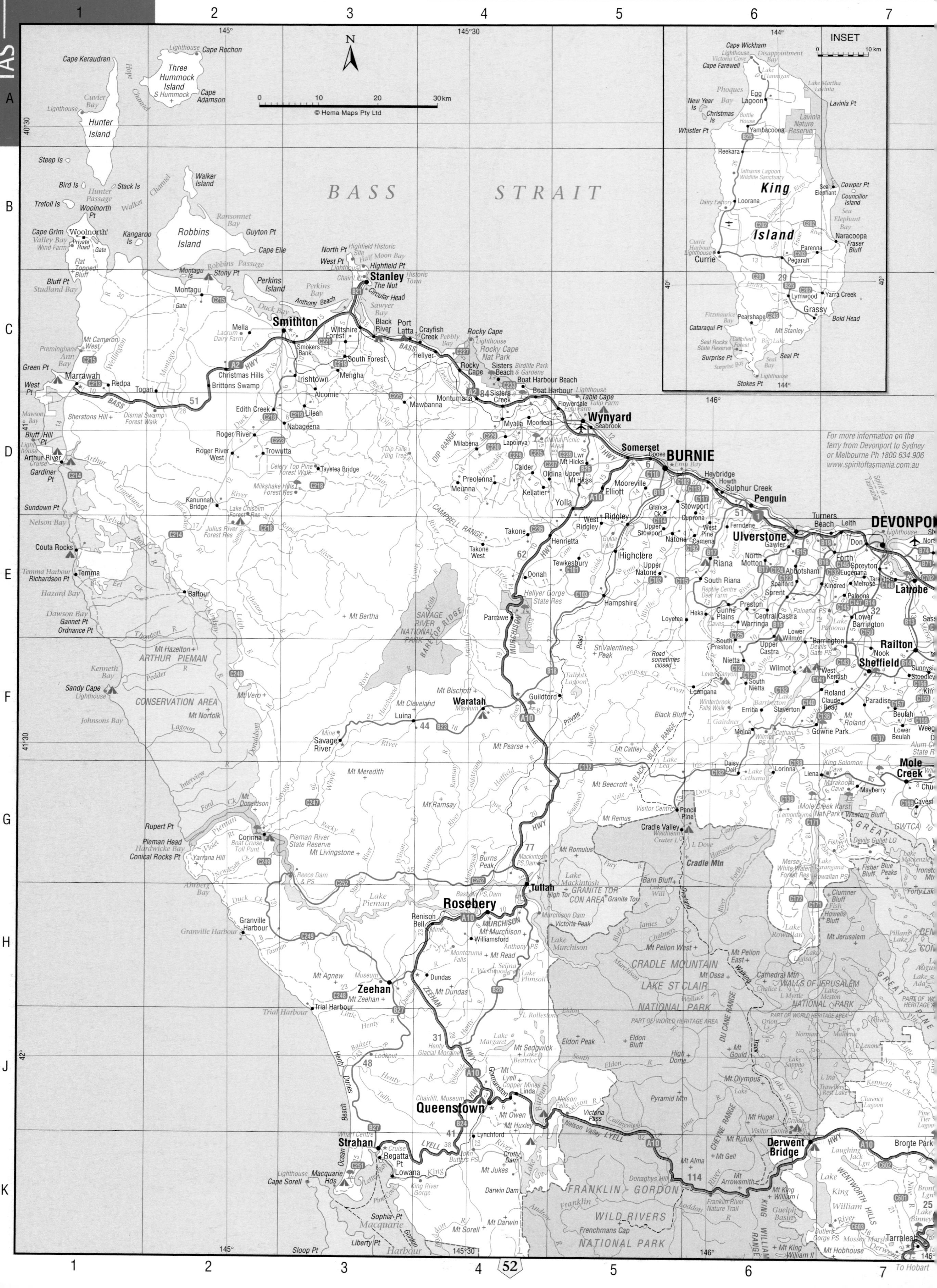

BASS STRAIT
© Hema Maps Pty Ltd
Three Hummock Island
Hunter Island
Robbins Island
Walker Island
Cape Rochon
Cape Adamson
Cape Keraudren
Steep Is
Bird Is
Stack Is
Trefoil Is
Hunter Passage
Woolnorth Pt
Cape Grim
'Woolnorth'
Valley Bay
Wind Farm
Kangaroo Is
Ransonnet Bay
Guyton Pt
Cape Elie
Robbins Passage
Montagu
Perkins Island
Perkins Bay
North Pt
West Pt
Highfield Historic Site
Half Moon Bay
Highfield Pt
Stanley
The Nut
Circular Head
Sawyer Bay
Anthony Beach
Smithton
Mella
Wiltshire Forest
Black River
Port Latta
Crayfish Creek
Rocky Cape
Rocky Cape Nat Park
Sisters Beach
Boat Harbour Beach
Boat Harbour
Table Cape
Wynyard
Somerset
BURNIE
Heybridge
Sulphur Creek
Penguin
Ulverstone
Turners Beach
Leith
DEVONPORT
Latrobe
Railton
Sheffield
Mole Creek
Marrawah
Green Pt
West Pt
Redpa
Togari
Christmas Hills
Brittons Swamp
Irishtown
Alcomie
Mengha
South Forest
Edith Creek
Lileah
Nabageena
Mawbanna
Montumana
Sisters Creek
Myalla
Moorleah
Flowerdale
Seabrook
Roger River
Roger River West
Trowutta
Tayatea Bridge
Arthur River
Bluff Hill Pt
Gardiner Pt
Sundown Pt
Nelson Bay
Couta Rocks
Temma
Balfour
Kanunnah Bridge
Julius River Forest Res
Milabena
Lapoinya
Calder
Oldina
Preolenna
Meunna
Kellatier
Mt Hicks
Elliott
Yolla
Mooreville
Ridgley
Takone
Takone West
Henrietta
West Ridgley
Highclere
Tewkesbury
Oonah
Hellyer Gorge State Res
Hampshire
Upper Natone
Natone
Riana
South Riana
Gunns Plains
Preston
Castra
Nietta
Loyetea
Hazard Bay
Dawson Bay
Gannet Pt
Ordnance Pt
Mt Bertha
SAVAGE RIVER NATIONAL PARK
Mt Hazelton
ARTHUR PIEMAN CONSERVATION AREA
Kenneth Bay
Sandy Cape
Johnsons Bay
Mt Vero
Mt Norfolk
Parrawe
Guildford
Mt Bischoff
Waratah
Mt Cleveland
Luina
Savage River
Mt Meredith
Mt Pearse
Mt Cattley
Black Bluff
Lake Gairdner
Moina
Wilmot
Gowrie Park
Lorinna
Mt Beecroft
Mt Remus
Cradle Valley
Cradle Mtn
Mt Donaldson
Rupert Pt
Pieman Head
Conical Rocks Pt
Corinna
Pieman River State Reserve
Mt Livingstone
Mt Ramsay
Burns Peak
Tullah
Reece Dam
Lake Pieman
Rosebery
Renison Bell
Williamsford
Mt Murchison
Mt Read
Granville Harbour
GRANITE TOR CON AREA
Lake Mackintosh
Lake Murchison
Mt Pelion West
Mt Pelion East
Mt Ossa
CRADLE MOUNTAIN LAKE ST CLAIR NATIONAL PARK
WALLS OF JERUSALEM NATIONAL PARK
Mt Jerusalem
Cathedral Mtn
Mt Agnew
Zeehan
Mt Zeehan
Dundas
Mt Dundas
Trial Harbour
Eldon Peak
Eldon Bluff
High Dome
Mt Olympus
Mt Gould
Lake Margaret
Mt Sedgwick
Mt Lyell
Gormanston
Linda
Queenstown
Mt Owen
Mt Huxley
Lynchford
Strahan
Regatta Pt
Lowana
Cape Sorell
Macquarie Hds
Sophia Pt
Macquarie Harbour
Liberty Pt
Sloop Pt
Mt Jukes
Darwin Dam
Mt Darwin
Mt Sorell
Nelson Falls
Victoria Pass
Pyramid Mtn
Mt Hugel
Mt Rufus
Mt Gell
Mt Alma
Mt Arrowsmith
Derwent Bridge
Bronte Park
Lake King William
FRANKLIN GORDON WILD RIVERS NATIONAL PARK
Frenchmans Cap
Tarraleah
To Hobart
INSET
King Island
Cape Wickham
Egg Lagoon
Currie
Naracoopa
Grassy
Stokes Pt
For more information on the ferry from Devonport to Sydney or Melbourne Ph 1800 634 906 www.spiritoftasmania.com.au

52

INSET

0   10 km

8   9   10   11   12   13   14

A   B   C   D   E   F   G   H   J   K

Flinders Island

FURNEAUX GROUP

Outer Sister Island
Inner Sister Island
Stanley Pt Lighthouse
Blyth Pt • Palana
Mt Killiecrankie • Killiecrankie
Cape Frankland   Mt Tanner
Roydon Is
Cape Frankland
Prime Seal Island
Safe Passage
Goose Is   Mt Chapple Is
CHAPPELL ISLANDS
Lighthouse   Unicorn Pt

Settlement Pt   Emita
Brougham St
Adelaide
Blue Rocks
Arthur Bay
Chalky Is
Marshall Bay
Lackrana
Long Point   Whitemark
Parrys Bay   43   Ranga
Big Green Is
East Kangaroo Is   Strzelecki Peaks
Trousers Pt   Strzelecki Nat Park
Pigs Head Pt
Anderson Is   Little Dog Is   Great Dog Is
Badger Is   Tin Kettle Is   Apple Orchard Pt
Puncheon Pt
Vansittart Is
Pot Boil Point
Lady Barron

Memana
Walkers LO
Mt Leventhorpe
The Patriarchs
Babel Island Lighthouse
Sellars Point
Sellars Lagoon
Cameron Inlet
Logan Lagoon

BASS   STRAIT

Banks Strait

Cape Barren Island

Long Is   Neds Pt   Deep Bay
Mt Munro   Kent Bay
Cape Sir John
Preservation Is   Wombat Pt   Sloping Pt   Kangaroo Is   Seal Pt   Cone Pt
Rum Is   Forsyth Is   Black Pt   Passage Is
Spike Bay   **Clarke Island**   Lookout Heads   Moriarty Bay   Moriarty Pt

Thunder & Lightning Bay   Armstrong Channel

Cape Portland   Lighthouse   Swan Is
Waterhouse Is   Lighthouse
Waterhouse Point
Ringarooma Bay
Croppies Pt
Sth Croppies Pt   Tomahawk
Waterhouse Conservation Area
West Sandy Point   Waterhouse
East Sandy Point   Boobyalla
Anderson Bay   Boobyalla Beach
Ninth Is
Double Sandy Point Coastal Res
Stony Head   Granite Point Con Area
Noland Bay
Big Waterhouse Lake
Little Waterhouse Lake
Ringarooma Coastal Res
Musselroe Bay Conservation Area
Rushy Lagoon   Poole
Cape Naturaliste
Stumpys Bay
Great Musselroe Bay
Cape Boulder
MOUNT WILLIAM NAT PARK   Purdon Bay
Mt William   God Bay
Eddystone Pt   Lighthouse
Ansons Bay   Policemans Pt
Bay of Fires Con Area
Bay of Fires

Bridport
Stony Head Artillery Range
Five Mile Bluff
Low Head Lighthouse   Weymouth   Bellingham
Lulworth   Beechford
Maritime Museum
Pipers River   Lefroy
Pipers Brook
Lavender Farm
Retreat   Golconda
Jetsonville
North Scottsdale
Scottsdale   Warrentina   Winnaleah   Gladstone
Forester   Mt Cameron
Telita   Herrick   Little Blue Lake
South Mt Cameron
Pioneer
Lietinna   Kamona
Springfield   Cuckoo   Legerwood   Tulendeena   **Derby**   Moorina
Branxholm   Weldborough
Ringarooma   Legunia   Lottah
Talawa   Goulds Country   The Gardens
Alberton   Pyengana   Goshen   Big Lagoon   Sloop Lagoon
St Columba Falls   Priory   Binalong Bay   Grant Pt
Trenah   Mt Victoria   Skeleton Bay
St Helens   St Helens Pt
Humbug Pt Conservation Area
St Helens Is   Dianas Basin   Stieglitz

George Town
Bell Bay   Beauty Pt   Kelso   Yorktown   Low Head
Ilfraville   Sidmouth   The Glen
Beaconsfield   Rowella   Kayena   Lebrina
Greens Beach   Badger Head
Hawley Beach   Bakers Beach
Port Sorell
NARAWNTAPU NAT PARK
East Sassafras   Holwell   Deviot
Flowery Gully   Rosevears   Turners Marsh
Winkleigh   Exeter   Gravelly Beach   Lalla   **Lilydale**   Lilydale Falls
West Frankford   Windermere   Karoola
Frankford   Glengarry   Dilston   Underwood   Hollybank Forest Res
Birralee   Notley Gorge   Myrtle Bank
Rosevale   Rocherlea   Patersonia   Nunamara
North Riverside   St Patricks River
LAUNCESTON   Didleum Plains
St Leonards   Tayene
Selbourne   White Hills   Mt Barrow
Westwood   Hadspen   Relbia
Carrick   Breadalbane   Burns Creek
Westbury   Pateena   Musselboro   Upper Blessington
Perth   Western Junction   34   Blessington
Evandale   Temple Bar   English Town
Deddington   Castle Hill
Longford   Clarendon   Ski Village
Cressy   Toiberry   Nile   Tower Hill   Mt Nicholas   Cornwall
Bishopsbourne   BEN LOMOND NATIONAL PARK   St Marys
Bracknell   Stacks Bluff   Mangana   Patricks Head
Mother Lords Plains   Clarendon House   Four Mile Creek
Poatina   Epping Forest   **Fingal**   Gray
Cleveland   Avoca   Ironhouse Pt
Conara   Rossarden   Wardlaws Pt
Isis   Storys Creek   Lagoons Beach   Chain of Lagoons
St Pauls Dome   Piccaninny Pt
Royal George   Mt St John
Millers Bluff   Mt Puzzler Forest Res   Long Pt Seymour
Snow Hill   DOUGLAS-APSLEY NATIONAL PARK
Campbell Town   Harding Falls Forest Res   Douglas River
Goldsmith   Mt Augusta   Waubs Harbour
Seaside Centre, Marine Res
Lake Leake   Apsley Gorge   Winery
Hobgoblin   Rawlinna   **Bicheno**
Ross   Lost Falls Forest Res   Cape Lodi
Cranbrook   Llandaff
Apslawn   FREYCINET NATIONAL PARK
Mona Vale   Mt Connection   Courland Bay   Butlers Pt
Tunbridge   Lake Leake   Friendly Beaches
Woodbury   Nine Mile Beach
Antill Ponds   Waterloo Pt   Cape Tourville Lighthouse
Oatlands   Hepburn Pt   Coles Bay
Swansea   Coles Bay   Sleepy Bay
Bark Mill, Wine & Wool Centre, Winery   The Hazards
Webber   Fleurieu Pt   Wineglass Bay
Spiky Bridge   Cape Forestier
Great   Mayfield Bay Con Area   Mt Freycinet   Promise Bay
Oyster Bay   Weatherhead Pt   **Freycinet Peninsula**
Buxton Pt   Cape Degerando

Deloraine   Exton   Hagley   Longford
Meander   Quamby Brook   Glenore   Oaks
Golden Valley   Quamby Bluff   Whitemore   Cluan
Liffey   Liffey Falls   Drys Bluff   Blackwood Creek
Breona   GREAT WESTERN TIERS CONSERVATION AREA
Liawenee   Cramps   Bradys Lookout
Shannon   Wilburville   Flintstone
Miena   Brazendale Is
Waddamana   Steppes
Interlaken   Tunbridge
Victoria Valley   Lake Crescent   Lake Sorell
Bothwell   Table Mtn
St Peters Pass
York Plains   Lemont   Pawtella

To Hobart

N

0   5   10km
© Hema Maps Pty Ltd

BASS STRAIT

West Sandy Point
East Sandy Point
St Albans Bay
Double Sandy Point Coastal Reserve
Granite Pt Con Area

To Gladstone

Stony Head
Lulworth
Weymouth
Bellingham
Bridport
Noland Bay

Five Mile Bluff
Beechford
Stony Head Artillery Range
Turquoise Bluff

C817
C816
C852
Pipers River
B82
12
Little Pipers River

Low Head
Low Head Lighthouse
Maritime Museum Penguin Rookery
West Head
Port Dalrymple

Greens Beach
Kelso
Clarence Point
George Town
+Mt George
Bell Bay
Lefroy
Pipers River
Winery
Pipers Brook Winery

C807
C808
C815
C819
C818
C826
C827

NARAWNTAPU NAT PARK
Asbestos Range
Yorktown
Ilfraville
Beauty Point
Beaconsfield
Gold & Heritage Museum

C721
C722
C741
C720
A8
B82
B83
B81

EAST TAMAR
River
A8
Winery Area Kayena
Rowella
Sidmouth
Batman Bridge
Deviot
Hillwood Winery
Mt Direction
+Mt Direction

The Glen
Lower Turners Marsh
Bangor
North Lilydale
Lilydale Falls
Retreat
Golconda
Lebrina Wineries Tunnel
Wyena
Nabowla
Lavender Farm

C809
C810
C812
C813
C814
C811
C820
C823
C827

Lilydale
Turners Marsh
Karoola
Lalla
Underwood
Mt Arthur
Myrtle Bank
Targa
St Patricks River
Patersonia

B81
C824
C829
C404
C827

Flowery Gully
Holwell Gorge
Stewarts Hill
Holwell
Winkleigh
Robigana
Paper Beach
Gravelly Beach
Exeter
Rosevears
Waterbird Haven
Brady's Lookout
Grindelwald Swiss Village
Legana
Rocherlea

WEST TAMAR ROAD
FRANKFORD
West Frankford
Frankford
Glengarry Winery
Notley Hills
Notley Gorge
Bridgenorth
North Riverside
Riverside

B71
C715
C717
C716
C718
B71
C730
C731
C769
A8
A7
B83
B81

Dilston

Black Sugarloaf
Birralee
Rosevale
Reedy Marsh
Selbourne
Westwood
Hadspen
Entally House

LAUNCESTON
Lake Trevallyn
Trevallyn State Rec Area
Norwood
St Leonards
Prospect
Country Club Casino
Silverdome
Youngtown
White Hills
Mowbray
Nunamara
Mt Edgecombe

C714
C732
C374
C735
C732
C738
C403
C401
A3

Deloraine
Exton
Hagley
Westbury
Carrick
Breadalbane
Launceston Airport
Western Junction
Historic Town
Evandale
Relbia Winery

BASS HWY
B54
B52
B41
C412
C413

To Devonport
To Golden Valley

Pateena
Perth
Glenore Winery
Whitemore
Oaks
West Lagoon
East Lagoon
Toilberry
Longford
Clarendon
Clarendon House
Glen Stuart
Nile

Quamby Brook
Cluan
Bishopsbourne
Bracknell
Brickendon
Woolmers
Symmons Plains Car Racing
Cressy

Golden Valley
Quamby Bluff Forest Res
Jackeys Marsh
Liffey
Liffey Forest Res
Liffey Falls
CENTRAL PLATEAU CON AREA
GREAT WESTERN TIERS CON AREA
CLUAN TIERS

MIDLAND HWY
A5
B51
B52

C503
C501
C505
C504
C513
C511
C513
C514
C517
C516
C518
C519
C520
C521
C416
C419
C420
C531

To Miena
To Poatina
To Campbell Town
To Scottsdale
To Upper Blessington

South Australia

Paddle Steamer Murraylands, Murray River (62 C5, 65 H13)

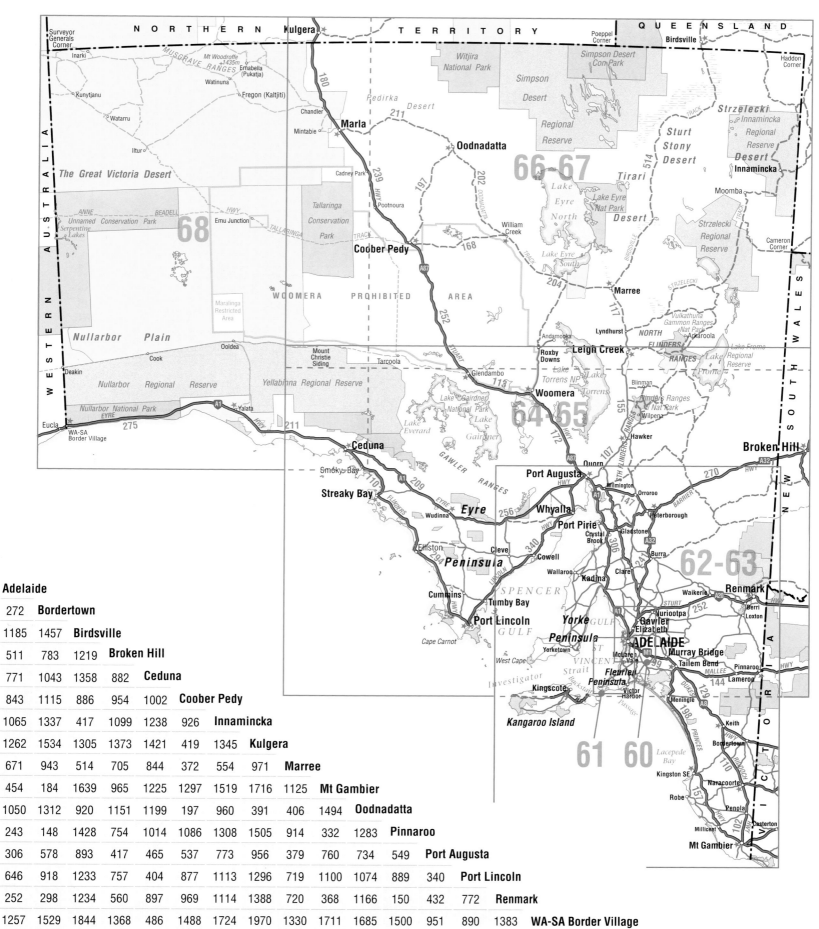

Adelaide

272	**Bordertown**														
1185	1457	**Birdsville**													
511	783	1219	**Broken Hill**												
771	1043	1358	882	**Ceduna**											
843	1115	886	954	1002	**Coober Pedy**										
1065	1337	417	1099	1238	926	**Innamincka**									
1262	1534	1305	1373	1421	419	1345	**Kulgera**								
671	943	514	705	844	372	554	971	**Marree**							
454	184	1639	965	1225	1297	1519	1716	1125	**Mt Gambier**						
1050	1312	920	1151	1199	197	960	391	406	1494	**Oodnadatta**					
243	148	1428	754	1014	1086	1308	1505	914	332	1283	**Pinnaroo**				
306	578	893	417	465	537	773	956	379	760	734	549	**Port Augusta**			
646	918	1233	757	404	877	1113	1296	719	1100	1074	889	340	**Port Lincoln**		
252	298	1234	560	897	969	1114	1388	720	368	1166	150	432	772	**Renmark**	
1257	1529	1844	1368	486	1488	1724	1970	1330	1711	1685	1500	951	890	1383	**WA-SA Border Village**

Distances are shown in kilometres and follow the most direct major sealed route where possible

LEGEND

Highway	National Highway No. A17
Major Road	Trailblazer Route No. A21
Street	
Lane / Walkway	
Railway, Station	Keswick
Tram, Busway	
Parkland Bikeway	
Picnic Area	
Post Office	
Major Building	
Govt Building	
Accommodation	
Theatre / Cinema	
Shopping	
Church	+
Hospital	+

0   200   400   600m

© Hema Maps Pty Ltd

Places of Interest

1 Adelaide Aquatic Centre A2
2 Adelaide Convention Centre C2
3 Adelaide Entertainment Centre A1
4 Adelaide Festival Centre B2
5 Adelaide Gondola B1
6 Adelaide Oval B2
7 Adelaide Town Hall C2
8 Art Gallery of South Australia C2
9 Ayers House C3
10 Bicentennial Conservatory B3
11 Botanic Gardens B3
12 Carclew Youth Arts Centre B2
13 Central Market/China Town C2
14 Government House B2
15 Hill-Smith Fine Art Gallery C2
16 Himeji Japanese Garden D3
17 Jam Factory Craft & Design Centre C2
18 Lights Vision B2
19 Memorial Drive Tennis Courts B2
20 Migration Museum B2
21 North Adelaide Golf Links B1
22 Old Adelaide Gaol - Museum B1
23 Old Parliament House - Museum C2
24 Parliament House C2
25 Performing Arts Collection of SA B2
26 Pop-eye Motor Launches B2
27 Sky City Casino C2
28 South Australian Museum C2
29 State Library of SA B2
30 Supreme Court Building C2
31 Tandanya Aboriginal Cultural Ctr C3
32 Victoria Park Raceway C3
33 War Memorial C2
34 Zoological Gardens B3

Railway Stations

64 North Adelaide A1
65 Mile End C1
66 Great Southern Rail Interstate Tml D1
67 Keswick D1

Accommodation

36 Adelaide Central YHA C2
37 Adelaide Hilton International C2
38 All Seasons Adelaide Meridien A3
39 Cannon Street Backpackers C2
40 Festival City Hotel/Motel C2
41 Franklin Central Apartments C2
42 Holiday Inn Adelaide C2
43 Hotel Adelaide International B2
44 Hotel Richmond C2
45 Hyatt Regency Adelaide C2
46 Majestic Roof Garden Hotel C3
47 Medina Grand Adelaide Treasury C2
48 Mercure Grosvenor Hotel Adelaide C2
49 Motel Adjacent Casino C2
50 Old Adelaide Inn A2
51 Old Lion Apartments B3
52 Pacific International Suites C2
54 Radisson Playford Hotel C2
55 Rendezvous Allegra Hotel C2
56 Rockford Adelaide C2
57 Rydges South Park Adelaide D1
58 Saville Park Suites C1
59 Stamford Plaza Adelaide C2
60 The Chancellor Adelaide C2
61 The Chifley on South Terrace D2
62 The Oakes Embassy C2

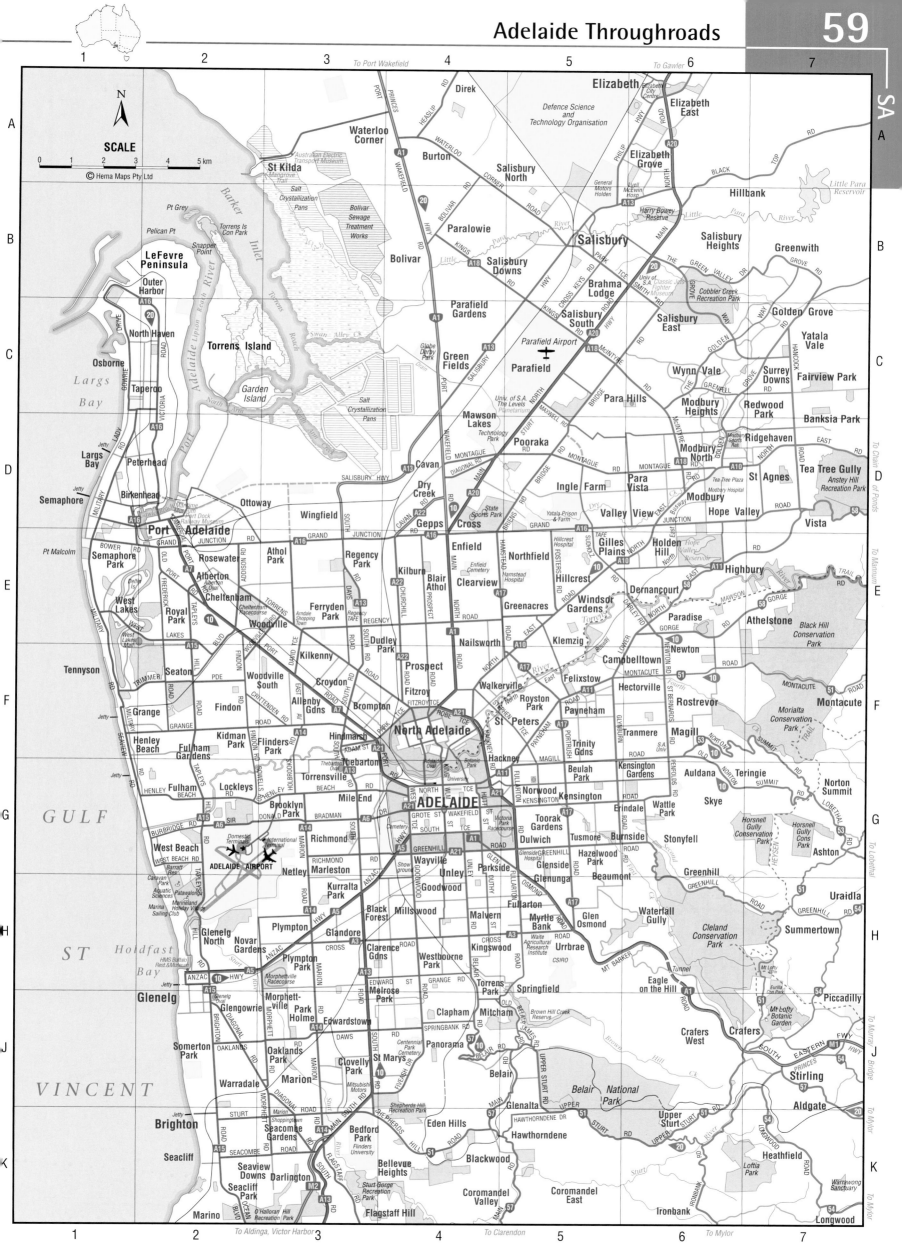

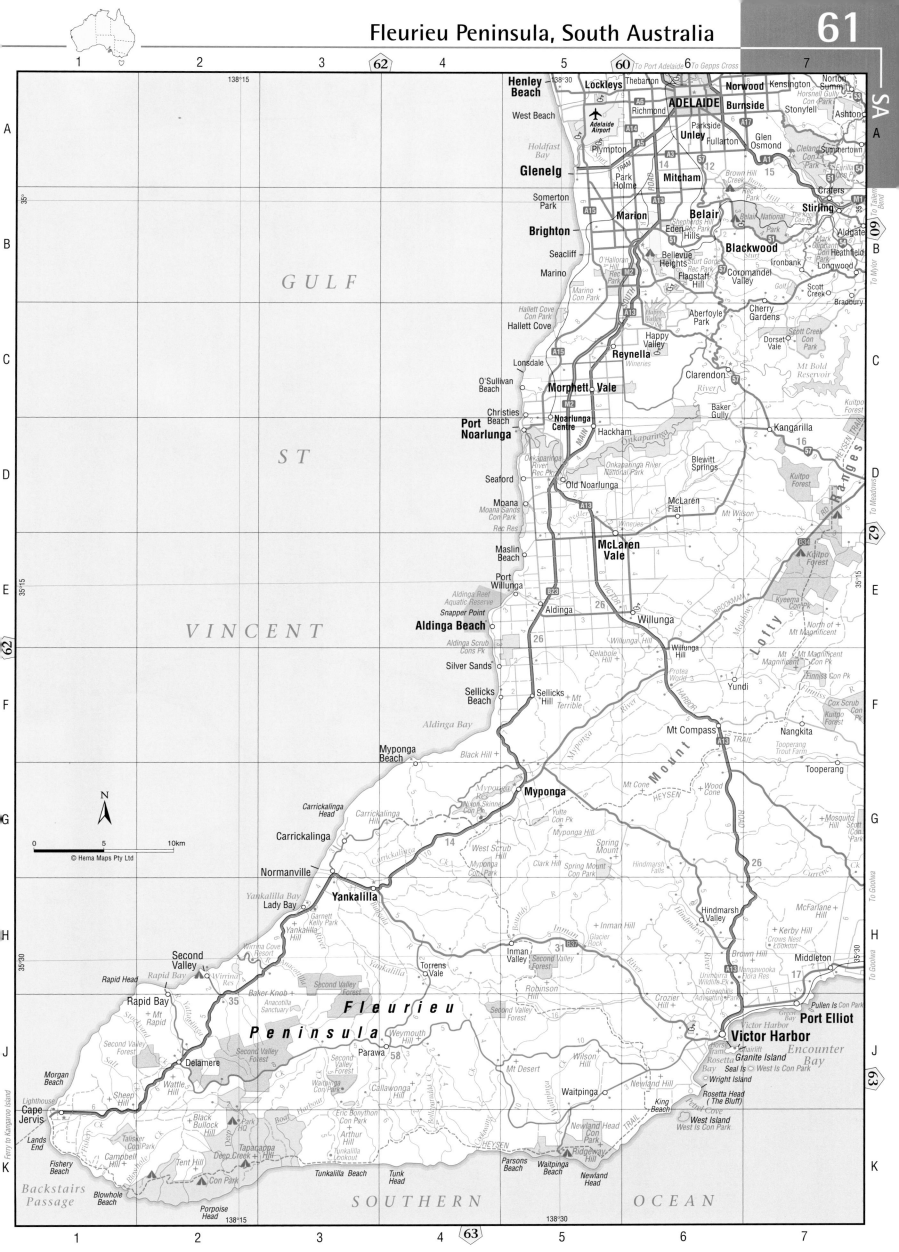

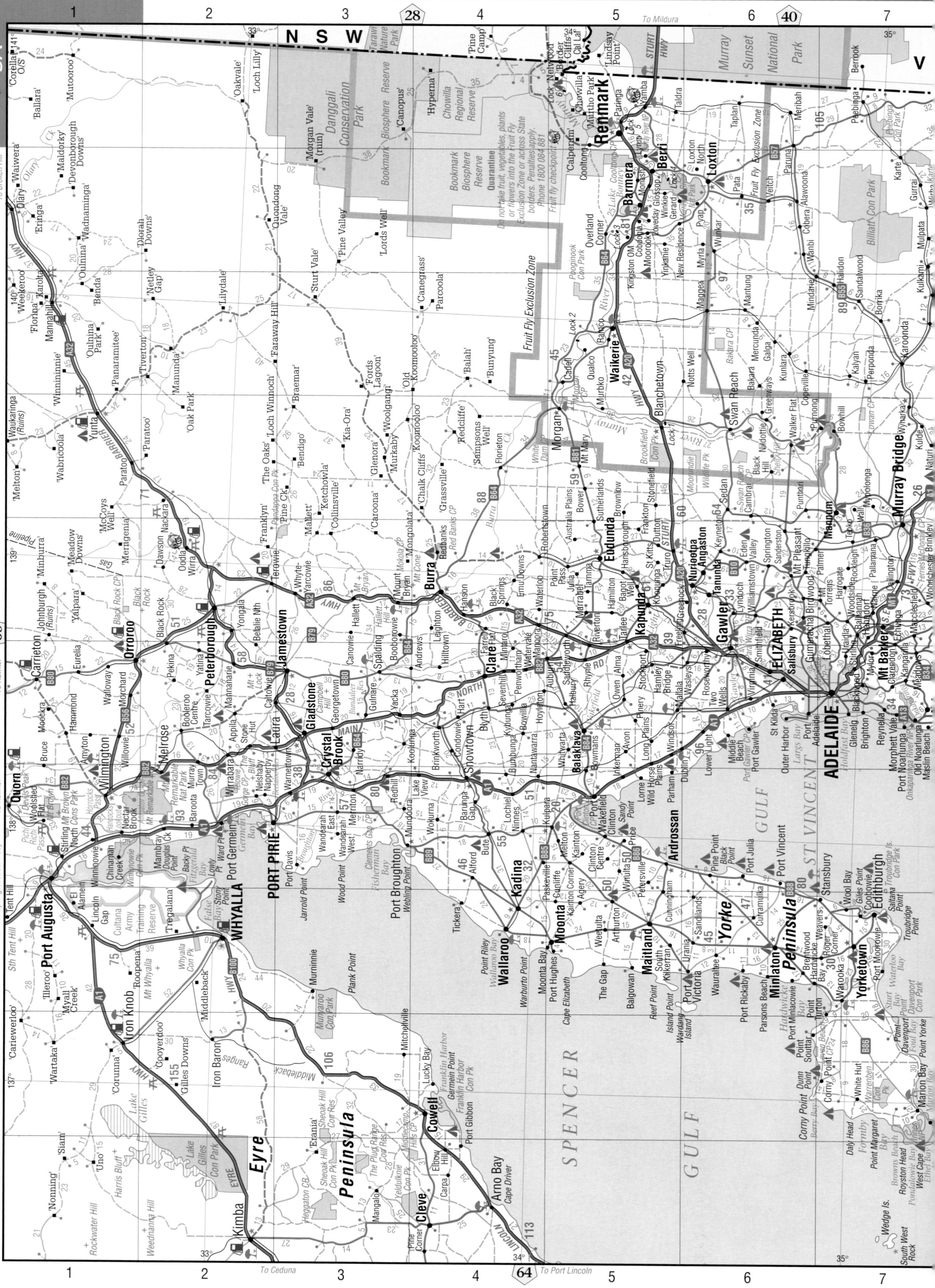

SA

VICTORIA

BIG DESERT

Wilderness Park

Big Desert Wilderness Park

Ngarkat Con Park 136

Scorpion Springs Con Park

Mt Shaugh Con Park

Red Bluff Nature Reserve

Mount Rescue Con Park

LITTLE DESERT

Little Desert National Park

Telopea Downs

Kaniva

Serviceton

Wolseley

Bordertown

Apsley

Edenhope

Langkoop

Casterton

GLENELG HWY

Nelson

Dartmoor

Mt Gambier

Millicent

Penola

Naracoorte

Kingston SE

Robe

Beachport

Carpenter Rocks

Port MacDonnell

Keith

Tintinara

Coonalpyn

Culburra

Meningie

Coorong National Park

Younghusband Peninsula

Salt Creek

Policemans Point

Woods Well

Lacepede Bay

Cape Jaffa

Boatswain Pt

Cape Thomas

Guichen Bay

Mount Benson

Nora Creina

Lake St Clair

Canunda Nat Park

Lake Bonney

Goolwa

Victor Harbor

Port Elliot

Middleton

Encounter Bay

Fleurieu Peninsula

Yankalilla

Normanville

Rapid Bay

Cape Jervis

Backstairs Passage

Kingscote

American River

Penneshaw

Kangaroo Island

Flinders Chase National Park

Cape Borda

Cape Couedic

Cape Gantheaume

Cape Gantheaume Con Park

Investigator Strait

SOUTHERN OCEAN

N

0 10 20 30 40 50 60 70 80km

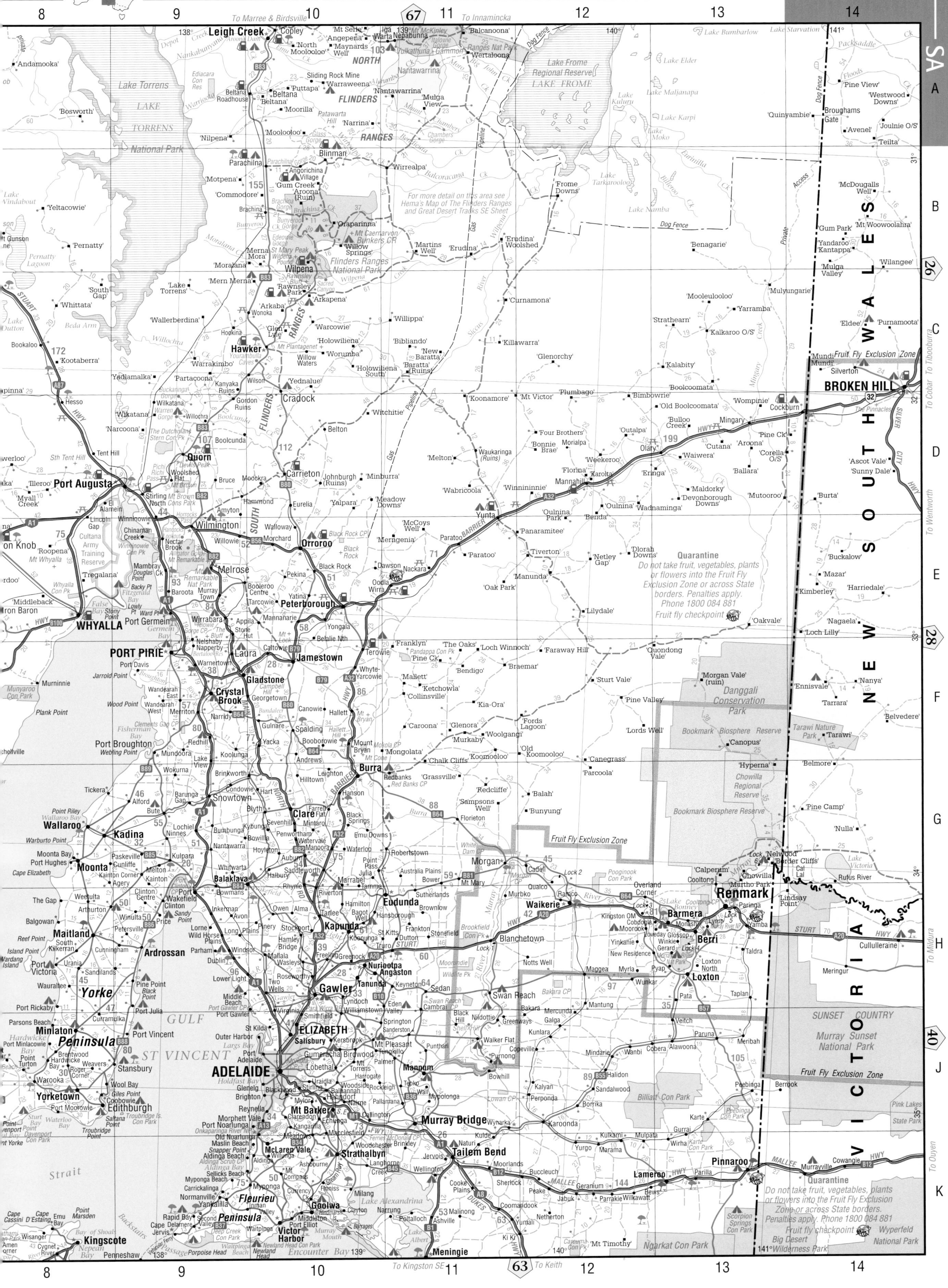
SA
NEW SOUTH WALES
VICTORIA
Leigh Creek
Lake Torrens
Lake Frome
Flinders Ranges National Park
Wilpena
Hawker
Quorn
Port Augusta
Whyalla
Port Pirie
Wilmington
Orroroo
Peterborough
Jamestown
Gladstone
Crystal Brook
Yunta
Olary
Mannahill
BROKEN HILL
Burra
Clare
Kadina
Wallaroo
Moonta
Maitland
Yorke Peninsula
Balaklava
Kapunda
Gawler
Tanunda
Angaston
ELIZABETH
ADELAIDE
Mt Barker
Murray Bridge
Tailem Bend
Strathalbyn
Goolwa
Victor Harbor
Kingscote
Fleurieu Peninsula
Morgan
Waikerie
Renmark
Barmera
Berri
Loxton
Pinnaroo
Lameroo
Meningie
Yorketown
Edithburgh
Minlaton
Quarantine
Do not take fruit, vegetables, plants or flowers into the Fruit Fly Exclusion Zone or across State borders. Penalties apply. Phone 1800 084 881
Fruit fly checkpoint
Fruit Fly Exclusion Zone
Murray Sunset National Park
Danggali Conservation Park
Ngarkat Con Park
For more detail on this area see Hema's Map of The Flinders Ranges and Great Desert Tracks SE Sheet
To Marree & Birdsville
To Innamincka
To Kingston SE
To Keith
To Mildura
To Ouyen
To Wentworth
To Cobar
To Tibooburra

SA

NORTHERN   TERRITORY

To Alice Springs
Kulgera
Mt Reynolds +
'Victory Downs'
'Mount Cavenagh'
Kulgera Rail Head
'Umbeara'
Umbeara Well
+ Mt Beddome
To Finke
Mt Grundy
'Charlotte Waters'
+ Mt Daer
+ Mt Etingambra
+ Walla Hills
Finke
Pmer Ulperre Ingwemirne Arletherre

Ilykuwaratja
Gosse Bore
Pine Ridge
'Sundown O/S'
Mt Cecil
Goyder
Tieyon'
Cunnbulla
Lindsay
Stevenson
Mt Anderson
Abminga (ruins)
Abminga
Bloods Creek
Blood Ck Bore
'Mount Dare'
Mt Crispe
Dalhousie Springs
Witjira National Park
Desert Parks Pass required
Freeth Junction
Purni Bore
French Line (FRN)
Rig
COLSON TRACK

Echo Hill
Echo Hill
'Agnes Creek' (De Rose Hill)
Marryat
'Mt Irwin'
Mt Britton
'Eringa' (Ruin)
'Hamilton'
Pedirka (ruins)
public access route
'Dalhousie' (Ruin)
Macumba Oil Well
Simps[on]

Moorilyanna Hill
Umerina
Indulkana (Iwantja)
Chandler
Emergency Telephone & Water
'Granite Downs'
Yoolperlunna Creek
Alberga
'Lambina'
Pedirka Desert
Conditions of outback roads can change dramatically after rain. Check road and track conditions with the nearest Police station, Park Ranger station or Dept. of Transport office.
'Mt Sarah'
Flood Detour
Fogarty Claypan
For more detail on this area, see Hema's Simpson Desert, Great Desert Tracks South East Sheet and Central Australia Map

Marla
Coongra Creek
'Todmorden'
211
OODNADATTA TRACK
'Macumba'

Mintabie Opal Field
Marla Bore
Wallatinna
'Welbourn Hill'
Olarinna
Neales River
North Branch Neales
'Oodnadatta'
'Allandale'

Anangu Pitjantjatjara Aboriginal Land
Amaroodinna Hill
'Wintinna'
private track
Arckaringa
Mt Arckaringa
Painted Desert
South Branch Neales River
Mt + Dutton
Mount Dutton (ruins)
Algebuckina Bridge
Algebuckina Waterhole

Cadney Homestead
Cadney Park
'Mt Willoughby'
Copper Hill
'Arckaringa'
San Marino Hut
Mt Kingston
Peak Creek Siding
'Peake Hill' public access route
Mt + Denison
Warrina (ruins)
'Peake'

Tallaringa Conservation Park
Desert Parks Pass required
Kulvergalinna
'Evelyn Downs'
Lora Creek
197
'Mount Barry'
Nilpinna
202
Edwards Creek (ruins)
Duff Ck (ruins)
'Nilpinna'
Mt Margaret
George Creek
Daventport Ck

To Emu Junction
ANNE BEADELL HWY
Tallaringa Well
239
Pootnoura
Pootnoura Creek
Emergency Telephone & Water
Algebullcullia
+ Darangunabula Hill
Amer Creek
Douglas Creek

Dog Fence
'Mount Clarence'
The Breakaways Lookout
Oolgelima Ck
Lake Cadibarrawirracanna
Worlds largest cattle property
Anna Creek
William Creek
public access route
OLD GHAN RAIL ROUTE

Mabel Creek
Manguri
WILLIAM CREEK
168
public access route
ROAD
Irrapatana (ruins)
Lake Callara

Coober Pedy
Opal Fields
91
Dog Fence
WILLIAM
Engoina
Warriner Creek
Strangways Springs Historic Site
Beresford (ruins)

Wilkinson Lakes
Pioneer Swamp
Lake Woorong
Lake Phillipson
204
Coward
Wabma Kadarbu Mound Springs Con /Park

Dog Fence
CENTRAL
Wirrida
Lake Wirrida
Ingomar
35
Dog Fence

WOOMERA   PROHIBITED   AREA
'Comet O/S'
Gina
'McDouall Peak'
Mirikata
'Billa Kalina'
Lake Anthony
Lake Bring
'Commonwealth Hill'
'Muckanippie O/S'
'Bradman O/S'
Carnes
'Bulgunnia'
252
Hoggard Hill
'Mount Eba'
'Millers Creek'
The Twins'
Mt Paisley
Curdilawidny Lagoon
Mattawarangala Lagoon

Mount Christie Corner
+ Mt Christie
'Mulgathing'
'Carne O/S'
Mt Sabine
'Mount Vivian'

Barton Siding
TRANS
Mount Christie Siding
ACCESS ROAD
Wynbring
Lyons
'Ambrosia'
'Gilbraltar O/S'
'Gilbraltar Rocks'
'Ealbara O/S'
'Mentor OS'
Emergency Telephone
'Bon Bon'
'Vivian Wells'
'Parakylia'
Olympic Dam Mine
Olympic Dam
Roxby Downs

Malbooma
'Malbooma O/S'
Tarcoola
Wilgena
'Wilgena'
Dog Fence
Ferguson
'North Well' Kingoonya
Mulga Well
Lake Labyrinth
Hickson Hill
Lake Patricia
Lake Younghusband
'Roxby Downs'
Purple Downs
Norris Ridge

Yellabinna Regional Reserve

0   50   100 km

© Hema Maps Pty Ltd

N

To Port Augusta

To Finke

QUEENSLAND

SA

Simpson Desert National Park
Permit Required from QNPWS
Simpson Desert Conservation Park — Desert Parks Pass required
Poeppel Corner
Lake Poeppel
Lake Thomas
French Line (FRM)
Approdinna Attora Knolls
Simpson Desert
Rig Road
Poolawanna No1 Oil Well
Poolawanna Lake
Peera Peera Poolanna Lake
Desert
QAA Line
Birdsville
'Roseberth'
Nappanerica Big Red Dune
'Durrie'
Betoota
'Planet Downs' Outstation
Haddon Corner
'Pandie Pandie'
'Cadelga' (Ruin)
Nullah OS
Lake Cooninnie
Moonda Lake
Lake Short
Lake Etamunbanie
'Alton Downs'
Andrewilla Waterhole
Strzelecki
Cordillo Downs' — Australia's Largest Shearing Shed
Goyder Lagoon
Desert
Lake Marraootanie
'Arrabury'
Warburton Crossing
'Clifton Hills'
Yelpawaralinna Track (YLP)
BIRDSVILLE TRACK
Apuninna
Lake Goyder
Lake Toontoowaranie
Coongie Lake
Mulga Bore
Candradecka
Leap Year Bore
Mt Gason Bore
Sturt
Lake Koonnanie
Lake Howitt
Stony
Desert
Patchawarra Bore
141
Innamincka Regional Reserve — Desert Parks Pass required
Innamincka No 2 Bore
Innamincka No 1 Bore
Nappa Merrie
Burke & Wills Dig Tree
'Cowarie'
Mira Mitta Bore
Walkers Crossing
Tirrawarra Oil & Gas Field
'Gidgealpa'
Cunyamurra Waterhole
'Kalamurina'
Lake Periguna
Lake Andree
Durrantie
Bunyeroo WH WH
Innamincka
'Mungeranie'
Mungerannie Roadhouse
Lake Kittakittaooloo
Lake Wancalanna
Moomba Oil & Gas Field
Della Gas Field
Innamincka No 3 Bore
Dullingari Oil & Gas Field
'Epsilon'
Tirari
Lake Ngapakaldi
Lake Mulapula
Desert
'Mulka'
Lake Puntawolona
Lake Killalpaninna
Lake Hope
Big Lake Moomba
Lake Merteree
'Merty Merty'
Lake Moomba
LAKE EYRE NATIONAL PARK — Desert Parks Pass required
LAKE EYRE NORTH
Lake Killalperpumna
'Etadunna'
Flood Bypass
Lake Koppermkppinna
Strzelecki
'Omicron'
Elliot Price Con Park
Madigan Gulf
Lake Florence
206
Lake Gregory
Strzelecki Crossing
'Bollards Lagoon'
Bollards Lagoon
The Corner Store
'Dulkaninna'
Strzelecki Regional Reserve
123
Cameron Corner
Dog Fence
'Lindon'
'Fort Grey'
Sturt National Park
Lake Ellen
public access route
'Muloorina'
'Clayton'
Lake Blanche
'Whitecatch House'
'Lake Stewart'
LAKE EYRE SOUTH
Lake Harry
'Lake Harry' (Ruin)
Dog Fence
Montecollina Bore
Munkartie Gate
Finniss Springs
Bopeechee
'Murnpeowie'
'Blanchewater' (Ruin)
'Hewart Downs'
Lake Arthur
'Mount Hopeless'
Lake Callabonna
'Old Tilcha' (ruins)
Alberrie Creek
Wongianna
Marree
'Mundowdna'
'Callanna'
Tilcha Gate
Winnathee
'Finniss Springs'
Fossil Reserve — S.A. Museum — No access to South Australia via Hawkers Gate Entry Permit required
Hawkers Gate
Mt Distance
Mt Freeling
Mt Babbage
'Moolawatana'
'Smithville House'
'Mulgaria'
'Witchelina'
Farina (Ruins)
'Mt Lyndhurst'
Mt Fitton
'Mt Freeling'
Mt Livingstone
North Mulga'
'Moorabie'
Lake Arthur
'Farina'
Avondale'
NORTH
Umberatana
Mt Neil
'Border Downs'
Lyndhurst
FLINDERS
Benbonyath Hill
Vulkathuna - Gammon Ranges Nat Park
'Arkaroola'
'Wooltana'
'Turleys House'
'Myrtle Springs'
Leigh Creek Coalfield
'Depot Springs'
'Mt Serle'
'Owieandana'
Mt McKinley
Balcanoona
'Pine View'
'Westwood Downs'
Andamooka
Leigh Creek
Copley
'North Moolooloo'
Iga Warta Nepabunna
Nantawarrina
'Wertaloona'
LAKE TORRENS
Sliding Rock Mine
RANGES
Beltana Roadhouse
Beltana
'Puttapa'
'Warraweena'
'Nantawarrina'
Lake Frome Regional Reserve
LAKE FROME
Lake Torrens National Park
Lake Maljanapa

QUEENSLAND
NSW

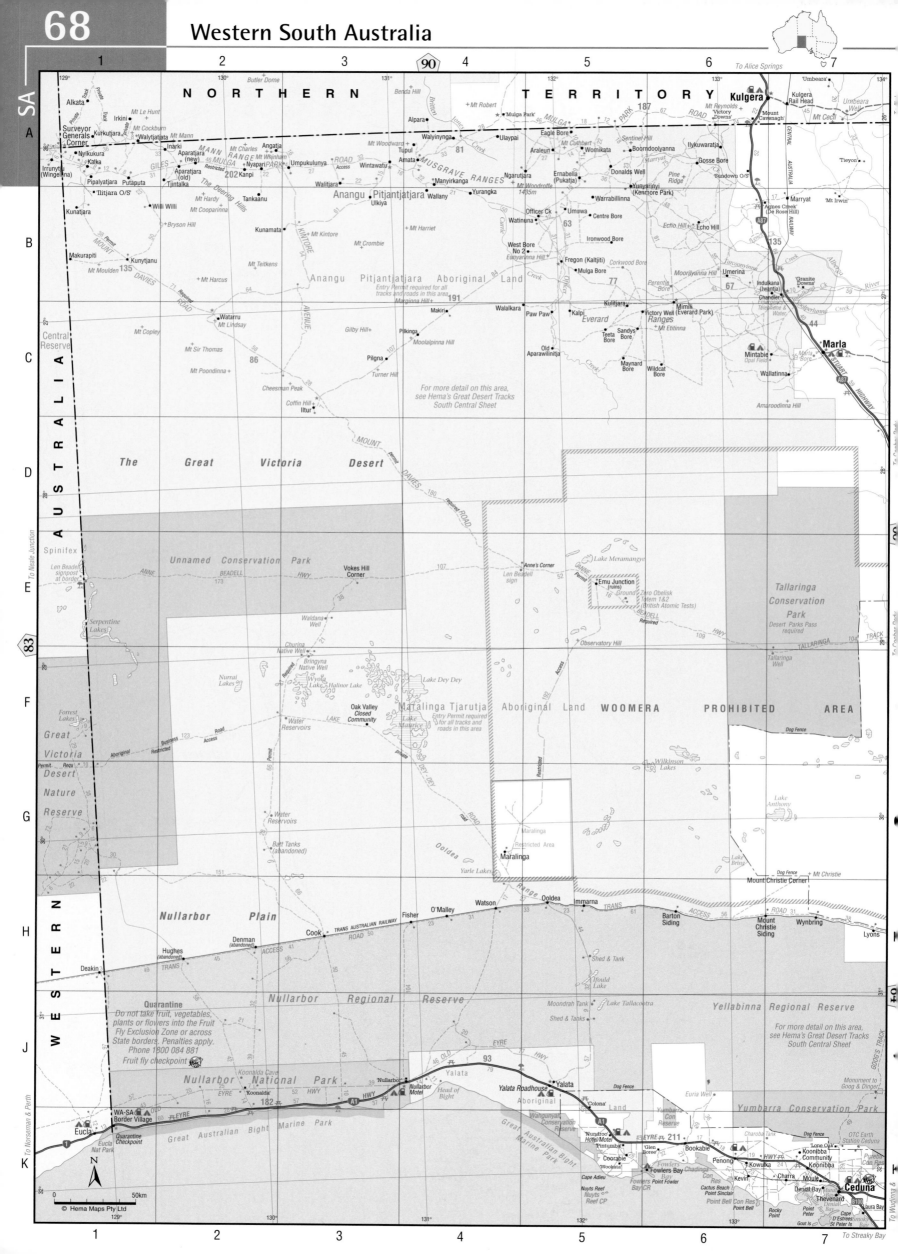

Western Australia

Sunrise, Geographe Bay, Dunsborough (73 J11, 74 G1)

Distances are shown in kilometres and follow the most direct major sealed route where possible

1401	2020	411	1564	939	3610	1977	805	835	483	1315	342	2618	**Albany**
3101	615	2245	1051	1676	1063	845	2197	1942	2589	1462	2427	**Broome**	
1585	1832	182	1376	751	3422	1748	774	606	667	1086	**Bunbury**		
2338	867	904	985	819	2457	662	1460	480	1625	**Carnarvon**			
918	1994	721	1538	1069	3584	2169	392	1145	**Esperance**				
1822	1347	424	964	339	2937	1142	980	**Geraldton**					
904	1602	592	1146	677	3192	1786	**Kalgoorlie**						
2690	259	1566	631	1256	1849	**Karratha**							
4096	1610	3240	2046	2671	**Kununurra**								
1597	1081	569	625	**Mt Magnet**									
2050	456	1194	**Newman**										
1434	1650	**Perth**											
2506	**Port Hedland**												
WA-SA Border Village													

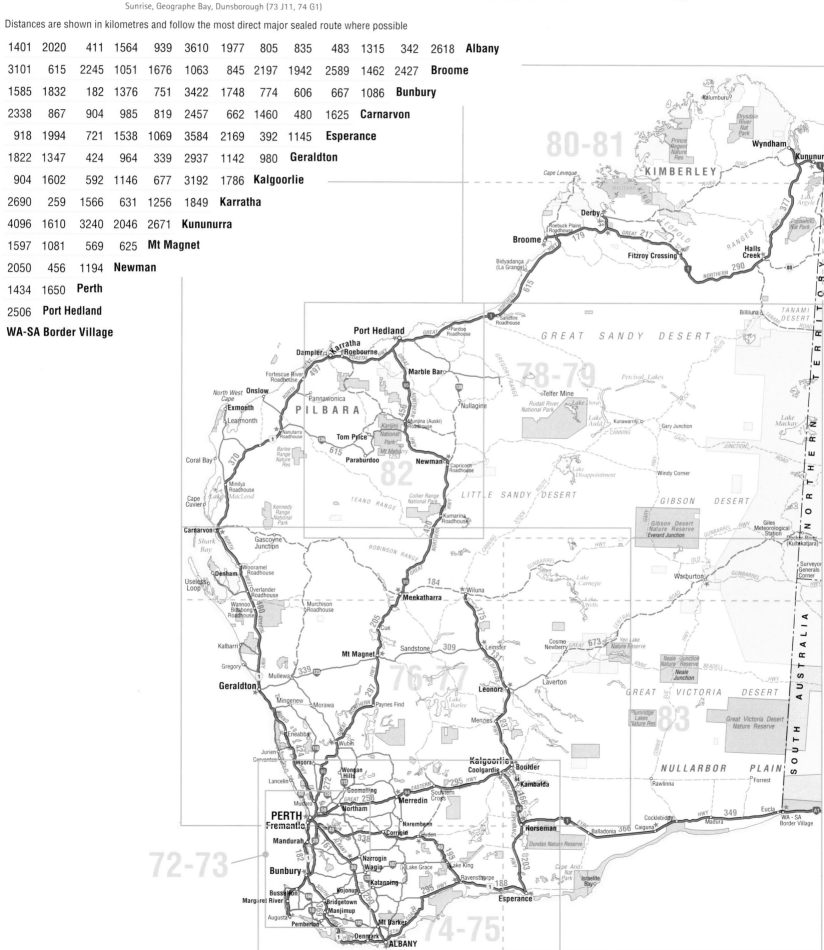

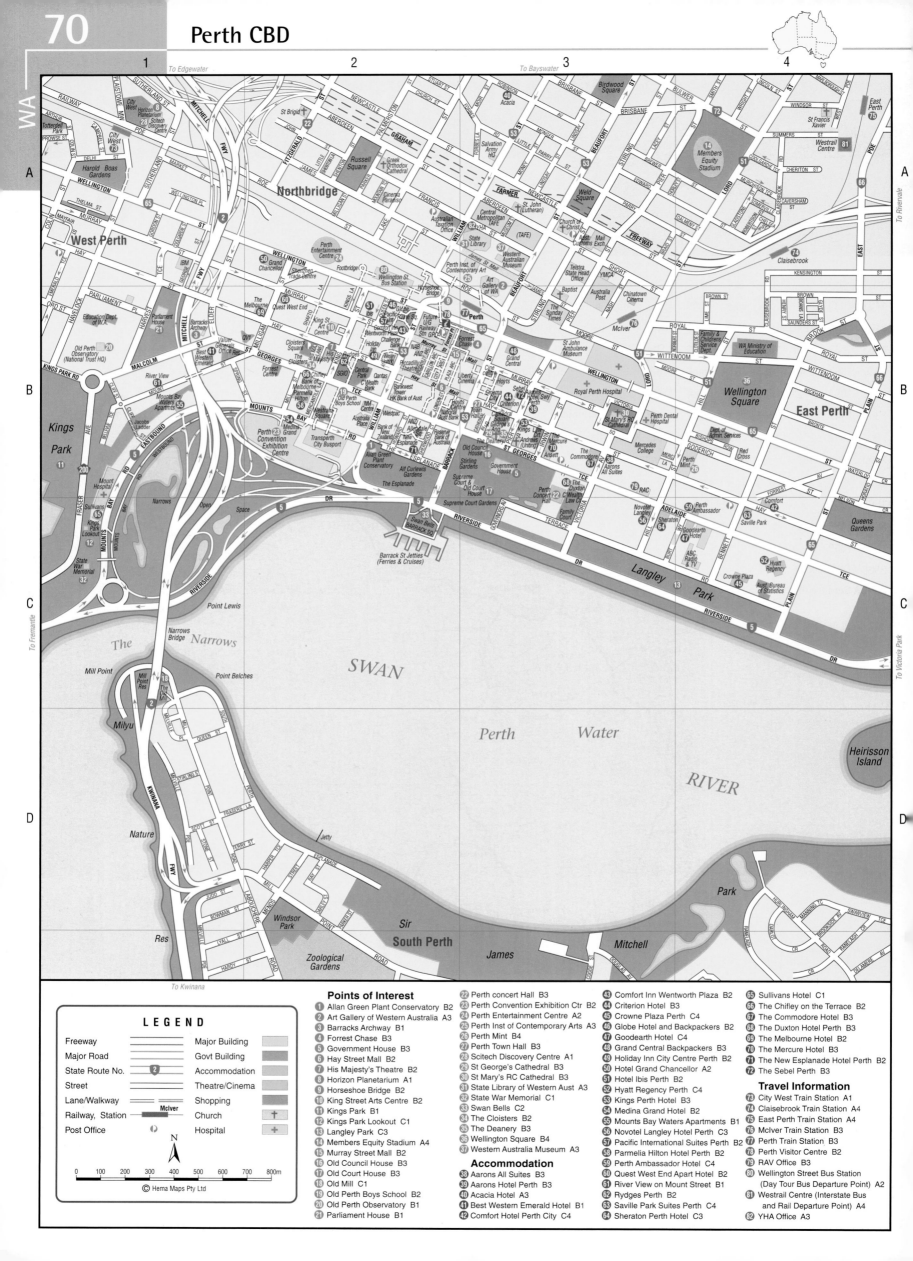

Points of Interest
1 Allan Green Plant Conservatory B2
2 Art Gallery of Western Australia A3
3 Barracks Archway B1
4 Forrest Chase B3
5 Government House B3
6 Hay Street Mall B2
7 His Majesty's Theatre B2
8 Horizon Planetarium A1
9 Horseshoe Bridge B2
10 King Street Arts Centre B2
11 Kings Park B1
12 Kings Park Lookout C1
13 Langley Park C3
14 Members Equity Stadium A4
15 Murray Street Mall B2
16 Old Council House B3
17 Old Court House B3
18 Old Mill C1
19 Old Perth Boys School B2
20 Old Perth Observatory B1
21 Parliament House B1
22 Perth concert Hall B3
23 Perth Convention Exhibition Ctr B2
24 Perth Entertainment Centre A2
25 Perth Inst of Contemporary Arts A3
26 Perth Mint B4
27 Perth Town Hall B3
28 Scitech Discovery Centre A1
29 St George's Cathedral B3
30 St Mary's RC Cathedral B3
31 State Library of Western Aust A3
32 State War Memorial C1
33 Swan Bells C2
34 The Cloisters B2
35 The Deanery B3
36 Wellington Square B4
37 Western Australia Museum A3

Accommodation
38 Aarons All Suites B3
39 Aarons Hotel Perth B3
40 Acacia Hotel A3
41 Best Western Emerald Hotel B1
42 Comfort Hotel Perth City C4
43 Comfort Inn Wentworth Plaza B2
44 Criterion Hotel B3
45 Crowne Plaza Perth C4
46 Globe Hotel and Backpackers B2
47 Goodearth Hotel C4
48 Grand Central Backpackers B3
49 Holiday Inn City Centre Perth B2
50 Hotel Grand Chancellor A2
51 Hotel Ibis Perth B2
53 Kings Perth Hotel B3
54 Medina Grand Hotel B2
55 Mounts Bay Waters Apartments B1
56 Novotel Langley Hotel Perth C3
57 Pacific International Suites Perth B2
58 Parmelia Hilton Hotel Perth B2
59 Perth Ambassador Hotel C4
60 Quest West End Apart Hotel B2
61 River View on Mount Street B1
62 Rydges Perth B2
63 Saville Park Suites Perth C4
64 Sheraton Perth Hotel C3
65 Sullivans Hotel C1
66 The Chifley on the Terrace B2
67 The Commodore Hotel B3
68 The Duxton Hotel Perth B3
69 The Melbourne Hotel B2
70 The Mercure Hotel B3
71 The New Esplanade Hotel Perth B2
72 The Sebel Perth B3

Travel Information
73 City West Train Station A1
74 Claisebrook Train Station A4
75 East Perth Train Station A4
76 McIver Train Station B3
77 Perth Train Station B3
78 Perth Visitor Centre B2
79 RAV Office B3
80 Wellington Street Bus Station
     (Day Tour Bus Departure Point) A2
81 Westrail Centre (Interstate Bus
     and Rail Departure Point) A4
82 YHA Office A3

LEGEND

Freeway		Major Building
Major Road		Govt Building
State Route No.	2	Accommodation
Street		Theatre/Cinema
Lane/Walkway		Shopping
Railway, Station	McIver	Church
Post Office		Hospital

0 100 200 300 400 500 600 700 800m

© Hema Maps Pty Ltd

WA

To Quinns Rocks

To Lancelot

To Geraldton

To Kalgoorlie

To Bunbury, Albany

To Rockingham

To Kwinana, Mandurah

To Oakford

To Armadale

SCALE

0 1 2 3 4 5km

© Hema Maps Pty Ltd

N

INDIAN

OCEAN

Swan River

Major localities:

Joondalup, Edgewater, Beldon, Mullaloo, Ocean Reef, Kallaroo, Craigie, Woodvale, Wanneroo, Hocking, Pearsall, Jandabup, Jandakot, Gnangara, Lexia, Ellenbrook, The Vines, Henley Brook, West Swan, Middle Swan, Herne Hill, Hillarys, Padbury, Kingsley, Greenwood, Marangaroo, Alexander Heights, Landsdale, Cullacabardee, Whiteman Park, Whiteman, Ballajura, Sorrento, Duncraig, Warwick, Girrawheen, Koondoola, Mirrabooka, Malaga, Beechboro, Caversham, Midland, Marmion, Carine, Hamersley, Balga, Westminster, Nollamara, Dianella, Noranda, Morley, Lockridge, Eden Hill, North Beach, Karrinyup, Balcatta, Stirling, Trigg, Scarborough, Innaloo, Osborne Park, Tuart Hill, Yokine, Bedford, Inglewood, Bayswater, Bassendean, Guildford, South Guildford, Bellevue, Hazelmere, Woodlands, Joondanna, Coolbinia, Mt Lawley, Maylands, Ashfield, Brighton Beach, Wembley Downs, Mt Hawthorn, North Perth, Highgate, Ascot, Redcliffe, Perth Airport, City Beach, Wembley, Floreat, Jolimont, Subiaco, West Perth, Northbridge, East Perth, Burswood, Belmont, Cloverdale, Newburn, High Wycombe, Maida Vale, Bold Park, Mt Claremont, Shenton Park, Kings Park, PERTH, Rivervale, Carlisle, Kewdale, Forrestfield, Swanbourne, Claremont, Nedlands, Crawley, South Perth, Victoria Park, East Victoria Park, Welshpool, Cottesloe, Peppermint Grove, Dalkeith, Como, Kensington, Bentley, Cannington, Wattle Grove, Mosman Park, Bicton, Attadale, Applecross, Mt Pleasant, Manning, Waterford, Salter Point, Shelley, Riverton, Ferndale, Beckenham, Orange Grove, North Fremantle, East Fremantle, Melville, Alfred Cove, Booragoon, Rossmoyne, Langford, Parkwood, Kenwick, Maddington, Fremantle, Palmyra, Winthrop, Bull Creek, Willetton, Thornlie, White Gum Valley, O'Connor, Kardinya, Leeming, Canning Vale, Forest Lakes, Huntingdale, Gosnells, South Fremantle, Hilton, Samson, Murdoch, Southern River, Westfield, Hamilton Hill, Spearwood, Bibra Lake, Jandakot, South Lake

Lake Joondalup, Lake Jandabup, Lake Gnangara, Lake Goollelal, Lake Karrinyup, Herdsman Lake, Lake Monger, Bibra Lake, North Lake, South Lake

Jandakot Airport

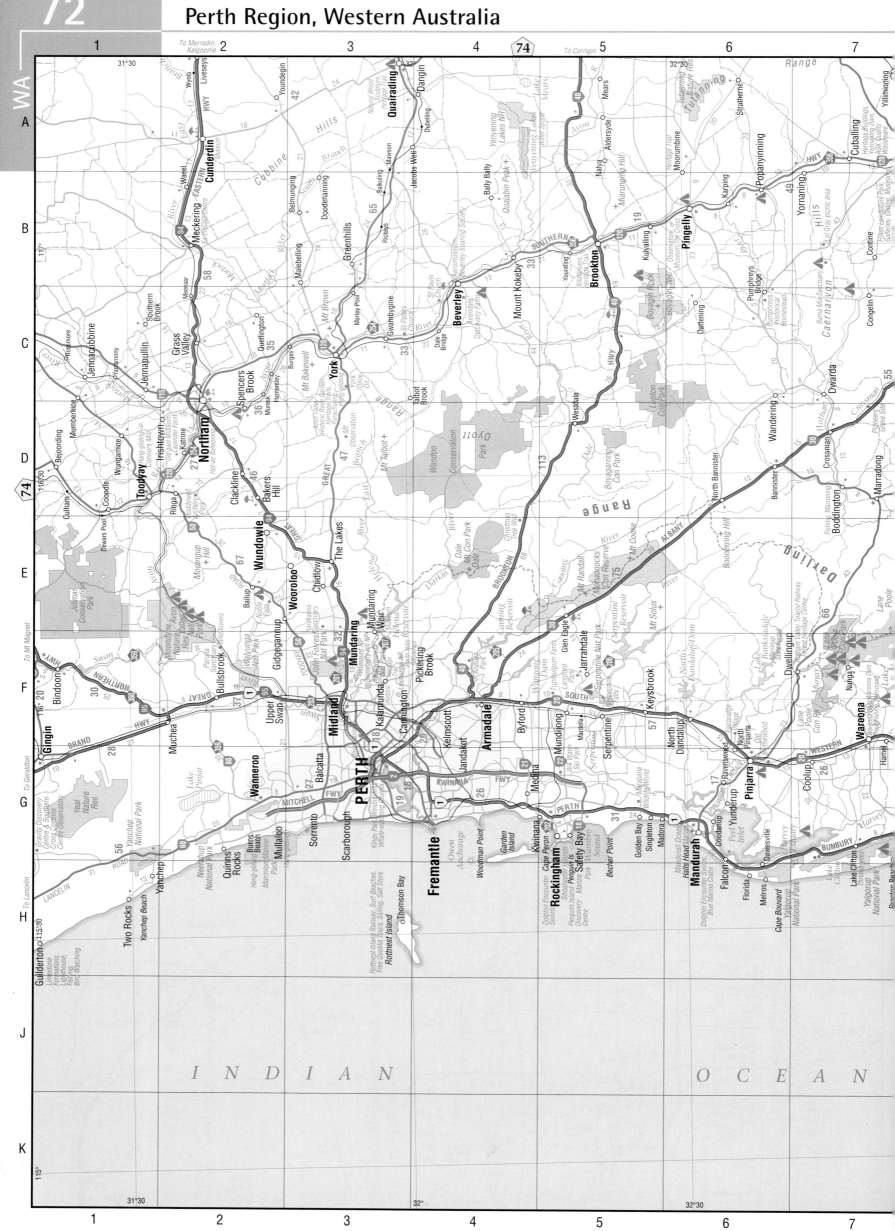

8 9 10 74 11 12 13 14

To Lake Grace To Albany HWY To Albany

Wagin
Williams
Kojonup
Frankland
Rocky Gully

Highbury
Dumbering
Geeralying
Plessville
Piesseville
Neeranup Pool
Quangalin
Dellyanine
Warup
Lime Lake
Norrin Lake
Flagstaff Lake
Mine Hill
Carrolup
Carlecatup
Flat Rocks
Borderdale
Boyacup
Campup
Yarralena

Quindanning
Josbury
Cuthin
Dardadine
Hillman
Bokal
Kylie
Beaufort
Boscabel
Cherry Tree Pool
Farrar
Euio Hill
Thornton Hill
Kenine Hill
Lumeah
Gracefield
Tunney
Yarralena
Lower Frankland

Williams
Quindanning
Boranup
Boraning
Darkan
Boolading
Duranillin
Capercup
Moodiarrup
Cordering
Kulikup
Dinninup
Qualeup
Muradup
Orchid Valley
Jingalup
Mobrup
Cooranup
Tonebridge
Mordalup
Chowerup
Hearttea

Collie
Shotts
Collie Cardiff
Allanson
Mumballup
Noggerup
McAlinden
Wiiga
Boyup Brook
Benjinup
Mayanup
Glentulloch
Strachan
Quinninup
Nyamup

Harvey
Wokalup
Benger
Brunswick Junction
Roelands
Burekup
Waterloo
Dardanup
Boyanup
Argyle
Donnybrook
Lowden
Grimwade
Mullalyup
Balingup
Hester
Greenbushes
Bridgetown
Yornup
Wilgarup
Palgarup
Balbarrup
Dingup
Manjimup
Deanmill
Jardee
Eastbrook
Collins
Pemberton

Myalup
Binningup
Australind
Eaton
Picton
Bunbury
Point Casuarina
Elgin
Capel
Ludlow
Wonnerup
Stratham
Gwindinup
Claymore
Tutunup
Yoongarillup
Cundinup
Jarrahwood
Cambray
Sussex Mill
Nannup
Carlotta
Barlee
Darradup
Jalbarragup
Peerabeelup

Busselton
Vasse
Dunsborough
Yallingup
Quindalup
Canal Rocks
Jindong
Treeton
Cowaramup
Metricup
Yelverton
Carbunup River
Wilyabrup
Osmington
Mowen
Margaret River
Witchcliffe
Prevelly
Alexandra Bridge
Karridale
Kudardup
Augusta
Flinders Bay

Cape Naturaliste
Cape Clairault
North Point
Gracetown
Ellensbrook
Cape Mentelle
Redgate Beach
Cape Freycinet
Hamelin Bay
Knobby Head
Cosy Corner
Cape Hamelin
Cape Leeuwin
White Point
Black Point

Geographe Bay

N
50km
40
30
20
10
0
© Hema Maps Pty Ltd

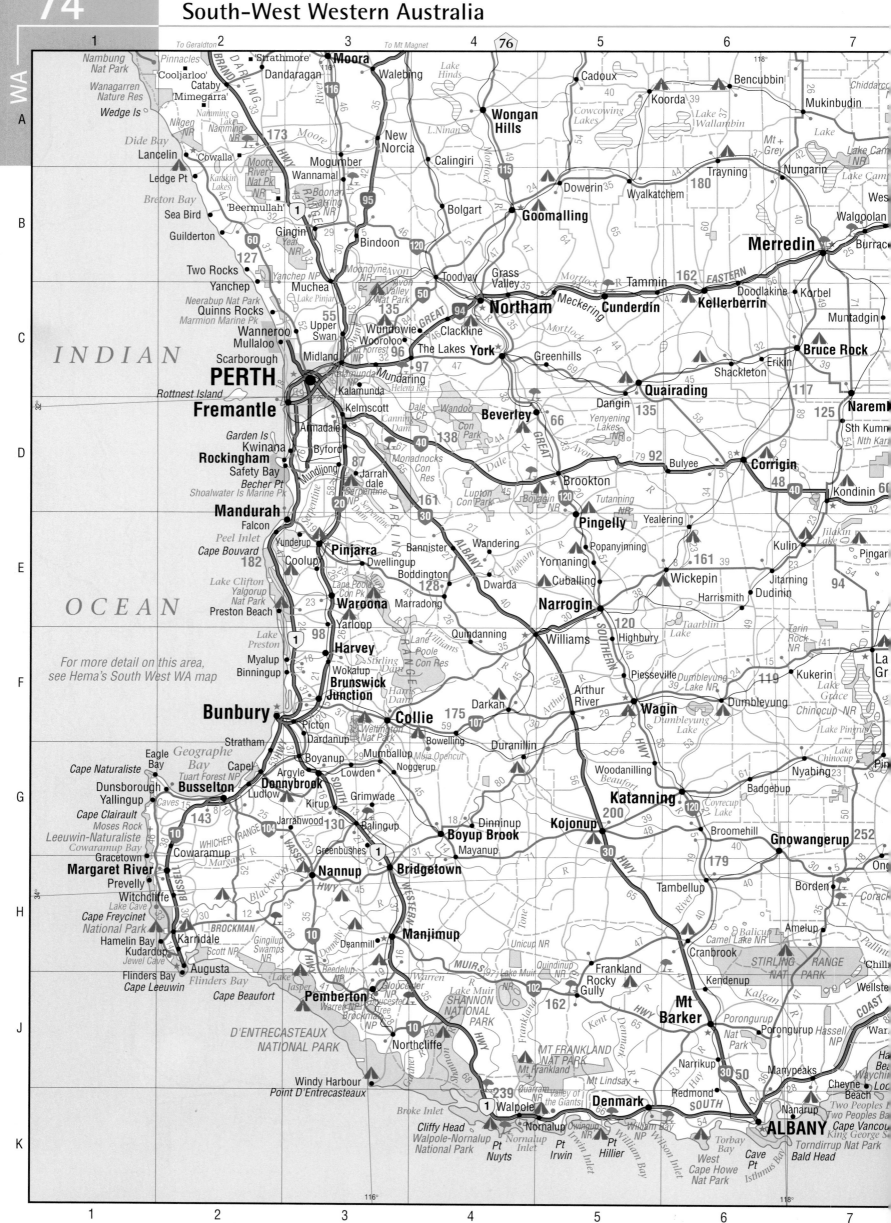

8 9 77 11 10 12 13 14

Kalgoorlie
Boulder
To Leonora
Bulong
'Hampton Hill'
Lake
Yindarlgooda
Lake Roe
Lake Deborah West
Lake Deborah East
'Jaurdi'
Mt Burgess
'Mt Burgess'
Kurrawang
39
Golden Ridge
Curtin
Randell
'Avoca Downs'
Karonie
Koolyanobbing
Kangaroo Rock
Bonnie Vale
Coolgardie
Randalls Mine
'Cowarna Downs'
Karonie Mine
Lake Seabrook
'Mt Monger'
'Woolubar'
A
Baladjie Lake NR
Bullabulling
94
29
Brown Lake
ALT
94
60
110
Bullfinch
Goldfields Woodlands Nat Park
25
Mt Marion
Kambalda NR
'Madoonia Downs'
Southern Cross
Weowanie + Rock
Yellowdine Nature Res
94
124
Goldfields Woodlands Cons Pk
Nepean
Nickel Mine
37
Kambalda
Kambalda West
B
185
Boorabbin Nat Park
Boorabbin
Victoria Rock
Victoria Rock Nature Res
Private Road Restricted Access
Bodallin
10
HWY
Moorine Rock
Yellowdine
Koorarawalyee
Burra Rock
'Mandilla'
Roysalt Siding
St Ives Mine
'Yalca Hill'
Strawberry Rocks
15
17
21
42
Widgiemooltha
Lake Lefroy
Marvel Loch
Thursday Rock
'Mareil'
Cockatoo Tank
Diamond Rock
Cave Hill Nature Res
166
Private Mining Road
Toomey Hills
Cave Hill
94
Mt Hampton
Higginsville
Higginsville Mine
Lake Cowan
C
174
JILBADJI NATURE RESERVE
Skeleton Rocks
Lake Barker
54
Wingarnie
Pioneer
'Buldania'
Welcome Hill
McDermid Rock
100
To Adelaide
Mt Thirsty
NORSEMAN
1
Sandalwood Rocks
46
Mt Day
38
Mt Norcott
32
Mt Holland
89
106
Norseman
D
TRACK
HOLLAND
King Rocks
Lake Johnston
Bromus
Woolyeenyer Hill
DUNDAS NATURE RESERVE
Wave Rock
Lake Carmody
28
69
Mt Gordon
Lake Dundas
Marble Rock
Modesty Rock
Lake Hope
BREMER RANGE
Lake Gilmore
40
65
Kerrigan Rocks
Lake Hurlstone
L Hurlstone NR
L Varley NR
Diggers Rock
Hatter Hill
Frank Hann National Park
Ninety Mile Tank
58
Kumarl
83
E
125
L Varley NR
Holt Rock
28
Mt Gibbs
258
Lake Sharpe
Peak Charles
203
Nature Res
Dragon Rocks NR
Mt Vernon
Varley
42
Lake Fox
Lake Tay
Peak Charles National Park
Salmon Gums
Mt Sheridan
Lake Camm
Lake Ace NR
Lake Mends
29
HWY
Lake Biddy
Lillian Stoke Rock
Swallow Rock
Pyramid Lake
1
Grass Patch
F
NEWDEGATE
115
Lake King NR
Lake King
115
'Karak Park'
'Kappi Ki'
Bishops Nature Res
Truslove Townsite
Mt Ridley
Beaumont NR
107
Newdegate
63
Lake Pallarup
Pallarup NR
One Mile Rocks NR
Griffiths Nature Res
Scaddan
Burdett South NR
Kau Rock NR
Breakaway Ridge NR
70
40
Lake Chidnup
Cheadanup Nature Res
Cascade
'Clare Downs'
'Lauriana'
'Zeehan'
'Wittenoom Hill'
Muntz NR
Lake Lockhart
Dunn Rock NR
Ravensthorpe
80
Munglinup
1
'Warrawoona'
'Veperey'
Lake Magenta
Lake Magenta Nature Res
West R
40
'Maydon'
'Nurragi'
188
59
'Dalyup'
Condingup
G
Fitzgerald
Kundip NR
Lake Shaster
Stokes Nat Park
'Fairfield'
Lake Gore
'Gerbryn'
'Peak Downs'
HWY
Annie Peak
Jerdacuttup Lakes NR
Shoal Cape
Butty Head
Pink Lake
Esperance
Cape Le Grand Nat Park
Mt Drummond
55
20
Jerdacuttup Lakes
Lake Shaster NR
Powell Pt
Stokes Inlet
Observatory Pt
Esperance Bay
Rossiter Bay
Hammer Head
amungup
FITZGERALD RIVER
Hopetoun
Mason Bay
WEST GROUP
Cape Le Grand
Mississippi Pt
H
295
NATIONAL PARK
Pt Charles
Pt Charles Bay
Pt Ann
West Mt Barren
Gordon Inlet
Mondrain Island
Recherche Archipelago Nature Reserve
1
Gairdner
Doubtful Islands Bay
Boxwood Hill
Bremer Bay
Hood Pt
'Minarup'
Pt Henry
Pt Irby
Cheyne Bay
Cape Knob
Cape Riche
J
aul Off Rock

SOUTHERN OCEAN

N

K

0 50 100km

© Hema Maps Pty Ltd

WA

INDIAN

OCEAN

N

0   50   100 km

© Hema Maps Pty Ltd

PERTH
Fremantle

Grid columns: 8 [82] 9 10 11 [79] 12 13 14

Rows: A B C D E F G H J K

To Newman · To Newman

CARNARVON RANGE · BRASSEY RANGE · Lake Brenner · Lake Keene

MUNGILLI · 'Mungilli Outstation' (Abandoned) · Mt William Lambert · Mangkili Claypan Nature Res · Mt Johnson

Three Rivers · 'Bryah' · Noonyereena Hill · Peak Hill · 'Doolgunna' · 'Neds Creek' · Lake Gregory

Mt Methwin · Mt Davis · Well 8 · Well 7 · private fee required · road · 'Glenayle' · Well 6 · Good Camp Rockhole · Mt Salvado · ROUTE · STOCK · Lake Burnside · Mt Nossiter

'Mooloogool' · 'New Springs' · Well 4A · Well 3 · Well 2A · 'Earaheedy' · 'Granite Peak' · Mt Moore · Mt Archie · 'Old Carnegie' · 'Carnegie' · BOODIE RANGE · Linke Lakes · Mingol Camp · Mt Archie

'Cunyu' (abandoned) · 'Diamond Well' · 'Paroo' · 'Yandil' · GUNBARREL · Wongawol · Lake Carnegie · Mt Lancelot · Mt O'Loughlin · Square Hill · Mt Smith

'Killara' · Paroo Siding · Mt Alice West · Kutkabubba · 'Jundee' · 'Millrose' · PRINCES RANGES · WELLINGTON RANGE · 'Lorna Glen' · Point Robert · Mt Laurie

'Murchison Downs' · Wiluna · Nganggarwili · 'Lake Violet' · 'Emu Farm' · 341 · 'Windidda' · Mt Dora · Point Katherine · IDA RANGE

Teodter O/P Mine · 'Noibla' · Mt Lawrence Wells · Lake Way · VAN TREUER TABLELAND · Lyell Brown Bluff · Lake Wells · Empress Spring

'Youno Downs' · 'Yarrabubba' · Walga Gunya · BARR SMITH RANGE · 175 · 'Lake Way' · 'Barwidgee' · 'Wonganoo' · 'Deleta' · Holroyd Bluff

192 · Errolls · 'Gidgee' · 'Yeelirrie' · Mt Keith Mine · 'Mt Keith' · Lake Maitland · De La Poer Range Nature Res · 'Lake Wells' · Tjukayirla Roadhouse · To Warburton

'Old Gidgee' · Montague · 'Albion Downs' · 'Mount Grey O/C' · 'Milurie O/C' · Mt Maiden · FARQUHARSON TABLELAND · ERNEST GILES RANGE · Lake Throssell

'Cogla Downs' · 'Barrambie' · 'Lake Mason' · 'Altona' · 'Yakabindie' · Mt Goode · 'Yandal' · 'Banjawarn' · 'Bandya' · COSMO NEWBERRY (NORTH)

'Black Range' · 'Kaluwiri' · Leinster Mine · Lake Miranda · 'Weebo' · GOLDFIELDS · 'Melrose' · YEO LAKE NATURE RESERVE · Yeo Lake

Sandstone · 'Leinster Downs' · 'Depot Springs' · Leinster · 425 · Cosmo Newbery · GREAT · ANNE · BEADELL

'Anketell' · 'Black Hill' · Agnew · Lawlers Mine · COSMO NEWBERRY (WEST) · 'Yamarna' · 'Yeo' (abandoned)

'Dandaraga' · Maninga Marley · Lawlers · Fairyland Mine · Ten Mile Outcamp · 'Erlistoun' · Point Salvation · COSMO NEWBERRY (EAST)

'Atley' · 'Daly Outcamp' · 'Pinnacles' · Teutonic Bore · Mt Redcliffe · 'Nambi' · 'Laverton Downs' · White Cliffs · Permit Required

'Youanmi Downs' · 'Yuinmery' · 'Bulga Downs' · Wildara Outcamp · 131 · 'Mt Clifford Outcamp' · West Terrace · Windarra · Mt Windarra · 'Korong' · [83]

'Youangarra' · Mt Forrest · 'Ida Valley' · 'Sturt Meadows' · Tarmoola · 'Mertondale' · Laverton · Craiggiemore · Lake Rason

'Cashmere Downs' · 'Perinvale O/C' · Kurrajong · Jasper Hill Dominion · 'Braemore' · Mount Morgans · Mt Weld · Burtville · Merolia

Mt Ida · 'Wilbah O/S' · Leonora · Malcolm · 'Minara' · 'Kowtah' · Mt Margaret · Granny Smith Mine · 'Coglia Well and Outcamp' · Hope Campbell Lake

Copperfield Mining Centre · Desdemona · 'Melita' · 'Glenorn' · Yundamindera · Sunrise Mine · Mt East · Lightfoot Lake

Lake Barlee · Tampa · 'Yundamindra' · Butcher Well North Mine · Lake Carey

'Lake Barlee' · 'Walling Rock' · 'Riverina Outcamp' · Lake Ballard · Kookynie · Niagara · Morapoi · 'Mt Colindina' · For more detail on this area, see Hema's Great Desert Tracks South West Sheet

'Mt Elvire' · 'Jeedamya' · 'Yerilla' · Yerilla · 'Mt Remarkable' · Lake Minigwal

'Diemals' · 'Riverina' · 'Mindana' · 'Mendleyarri' · 'Mt Celia' (abandoned)

Evanston · Menzies · 'Yundaga' · Lake Marmion · Porphyry Mine · Edjudina Mine

Pigeon Rocks · Yundaga · 'Menangina' · 'Yarri' · 'Edjudina'

MOUNT MANNING RANGES NATURE RESERVE · Mulline · Comet Vale · Goongarrie Nat Park · 'Kirgella Rocks' · QUEEN VICTORIA SPRING NATURE RESERVE

'Mt Jackson' · Mt Jackson · Davyhurst · Goongarrie · Carr-Boyd · 'Pinjin' · Queen Victoria Spring · Streich Mound

Hammersley Lakes · MT HUNT RANGE · Bardoc Mine · Callion · Canegrass · Scotia Mine · Gindalbie Woolshed · 'Arcoona' · 'Yindi' · 'Old Pinjin'

Lady Jane -Orabanda Mine · Mt Carnage · Bardoc · 'Mt Vetters' · Silver Swan · Gindalbie · CUNDEELEE

Lake Deborah East · Ora Banda · Broad Arrow · Paddington Siding · 'Credo' · Kanowna · Cundeelee (abandoned)

Koolyanobbing · 'Carbine' · 'Black Flag' · 'Kintore' · 'Perkolilli' · SPINIFEX RANGE · Lake Roe

Bullfinch · Kangaroo Rock · Baladjie Lake · 'Jaurdi' · 'Kunanalling' · Kundana · Kalgoorlie · Boulder · Bulong · Lake Yindarlgooda · Cundeelee

Lake Seabrook · Mt Burgess · 'Mt Burgess' · Kurrawang · 'Hampton Hill' · Golden Ridge · Curtin · Randall · 'Avoca Downs' · Karonie · Chifley · Coonana · Kitchener · TRANSCONTINENTAL RAILWAY · 913 Mile

Southern Cross · Coolgardie · Bonnie Vale · 94 · Randalls Mine · 'Cowarna Downs' · Karonie Mine · Zanthus · COONANA

Weowanie Rock · Yellowdine Nature Res · Bullabulling · 'Woolubar' · 'Mt Monger'

Bodallin · Moorine Rock · Yellowdine · Boorabbin Nat Park · Boorabbin · Kooraravalyee · Nepean Nickel Mine · Kambalda · 'Madoonia Downs' · Lake Boonderoo

Marvel Loch · Cockatoo Tank · Victoria Rock · Kambalda West · Burra Rock · St Ives Mine · 'Mareil' · Yalca Hill

JILBADJI NATURE RESERVE · Diamond Rock · Mandilla Rock · Roysalt Siding · Private Mining Road

Noombenberry Rock · Mt Hampton · Thursday Rock · Widgiemooltha · 166 · Binneringie Nature Res

Skeleton Rocks · McDermid Rock · Cave Hill · Higginsville · Higginsville Mine · Wingarnie · Lake Cowan

Welcome Hill · Sandalwood Rocks · Mt Day · Mt Johnston · Pioneer · 'Buldania' · 'Fraser Range' · ESPERANCE HWY · EYRE HWY

To Norseman, Esperance · Mt Norcott · To Adelaide · Wyralinu Hill · [83]

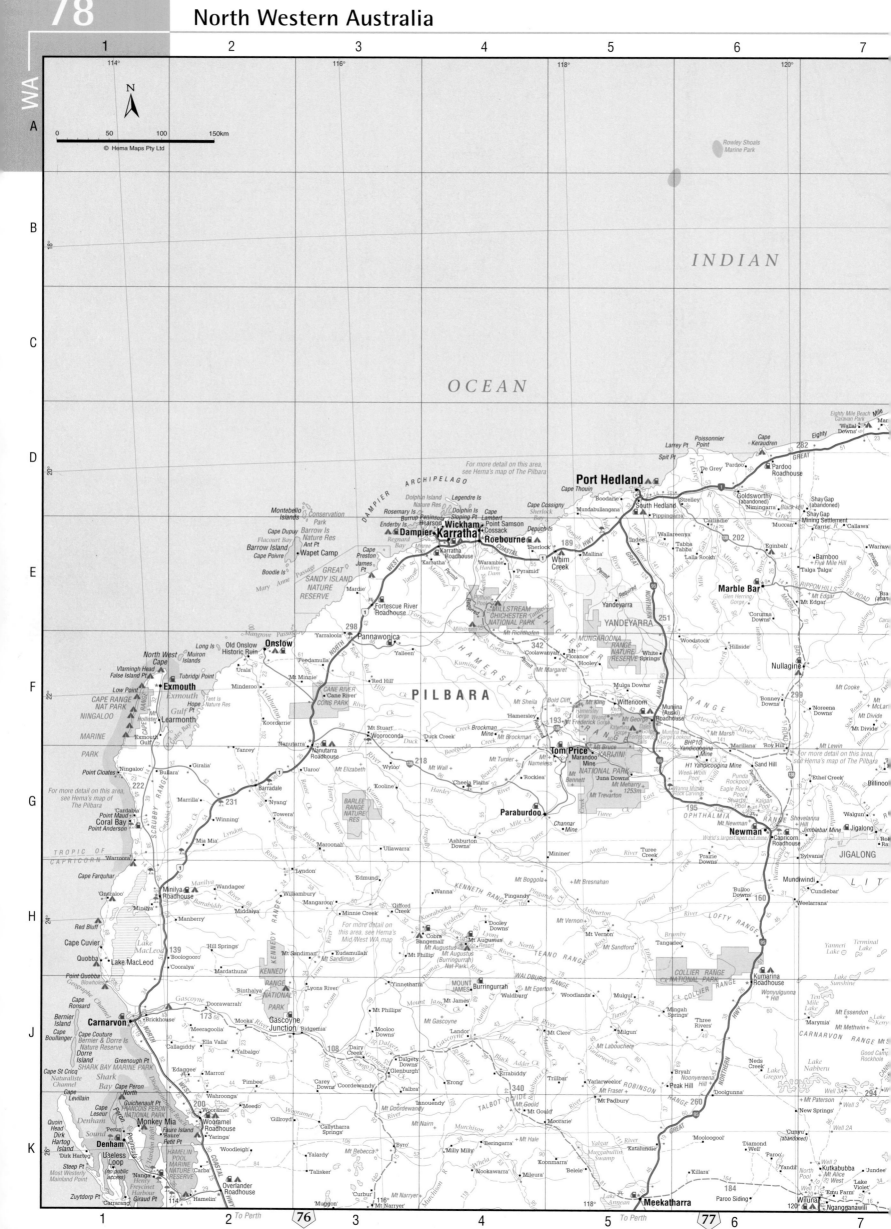

GREAT SANDY DESERT

GIBSON DESERT

TANAMI DESERT

KIMBERLEY

BEAGLE BAY

Broome
Gantheaume Point
Cable Beach
Roebuck Bay

Derby
Mowanjum
Meda

Fitzroy Crossing
Ngurtuwarta
Eight Mile
Bayulu

Halls Creek
Old Halls Creek

Warmun (Turkey Creek)
VIOLET VALLEY

PURNULULU NAT PARK
Purnululu Con Res

KING LEOPOLD RANGES

DURACK RANGES

LEOPOLD RANGES

To Kununurra

To Katherine

To Alice Springs

To Yulara

To Kalgoorlie

Telfer Mine

RUDALL RIVER NATIONAL PARK
Lake Dora
Punmu

LAKE GREGORY
Balgo
Mulan

BILILUNA
Billiluna (Mindibungu)

GIBSON DESERT NATURE RESERVE
Lake Blair
+ Mt Cox
Lake Newell

MUNGILLI

TJIRRKARLI

WARBURTON
Warburton Range

KIWIRRKURRA
Jupiter Well
Kiwirrkurra

MARUWA

KURLKUTA

NGAANYATJARRA LAND COUNCIL

Walungurru (Kintore)

Haasts Bluff

CENTRAL AUSTRALIA
Lake Mackay

CENTRAL RESERVE

Warakurna Roadhouse

Docker River (Kaltukatjara)

BALGO

Mangkururrpa (Tanami Downs)
Yiningarra

Mount Frederick
Mount Frederick No2

Warning to travellers
Travelling in Australia's arid regions can be extremely hazardous, especially during the summer months (October-March). Always seek local advice as to road conditions and notify the police of your intended destination and ETA. Always carry plenty of fuel and water. In the event of a breakdown, remain near your vehicle.

For more detail on this area, see Hema's Great Desert Tracks North West Sheet

CANNING STOCK ROUTE

GARY HIGHWAY

GUNBARREL HIGHWAY

TALAWANA TRACK

TANAMI ROAD

WA

N

0   50km

© Hema Maps Pty Ltd

14°

122°

124°

A
B
C

I N D I A N

HEYWOOD
ISLANDS

Corona
Isl

Brunswie

Champagny Is

Augustus Is

Camden Sound

Wilson Point

Kuri Bay

KUNM

D

For more detail on this area,
see Hema's map of The Kimberley

Deception Bay
Hall Point

Wedge Hill

George Water

Mt

16°

Montgomery
Islands

E

BUCCANEER ARCHIPELAGO

Cockatoo Cockatoo
Is

Koolan Is
Koolan

Kingfisher
Is

Doubtful Bay

Collier
Bay

ONE ARM
POINT

Cape Leveque
Kooljaman Resort

Sunday
Is

One Arm Pt

SUNDAY IS

Yampi Sound

Goose Channel

Hidden Is

WOTJALUM

LOMBADINA
Bygnunn

Lombadina Pt   Lombadina

Thomas Bay

Strickland
Bay

Cone Bay

Talbot Bay

Horizontal
Waterfall

Yule
Entrance

Walcott Inlet

F

O C E A N

Cape Borda

Pender
Bay

Willie Pt

Cognet Bay

Cunningham Pt

Cascade Bay

Compass Hill

McLARTY RANGE

Mt Disaster

YAMPI

'Oobagooma'

TRAINING
AREA
(Restricted Access)

Emeriau Pt
Middle Lagoon

Gurrbalgun

Beagle
Bay

KIMBOLTON RA

WYNDHAM RA

Lacepede Islands

Sandy
Pt

Beagle
Bay

La-Djardarr
Bay

Maddarr

Comambie Pt

Disaster
Bay

KING

Robinson R

Lacepede Channel

BEAGLE BAY

SOUND

NAPIER

G

Cape Baskerville

Carnot Bay

Cape Bertholet

Coulomb Point

James Price Pt

Quondong Pt

Cape Boiliau

Coulomb Point
Nature Reserve

Lurujarri
Heritage
Trail

'Country Downs'

North Cliffs

Fraser

Stony Hill

River

Reeves' Hill

'Mt Jowlaenga'

Point
Torment

Stokes Bay

Malaburra

Christine Pt

Derby

Boab Prison Tree

Mowanjum

public access

Alexander Ck

Meda R

'Birdwood
Downs'

'Meda'

May R

Robinson R

'Napie
Down

Kimberley Downs'

Blina
Oil & Gas Field

'Napier

private road
no access

recommended

4WD

Curtin
Air Base

H

18°

Willie Creek Pearl Farm

'Waterbank'

Cable Beach

Broome

Gantheaume Point

Entrance Pt

Roebuck Bay

'Kilto'

Deep Ck

179

GREAT

Roebuck Plains
Roadhouse

'Roebuck
Plains'

Bedunburra

Willare Bridge
Roadhouse

'Yeeda'

Minnie Bridge
Willare Bridge

Pandanus Park

'Debesa'

'Blina'

Fitzroy

NORTHERN

217

Jimba

Bush Pt

Thangoo

private
station

'Yakka Munga'

'Udialla'

'Mt Anderson'

Jarlmadangah
Burr

Camballin

Looma

'Liveringa'

LOOMA

New
Looma

'Paradise'

'Calwy
(aban

'Myroodah'

J

Cape Villaret
'Barn Hill'

Cape Latouche Treville

Port Smith

Port Smith Caravan Park
False Cape Bossut

Lagrange Bay

(Lagrange)

Cape Bossut
Bidyadanga

Admiral Bay

'Frazier Downs'

'Shamrock'

HWY

'Dampier Downs
O/C'

track

Near Hill

'Dampier
Downs'

Barbrongan Tower

Mt Collins

Frome Rocks

Collins Pool

Bulanjarr
(Mowla Bluff)

Mt Jarlemai

EDGAR

'Luluigul'
(abandoned)

Greegory

'Nerrima'

'Kalyeeda'

'Noonkanba

'Koorr

Mt Tuck

K

Geoffrey Bay

Cape Jaubert
Desault Bay
Cape Missiessy

'Nita Downs'
(ruins)

323

Mowla Bluff

RANGES

'Anna
Plains'

WA

8 9 10 11 12 13 14

A

Troughton Is
Cape Bougainville
Cassini Is
Gibson Pt
Troughton Passage
Cape Talbot
Napier Broome Bay
Sir Graham Moore Islands
Cape Londonderry
Cape Ruthieres
Cape Bernier

ARCHIPELAGO
Cape Voltaire
Montesquieu Islands
Borda Is
Vansittart Bay
Honeymoon Beach
Cone Mtn
McGowans Island
Pago Mission (ruins)
The Bush Camp Faraway Bay
King George Falls

Maret Islands
Biggs Island
Cape Pond
York Sound
Admiralty Gulf
Walmesly Bay Gulf
Kalumburu (permit req.)
'Barton Plains' Outcamp (ruins)
Barton R
King George R

B

Joseph Bonaparte Gulf

Cape St Lambert
SEPPELT RANGE
Casuarina R
Buckie Head
Cape Dussejour
Lacrosse Is
C. Domett

Crystal Head
Kimberley Coastal Camp
Surveyors Pool
LAWLEY RIVER NAT PARK
Mt Connor
Mt Reid
'Carson River' private track
Solea Falls
DRYSDALE RIVER NAT PARK
COLLISON RANGE
CAMPBELL RANGE
Mt Nicholls
OOMBULGURRI
Mt Carty

C

ADMIRALTY GULF
Cape Frederick Harbour
Mitchell Falls
Camp Creek CP
Kandiwal
Laterite Cons Park
MITCHELL RIVER NAT PARK
Mt Anderson
Enid Falls
'Theda'
private track
'Old Theda'
Morgan R
COACHMAN RANGE
ESCARPMENT Drysdale
CARSON RANGE
Carson R
Mt Mongona
Berkeley R
Forrest R
Viotti Peak
Cambridge Gulf
Dome Hill
Ord River Nature Res
Elephant Hill
'Nimbing'

Mt Knight
Mt Trafalgar
PRINCE REGENT NATURE RESERVE
Mt York
Roe R
Mt Bradshaw
Marunbabidi
'Doongan'
Oombulgurri (closed community)
Mt Connection
Adolphus Island
'Carlton Hill'
Quarantine. Do not take fruit, vegetables, plants or flowers across State and quarantine borders. Penalties Apply. Ph 1800 084 881

D

King Cascades
Prince Regent R
Spong Pyramid
Mt Hann
Miners Pool
'Drysdale River'
Drysdale R
Maitland R
Gibb R
Mt Jameson
KIMBERLEY
Woodhouse R
MULLIGAN RANGE
Durack R
'Home Valley'
Mt Cockburn North
The Grotto
'The Diggers Rest'
Boab Prison Tree
Parry Lagoons Nature Res
Wyndham
Ord R
Ivanhoe
Mirima Nat Pk
Research Stn
Kununurra
Keep River Nat Pk
Border Quarantine Check Point
VICTORIA

E

EDKINS RANGE
BLYTHE CREEK
Daglish R
Charnley R
Calder R
MINJA
Mt Lacy
'Mt Elizabeth'
'Gibb River'
Dodnun
588
Chapman R
ROAD
Oomaloo Falls
'Karunjie' (Pentecost Downs) (abandoned)
private track
PENTECOST RANGE
Salmond R
Chamberlain Gorge
El Questro Gorge
El Questro Wilderness Park
Emma Gorge Resort
DUNHAM HWY
Dunham R
Dunham Pilot Dam
Lake Kununurra
Lake Argyle Village
'Argyle' Museum
Ord Dam
Lake Argyle
To Timber Creek Katherine

F

Hart Wilderness Lodge
LEOPOLD RANGES
Mt Hart
Bell Gorge
CONSERVATION PARK
'Silent Grove'
Mt Frank
Imintji
MAURICE CREEK
Old Beverley Springs (ruins)
'Mt Barnett' Roadhouse
Galvans Gorge
Manning Gorge
Barnett River Gorge
'Charnley River'
Kupungarri
SYNNOT RANGE
PHILLIPS RANGE
Adcock Gorge
Moll Gorge (private)
Mount House (no access)
GIBB RIVER ROAD
Gladstone Lake
'Marion'
Blackfellow R
BLUE FACE RANGES
DURACK RANGES
Durack R
'Kachana Station'
Wilson R
Crocodile Hole
Mt Nyulasy
Pompeys Pillar
Argyle Diamond Mine no public access
'Bow River'
Bow R
'Glen Hill'
CARR BOYD RANGE
O'DONNELL RANGE
Doon Doon Roadhouse
Dunham River
'Rosewood'
'Argyle Downs'
'Lissadell'
'Spring Creek'
Mt Behn

G

Mt Ord
'Millie Windie'
Mt Behn
Richenda R
'Glenroy'
'Old Glenroy'
Mornington Wilderness Camp
'Mornington'
Glenroy Meatworks (abandoned)
NARRIE RANGE
Pittard Bluff
Dimond Gorge
Tablelands Track
'Tableland'
Yulumbu
The Tablelands Track between Yulumbu (Tablelands) and Bedford Downs homesteads has been closed until further notice.
Mt Lush
Mt Remarkable
'Bedford Downs'
Terannis R
Mt Wells
no public access road
'Lansdowne'
Ord R
'Mabel Downs'
VIOLET VALLEY
377
Warmun (Turkey Creek)
NORTHERN HWY
Lumuku
Osmond Valley
Echidna Chasm
GREAT
'Texas Downs'
Mt Parker
Purnululu Con Res
BUNGLE BUNGLE RANGE
Visitors Centre
PURNULULU NAT PARK
Cathedral Gorge
WORLD HERITAGE AREA
Ord R
'New Ord River'
Malangan
'Old Ord River'
Darlu Darlu
'Mistake Creek'
Mt Napier

H

OSCAR RANGE
167
'Leopold Downs'
King Leopold R
Sandy Ck
RANGES
Mt Frederick
Conical Peak
Little R
Gold R
Watery R
'Alice Downs'
KING
'Springvale'
Springvale Hill
Mt Coghlan
Panton R
'Turner'
Turner Hill
'Kirkimbie'
'Bunda'

I (J)

'Laurel Downs'
Brooking Gorge Con Pk
Brooking Springs
Geikie Gorge Nat Park
Junjuwa
Mudludja
Fitzroy Crossing
Ngurtuwarta
Bayulu
Eight Mile
'Fossil Downs'
Geikie Gorge
Fitzroy R
Mt Winifred
O'Donnell R
MUELLER RANGES
Margaret R
Mt Cummings
Mt Amhurst
Mt Ball
'Moola Bulla'
China Wall
Halls Creek
Nicholson Camp
'Rockhole'
Old Halls Creek
'Sophie Downs'
Marella Hole
Nicholson
BUNTINE HWY
'Wallamunga' (Ruin)

J

'Jubilee Downs'
'Quanbun'
'Dukes Down'
Yakanara
Ngalingkadji
Galeru Gorge
Galeru Gorge
PILLARA RANGE
SPARKE RANGE
(Savannah HWY 45)
Mt Bertram
Margaret River
Mt Huxley
'Louisa Downs'
Yiyili
'Mt Amhurst'
'Lamboo'
290
'Dellinger'
Koongie Pk
Nicholson Camp
'Old Elvire'
Wungu
Leedawooloo
'Old Flora Valley'
Elvire R
Saw Tooth (Sawpit) Gorge
'Ruby Plains'
Wolfe R
DUNCAN ROAD
80
'Windoo Hill'

K

'Christmas Creek'
Wangkatjungka
'Cherrabun'
Djugerari
Mt Talbot
Ngumpan
Moongardie
'Larrawa'
'Bohemia Downs'
JONES RANGE
CUMMINS RANGE
Berrangi Bridge
Ngunjiwirri
Mt Dockrell
McCLINTOCK RANGE
TANAMI ROAD
Wolfe Creek Meteorite Crater
Wolfe Creek Crater NP
'Sturt Creek'
Sturt R
'Gordon Downs' (Abandoned)
Kandat Djaru
GARDNER RANGE
Western Desert
Kartangarurru, Walpiri & Walmajert
NORTHERN TERRITORY

To Alice Springs
79
To Top Springs

170
'Carranya'
290

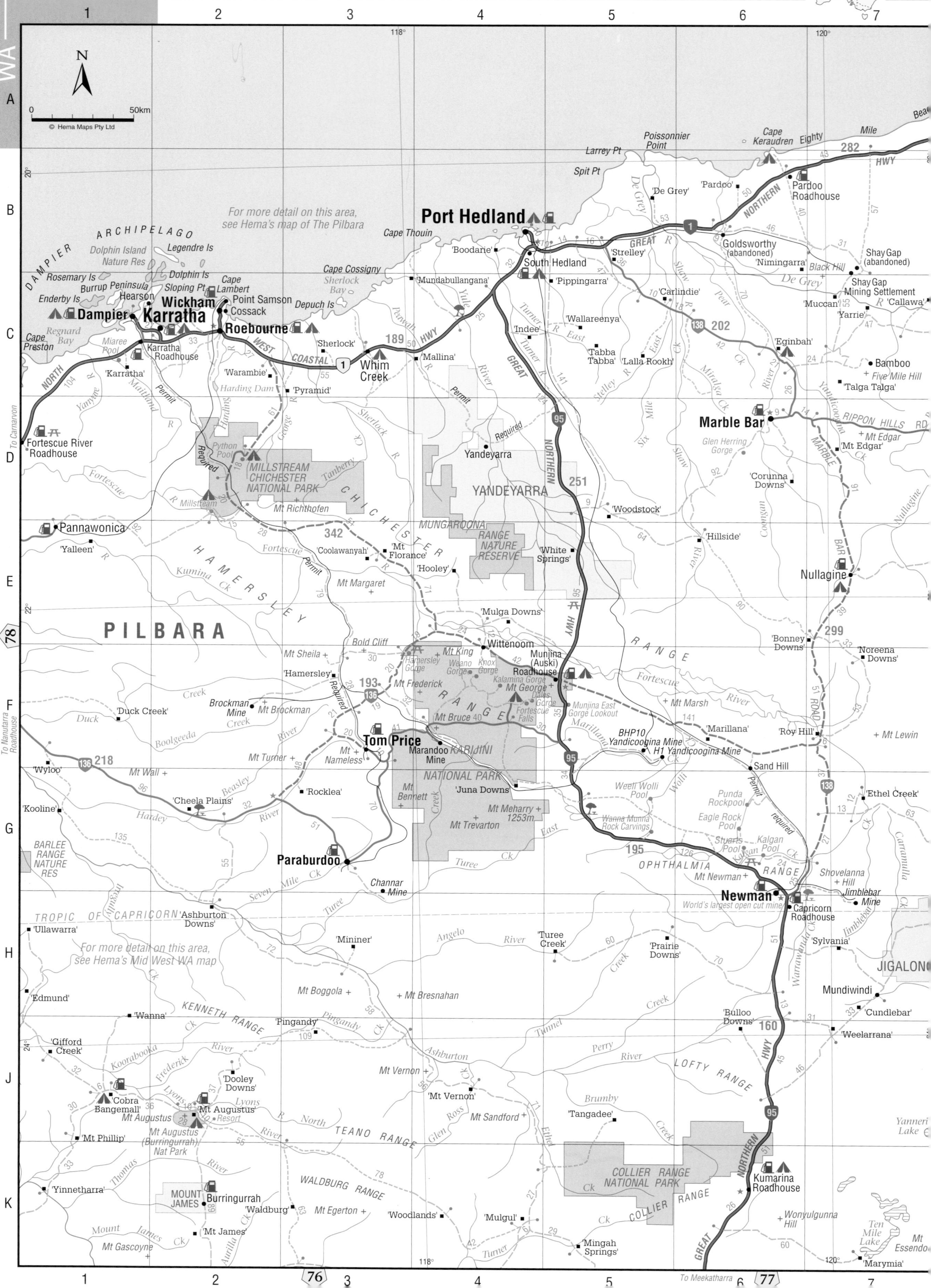
WA
N
0 50km
© Hema Maps Pty Ltd
PILBARA
For more detail on this area, see Hema's map of The Pilbara
For more detail on this area, see Hema's Mid West WA map
DAMPIER ARCHIPELAGO
Dolphin Island Nature Res
Legendre Is
Rosemary Is
Dolphin Is
Burrup Peninsula
Enderby Is
Hearson
Sloping Pt
Cape Lambert
Point Samson
Cossack
Wickham
Dampier
Karratha
Roebourne
Karratha Roadhouse
'Karratha'
Regnard Bay
Cape Preston
Miaree Pool
Depuch Is
Cape Cossigny
Sherlock Bay
Cape Thouin
Port Hedland
South Hedland
'Boodarie'
'Pippingarra'
'Mundabullangana'
Larrey Pt
Spit Pt
Poissonnier Point
Cape Keraudren
Eighty Mile Beach
'De Grey'
'Pardoo'
Pardoo Roadhouse
Goldsworthy (abandoned)
'Nimingarra'
Shay Gap (abandoned)
Shay Gap Mining Settlement
'Strelley'
'Carlindie'
'Muccan'
'Yarrie'
'Callawa'
'Wallareenya'
'Indee'
'Tabba Tabba'
'Lalla Rookh'
'Eginbah'
Bamboo
Five Mile Hill
'Talga Talga'
Marble Bar
Mt Edgar
'Mt Edgar'
Glen Herring Gorge
'Corunna Downs'
'Sherlock'
'Mallina'
Whim Creek
'Warambie'
'Pyramid'
Harding Dam
Fortescue River Roadhouse
To Carnarvon
Python Pool
MILLSTREAM CHICHESTER NATIONAL PARK
Millstream
Mt Richthofen
CHICHESTER RANGE
Yandeyarra
YANDEYARRA
MUNGAROONA RANGE NATURE RESERVE
'White Springs'
'Woodstock'
'Hillside'
Pannawonica
'Yalleen'
'Coolawanyah'
'Mt Florance'
'Hooley'
Mt Margaret
HAMERSLEY RANGE
Nullagine
'Mulga Downs'
Wittenoom
Bold Cliff
Mt Sheila
'Hamersley'
Mt King
Hamersley Gorge
Weano Gorge
Knox Gorge
Kalamina Gorge
Munjina (Auski) Roadhouse
Mt George
Dales Gorge
Fortescue Falls
Munjina East Gorge Lookout
Mt Frederick
'Bonney Downs'
'Noreena Downs'
Mt Marsh
'Duck Creek'
Brockman Mine
Mt Brockman
Mt Bruce
Tom Price
Marandoo Mine
Mt Nameless
KARIJINI NATIONAL PARK
BHP10 Yandicoogina Mine
H1 Yandicoogina Mine
'Marillana'
'Roy Hill'
Mt Lewin
Sand Hill
To Nanutarra Roadhouse
'Wyloo'
Mt Wall
Mt Turner
'Rocklea'
'Cheela Plains'
'Juna Downs'
Mt Bennett
Weeli Wolli Pool
Punda Rockpool
Eagle Rock Pool
Wanna Munna Rock Carvings
Mt Meharry 1253m
Mt Trevarton
'Ethel Creek'
'Kooline'
BARLEE RANGE NATURE RES
Paraburdoo
Stuarts Pool
Kalgan Pool
OPHTHALMIA RANGE
Mt Newman
Newman
World's largest open cut mine
Capricorn Roadhouse
Shovelanna Hill
Jimblebar Mine
Channar Mine
TROPIC OF CAPRICORN
'Ashburton Downs'
'Ullawarra'
'Mininer'
'Turee Creek'
'Prairie Downs'
'Sylvania'
JIGALONG
Mundiwindi
'Cundlebar'
'Edmund'
Mt Boggola
Mt Bresnahan
'Wanna'
KENNETH RANGE
'Pingandy'
'Bulloo Downs'
'Weelarrana'
'Gifford Creek'
Mt Vernon
'Mt Vernon'
LOFTY RANGE
'Dooley Downs'
'Cobra Bangemall'
Mt Augustus
'Mt Augustus' Resort
Mt Augustus (Burringurrah) Nat Park
TEANO RANGE
Mt Sandford
'Tangadee'
Yanneri Lake
'Mt Phillip'
COLLIER RANGE NATIONAL PARK
Kumarina Roadhouse
WALDBURG RANGE
'Yinnetharra'
MOUNT JAMES
Burringurrah
'Waldburg'
Mt Egerton
'Woodlands'
'Mulgul'
Wonyulgunna Hill
COLLIER RANGE
Ten Mile Lake
Mt Essendon
Mt Gascoyne
'Mt James'
'Mingah Springs'
'Marymia'
To Meekatharra
NORTH WEST COASTAL HWY
GREAT NORTHERN HWY
RIPPON HILLS RD
MARBLE BAR ROAD
Fortescue River
Ashburton River
De Grey River
Yule River
Turner River
Sherlock River
Harding River
Maitland River
George River
Peawah River
Shaw River
Coongan River
Nullagine River
Oakover River
Hardey River
Beasley River
Duck Creek
Boolgeeda Creek
Turee Creek
Seven Mile Ck
Angelo River
Kumina Ck
Marillana Ck
Weeli Wolli Ck
Perry River
Tunnel Creek
Brumby Creek
Frederick River
Lyons River
Thomas River
Ethel River
Kooraboooka Creek
118°
120°
20°
22°
24°
1 2 3 4 5 6 7
A B C D E F G H J K
1 95 138 136 202 189 342 193 218 251 282 299 195 160 78 76 77

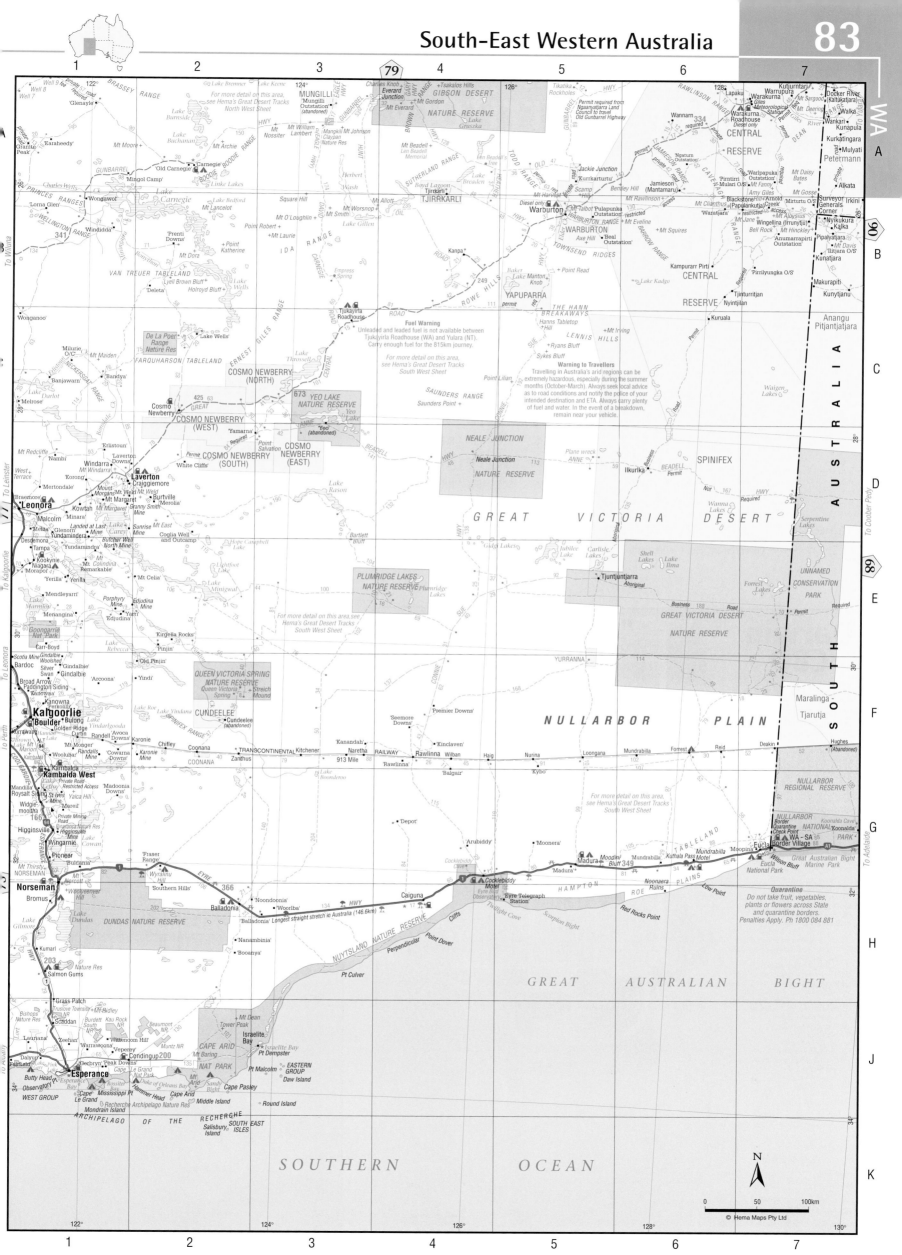

Northern Territory

Chambers Pillar (91 H8)

	Alice Springs	Ayers Rock	Barrow Creek	Borroloola	Camooweal	Darwin	Jabiru	Katherine	Kulgera	Mataranka	Nhulunbuy
Ayers Rock	443										
Barrow Creek	725	282									
Borroloola	922	1647	1204								
Camooweal	748	694	1419	976							
Darwin	1434	986	1234	1959	1516						
Jabiru	254	1410	962	1210	1935	1492					
Katherine	300	324	1110	662	910	1635	1192				
Kulgera	1465	1765	1789	1249	1477	555	318	273			
Mataranka	1360	105	405	429	1005	557	805	1530	1087		
Nhulunbuy	708	2068	705	1005	1029	1713	1265	1513	2238	1795	
Tennant Creek	1290	582	778	687	987	1011	471	699	223	948	505

Distances are shown in kilometres and follow the most direct major sealed route

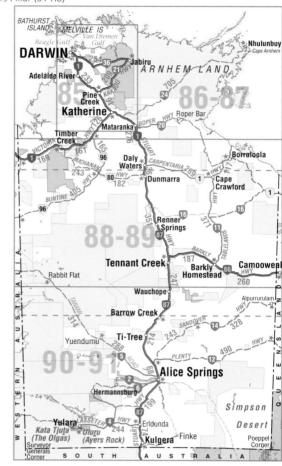

Darwin CBD

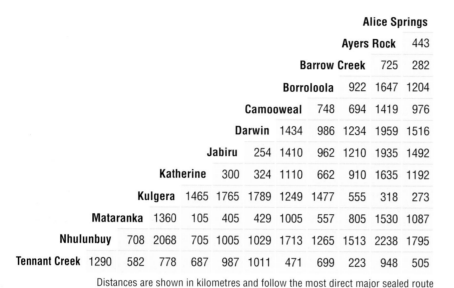

Points of Interest
1. Aboriginal Fine Arts Gallery
2. Aquascene Fish Feeding
3. Australian Pearling Exhibition
4. Chinese Temple & Museum
5. Darwin Theatre Company
6. Indo Pacific Marine
7. Joy Flights
8. Lyons Cottage
9. Old Admiralty House
10. Survivors Lookout
11. The Cenotaph / War Memorial
12. The Deckchair Cinema
13. The Old Court House & Police Station
14. The Old Town Hall
15. The Tree of Knowledge
16. USS Peary Memorial / USAAF Memorial
17. WWII Oil Storage Tunnels

Accommodation
1. Air Raid City Lodge
2. Alatai Quest Apartments
3. Banyan View Lodge
4. Cherry Blossom Motel
5. Chilli's Backpackers
6. City Garden Apartments
7. Crowne Plaza Darwin
8. Darwin Central Hotel
9. Darwin City YHA Hostel
10. Elke's Inner City Backpackers Lodge
11. Frog Hollow Backpackers Resort
12. Globetrotters Backpackers Lodge
13. Holiday Inn Darwin
14. Holiday Inn Esplanade Darwin
15. Luma Luma Holiday Apartments
16. Marrakai Apartments
17. Mediterranean All Suites Hotel
18. Melaleuca On Mitchell Backpackers
19. Mirambeena Resort Darwin
20. Novotel Atrium Darwin
21. Palms City Resort
22. Poinciana Inn
23. Quest Apartments
24. Saville Park Suites
25. The Cavenagh Hotel Motel
26. The Metro
27. Ti-Tree Apartments
28. Top End Hotel
29. Value Inn
30. Wilderness Lodge

LEGEND
Major Road
Minor Road
Lane / Path
Major Building
Govt Building
Accommodation
Theatre/Cinema
Shopping
Church
Information

© Hema Maps Pty Ltd

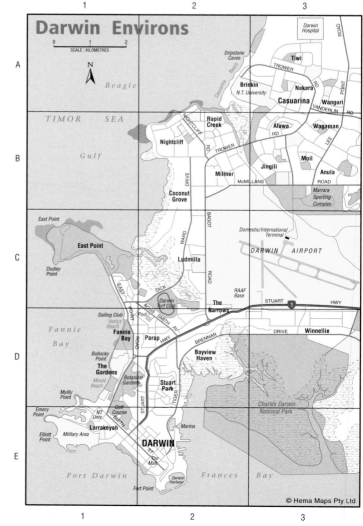

Darwin Environs

© Hema Maps Pty Ltd

MELVILLE ISLAND

Tiwi 131°

Paru
Nguiu
Pickertaramoor

Napier Bay
Cape Keith
Cobham Bay
Conder Pt

GARIG GUNAK BARLU NAT PARK
Greenhill Is
Morse Is
Endyalgout Is

Murgenella 133°

WELLINGTON RANGE

Mt Permain +
Tor Rock +

Van Diemen Gulf

Cape Gambier

Clarence Strait

12°

NW Vernon Is
SW Vernon Is
East Vernon Is
Cape Hotham Forestry Res
Djukbinj Nat Park
Cape Hotham
Cape Hotham Sector
Chambers Bay
Pt Stuart Coastal Res
Pt Stuart
Finke Bay
West Alligator Head
Field Is
Barron Is
Pt Farewell

Kakadu

Mt Borradaile +

Beagle Gulf

Gunn Pt
Shoal Bay
Lee Pt
Hope Inlet

'Koolpinyah'
'Woolner'
'Lake Finnis'
Lake Finnis
'Swim Ck'
Swim Ck Con Res
Shady Camp
'Carmor Plain'

Gunbalanya (Oenpelli)
Cannon Hill
Ubirr
Jabiluka
Border Store
Boat Cruise

DARWIN

Radio Aust Transmitting Stn
Mandorah
COX PENINSULA
Belyuen
Palmerston
Channel Is
Howard Springs
Nature Park
Humpty Doo
Middle Point
Djukbinj Nat Park
Marrakai Sector
'Helens Ck'
'Melaleuca'
Pt Stuart Wilderness Lodge
'Opium Ck'

KAKADU
'Munmarlary'
MAGELA PLAIN
'Mudginberri'
Jabiluka Mineral Lease
Ranger Mineral Lease

C

Ida Bay
Burge Pt
Bynoe
Berry Springs
Wildlife Park
Noonamah
Tumbling Waters
Manton Res

Bird Sanc Beatrice Hill
Corroboree Billabong
Rockhole
Wildman Sector

Alecs Hole
Four Mile Hole
Two Mile Hole

Bowali Visitor Centre
Aurora Kakadu
Jabiru
Gagudju Crocodile Holiday Inn
Mt Brockman +
Koongarra Mineral Lease

'Finniss'
Mt Finniss
Darwin River Dam
Manton Dam Pk
Acacia Store
Rum Jungle
Corroboree Park Inn
Delta Sector
Mary River
Bark Hut Inn
'Annaburroo'
McKinlay Sector

219
36

JIM JIM ROAD

Gagudju Lodge Cooinda
Yellow Water
Nourlangie Rock
Jim Jim Billabong
Spring Peak
Mundogie Hill
+ Mt Partridge

NATIONAL

Mt Cahill +
Mt Basedow +
Table Top
Mt Gilruth +

13°

'Woolaning'
'Wangi'
Walker Creek
Florence Falls
Wangi Falls
Tolmer Falls
Batchelor
Banyan
'Sargents'
'Stapleton'
'Mt Bundey'
'Mt Ringwood'
Mt Ringwood
McKinlay
Mt Douglas +
Mt Masson +
Mt George +

KAKADU

Maguk Gorge
Deaf Adder Ck
Mt Adder +
Jim Jim Falls
Twin Falls

PARK

LITCHFIELD NAT PARK

Mt Raymond
War Cemetery
Adelaide River
Mt Tymn +
Mt Paqualin +
Pipeline
Mt Ellison +
'Ban Ban Springs'
Robin Falls
Brooks Creek
Grove Hill
'Mary River'
Mary River Roadhouse
Gunlom (UDP) Falls
Koolpin Gorge (Jarrangbarnmi)
'El Sherana'
Coronation Hill +
Gunlom
Mt Evelyn +

28
23
120
STUART

Mt Smith
Hayes Creek
'Douglas'
Tjuwaliyn (Douglas) Hot Springs Nature Pk
Emerald Springs
'Esmerelda'
Tent Hill
Mt Davis +
Mt Gardiner +
Coronet Hill +

KAKADU

Mt Porter +
McCarthy Hill +

'Woolianna'
Mt Thomas +
Mt Haywood +
'Banyan Farm'
'Perry's'
Nauiyu
'Mango Farm'
Daly River
Mt Nancar +
'Mt Pleasant'
'Tipperary'
Butterfly Gorge Nature Park
Douglas Daly Exp Stn
Douglas Daly Park
Pine Creek
'Bonrook'
Ranford Hill +
Two Sisters +
Mt Stow +
Mt Ebsworth +

NITMILUK (Katherine Gorge) NATIONAL PARK

'Fish River'
Mt Boulder +
'Oolloo'
Mt Muriel +
Mt Briggs +
'Jindare'
'Lewin Springs'
Cullen
Umbrawarra Gorge
Mt Giles +
Barnjarn
Mt Todd +
Edith Falls
Mt Harvey +
Mt David +
Manyallaluk
Mt Felix +
Manyallaluk (Eva Valley)

14°

Oolloo Crossing
91 HWY
Jawoyn
Katherine
Nitmiluk Gorge
Jawoyn
Maranboy
Barunga
Beswick

WINGATE MOUNTAINS
Upper Daly
Daly
Bamboo Ck
Fish River Reserve
Ferguson R
'Claravale'
Wagiman
'Florina'
Hornet Hill +
Katherine
Historic Springvale Homestead
'Manbulloo'
Mt Shepherd +
Dook Ck

'Dorisvale'
Yubulyawun
Mt Pearce +
Mullens Ridge
Mt Armstrong +
Flora River Nature Park
Croker Hill +
'Scott Creek'
'Claravale'
Tindal RAAF Base
Cutta Cutta Caves
STUART
105

15°

'Wombungi'
Mt Barwolla +
Mt Freda +
Butchers Hill +
'Mataranka'
Mataranka

Bradshaw Field Training Area
Fitzmaurice River
VICTORIA
King River
'Lakefield'

N

© Hema Maps Pty Ltd

0   50km

NT

Quarantine
Do not take fruit, vegetables, plants or flowers across State and quarantine borders.
Penalties Apply. Ph 1800 084 881

For more detail on this area, see Hema's Kakadu National Park map

For more detail on this area, see Hema's map of The Top End & Western Gulf & Cairns to Broome

8 9 10 11 12 13 14

134° 135° 136° 137°

A

11°

Rimbija Is
Cape Wessel

B

Wessel Islands
Marchinbar Is

Cumberland Strait

Stevens Is
Guluwuru Is

ARAFURA SEA

North West Crocodile Is
Drysdale Is
Raragala Is
Truant Is

C

12°

Cuthbert Pt
Braithwaite Pt
Junction Bay
Rolling Bay
Hawkesbury Pt
Nth East Pt
Skirmish Pt
False Pt
Cape Stewart
Rabuma Is
Mooroongga Is
Elcho Is
Pt Napier
Inglis Is
Cunningham Islands
Alger Is
Wigram Is
The English Company's Islands
Bromby Islands
Cape Wilberforce
Maley Road

Goomadeer
Maningrida
Boucaut Bay
Ji-Marda
Milingimbi
Howard Is
Galiwinku
Flinders Pt
Probable Is
Mallison Is
Everett Is
Rorruwuy
Bremer Is

Nhulunbuy
Yirrkala

Gochin Jiny Jirra
Castlereagh Bay
Banyan Is
Mapurru
Buckingham Bay
GOVE PENINSULA
Cape Arnhem

Yathalamarra

D

13°

Closed to all non-local traffic
Ramingining
Nangalala
'Old Arafura' (ruins)
Lake Evella
Gapuwiyak
Dhalinybuy
Port Bradshaw
Arnhem Bay

Manmoyi
Mirrnatja
FREDERICK HILLS
Gurrumuru
'Mt Alexander' (ruins)

ROAD
Birany Birany
Garrthalala
Pt Alexander

MITCHELL RANGE
Required
Mt Caledon
Cape Grey

ARNHEM LAND
Arnhem Land
CENTRAL
Govder R
Gan Gan
Koolatong R
Dial Bay
Bald Pt

E

GULF

Emu Springs
Mt Flemming
BATH RANGE
Baniyala
Round Hill Is
Pt Arrowsmith
Cape Shield

Mt Marumba
PARSONS RANGE
Mt Ranken
Blue Mud Bay
Isle Woodah
Nicol Is

Weemol
Bulman
Black Mountain
Morgan Is
Burney Is
Hawknest Is
North Point Is
North East Isles

F

14°

Mt Catt
Mt Catt
Cape Barrow
Bustard Is
Chasm Is
Bickerton Is
Winchelsea Is

Mainoru Store
Mt Bridges
Mt Stretton
Milyakburra
GROOTE EYLANDT
Alyangula
Umbakumba

'Mountain Valley'
'Mainoru'
Mt Bray
Mt Leane
Rose R
Angurugu
Ilyungmadja Pt
OF

Mt Throsby
'Wongolara'
Mt Furner
Three Graces
Required

G

Mt Bagster
Mt Phillip
Tasman Pt
South Pt
Cape Beatrice

Mt Favenc
Phelp R
Numbulwar

Mt Chapman
DOWNERS RANGE
Mt Warrington
Sandy Is
Edward Is
CARPENTARIA

Buddawarka
Urapunga
Ngukurr
Port Roper
For more detail on this area, see Hema's Top End & Western Gulf map and Cairns to Broome map

H

15°

'Moroak'
Mt Eleanor
Roper Bar
Yutpundji-Djindiwirritj
'St Vidgeon' (ruins)
Mt Boxall
Roper R
Limmen Bight
Maria Is
N

Mt Price
Bringung
'Roper Valley'
Mt Eclipse
Marra

Mt St Vidgeon
0 50 100km

Mt Forrest
Mt Hughes
© Hema Maps Pty Ltd

Mt Davidson
Hodgson Downs
Mt Kelly
Beatrice Is

Miniyeri
'Hodgson Downs'
Mason Bluff
Proposed Limmen National Park
Limmen River Fishing Camp
Maria Lagoon

J

'Hodgson River'
Rosie Creek Fishing Camp
Wurralibi
Sir Edward Pellew Group

'Nutwood Downs'
The Four Archers
'Nathan River'
Port for McArthur River Mine
West Island
Watson North Is
Barranyi (North Island) Nat Park
Cape Vanderlin

'Minamia' (Cox River)
Alawa
'Bing Bong'
Bing Bong Loading Facility
Centre Is
Vanderlin Is
Wurralibi

'Lorella Springs'
South West Is
Port McArthur

K

16°

Borroloola
King Ash Bay
'Manangoora'

Jandanku
Narwinbi
Mt Feathertop
Warby
'Greenbank'

'Tawallah'
'Bauhinia Downs'
'Billengarrah'
Caranbinni Con Res
Buckaroo Rock
McLEOD RANGE

CARPENTARIA
'Broadmere'
'Tanumbirini'
McArthur River Mine(HYC)
'Seven Emu'

134° 135° 136° 137° 138°

NT

1 2 3 4 5 6 7

To Katherine 86

A
To Kununurra
129° 130°
'Bullo River' 'Coolbah' 131° Illari Hill 132° 133° Wubalawun
Keep River 'Auvergne' + Mt Goose Larrima
National Park **Timber** 'Fitzroy' 'Gorrie' WWII
Creek Mt Gregory 171
Quarantine Mayat Ngaliwurru/ 161 **Victoria** 'Delamere' 'Western' Maryfield
Checkpoint Bulla Nungali RANGE **River** 96 Creek' Alexander Forrest Cairn
Mt Sellars Mt Peaka 165 'Sunday
'Newry' 15 51 Wanimiyn Romula Knob 'Dillinya' 'Gilnockie' Creek' 'Kala
169 Drovers Mt Sandiman Dillinya **Daly Waters**
Rest Wambardi Mt Compton Gallery Hiway Inn
Quarantine 30 Limestone Jasper + Price Hill + Hill
Do not take fruit, vegetables, Gorge 'Kidman Romula Knob

B
plants or flowers across State Springs' Mt Compton 'Killarney' 'Hidden
and quarantine borders. 46 Station Hill Mt Compton Fraynes 'Birrimba' Valley'
Penalties Apply. Ph 1800 084 881 Humbert Yarralin 243 'Mooloooloo' + Knob HWY
Byrnes Hill Amanbidji **GREGORY** 'Humbert Yarralin 80 Mt Sullivan Dunmar
'Rosewood' + Mt Duncan Nagurunguru River' 'Victoria River **Top Springs**
'Waterloo' **NATIONAL** Mt Warburton Downs' Yingawunarri
Mt Mary + Tee Dee Hill **PARK** + Mt Mudbura 'Dungowan'
Flour Hill Mt Hodgson Mt Mervin Montejinni BUCHANAN
+ Mt Behn View Hill Gregorys Stoney Knob 182

C
263 Remarkable Pillar Hawk Knob
Bamboo Malngin 2 Mt Wickham Cusack Rock Pigeon + Lovell Hill **Murranji**
Spring Mt Kimon + Mt Sanford Hole Mt Northcote 96
'Mt Sanford' 'Camfield' + Mt Williams 'Murranji'
81 Mistake Warriki Hill 'Camfield' 171 Biri Hill
Mt Wickham 76

D
Mistake Creek Blackgin Hill + Daguragu 'Wave Hill'
'Nelson (Closed
Springs' 'Limbunya' Community) 'Cattle Creek O/S'
Malngin Mt Copley Kalkaringi Wampana-
(Mistake Creek) Amos Knob Red Hill Karlantijpa
Mt Panton Daguragu Mt Gordon
Mt Rose (Gurindji) Mt Seale Lake
New Ord Mt Maivo 96 Toms + Gap Hill Woo
River Rock 234 + Mt Barton
'Kirkimbie' Inverway Mt Farquharson + Mt Watson
'Riveren' + Mt Reid

E
Nicholson 'Bunda' + Mt Archie Hooker
BUNTINE Creek For more detail on this area,
see Hema's Great Desert Tracks
Nongra North Central Sheet
'Wallamunga' Lake RAILWAY
(ruin) Lajamanu
'Birrindudu' Lul-Tju

F
Western Desert 'Parnta' Kulingalimpa
Mt Winnecke Mirirrinyungu Karlantijpa North
Pielegia (Duck Ponds) (Warlmanpa, Warlpiri,
Mirrindi Lothari Hill Mudbura & Warumungu)

G
Kartangarurru, 'Supplejack
Walpiri & Downs' 295
Walmajert
Mallee Hill

79
Mt Frederick
(Western Desert) 'Talbot Well O/S'
'Mt Frederick O/S' Coomarie Spring

H
'Picaninny O/S' The Black Hills
125
Mt Tanami + Tanami Mine Central Desert
Mt Frederick No2 (Warlpiri & Kartagmarruru Lake
(Western Desert South) Kurintji) Surprise Karlantijpa South
Rabbit Flat
Roadhouse

J
'Ngulupi' Locked + Mt Davidson
Gate 'Mt Davidson
Mangkururrpa 'Tanami The Granites Outstation'
(Tanami Downs) Downs' Mine + Mt Solitaire
Lake + Mt Bennett Wirliyajarrayi
Jeavons Hordern Jarra Jarra
Hills

K
Lake White + McDairmid Hill Willowra
314
SYDNEY MARGARET RANGE Renahans Bore
129° 'Puyurra' Mt Theo + 'Mt Theo + Mt Windajong
130° 131° Outstation' 132° 133°
To Alice Springs

1 2 3 4 90 5 6 7

To Katherine

GULF OF CARPENTARIA

8 9 10 11 12 13 14

© Hema Maps Pty Ltd

0 50km

N

134° 135° 136° 137° 138°

A

'Hodgson River'
'Nutwood Downs'
'Minamia' (Cox River)
Alawa
Proposed Limmen National Park
To Roper Bar 87
372
'Nathan River'
Rosie
Sir Edward Pellew Group
Barranyi (North Island) Nat Park
Watson Is
North Is
West Island
Cape Vanderlin
Vanderlin Is
Wurralibi
Port for McArthur River Mine
Bing Bong
Bing Bong Loading Facility
South West Is
Centre
Manangoora
'Lorella Springs'
King Ash Bay
Port McArthur

B
'Amungee Mungee'
'Tanumbirini'
HWY 1
269
'O.T. Downs'
Broadmere'
Jandanku
'Bauhinia Downs'
'Billengarrah'
Tawallah Range
'Tawallah'
McArthur River Mine (HYC)
Carananbirini Con Res
Bukalara Rock
117
Borroloola
Narwinbi
Mt Feathertop
'Bing Bong'
Warby
'Greenbank'
'Spring Creek'
Garawa
254
'Seven Emu'
'Pungalina'

C
'Beetaloo'
CARPENTARIA
Favenc Range
Cape Crawford
'McArthur River'
'Balbirini'
Abner Range
'Mallapunyah'
Robinson River
'Calvert Hills'
HWY 1
Wollogorang
To Burketown

D
'Ucharonidge'
Wampaya
Lija
Shandon Downs' (Ruins)
'Wallhallow'
11
16
China Wall
Permit Required
To Mt Isa

E
'Powell Creek (Jangirulu)'
'Mungabroom'
'Eva Downs'
STOCK ROUTE
371
'Anthony Lagoon'
'Cresswell Downs'
Calvert Road
'Benmara'
Nicholson R
Waahyi / Garawa
Murun Murula

F
Renner Springs
'Helen Springs'
'Muckaty'
'Banka Banka'
'Brunchilly'
BARKLY
'Rockhampton Downs'
Corella Creek
'Brunette Downs'
Fish Creek
Hole Creek
Connells Lagoon Conservation Reserve
'Connell Lagoon'
Mittiebah
Mittiebah Range
'Mittiebah'
Carrara Range
'Old Herbert Vale'

G
Whittington Range
Short Range
'Phillip Creek'
Warumungu
Likkaparta
BARKLY
John Flynn Memorial
Gecko Mine
Three Ways
187
66
Prentice Lake
'Alroy Downs'
'Alexandria'
11
TABLELANDS
Buchanan
Burudu
'Gallipoli'
'Herbert Vale'

H
Warrego Mine
MGDOUALL RANGE
'Orlando'
Peko Mine
Tennant Creek
'Tennant Creek'
Mt Samuel
138
Kanturrpa
Copper & Gold Mines
Barkly Homestead
66
Wakaya
Wunara
'Soudan'
260
BARKLY HWY
'Avon Downs'
'Rocklands'
Camooweal
Camooweal Caves Nat Park
Nowranie
To Mt Isa

Q
Arruwurra
'Old Wootoona'
164
'Wooroona'

J
McLaren Creek
Mungkarta
Bonney Well
Devils Marbles Con Reserve
Mt Cairns
'Kurundi'
'Epenarra'
Wutunugurra
Anurrete
Seantree Bore
Canteen Creek (Orwaitilla)
'Burramurra' (ruin)
'Austral Downs'
Wauchope
'Singleton'
Whistle Duck Creek
Davenport Range Nat Park
Old Police Stn Waterhole (Ruins)
'Hatches Creek' (Ruins)
Mt Michael
'Arcadia' (ruin)
Wycliffe Well
Ali-Curung (Closed Community)
Warrabri
'Murray Downs'
'Elkedra'
Elkedra River
Alpurrurulam
'Lake Nash'

K
109
STUART
RAILWAY
'Annitowa'
Scarr Hill
SANDOVER HWY
'Georgina'
Georgina R
87
To Alice Springs
91
To Alice Springs

88

To Halls Creek

1 2 3 4 5 6 7

A
'Ngulupi'
129°
Locked Gate
Permit Required
Mangkururrpa 94 (Tanami Downs)
'Tanami Downs'
The Granites Mine
Private Track
Track
+ Mt Davidson 131°
'Mt Davidson Outstation'
+ Mt Solitaire
+ Mt Windajong
Jarra Jarra
Lake Jeavons
Lake Dennis
Iningarra Range
Hordern Hills
132°
Yiningarra (Walpiri-Kukaja-Ngarti)
+ Mt Bennett
Wirliyajarrayi
133°

B
Lake White
Sydney Margaret Range
314
Renahans Bore
'Puyurra'
Chilla Well (Abandoned)
+ Mt Theo
'Mt Theo Outstation'
+ Mt Patricia
Willowra
McDairmid Hill
Sowden Hill
'Chilla Well'
Mala (Tjilla-Warlpiri)
Mount Barkly (Pawu) (Private Road)
+ Mt Renhie
+ Mt Peake
Pawu
+ Mt Campbell
Mt Leichhardt
'Anningie'

C
Lake Mackay
Warning to Travellers
Travelling in Australia's arid regions can be extremely hazardous, especially during the summer months (October-March). Always seek local advice as to road conditions and notify the police of your intended destination and ETA. Always carry plenty of fuel and water. In the event of a breakdown, remain near your vehicle.
22°
Mt Singleton
'Mt Doreen' (Ruins)
Mt Hardy
'Mt Denison'
Mt Treachery
'Coniston'
Quartz Hill
Mt Stafford
Nancy Hill
'Ti-Tree' (Nturiya)
Ti-
Yuendumu
Giles Range
Reynolds Range

D
Lake Mackay
Ethel Ck
'Vaughan Springs'
Treuer Range
Mt Nicker +
Mt Davenport
176
17
Yuendumu
28
Yuelamu
Uldirra Hill
Yalpirakinu (Mount Allen)
Mt Finniss
'Pine Hill'
Yunkanjini
Nirrippi 12
'Wayililinypa O/S'
Mt Gardiner
Laramba
'Napperby'
Mt Freeling
Mt Boothby
Waite Creek Settlement
'Yarripilangu O/S'
+ Mt Gurner
'Newhaven'
Central Mount Wedge
118
West Bluff
Mt Hammond
Tilmouth Roadhouse
+ Mt Carey
Ngalurrtja
+ Central Mt Wedge

E
23°
+ Mt Morris
+ Mt Redvers
Lake Bennett
Mt Harris
For more detail on this see Hema's maps 'The Re and 'Central Austra
Junction Road
16
Ininti 24
'Pinpirnga'
Len Beadell marker
Sandy Blight Junction 'Tinki'
Willie Rockhole
Permit Required
'New Bore'
Illili
Papunya
'Derwent'
110
Narwietooma
Rubunja
Walungurru (Kintore)
Mt Strickland
Mt Leisler
'Warren Creek Bore'
Mount Liebig (diesel only)
+ Mt Liebig
'Blackwater'
'Mt Larrie'
'Ulambaura'
Bunghara
Mt Zeil 1531m
Mt Chapple
'Milton Park'
'Anburla
Tietkens Tree
188
255
Mt Edward +
Glen Helen
Mt Hay

F
79
Tropic of Capricorn
Mt Crawford +
Ikuntji (Haasts Bluff)
14
Macdonnell Ranges
'Hamilton Downs'
Lake Macdonald
Mt Mein
'Ualki'
Neunman
Ehrenberg Range
Haasts Bluff
+ Mt Udor
Deerings Ck
Mereenie Bluff
'Yatemans Bore' Gas
Camels Hump
Kulpitarra
West Macdonnell National Park
Redbank Gorge Mt Sonder
71
Glen Helen Resort
Glen Helen Gorge
Ellery Ck Big Hole
Bonython Range
Sandy Blight Junction
Permit Required
331
+ Mt Forbes
'Kunkayunti'
Mt Solitary
Pipeline
154
Gardiner Range
Tnorala Gosse Bluff Con Reserve
Ellery Creek Nature Park
Rodna
Roulpmaulpma
Laapinta
+ Worman Rocks
+ Mt Winter
Laycocks Hill
Ltalaltuma
43
Hermannsburg
Ntaria
Injarrtnama

G
Lake Hopkins
24°
Tjukurla (Closed Community)
+ Mt Cowle
Lake Neale
+ Mt Murray
Mt Tucker
Kings Canyon Resort
Kings Canyon
Watarrka National Park
+ Mt Olifent
+ Tent Hill
Urrampinyu Illjitjarra
Mt Lewis
Illamurta Springs Police Station (Ruins)
Illamurta Con Res
Illpurta
Finke Gorge National Park
James Range
Wallace Rockhole
Boggy Hole
'Kings Creek'
100
George Gill Range
Petermann
Tempe Downs'
Ipolera
Areyonga (Permit Only)
Pitjantjatara Bluff
Uruna
Palm Valley
Henbury Meteorite Con Res
'He
Docker River
Mt Harris +
+ Mt Carruthers
Lake Amadeus
Mt Levi
Yow a
60
Giles
99
Finke River

H
Bloods Range (Puntitjata)
Kulail
Mt Taylor
Tjuninanta
Karukaki
Bloods Range
Walu
Petermann
Fuel Warning
Unleaded and leaded fuel is not available between Tjukayirla Roadhouse (WA) and Yulara (NT). Carry enough fuel for the 815km journey.
25°
Warrupura
Kutjurntari
Kaltukatjara (Docker River) (Diesel only)
Tjunti
Lasseters Cave
Mt Currie +
Katiti
67
'Angas Downs'
Basedow Range
Ippia Hill
Mount Ebenezer
Erldunda
Permit Required
Private Tracks
259
Tjukaruru Road
Mt Ebenezer
Imanpa
Desert
Kernot Range
Lasseter Hwy
Stuart Hwy

J
Mt Deering
Walka
Wankari
Kunapula
Mt Curdie
Puta Puta
Ngarnurr
Mt Bowley
Mt Phillips
Mt McCulloch
Uripila
Pitalu
Pilakatal
Olia Chain
Kata Tjuta (The Olgas)
Uluru
Pirrulpakalarintja
Katamala Cone
Stevenson Peak
Uluru - Kata Tjuta National Park
Yulara Resort
Connellan Airport
Lasseter Hwy
4
136
Curtin Springs
'Mount Ebenezer'
108
Erldunda
Karinga
Kata Tjuta
Uluru (Ayers Rock)
43
Mt Conner +

K
Mt Daisy Bates +
Alkata Track
26°
Mt Gosse
'Mirturtu O/S'
Ukatjupa
Surveyor Generals Corner
Irkini
Mt Cockburn
Mt Le Hunt
+ Butler Dome
Benda Hill
Mt Robert +
'Mulga Park'
188
Mt Reynolds
'Victory Downs'
Kulgera
A87
Nyikukura
Kurkutjara
Walytjatjata
Mt Mann
Mt Charles
Angatja
Alpara
Eagle Bore
Araleun
Mt Cuthbert
Sentinel Hill
Iykuwaratja
'Mou Caver
Irrunytju (Wingellina)
Kalka
Inarki
Aparatjara (new)
Nyapari
Umpukulunya
Wintawatu
Amata
Ulaypai
Donalds Well
Pukatja (Ernabella)
'Sundown O/S
'Anumarrapirti O/S'
Pipalyatjara
Putaputa
Aparatjara (old)
Kanpi
Tjintalka
Mann Range
Giles Range
129°
Kunatjara
Willi Willi
Tankaanu
130°
Anangu Pitjantjatjara
Ulkiya
Wallany
131°
Yurangka
Mt Woodroffe 1435m
Manyikanga
Musgrave Ranges
Yunyarinyi (Kenmore Park)
Warrabillinna
132°
Ngarutjara
Pine Ridge
133°
Gosse Bore
Agne (De F
SOUTH
Tomkinson Range

79

68

To Coob

8   9   89 11   12   13   14

NT
A

To Tennant Creek

134°
'Kurundi'
Devils Marbles
Devils Marbles Con Reserve
Wauchope
'Singleton'
Mt Cairns
Whistle Duck Creek
135°
Canteen Creek (Orwaitilla)
136°
137°
'Burramurra' (ruin)
138° 'Wooroona'
'Austral Downs'
Arruwurra

magalong'
Wycliffe Well
Road
Old Police Stn.
Waterhole
Mine Ruins
DAVENPORT RANGE NAT PARK
Anurrete
Mt Michael
'Arcadia' (ruin)

109
Ali-Curung (Closed Community)
Warrabri
'Murray Downs'
'Hatches Creek' (Ruins)
Anurrete
Alpurrurulam 'Lake Nash'
HWY
21°

52
'Elkedra'
Elkedra River
'Annitowa'
'Georgina'
B

Nelson
Tara Neutral Junction
87
arrow Creek
Mt Gwynne
RAILWAY
STUART
307
SANDOVER
+ Scarr Hill
Mt Hogarth +

Stirling
'Stirling'
Wilora
90
Mt Tops +
Alyawarra & Katitja private road
Ampilatwatja
Antarrengenge
'Ammaroo'
Ermarne Irrmarne
'Argadargada'
For more detail on this area, see Hema's Great Desert Tracks North East Sheet
D

Mt Octy
HWY
River
River
14
'Ooratippra'
Mt Hogarth +
22°
C

'emorial
Mt Harper
keye (Ti-Tree)
Atnelyey
Ariparra Store (Diesel only)
Angarapa
Urapuntja (Utopia)
'Derry Downs'
Mt Stott
Lucy Ck
'Manners Creek'

Solitary
'Woolla Downs' (ruins)
Mt Skinner
+ Mt Skinner
+ Ledan Peak
243
'MacDonald Downs'
'Arapunya'
Arltur
'Tobermorey'

'Chianina'
14
'Woodgreen'
'Waite River'
'Delmore Downs'
Mt Ida
MacDonald Downs Outstation
DULCIE RANGES NAT PARK
'Lucy Creek'
Anatye 219
Mt Pozieres
'Urlampe'
D

Arno Peak +
Red Cliff
'Mount Swan'
Box Hole Meteorite Crater
Mt Ultim
PLENTY
HWY
Tarlton Downs'
12

Mendip Hill +
+ Mt Byrne
Engawala
'Alcoota'
'Delny'
'Dneiper'
+ Mt Sainthill
+ Mt Swan
JERVOIS RANGE
Bonya (Orrtipa-Thurra)
'Marqua'
23°

'Bushy Park'
Gem Tree Caravan Park
12
'Mount Riddoch'
Harts Range
Irriliree
'Huckitta'
'Jinka'
'Jervois'
TARLTON RANGE
Marshall River
+ Mt Reinecke
TOKO RANGE
E

69
+ Mt Strangways
Mt Pfitzner
Attitjere
HARTS
RANGE
202
+ Mt Eaglebeak
80
+ Mt Tietkens
Mt Smith
Mt Woods
Mt Wooldridge +

37
'Yambah'
Mt Riddoch +
Mt Campbell
Mt Palmer
+ Mt Mary
Plenty
Mt Winnecke +
Mt Barrington +
Twin Hills

68
Mt Laughlen +
The Garden
'Quartz Hill' (ruins)
+ Mt Lionel
+ Mt Ruby
'Atula'
Mt Knuckey +
Cravens Peak +
12
Two Hills +

Mt Everard +
'Ambalindum'
'Claraville'
Arltunga
Mt Gardner +

'Bond Springs'
106
Trephina Gorge Nat Pk
Arltunga Resort
Historic Reserve
Ruby Gap Nature Pk
Atnetye

Alice Springs
Ross River Resort
'Atnarpa'
N'dhala Gorge Nat Park
MACDONNELL RANGES
Lake Caroline
Mt Gardner +
F

Pine Gap
Amoonguna
Emily & Jessie Gaps Nature Park
Corroboree Rock Cons Res
'Todd River'
'Ringwood'
'Limbla'
FERGUSON RANGE
River

81
Ltyentye Apurte (Santa Teresa)
'Numery'
24°

106
Santa Teresa
Todd River Downs'
Pmere Nyente
For more detail on this area, see Hema's Central Australia map, Great Desert Tracks NE Sheet & Simpson Desert map
G

'Deep Well'
Mowelanne 'Oak Valley'
'Allambi'
private track
Hale River
Oneill Point
RODINGA RANGE

Hugh River
Rodinga (ruin)
238
OLD ANDADO TRACK
COLSON
SIMPSON

'Maryvale'
Mt Frank +
4WD only
Warning to Travellers
Travelling in Australia's arid regions can be extremely hazardous, especially during the summer months (October-March). Always seek local advice as to road conditions and notify the police of your intended destination and ETA. Always carry plenty of fuel and water. In the event of a breakdown, remain near your vehicle.
H

Mt Charlotte +
Titjikala
137
Bundooma (ruin)
MAC CLARK (ACACIA PEUCE) CONSERVATION RESERVE
25°

Chambers Pillar Historical Reserve
Pinnacle Hills
'Idracowra'
Chambers Pillar
GHAN
SIMPSON DESERT NATIONAL PARK

'Horseshoe Bend'
+ Colson Pinnacle
Simpson
Desert

Rumbalara (ruin)
'Old Andado'
Q

122
'Andado'
N

'Lilla Creek'
HILL RANGE
Finke (Apatula)
Lambert's Centre of Australia
Mt Peebles +
Finke
0   50   100km

Mt Gordon +
Apatula
RAIL
'New Crown'
Pmer Ulperre Ingwemirne Arletherre
© Hema Maps Pty Ltd
J

148
+ Mt Beddome
Charlotte Waters'
+ Mt Daer
Mt Etingambra
'beara'
Goyder
+ Mt Grundy
+ Mt Wilyunpa
+ Walla Hills
26°

'Tieyon'
'Mt Irwin' 134°
Mt Parlue +
Mt Mead +
Mt Dare'
Finke
Mt Alinerta
FRENCH
LINE
Poeppel Corner

Abminga (ruin)
'Eringa' (abandoned)
Bloods Creek
WITJIRA NATIONAL PARK
Mt Bagot
Purni Bore
Freeth Junction
SIMPSON DESERT CONSERVATION PARK
K

AUSTRALIA
Ilbunga (ruin) 135°
Dalhousie Springs
Desert Parks Pass required
136°
SIMPSON DESERT REGIONAL RESERVE
137°
Permit Required from DNPWS
138°

8   9   66 10   11   67 13   14

92 913 Mile – Bellata

A

913 Mile WA 77 J14 83 F3
A1 Mine Settlement VIC 42 H6 44 A7 46 C1
Abbeyard VIC 43 F8
Abbotsbury NSW 21 E9
Abbotsford NSW 19 E4
Abbotsham TAS 54 E6
Aberbaldie Nature Res NSW 25 J8
Abercorn QLD 7 A9
Abercrombie NSW 22 H5
Abercrombie River Nat Park NSW 22 J6 30 A5
Aberdeen NSW 23 C8
Aberfeldy VIC 42 J7 44 B7 46 D1
Aberfoyle Park SA 60 J2 61 C6
Abergowrie QLD 11 F13
Abminga SA 66 A4 91 K9
Acacia Ridge QLD 3 H4 5 E9
Acacia Store NT 85 D2 86 D4
Acheron VIC 42 G4
Acland QLD 7 F10
Acraman Creek Con Park SA 64 D3
Actaeon Island TAS 53 K9
Acton ACT 31 A1 32 D4
Adaminaby NSW 30 F2
Adamsfield TAS 52 F7
Adavale QLD 13 K11 15 C11
Addington VIC 39 D10
Adelaide SA 59 G4 60 G2 61 A6 62 F7 65 J10
Adelaide CBD SA 58
Adelaide River NT 85 E2 86 E4
Adelong NSW 29 H14 30 D1
Adjungbilly NSW 30 D1
Admiral Bay WA 79 C8 80 J2
Adolphus Island WA 81 C13
Advancetown QLD 5 C13
Adventure Bay TAS 53 J10
Afterlee NSW 25 B12
Agery SA 62 H5 65 G9
Agnes Banks NSW 20 G7
Agnes Banks Nature Res NSW 20 G7 23 G8
Agnes Water QLD 9 J12
Agnew WA 77 E10
Ahrberg Bay TAS 54 H2
Aileron NT 90 D7
Ailsa VIC 40 K6
Ainslie ACT 32 D5
Aireys Inlet VIC 36 K1 39 J11
Airlie VIC 45 D11 46 E4
Airlie Beach QLD 9 B8
Akuna Bay NSW 19 A6
Alawa NT 84 B3
Alawoona SA 62 B6 65 J13
Albacutya VIC 28 K3 40 H4
Albany WA 74 K6
Albany Creek QLD 3 B2 4 F7
Albany Island QLD 16 B2
Albatross Bay QLD 16 F1
Alberrie Creek SA 67 H8
Albert NSW 22 C1 27 K13 29 A13
Albert Park VIC 36 D7
Alberton QLD 5 C10
Alberton SA 59 E2 60 F1
Alberton TAS 55 E12
Alberton VIC 45 G9 46 H2
Albion QLD 3 D4
Albion VIC 36 C6 39 F13 42 K1 44 B1
Albury NSW 29 K12 43 B9
Alcomie TAS 54 C3
Alderley QLD 3 D3
Aldersyde WA 72 A5
Aldgate SA 59 J7 60 H4 61 B7
Aldinga SA 61 E5 62 F7 65 K10
Aldinga Beach SA 61 E4 62 F7 65 K9
Aldinga Scrub Con Park SA 61 E4 65 K9
Alectown NSW 22 E2
Alexander Heights WA 71 C4
Alexander Morrison Nat Park WA 76 H4
Alexandra VIC 42 G4
Alexandra Bridge WA 73 J13
Alexandra Headland QLD 4 D1 7 E13
Alexandra Hills QLD 5 D8
Alford SA 62 G4 65 G9
Alfords Point NSW 19 H3
Alfred Cove WA 71 H3
Alfred Nat Park VIC 47 C12
Alfred Town NSW 29 H13
Algebuckina Bridge SA 66 E5
Alger Island NT 87 C11
Algester QLD 3 J4
Alice NSW 7 K12 25 C12
Alice QLD 8 H3 13 F13
Alice Springs NT 91 F8
Ali-Curung NT 89 K9 91 A9
Alkata NT 68 A1 79 K14 83 A7 90 J1
Allambie NSW 19 D6
Allans Flat VIC 43 C9
Allansford VIC 38 H7
Allanson WA 73 F9
Alleena NSW 29 E13
Allen Island QLD 10 D3
Allenby Gardens SA 59 F3
Allendale East SA 38 G1 63 B14
Allestree VIC 38 H4
Allies Creek QLD 7 D9
Allora QLD 7 H11
Allworth NSW 23 D11
Alma SA 62 F5 65 H10
Almaden QLD 11 E11
Almonds VIC 42 C6
Almoola QLD 8 C6
Almurta VIC 37 K12 44 F4
Alonnah TAS 53 J10
Aloomba QLD 11 D13
Alpara NT 68 A4 90 K4
Alpha QLD 8 H4 13 F14
Alpine Nat Park VIC 30 J1 43 F10 46 B3
Alpurrurulam NT 12 A1 89 K14 91 A14
Alstonville NSW 7 K13 25 C14
Althorpe Islands SA 63 J8 64 K7
Alton QLD 6 H6
Alton Nat Park QLD 6 H6
Altona VIC 35 E1 36 D6 39 F13 42 K1 44 C1
Altona Meadows VIC 35 E1
Alum Cliffs State Res TAS 54 F7
Alva Beach QLD 8 A6
Alvie VIC 39 H9
Alyangula NT 87 F12
Amamoor QLD 7 D12
Amanbidji NT 86 K2 88 B2
Amaroo ACT 32 A5
Amata SA 68 A4 90 K4
Ambarvale NSW 21 E11
Amberley QLD 5 H9
Ambleside SA 60 H4
Amboola QLD 6 D3
Amboyne VIC 43 G14 47 A9
Ambrose QLD 9 H11
Amby QLD 6 E4
Amelup WA 74 H7
Amen Corner SA 63 J8 65 K8
American River SA 63 H9
Amherst VIC 39 C10
Amity QLD 4 B7 7 G13
Amoonguna NT 91 F8
Amosfield NSW 25 B10
Amphitheatre VIC 39 C9
Ampilatwatja NT 91 C10
Amyton SA 62 F1 65 D9
Anakie QLD 8 H6
Anakie VIC 36 E2 39 F12
Anakie East VIC 36 E2
Anakie Junction VIC 36 D2 39 F12
Ancona VIC 42 F5
Andamooka SA 67 K8
Anderson VIC 44 G3
Anderson Island TAS 55 C9
Ando NSW 30 H3
Andover TAS 53 D11
Andrews QLD 5 B14
Andrews SA 62 F4 65 F10
Anembo NSW 30 F4
Angahook Lorne State Park VIC 39 J11
Angaston SA 60 A7 62 E6 65 H10
Angatja SA 68 A2 90 K3
Angellala QLD 6 D1 13 K14
Angip VIC 40 J5
Angle Vale SA 60 C3
Anglers Rest VIC 43 F11 46 A5
Anglesea VIC 36 K2 39 H11
Angorichina Village SA 65 B10
Angourie NSW 25 E13
Angove Con Park SA 60 E3
Angurugu NT 87 F12
Anna Bay NSW 23 E11
Anne's Corner SA 68 E5
Annerley QLD 3 F4 5 E8
Annuello VIC 28 G5 40 D7
Anser Group VIC 44 K7 46 K1
Anson Bay NT 86 E2
Ansons Bay TAS 55 D14
Antarrengenge NT 91 C9
Antill Plains QLD 8 A5 11 H14
Antill Ponds TAS 53 C11 55 K11
Antwerp VIC 40 K5
Anula NT 84 B3
Anxious Bay SA 64 F4
Aparatjara (new) SA 68 A2 90 K2
Aparatjara (old) SA 68 A2 90 K2
Apollo Bay VIC 39 K10
Appila SA 62 F2 65 E10
Appin NSW 21 E12 23 J8 30 A7
Appin VIC 41 H10
Appin South VIC 41 H10
Apple Tree Flat NSW 22 D6
Applecross WA 71 H3
Apslawn TAS 53 B13 55 J13
Apsley TAS 53 D10
Apsley VIC 38 C2
Aquila Island QLD 9 E9
Arabella QLD 13 K14 15 D14
Arakoola Nature Res NSW 24 D7
Arakoon NSW 25 J12
Arakwal Nat Park NSW 25 B14
Araleun SA 68 A5 90 K5
Araluen NSW 30 E5
Araluen Nature Res NSW 30 E5
Aramac QLD 8 G2 13 E12
Aramara QLD 7 C11
Arana Hills QLD 3 C2
Aranda ACT 32 D4
Ararat VIC 39 D8
Aratula QLD 5 J12 7 H12
Arawata VIC 37 J14
Arcadia NSW 19 A3 20 D6
Arcadia VIC 42 D3
Archdale VIC 39 B9
Archer River Roadhouse QLD 16 G3
Archerfield QLD 3 G3 5 E9
Archies Creek VIC 44 G4
Ardeer VIC 35 D1
Ardglen NSW 23 B8
Ardlethan NSW 29 F12
Ardno VIC 38 F2
Ardrossan SA 62 G5 65 H9
Areyonga NT 90 G6
Argents Hill NSW 25 H12
Argyle WA 73 G10 74 G3
Ariah Park NSW 29 F13
Aringa VIC 38 H5
Arkaroola SA 67 J11
Arkona VIC 40 K5
Arlparra NT 91 C9
Arltunga NT 91 F9
Arltunga Historic Res NT 91 F9
Armadale VIC 35 E4
Armadale WA 72 F4 74 D3
Armatree NSW 22 A3 24 K1
Armidale NSW 25 G9
Armstrong VIC 38 D7
Armuna QLD 8 B6
Armytage VIC 39 H10
Arncliffe NSW 19 G4
Arno Bay SA 62 K4 64 G7
Arnold VIC 39 A10
Arrino WA 76 G4
Artarmon NSW 21 C8
Arthur East WA 73 B10
Arthur Pieman Con Area TAS 54 F2
Arthur Point QLD 9 F9
Arthur River TAS 54 D1
Arthur River WA 73 B9 74 F5
Arthurs Creek VIC 37 A9
Arthurs Lake TAS 53 B9 55 J9
Arthurs Seat State Park VIC 36 J7 39 H14 44 F1
Arthurton SA 62 H5 65 H8
Arthurville NSW 22 D3
Arundel QLD 5 B12
Ascot QLD 3 D4 4 E7
Ascot VIC 39 D10
Ascot WA 71 F5
Ashbourne SA 63 F8 65 K10
Ashbury NSW 21 C9
Ashfield NSW 21 C9
Ashfield WA 71 E5
Ashford NSW 25 D8
Ashgrove QLD 3 D3
Ashley NSW 24 D5
Ashmore QLD 5 B12
Ashton SA 59 G7 60 G4 61 A7
Ashville SA 63 D8 65 K11
Aspen Island ACT 31 C4
Aspendale VIC 37 F8
Aspley QLD 3 B4 4 E7
Aspley VIC 63 A12
Asquith NSW 20 D7
Astrebla Downs Nat Park QLD 12 G5
Athelstone SA 59 E7 60 F3
Atherton QLD 11 D12
Athlone VIC 37 H13 44 E5
Athol Park SA 59 E3
Atitjere NT 91 E10
Atnelyey NT 91 C9
Attadale WA 71 H2
Attunga NSW 24 H7
Aubigny QLD 7 G10
Aubrey VIC 40 K5
Auburn NSW 19 F3 21 D9
Auburn SA 62 F5 65 G10
Auburn River Nat Park QLD 7 C9
Audley NSW 19 K3 21 C10
Augathella QLD 6 C1 13 J14 15 C14
Augusta WA 73 J14 74 H2
Augustus Island WA 80 D7
Auldana SA 59 G6
Aurora Kakadu NT 85 D6 86 D6
Aurukun Community QLD 16 G1
Austinmer NSW 21 C13
Austinville QLD 5 C14
Austral NSW 21 F10
Australia Plains SA 62 E5 65 G11
Australind WA 73 G9
Avalon NSW 20 B6
Avalon Beach VIC 36 F3
Avenel VIC 42 F3
Avenue SA 63 C12
Avisford Nature Res NSW 22 D5
Avoca TAS 53 A12 55 H12
Avoca VIC 39 C9
Avoca Beach NSW 20 B4
Avoid Bay SA 64 H5
Avon SA 62 F5 65 H9
Avon Plains VIC 38 A7
Avon Valley Nat Park WA 72 E2 74 C3 76 K5
Avondale QLD 7 A11 9 K12
Avonsleigh VIC 37 E11
Awabakal Nature Res NSW 23 E10
Axedale VIC 39 B12
Ayr QLD 8 A6
Ayrford VIC 38 J7
Ayton QLD 11 B12

B

Baalijin Nature Res NSW 25 G11
Baan Baa NSW 24 G5
Babel Island TAS 55 B10
Babinda QLD 11 E13
Bacchus Marsh VIC 36 B3 39 E12
Back River Nature Res NSW 23 A9 25 K8
Backstairs Passage SA 61 K1 63 G8
Backwater NSW 25 F10
Baddaginnie VIC 42 D5
Baden TAS 53 D11
Badgebup WA 74 G6
Badger Island TAS 55 C8
Badgerys Creek NSW 21 F9
Badgingarra WA 76 H4
Badgingarra Nat Park WA 76 H4
Badja NSW 30 F4
Badja Swamps Nature Res NSW 30 F4
Badu Island QLD 16 A1
Baerami NSW 23 D8
Baerami Creek NSW 22 D7
Bagdad TAS 53 E10
Bago Bluff Nat Park NSW 23 A13 25 K11
Bagot Well SA 62 E5 65 H10
Bailieston VIC 39 A14 42 E2
Bailup WA 72 E2
Baird Bay SA 64 E3
Bairnsdale VIC 43 K11 45 C13 46 D6
Bajool QLD 9 H10
Bakara SA 62 C6 65 J12
Bakara Con Park SA 62 C6 65 H12
Baker VIC 40 J3
Baker Gully SA 60 J2 61 C6
Baker Lake WA 83 B5
Bakers Creek QLD 9 D8
Bakers Hill WA 72 D2
Bakers Swamp NSW 22 E4
Baking Board QLD 7 E8
Baladjie Lake Nature Res WA 75 A8 77 J8
Balaklava SA 62 F5 65 G9
Balbarrup WA 73 E13
Balcatta WA 71 D3 72 G3
Bald Hills QLD 3 A3
Bald Island WA 74 K7
Bald Knob NSW 25 E10
Bald Knob QLD 4 F2
Bald Rock VIC 28 K7 41 J11
Bald Rock Nat Park NSW 7 K11 25 C10
Baldry NSW 22 E3
Balfe's Creek QLD 8 B3 11 J13
Balfour TAS 54 E2
Balga WA 71 D3
Balgo WA 79 D13
Balgowan SA 62 H5 65 H8
Balgowlah NSW 19 D6 21 B8
Balgownie NSW 21 D14
Balhannah SA 60 G5 62 E7 65 J10
Balingup WA 73 F11 74 G3
Balkuling WA 72 B3
Balladonia WA 83 H2
Balladoran NSW 22 B3
Ballajura WA 71 C5
Ballalaba NSW 30 E4
Ballan VIC 36 B2 39 E11
Ballan North VIC 36 A2
Ballandean QLD 25 B10
Ballangeich VIC 38 H7
Ballarat VIC 39 E10
Ballark VIC 36 C1
Ballbank NSW 28 J7 41 F11
Balldale NSW 29 K11 42 A7
Ballendella VIC 41 K13 42 C1
Balliang VIC 36 D3 39 F12
Balliang East VIC 36 D3 39 F12
Ballidu WA 76 H6
Ballimore NSW 22 C4
Ballina NSW 7 K14 25 C14
Ballina Nature Res NSW 25 C14
Bally Bally WA 72 B4
Balmain NSW 19 F5 21 C8
Balmattum VIC 42 E4
Balmoral NSW 19 E6 21 B8 21 G14
Balmoral QLD 3 E5
Balmoral VIC 38 D4
Balnarring VIC 37 J8 39 H14 44 F2
Balnarring Beach VIC 37 J8
Balook VIC 45 F8 46 G2
Balranald NSW 28 G6 41 C9
Balwyn VIC 35 D5 37 D8
Bamaga QLD 16 B2
Bamarang Nature Res NSW 30 C5
Bamawm VIC 41 K13 42 C1
Bamawm Extension VIC 41 J13 42 B1
Bambaroo QLD 11 G13
Bambill VIC 28 G2 40 B3
Bamboo WA 78 E7 82 C7
Bamboo Spring NT 88 C1
Bamborough Island QLD 9 E10
Bambra VIC 39 H11
Ban Ban Springs QLD 7 C10
Banana QLD 9 K10
Bancroft QLD 7 A9 9 K11
Bandiana VIC 43 B9
Bandon NSW 22 G2
Bandon Grove NSW 23 C10
Banealla SA 63 B9
Bangadilly Nat Park NSW 22 K7 30 B6
Bangalow NSW 7 K13 25 B14
Bangerang VIC 40 J6
Bangham SA 38 A1
Bangham Con Park SA 38 A1 63 A11
Bangholme VIC 35 H6
Bangor NSW 21 C10
Bangor TAS 55 E10 56 D5
Baniyala NT 87 E12
Banks ACT 32 K4
Banks Strait TAS 55 B13
Banksia Beach QLD 4 D4
Banksia Park SA 59 D7
Banksmeadow NSW 19 H6
Bankstown NSW 19 G2 21 D9
Bannaby NSW 22 K6 30 B5
Bannerton VIC 28 G5 40 C7
Bannister NSW 22 K5 30 B4
Bannister WA 72 D6 74 E4
Bannockburn VIC 36 F1 39 G11
Banora Point NSW 5 A14
Banyabba Nature Res NSW 25 D12
Banyan VIC 28 J5 40 G7
Banyan Island NT 87 C10
Banyena VIC 38 A7
Banyenong VIC 41 K8
Banyo QLD 3 C5
Barabon QLD 13 A9
Baradine NSW 24 H3
Barakee Nat Park NSW 23 A11
Barakula QLD 7 D8
Baralaba QLD 9 J9
Baranduda VIC 43 B9
Barcaldine QLD 8 H2 13 F12
Bardoc WA 77 H11 83 F1
Bardoc Mine WA 77 G10
Bardon QLD 3 E3
Barduthulla QLD 13 K14 15 C14
Barellan NSW 29 F12
Barfold VIC 39 C12
Bargara QLD 7 A12 9 K13
Bargo NSW 21 F13 22 J7 30 A7
Bargo State Con Area NSW 21 G14
Barham NSW 28 J7 41 G11
Baring VIC 40 F5
Baringhup VIC 39 C11
Barjarg VIC 42 F5
Bark Hut Inn NT 85 D4 86 E5
Barkly Homestead NT 89 H11
Barkstead VIC 39 E11
Barlee WA 73 G13
Barlee Range Nature Res WA 78 G3 82 G1
Barmah VIC 29 K9 41 H14 42 A2
Barmah Island VIC 41 H14 42 A2
Barmah State Park VIC 41 H14 42 A2
Barmedman NSW 29 F13
Barmera SA 62 B5 65 H13
Barmundu QLD 9 J11
Barnawartha VIC 43 B8
Barnes Bay TAS 50 H6 53 H10
Barneys Lake NSW 28 D7
Barongarook VIC 39 J10
Barooga NSW 29 K10 42 A4
Barool Nat Park NSW 25 E11
Baroota SA 62 G2 65 E9
Barossa Valley SA 60 A6
Barpinba VIC 39 G10
Barraba NSW 24 G7
Barrabool VIC 36 G2 39 G11
Barradale WA 78 G2
Barramunga VIC 39 J10
Barranyi (North Island) Nat Park NT 87 J13 89 A13
Barraport VIC 41 J10
Barratta QLD 8 A5
Barren Grounds Nature Res NSW 23 K8 30 C7
Barrington NSW 23 B11
Barrington TAS 54 F7
Barrington Tops Nat Park NSW 23 C10
Barringun NSW 15 K13 27 B10
Barrogan NSW 22 F3
Barron Gorge Nat Park QLD 11 D12
Barron Island NT 85 B5 86 C6
Barrow Creek NT 91 B8
Barrow Island WA 78 E2
Barrow Island Nature Res WA 78 E3
Barry NSW 22 G5 23 A10 25 K8
Barrys Beach VIC 44 H7 46 H1
Barrys Reef VIC 39 E12
Barton ACT 31 D3 32 E5
Barton SA 68 H6
Barton VIC 38 D7
Barton Nature Res NSW 22 F4
Barton Siding SA 66 K1
Barunga NT 85 J7 86 G7
Barunga Gap SA 62 G4 65 G9
Barwell Con Park SA 64 F5
Barwell Con Res SA 64 F5
Barwon Downs VIC 39 J10
Barwon Heads VIC 36 H4 39 H12
Baryulgil NSW 25 D12
Bascombe Well Con Park SA 64 F5
Bascombe Well Con Res SA 64 G5
Basket Range SA 60 G4
Basket Swamp Nat Park NSW 7 K11 25 C11
Bass VIC 37 K11 44 F3
Bass Hill NSW 21 D9
Bass Landing VIC 37 K11
Bass Strait 39 K12 44 K5 54 B3 56 A3
Bassendean WA 71 E6
Batchelor NT 85 E2 86 E4
Batchica VIC 40 J6
Bateau Bay NSW 20 B3
Batehaven NSW 30 F6
Batemans Bay NSW 30 F5
Batesford VIC 39 G12
Bathumi VIC 42 B6
Bathurst NSW 22 F5
Bathurst Bay QLD 16 H5
Bathurst Island NT 86 B2
Batlow NSW 29 J14 30 E1
Battery Point TAS 49 C2
Bauhinia QLD 9 K8
Baulkham Hills NSW 19 D2 21 E8
Bauple QLD 7 C12
Baw Baw Nat Park VIC 42 K6 44 B7 46 D1
Bawley Point NSW 30 E6
Baxter VIC 37 G9
Bay of Fires Con Res TAS 55 E14
Bay of Islands Coastal Park VIC 38 J7
Bayles VIC 37 G12 44 E4
Bayley Island QLD 10 D3
Baynton VIC 39 C13 42 G1
Bayswater VIC 35 E7 37 D9
Bayswater WA 71 E5
Bayulu WA 79 B11 81 J9
Bayview NSW 19 B7 20 B6
Bayview Haven NT 84 D2
Beachamp VIC 41 G9
Beachmere QLD 4 E5
Beachport SA 63 C13
Beachport Con Park SA 63 C13
Beacon WA 76 H7
Beaconsfield NSW 19 G5
Beaconsfield TAS 55 E8 56 D2
Beaconsfield VIC 37 F10 44 D3
Beaconsfield Upper VIC 37 F11
Beagle Bay WA 79 A9 80 F4
Beagle Gulf NT 85 B1 86 C3
Bealiba VIC 39 B9
Bearbung NSW 22 A4 24 K2
Beardmore VIC 42 K7 45 C8 46 D2
Beargamil NSW 22 E2
Bearii VIC 42 A3
Bears Lagoon VIC 41 K11
Beatrice Island NT 87 H11
Beaudesert QLD 5 E12 7 H13
Beaufort VIC 39 E9
Beaufort WA 73 B10
Beaumaris TAS 55 F14
Beaumont SA 59 H5
Beaumont Nature Res WA 75 F14 83 J2
Beauty Point TAS 55 E9 56 D2
Beazleys Bridge VIC 39 A8
Bebeah NSW 20 D1
Beckenham WA 71 H6
Beckom NSW 29 F12
Bedarra Island QLD 11 F13
Bedford WA 71 E4
Bedford Park SA 59 K3
Bedgerebong NSW 22 F1 29 D14
Bedourie QLD 12 G4
Bedunburra WA 79 B9 80 H5
Beeac VIC 39 H10
Beech Forest VIC 39 J10
Beechboro WA 71 D5
Beechford TAS 55 D9 56 B3
Beechmont QLD 5 D14
Beechwood NSW 23 A13 25 K11
Beechworth VIC 43 C8
Beechworth Historic Park VIC 43 C8
Beecroft NSW 20 D7
Beecroft Head NSW 30 D7
Beedelup Nat Park WA 73 F14 74 J3
Beekeepers Nature Res WA 76 G3
Beela WA 73 F9
Beenak VIC 37 D12
Beenleigh QLD 5 D10 7 G13
Beerburrum QLD 4 F3 7 F13
Beerwah QLD 4 F2 7 E12
Bees Nest Nature Res NSW 30 C5
Bega NSW 30 H5
Beggan Beggan NSW 22 K2 30 B1
Beilpajah NSW 28 C6
Bejoording WA 72 D1
Belair SA 59 J4 60 H2 61 B6
Belair Nat Park SA 59 J5 60 H3 61 B7
Belalie North SA 62 E2 65 E10
Belaringar NSW 22 B1 27 J13
Belbora NSW 23 C12
Belconnen ACT 30 D3 32 C3
Belconnen Town Centre ACT 32 C3
Beldon WA 71 A1
Belford Nat Park NSW 23 D9
Belgrave VIC 37 E10 42 K3 44 C3
Bell NSW 22 G7
Bell QLD 7 E10
Bell Bay TAS 55 D9 56 C2
Bellambi NSW 21 C13
Bellara QLD 4 D4
Bellarine VIC 36 G5 39 G13
Bellarwi NSW 29 F13
Bellata NSW 24 E5

Bellbird – Broomehill 93

Bellbird NSW 23 E9
Bellbird Creek VIC 47 D10
Bellbird Park QLD 5 F9
Bellbrae VIC 36 J2 39 H12
Bellbridge VIC 43 B9
Bellbrook NSW 25 H11
Bellenden Ker QLD 11 D13
Bellerive TAS 50 C6 53 F11
Bellevue WA 71 E7
Bellevue Heights SA 59 K4 60 H2 61 B6
Bellingen NSW 25 G12
Bellinger River Nat Park NSW 25 G12
Bellingham TAS 55 D10 56 B5
Bellmere QLD 4 F4
Bellmount Forest NSW 30 C3
Belltrees NSW 23 B9
Belmont NSW 23 F10
Belmont QLD 3 F6
Belmont VIC 36 G2
Belmont WA 71 F5
Belmore NSW 19 G4 21 C9
Belmunging WA 72 B3
Beloka NSW 30 H2
Belowra NSW 30 G4
Belrose NSW 20 B7
Belsar Island VIC 40 C7
Beltana SA 65 A10 67 K10
Beltana Roadhouse SA 65 A10 67 K10
Belton SA 65 D10
Belyando Crossing QLD 8 E5 13 B14
Belyuen NT 85 C1 86 D3
Bemboka NSW 30 H4
Bemm River VIC 47 D10
Ben Boyd Nat Park NSW 30 J5 47 A14
Ben Bullen NSW 22 F6
Ben Halls Gap Nat Park NSW 23 A9
Ben Lomond NSW 25 F9
Ben Lomond Nat Park TAS 55 G12
Bena NSW 29 D13
Bena VIC 37 K13 44 F5
Benalla VIC 42 D5
Benambra VIC 43 F11
Benambra Nat Park NSW 29 K13 43 A9
Benandarah NSW 30 E6
Benaraby QLD 9 J11
Benayeo VIC 38 C2
Bencubbin WA 74 A6 76 J7
Bendalong NSW 30 D6
Bendeela NSW 22 K7 30 C6
Bendemeer NSW 25 H8
Bendick Murrell NSW 22 J3 30 A2
Bendidee Nat Park QLD 7 H8 24 A7
Bendigo VIC 39 B12
Bendoc VIC 30 K3 47 A10
Bendoc North VIC 47 A11
Bendoc Upper VIC 30 K3
Bendolba NSW 23 D10
Beneree NSW 22 G4
Benetook VIC 28 F3 40 B4
Benger WA 73 G9
Bengerang NSW 6 K6 24 C4
Bengworden VIC 45 C12 46 E5
Beni NSW 22 C4
Benjeroop VIC 41 F10
Benjinup WA 73 E11
Benlidi QLD 8 K2 13 G11
Bennison Island VIC 44 H7 46 J1
Benowa QLD 5 B13
Bensville NSW 20 B4
Bentinck Island QLD 10 D3
Bentley NSW 25 B13
Bentley WA 71 H5
Bentleys Plain VIC 43 G12 46 B7
Benwerrin VIC 39 J11
Berajondo QLD 9 K12
Berala NSW 21 D9
Berambing NSW 20 J7 22 G7
Beremboke VIC 36 C2
Beresfield NSW 23 E10
Beresford SA 66 G7
Bergalia NSW 30 F5
Berkeley Vale NSW 20 B3
Berkshire Park NSW 20 F7
Bermaguee Nature Res NSW 30 H5
Bermagui NSW 30 H5
Bermagui South NSW 30 H5
Bernacchi TAS 53 A8 55 H8
Bernier and Dorre Island Nature Res WA 76 A1 78 J1
Bernier Island WA 76 A1 78 J1
Berowra NSW 19 A4 20 C6
Berowra Heights NSW 19 A5
Berowra Valley Regional Park NSW 19 A4 20 D7
Berowra Waters NSW 20 D6
Berri SA 28 F1 62 B5 65 H13
Berridale NSW 30 G2
Berriedale TAS 50 B5
Berrigan NSW 29 J10
Berrilee NSW 20 D6
Berrima NSW 22 K7 30 B6
Berringa VIC 39 F10
Berringama VIC 43 C11
Berriwillock VIC 28 J5 41 G8
Berrook VIC 28 H1 40 D1 62 A7 65 J13
Berry NSW 30 C7
Berry Springs NT 85 D2 86 D4
Berrybank VIC 39 G9
Berwick VIC 37 F10 44 D3
Bessiebelle VIC 38 H5
Bet Bet VIC 39 B10
Beta QLD 8 H4 13 F13
Bete Bolong VIC 43 K14 47 D8
Bethanga VIC 43 B9
Bethania QLD 3 K6
Bethany SA 60 B6
Bethungra NSW 22 K1 29 G14
Betoota QLD 12 J5 14 C3 67 A14
Betsey Island TAS 51 G8 53 G11
Beulah TAS 54 F7
Beulah VIC 28 K4 40 H6
Beulah East VIC 40 H6
Beulah Park SA 59 G5
Beulah West VIC 40 H5
Bevendale NSW 22 K4 30 B3
Beverford VIC 28 H6 41 E9
Beveridge VIC 39 E14 42 H2
Beveridge Station (site) VIC 43 F9
Beverley WA 72 C4 74 D4
Beverly Hills NSW 19 G4 21 C9
Bewong NSW 30 D6
Bews SA 63 B8 65 K12
Bexhill NSW 25 B13
Bexley NSW 21 C9
Beyal VIC 40 J7
BHP 10 Yandicoogina Mine WA 78 F6 82 F5
Biala NSW 22 K4 30 B3
Biamanga Nat Park NSW 30 H5
Bibbenluke NSW 30 J3
Biboohra QLD 11 D12
Bibra Lake WA 71 K3
Bicheno TAS 53 A14 55 H14
Bickerton Island NT 87 F12
Bicton WA 71 H2
Biddaddaba QLD 5 D12
Biddon NSW 22 A4 24 K2
Bidgeemia NSW 29 J11
Bidijul WA 79 C11 81 J8
Bidyadanga (Lagrange) WA 79 C8 80 J2
Big Bush Nature Res NSW 29 F13
Big Desert Wilderness Park VIC 28 J2 40 G2 63 A9 65 K14
Big Green Island TAS 55 C9
Big Heath Con Park SA 63 B12
Big Pats Creek VIC 37 C13
Bigga NSW 22 H4 30 A3
Biggara VIC 43 C13
Biggenden QLD 7 B11
Biggs Flat SA 60 H4
Biggs Island WA 81 B8
Bilambil NSW 5 B14 25 A14
Bilbaringa SA 60 C4
Bilgola NSW 20 B6
Billiatt Con Park SA 28 H1 62 B7 65 J13
Billiluna (Mindibungu) WA 79 D13
Billimari NSW 22 G3
Billinga QLD 5 A14
Billinooka WA 78 G7
Billinudgel Nature Res NSW 25 B14
Billinudgell NSW 25 B14
Billys Creek NSW 25 F11
Biloela QLD 9 J10
Bilpin NSW 20 J6 23 G8
Bilyana QLD 11 F13
Bimberamala Nat Park NSW 30 E6
Bimbi NSW 22 H2 29 E14
Binalong NSW 22 K3 30 B2
Binalong Bay TAS 55 E14
Binaronca Nature Res WA 75 C13 77 K11 83 G1
Binbee QLD 8 B6
Binda NSW 22 J5 30 A4
Bindango QLD 6 E4
Bindarri Nat Park NSW 25 G12
Bindi VIC 43 G12 46 A7
Bindi Bindi WA 76 H5
Bindoon WA 72 F1 74 B3 76 K5
Bingara NSW 24 E7
Bingil Bay QLD 11 E13
Binginwarri VIC 45 G8 46 H2
Biniguy NSW 24 D6
Binjour QLD 7 B10
Binjura Nature Res NSW 30 G3
Binna Burra QLD 5 D14 7 H13 25 A13
Binnaway NSW 22 A5 24 K4
Binnaway Nature Res NSW 22 A5 24 K4
Binningup WA 73 G9 74 F2
Binnu WA 76 E3
Binnum SA 38 B1 63 A11
Binya NSW 29 F11
Birany Birany NT 87 D12
Birchip VIC 28 K5 40 H7
Birchs Bay TAS 50 J4 53 H10
Bird Island TAS 54 B1
Birdsville QLD 12 K3 14 C1 67 A11
Birdwood NSW 23 A12 25 K11
Birdwood SA 60 E6 62 E6 65 J10
Birdwoodton VIC 28 F3 40 A4
Biriwal Bulga Nat Park NSW 23 A12 25 K10
Birkdale QLD 3 F7 5 D8
Birkenhead SA 59 D1
Birnam Range QLD 5 E12
Birralee QLD 8 C6
Birralee TAS 55 F8 56 G2
Birrego NSW 29 H12
Birregurra VIC 39 H10
Birri Lodge QLD 10 C3
Birriwa NSW 22 C5
Birrong NSW 19 F2
Birru QLD 5 J9
Bishops Nature Res WA 75 F12 83 J1
Bishopsbourne TAS 55 G9 56 J3
Bittern VIC 37 J9
Black Andrew Nature Res NSW 30 C2
Black Forest SA 59 H3
Black Hill SA 62 D6 65 J11
Black Hill Con Park SA 59 E7 60 F3
Black Hills TAS 50 A2 53 F9
Black Jungle Con Res NT 85 C2 86 D4
Black Mountain NSW 25 G9
Black Mountain Nat Park QLD 11 B12 16 K6
Black Point NT 86 B5
Black Range State Park VIC 38 C5
Black River TAS 54 C3
Black Rock SA 62 E2 65 E10
Black Rock VIC 35 G4 36 E7
Black Rock Con Park SA 62 E1 65 E10
Black Springs NSW 22 H6
Black Springs SA 62 E4 65 G10
Black Swamp NSW 25 C11
Blackall QLD 8 J3 13 G12
Blackbraes Nat Park QLD 8 A1 11 H10
Blackbull QLD 10 F7
Blackburn VIC 35 D6
Blackbutt QLD 7 E11
Blackdown Tableland Nat Park QLD 9 H8
Blackfellows Caves SA 63 B14
Blackheath NSW 21 K8 22 G7
Blackmans Bay TAS 50 F6 53 G10
Blacksmith Island QLD 9 C8
Blackstone (Papulankutja) WA 79 K13 83 B7
Blacktown NSW 19 D1 21 E8
Blackville NSW 22 A7
Blackwater QLD 9 H8
Blackwood SA 59 K4 60 H3 61 B6 62 F7 65 J10
Blackwood VIC 39 E12
Blackwood Creek TAS 53 A9 55 H9
Blackwood Forest VIC 37 K12
Blackwood Nat Park QLD 8 D5 13 B14
Bladensburg Nat Park QLD 13 D9
Blair Athol QLD 8 F6
Blair Athol SA 59 E4
Blairgowrie VIC 36 J6
Blakehurst NSW 19 H4 21 C10
Blakeview SA 60 C3
Blakeville VIC 36 A2 39 E11
Blakney Creek NSW 22 K4 30 B3
Blanchetown SA 62 D5 65 H11
Bland NSW 22 H1 29 E13
Blandford NSW 23 B9
Blanket Flat NSW 22 J4 30 A3
Blaxland NSW 21 H8 23 G8
Blaxlands Ridge NSW 20 G6
Blayney NSW 22 G5
Blessington TAS 55 G11
Blewitt Springs SA 60 K2 61 D6
Bligh Park NSW 20 F7
Blighty NSW 29 J9
Blinman SA 65 B10
Bloods Creek SA 66 A4 91 K9
Bloods Range (Puntitjata) NT 79 J14 90 H1
Bloomfield QLD 11 B12
Bloomsbury QLD 8 C7
Blow Clear NSW 22 E1 29 C14 29 E13
Blue Bay NSW 20 A3
Blue Lake Nat Park QLD 5 B8 7 G14
Blue Mountains Nat Park NSW 21 H9 22 H7 30 A5
Blue Mud Bay NT 87 F11
Blue Rocks TAS 55 B9
Bluewater QLD 8 A4 11 H14
Bluewater Springs Roadhouse QLD 8 A3 11 H13
Bluff QLD 9 H8
Bluff River Nature Res NSW 25 C10
Blyth SA 62 F4 65 G10
Blythdale QLD 6 E5
Boambee NSW 25 G13
Boat Harbour TAS 54 D4
Boat Harbour Beach TAS 54 C4
Boatswain Point SA 63 D12
Bobadah NSW 27 K12 29 A12
Bobbin Head NSW 19 A5 20 C6
Bobin NSW 23 B12
Bobundara Nature Res NSW 30 H3
Bodalla NSW 30 G5
Bodallin WA 75 B8 77 J8
Bodangora NSW 22 D4
Boddington WA 72 D7 74 E4
Bogan Gate NSW 22 E1 29 C14
Bogandyera Nature Res NSW 29 K14 30 F1 43 A12
Bogangar NSW 25 A14
Bogantungan QLD 8 H5
Bogee NSW 22 E7
Boggabilla NSW 6 J7 24 B6
Boggabri NSW 24 H5
Boginderra Hills Nature Res NSW 22 J1 29 F13
Bogolong Creek NSW 22 H2 29 E14
Bogong VIC 43 E10
Boho VIC 42 E5
Boho South VIC 42 E5
Boigbeat VIC 40 G7
Boinka VIC 28 H2 40 E3
Boisdale VIC 43 K9 45 C10 46 E4
Bokal WA 73 C10
Bokarina QLD 4 D1
Bolgart WA 74 B4 76 J5
Bolinda VIC 39 D13 42 H1
Bolivar SA 59 B4 60 D2
Bolivia NSW 25 D10
Bolivia Hill Nature Res NSW 25 D10
Bollanolla Nature Res NSW 25 H12
Bollon QLD 6 H2
Bolton VIC 28 H5 40 D7
Boltons Beach Con Area TAS 53 D13
Bolwarra VIC 38 H4
Bolwarrah VIC 36 A1 39 E11
Bomaderry NSW 30 C7
Bombala NSW 30 J3
Bombo NSW 23 K8 30 B7
Bomera NSW 22 A6 24 K5
Bonalbo NSW 7 K12 25 B12
Bonang VIC 30 K2 47 A10
Bonbeach VIC 37 F8
Bondi NSW 19 F7 21 B8
Bondi Gulf Nature Res NSW 30 K3 47 A11
Bondi Junction NSW 19 F6
Bonegilla VIC 29 K12 43 B9
Boneo VIC 36 K7
Bongaree QLD 4 D4 7 F13
Bongil Bongil Nat Park NSW 25 G13
Bonnells Bay NSW 20 B1
Bonnet Bay NSW 19 J3
Bonnie Doon VIC 42 F5
Bonnie Rock WA 76 H7
Bonnie Vale WA 75 A12 77 J11
Bonny Hills NSW 23 A13
Bonnyrigg NSW 21 E9
Bonogin QLD 5 C14
Bonshaw NSW 7 K9 25 C8
Bonville NSW 25 G12
Bonya (Orrtipa-Thurra) NT 91 D12
Bonython ACT 32 J3
Booborowie SA 62 G3 65 F10
Boobyalla TAS 55 C12
Booderee Nat Park ACT 30 D7
Boodie Island WA 78 E2
Boodjamulla (Lawn Hill) Nat Park QLD 10 G2
Bookabie SA 64 C1 68 K6
Bookaloo SA 65 C8
Bookar VIC 39 G8
Booker Bay NSW 20 B5
Bookham NSW 30 C2
Bookin QLD 10 K6 12 A6
Bool Lagoon SA 38 D1 63 B12
Boolading WA 73 D9
Boolarra VIC 44 F7 46 G1
Boolba QLD 6 H3
Boolburra QLD 9 H9
Boolcunda SA 65 D9
Booleroo Centre SA 62 F2 65 E10
Booligal NSW 29 E8
Boolite VIC 40 K7
Boomi NSW 6 J6 24 B4
Boomi Nature Res NSW 24 B4
Boomi West Nature Res NSW 24 B4
Boonah QLD 5 H12 7 H12
Boonanarring Nature Res WA 74 B3 76 J5
Boonanghi Nature Res NSW 25 J11
Boonarga QLD 7 E8
Boondall QLD 3 B5 4 E7
Boondooma QLD 7 D9
Boonmoo QLD 11 D12
Boonoo Boonoo NSW 25 C10
Boonoo Boonoo Nat Park NSW 7 K11 25 B11
Boonooroo QLD 7 C13
Boorabbin WA 75 B10 77 J10
Boorabbin Nat Park WA 75 A10 77 J9
Booragoon WA 71 J3
Booral NSW 23 D11
Boorcan VIC 39 H8
Boorganna Nature Res NSW 23 A12
Boorhaman VIC 42 C6
Boorindal NSW 27 E11
Boorndoolyanna SA 68 A5 90 K6
Boorongie North VIC 28 H4 40 E6
Booroolong Nature Res NSW 25 G9
Booroopki VIC 38 B2
Booroorban NSW 29 G8 41 D13
Boorowa NSW 22 J3 30 B2
Boort VIC 28 K6 41 J10
Boosey VIC 42 B5
Booti Booti Nat Park NSW 23 C13
Booyal QLD 7 B11
Bopeechee SA 67 H8
Boppy Mount NSW 27 H11
Borallon QLD 5 H8
Borambil NSW 22 B6
Borambola NSW 29 H14
Boraning WA 73 C8
Borda Island WA 81 B9
Borden WA 74 H7
Border Island QLD 9 B8
Border Ranges Nat Park NSW 7 J12 25 A12
Border Store NT 85 C7 86 D7
Borderdale WA 73 A12
Bordertown SA 40 K1 63 B10
Boree NSW 22 F4
Boree QLD 13 A10
Boree Creek NSW 29 H12
Boreen Point QLD 7 D13
Boro NSW 30 D4
Boronga Nature Res NSW 24 B5
Boronia VIC 37 D9
Boronia Heights QLD 3 K4
Boroobin QLD 4 G2
Bororen QLD 9 J11
Borrika SA 62 C7 65 J12
Borroloola NT 87 K12 89 B12
Borung VIC 41 K10
Boscabel WA 73 B11
Bossley Park NSW 21 E9
Bostobrick NSW 25 G11
Boston Island SA 64 H6
Botany NSW 19 H6 21 B9
Botany Bay NSW 19 H5 21 B9
Botany Bay Nat Park NSW 19 J6 21 B10 23 H9
Bothwell TAS 53 D9
Boucaut Bay NT 87 C9
Bouddi Nat Park NSW 20 B5 23 G10
Boulder WA 75 A12 77 J11 83 F1
Bouldercombe QLD 9 H10
Boulia QLD 12 E4
Boundain WA 73 A8
Boundary Bend VIC 28 G5 41 C8
Bountiful Island QLD 10 D4
Bourke NSW 27 E10
Bournda Nat Park NSW 30 J5
Bow NSW 22 C7
Bowden SA 58 A1
Bowelling WA 73 D10 74 F4
Bowen QLD 8 B7
Bowen Mountain NSW 20 H7
Bowen Park NSW 22 F4
Bowenvale VIC 39 C10
Bowenville QLD 7 F10
Bower SA 62 D5 65 G11
Boweya VIC 42 C6
Bowhill SA 62 D7 65 J11
Bowillia SA 62 F4 65 G9
Bowling Alley Point NSW 23 A9 25 K8
Bowling Green Bay QLD 8 A5
Bowling Green Bay Nat Park QLD 8 A6
Bowman QLD 9 F9
Bowmans SA 62 F5 65 H9
Bowna NSW 29 K13 43 A10
Bowning NSW 22 K4 30 C2
Bowral NSW 22 K7 30 B6
Bowraville NSW 25 H12
Box Hill NSW 20 F7
Box Hill VIC 35 D6 37 D9 39 F14 42 K2 44 B2
Boxwood Hill WA 75 H8
Boyacup WA 73 A13
Boyagarring Con Park WA 72 D5
Boyagin Nature Res WA 72 C6 74 D4
Boyanup WA 73 G10 74 G3
Boydtown NSW 30 K5 47 A14
Boyeo VIC 40 K3
Boyer TAS 50 A3 53 F10
Boyland QLD 5 D12
Boyne Island QLD 9 J11
Boynedale QLD 9 J11
Boyup Brook WA 73 E11 74 G4
Bracalba QLD 4 G4
Brachina SA 65 B10
Bracken Ridge QLD 3 A4 4 E6
Brackendale NSW 25 J9
Bracknell TAS 55 G9 56 K3
Bradbury NSW 21 E11
Bradbury SA 60 H4 61 B7
Braddon ACT 32 D5
Bradvale VIC 39 F9
Braefield NSW 23 A8 24 K7
Braeside VIC 35 H5 37 F8
Brahma Lodge SA 59 B5
Braidwood NSW 30 E5
Bramfield SA 64 F4
Brampton Island QLD 9 C8
Brampton Islands Nat Park QLD 9 C8
Bramston Beach QLD 11 E13
Bramwell Junction QLD 16 D2
Brandon QLD 8 A5
Brandy Creek VIC 37 G14
Branxholm TAS 55 E12
Branxholme VIC 38 F4
Branxton NSW 23 D10
Brawlin NSW 22 K2 29 G14 30 B1
Bray Junction SA 63 C12
Braybrook VIC 35 C1
Brayfield SA 64 G6
Brayton NSW 22 K6 30 B5
Brazendale Island TAS 53 B9 55 J9
Breadalbane NSW 30 C4
Breadalbane TAS 55 G10 56 H5
Break O'Day VIC 42 H3
Breakaway Ridge Nature Res WA 75 F8
Breakfast Creek NSW 22 D6 22 J3 30 A2
Breaksea Island TAS 52 J5
Bream Creek TAS 51 B12 53 F12
Breamlea VIC 36 H3
Bredbo NSW 30 F3
Breelong NSW 22 B4
Breeza NSW 24 J6
Bremer Bay WA 75 H9
Bremer Island NT 87 C13
Brendale QLD 3 A3
Brentwood SA 62 H6 65 J8
Brentwood VIC 40 H5
Breona TAS 53 A8 55 H8
Bretti NSW 23 B11
Bretti Nature Res NSW 23 B11
Brewarrina NSW 27 D12
Brewer NSW 29 D11
Brewster VIC 39 E9
Briaba QLD 8 C6
Briagolong VIC 43 K9 45 C11 46 D4
Bribbaree NSW 22 H1 29 F14
Bribie Island QLD 4 D3 7 F13
Bribie Island Nat Park QLD 4 E3 7 F13
Bridge Creek VIC 42 F6
Bridgeman Downs QLD 3 B3
Bridgenorth TAS 55 F9 56 F4
Bridgetown WA 73 F12 74 H3
Bridgewater SA 60 H4
Bridgewater TAS 50 A5 53 F10
Bridgewater VIC 39 A11
Bridport TAS 55 D11 56 B7
Brigalow QLD 7 E9
Bright VIC 43 E9
Brighton QLD 3 A4 4 E6
Brighton SA 59 K2 60 H1 61 B5 62 F7 65 J10
Brighton TAS 53 F10
Brighton VIC 35 F3 36 E7
Brighton-Le-Sands NSW 19 H5 21 B9
Brightview QLD 5 K8
Brightwaters NSW 20 B1
Brim VIC 40 J6
Brimbago SA 63 B10
Brimboal VIC 38 D3
Brimpaen VIC 38 C5
Brindabella NSW 30 D2
Brindabella Nat Park NSW 30 D2
Brinerville NSW 25 G11
Bringalbert VIC 38 B2
Bringelly NSW 21 F10
Bringung NT 87 H8
Brinkin NT 84 A2
Brinkley SA 62 E7 65 K11
Brinkworth SA 62 F4 65 G9
Brisbane QLD 3 E4 5 E8 7 G13
Brisbane CBD QLD 2
Brisbane Forest Park QLD 3 D1 4 G7
Brisbane Ranges Nat Park VIC 36 D2 39 F12
Brisbane Water Nat Park NSW 20 C5 23 G9
Brit Brit VIC 38 E4
Britannia Creek VIC 37 C12
Brittons Swamp TAS 54 C2
Brixton QLD 8 H2 13 E11
Broad Arrow WA 77 H11 83 F1
Broad Sound QLD 9 F9
Broad Sound Island Nat Park QLD 9 E9
Broadbeach QLD 5 B13 7 H13
Broadford VIC 39 C14 42 G2
Broadmarsh TAS 53 E10
Broadmeadows SA 60 D3
Broadmeadows VIC 35 B3 36 B7
Broadmont QLD 9 H10
Broadwater NSW 7 K13 25 C14
Broadwater VIC 38 G5
Broadwater Nat Park NSW 7 K13 25 C14
Brocklehurst NSW 22 C3
Brocklesby NSW 29 J12 43 A8
Brockman WA 73 F14
Brockman Mine WA 78 F4 82 F2
Brockman Nat Park WA 74 J3
Brodribb River VIC 43 K14 47 D9
Brogo NSW 30 H5
Broke NSW 23 E9
Broken Bay NSW 20 B5 23 G9
Broken Hill NSW 26 J2 28 A2 65 C14
Bromby Islands NT 87 C12
Bromelton QLD 5 F12
Brompton SA 59 F3
Bromus WA 75 D13 83 H1
Bronte NSW 21 B9
Bronte Park TAS 52 C7 54 K7
Bronzewing VIC 28 H4 40 E6
Brookdale NSW 29 H12
Brooker SA 64 G6
Brookfield NSW 23 D11
Brookfield QLD 3 E1 5 G8
Brookfield Con Park SA 62 D5 65 H11
Brookhampton WA 73 F11
Brooking Gorge Con Park WA 79 B11 81 H8
Brooklands QLD 5 F11
Brooklyn NSW 20 C5
Brooklyn VIC 35 D1
Brooklyn Park SA 59 G3
Brooks Creek NT 85 F3 86 E4
Brooksby VIC 38 C4
Brookstead QLD 7 G10
Brookton WA 72 B5 74 D5
Brookvale NSW 19 D6 20 B7
Brookville VIC 43 H11 46 B6
Brooloo QLD 7 E12
Brooman NSW 30 E6
Broome WA 79 B8 80 H3
Broomehill WA 74 G6

94 Brooms Head – Cathundral

Brooms Head NSW 25 E13
Brooweena QLD 7 C11
Broughton VIC 40 J2
Broughton Island NSW 23 D12
Broula NSW 22 H3
Broulee NSW 30 F6
Brovinia QLD 7 C9
Brownlow SA 62 D5 65 H11
Brownlow Hill NSW 21 F11
Browns Creek NSW 22 G4
Browns Plains QLD 3 K4 5 E10
Bruarong VIC 43 C8
Bruce ACT 32 C4
Bruce SA 62 F1 65 D9
Bruce Rock WA 74 C7 76 K7
Brucknell VIC 39 J8
Bruinbun NSW 22 F5
Brukunga SA 60 H6
Brungle NSW 30 D1
Brunswick VIC 35 C3 36 C7
Brunswick Bay WA 80 C7
Brunswick Heads NSW 7 J14 25 B14
Brunswick Junction WA 73 G9 74 F3
Bruthen VIC 43 K12 45 B14 46 D7
Bryden QLD 4 J6
Buangor VIC 39 D8
Bucasia QLD 9 D8
Buccarumbi NSW 25 E11
Buccleuch SA 63 C8 65 K12
Buchan VIC 43 J13 47 C8
Buchan South VIC 43 J13 47 C8
Bucheen Creek VIC 43 D11
Buchfelde SA 60 B3
Buckaroo NSW 22 D6
Buckenderra NSW 30 G2
Bucketty NSW 20 E1 23 F9
Buckingham SA 63 B10
Buckingham WA 73 E10
Buckland TAS 53 E12
Buckland VIC 43 E8
Buckland Junction VIC 43 F8
Buckleboo SA 64 E6
Buckley VIC 36 H1 39 H11
Buckley Swamp VIC 38 F5
Buckrabanyule VIC 41 K9
Budawang Nat Park NSW 30 E5
Buddabaddah NSW 27 J13
Buddawarka NT 87 G9
Budderoo Nat Park NSW 23 K8 30 B7
Buddigower NSW 29 E12
Buddigower Nature Res NSW 29 E12
Buddina QLD 4 D1
Buderim QLD 4 E1 7 E13
Budgee Budgee NSW 22 D6
Budgeree VIC 44 F7 46 G1
Budgerum VIC 41 H9
Budgerum East VIC 41 H10
Budgewoi NSW 20 A2 23 F10
Buenba Flat (site) VIC 43 E12
Buff Point NSW 20 A2
Buffalo VIC 44 G6
Buffalo River VIC 43 E8
Bugaldie NSW 24 J3
Bugan Nature Res NSW 23 A11
Bugilbone NSW 24 F2
Bugong Nat Park NSW 30 C6
Builyan QLD 9 K11
Bukalong NSW 30 J3
Bukkulla NSW 25 D8
Bulahdelah NSW 23 D12
Bulanjarr (Mowla Bluff) WA 79 C10 80 J5
Bulart VIC 38 E4
Buldah VIC 47 B11
Bulga NSW 23 D9
Bulgandry NSW 29 J12
Bulimba QLD 3 D4 5 E8
Bull Creek WA 71 J4
Bull Swamp VIC 37 H14
Bulla NT 86 J2 88 A2
Bulla VIC 35 A1 36 B6 39 E13 42 J1 44 A1
Bullabulling WA 75 A11 77 J10
Bullaburra NSW 21 J9
Bullagreen NSW 22 A2 24 K1 27 H14
Bullarah NSW 24 D3
Bullarook VIC 39 E11
Bullarto VIC 39 D11
Bullea Lake NSW 26 E2
Bulleen VIC 37 C8
Bullen Range Nature Res ACT 32 H1
Bullenbung NSW 29 H12
Bullengarook VIC 36 A4
Bulleringa Nat Park QLD 11 E10
Bullfinch WA 75 A8 77 J8
Bullhead Creek VIC 43 C10
Bulli NSW 21 C13 23 J8 30 B7
Bullio NSW 22 J7 30 A6
Bullioh VIC 29 K13 43 B10
Bullock Creek QLD 11 E11
Bullsbrook WA 72 F2
Bullumwaal VIC 43 J11 45 B12 46 D6
Bullyard QLD 7 A11 9 K12
Bulman NT 87 F9
Buln Buln VIC 37 F14 44 D6
Bulong WA 75 A13 77 J11 83 F1
Bulwer QLD 4 B4
Bulwer Island QLD 3 C6
Bulyee WA 74 D6
Bumbaldry NSW 22 H3
Bumberry NSW 22 F3
Bumbunga SA 62 G4 65 G9
Bunbartha VIC 42 B3
Bunburra QLD 5 H13
Bunbury WA 73 G9 74 F2
Bunbury Con Res SA 63 C10
Bundaberg QLD 7 A12 9 K13
Bundalaguah VIC 45 D10 46 E4
Bundall QLD 5 B12
Bundalong VIC 42 B6
Bundanoon NSW 22 K7 30 B6
Bundarra NSW 25 F8
Bundeena NSW 19 K5 21 B10 23 J9
Bundella NSW 22 A6 24 K5
Bunding VIC 36 A1
Bundjalung Nat Park NSW 25 D13
Bundook NSW 23 B11
Bundooma NT 91 H9
Bundoora VIC 35 B5 37 B8
Bundure NSW 29 H11
Bung Bong VIC 39 C9
Bunga NSW 30 H5
Bungabbee Nature Res NSW 25 B13
Bungador VIC 39 H9
Bungal VIC 36 C1 39 F11
Bungallen QLD 12 B4
Bungarby NSW 30 H3
Bungaree VIC 39 E11
Bungawalbin Nat Park NSW 7 K13 25 C13
Bungawalbin Nature Res NSW 25 D13
Bungeet VIC 42 C6
Bungendore NSW 30 D4
Bungil VIC 43 B10
Bungonia NSW 30 C5
Bungowannah NSW 29 K12 43 A8
Bungulla NSW 25 C10
Bunguluke VIC 41 J9
Bungunya QLD 6 J6 24 A4
Bungwahl NSW 23 D12
Buninyong VIC 39 E10
Bunjurgen QLD 5 H13
Bunker Group QLD 9 J13
Bunkers Con Res SA 65 B10
Bunnaloo NSW 29 J8 41 H13
Bunnan NSW 23 C8
Buntine WA 76 H5
Bunya NSW 23 C12
Bunya QLD 3 C2
Bunya Mountains Nat Park QLD 7 E10
Bunyan NSW 30 G3
Bunyaville State Forest Park QLD 3 C2
Bunyip VIC 37 F13 44 D5
Bunyip State Park VIC 37 E13 42 K4 44 C4
Buraja NSW 29 K11 42 A7
Burakin WA 76 H6
Burbank QLD 3 G6 5 D8
Burcher NSW 29 D13
Burdett South Nature Res WA 75 F13 83 J1
Burekup WA 73 G9
Burford Island NT 86 B5
Burges WA 72 C3
Burgooney NSW 29 D12
Burke and Wills Roadhouse QLD 10 H5
Burketown QLD 10 E3
Burleigh VIC 37 D11
Burleigh Head Nat Park QLD 5 B13
Burleigh Heads QLD 5 B13 7 H13
Burma Road Nature Res WA 76 F4
Burnbank VIC 39 D10
Burndale VIC 37 K12
Burney Island NT 87 F12
Burnie TAS 54 D5
Burning Mountain Nature Res NSW 23 B9
Burns Beach WA 72 G2
Burns Creek TAS 55 F11
Burnside SA 59 G6 60 G3 61 A6
Burnt Bridge NSW 25 J12
Burnt School Nature Res NSW 30 F4
Burnt-Down Scrub Nature Res NSW 25 D11
Buronga NSW 28 F3 40 A5
Burpengary QLD 4 F5
Burra NSW 30 E3
Burra QLD 8 C2 11 K12 13 A12
Burra SA 62 E4 65 G10
Burraboi NSW 28 J7 41 F12
Burracoppin WA 74 B7 76 J7
Burraga NSW 22 H5
Burragate NSW 30 J4 47 A13
Burragorang State Con Area NSW 21 H11
Burramine North VIC 42 A5
Burramine South VIC 42 B5
Burrandana NSW 29 J13
Burraneer NSW 19 K4
Burrapine NSW 25 H11
Burrell Creek NSW 23 B12
Burren Junction NSW 24 F3
Burrendong Dam NSW 22 D5
Burrill Lake NSW 30 E6
Burringbar NSW 25 A14
Burringurrah WA 78 J4 82 K2
Burrinjuck NSW 30 C2
Burrinjuck Dam NSW 30 C2
Burrinjuck Nature Res NSW 30 C2
Burroin VIC 40 G5
Burrowa-Pine Mountain Nat Park VIC 29 K14 43 B12
Burrowye VIC 29 K13 43 B11
Burrum VIC 38 A7
Burrum Coast Nat Park QLD 7 A12
Burrum Heads QLD 7 B12
Burrumbeet VIC 39 E10
Burrumboot VIC 39 A13 42 D1
Burrumbuttock NSW 29 K12 43 A8
Burrup Peninsula WA 78 D4 82 C1
Burswood WA 71 F4
Burton SA 59 A4 60 D2
Burtville WA 77 F12 83 D2
Burwood NSW 19 F4 21 C9
Burwood VIC 35 E5 37 D8 39 F14 42 K2 44 C2
Burwood East VIC 35 E6
Busbys Flat NSW 25 C12
Bushfield VIC 38 H6
Bushy Park TAS 53 F9
Bushy Park VIC 43 K9 45 C10 46 E4
Busselton WA 73 J11 74 G2
Bustard Bay QLD 9 J12
Bustard Island NT 87 F12
Butcher Well North Mine WA 77 F12 83 E1
Butchers Ridge VIC 43 H13 47 B8
Bute SA 62 G4 65 G9
Butler Tanks SA 64 G6
Butru QLD 12 B4
Butterfly Gorge Nature Park NT 85 G3 86 F5
Butterleaf Nat Park NSW 25 D10
Buxton NSW 21 G13
Buxton VIC 42 H4
Buxtonville QLD 7 B12
Byabarra NSW 23 A13 25 K11
Byaduk VIC 38 G5
Byaduk North VIC 38 F5
Byawatha VIC 42 C7
Byee QLD 7 D10
Byfield QLD 9 G10
Byfield Nat Park QLD 9 G11
Byford WA 72 F4 74 D3
Bygnunn WA 79 A9 80 E5
Bylong NSW 22 D7
Byrnes Scrub Nature Res NSW 25 F12
Byrneside VIC 41 K14 42 C3
Byrnestown QLD 7 B10
Byrock NSW 27 F11
Byron Bay NSW 7 K14 25 B14
Bywong NSW 30 D4

C

Cabanandra NSW 47 A9
Cabanda QLD 5 J9
Cabawin QLD 7 F8
Cabbage Tree Creek VIC 47 D10
Cabbage Tree Palms Res VIC 47 D9
Caboolture QLD 4 F4 7 F12
Caboonbah QLD 4 K5
Cabramatta NSW 19 F1 21 E9
Cabramurra NSW 30 F1 43 A14
Caddens Flat VIC 38 D4
Cadell SA 62 C5 65 G12
Cadney Homestead SA 66 E3
Cadney Park SA 66 E3
Cadoux WA 74 A5 76 J6
Caiguna WA 83 H4
Cairns QLD 11 D13
Cairns Bay TAS 50 J1 53 H9
Cal Lal NSW 28 F1 40 A1 62 A5 65 G14
Calamvale QLD 3 J4 5 E9
Calca SA 64 E3
Calcifer QLD 11 D11
Calcium QLD 8 A5 11 H14
Calder TAS 54 D4
Calder Island QLD 9 C9
Caldermeade VIC 37 H12
Caldwell NSW 29 J8 41 G12
Calen QLD 9 C8
Calga NSW 20 C4
Calingiri WA 74 A4 76 J5
Calivil VIC 41 K11
Callanna SA 67 H9
Callaroy NSW 22 C7
Callawadda VIC 38 B7
Calleen NSW 29 E12
Callide QLD 9 J10
Callide Coalfields QLD 9 J10
Callington SA 60 J7 62 E7 65 J10
Callion WA 77 H10
Calliope QLD 9 J11
Caloona NSW 6 K6 24 B3
Caloundra QLD 4 D2 7 E13
Calpatanna Waterhole Con Park SA 64 E3
Caltowie SA 62 F2 65 F10
Calulu VIC 43 K11 45 B12 46 D5
Calvert QLD 5 J10
Calvert VIC 38 E7
Calwell ACT 32 J4
Camballin WA 79 B10 80 H6
Cambalong NSW 30 J3
Cambarville VIC 37 A14 42 J5 44 A5
Camberwell NSW 23 D9
Camberwell VIC 35 D5 37 D8
Cambewarra Range Nature Res NSW 30 C6
Camboon QLD 7 A8 9 K10
Cambooya QLD 7 G10
Cambrai SA 62 D6 65 H11
Cambray WA 73 G12
Cambrian Hill VIC 39 E10
Cambridge NSW 21 G8
Cambridge TAS 50 C7 53 F11
Cambridge Gulf WA 81 C13
Cambridge Ruins QLD 11 K9
Camden NSW 21 F11 23 H8 30 A7
Camden South NSW 21 F11
Camel Lake Nature Res WA 74 H6
Camels Hump Nature Res NSW 23 B11
Camena TAS 54 E6
Cameron Corner NSW QLD SA 14 K4 26 C1 67 G14
Camerons Gorge Nature Res NSW 23 B9
Camira QLD 3 J1 5 F9
Camira Creek NSW 25 D12
Camooweal QLD 10 J1 89 H14
Camooweal Caves Nat Park QLD 10 J2 89 H14
Camp Creek Con Park WA 81 C9
Camp Hill QLD 3 F5 5 E8
Camp Mountain QLD 3 C1 4 G7
Campania TAS 53 E11
Campbell ACT 31 B4 32 E5
Campbell Town TAS 53 B11 55 J11
Campbellfield VIC 35 B3 36 B7
Campbells Bridge VIC 38 B7
Campbells Creek VIC 39 C11
Campbells Forest VIC 39 A11
Campbelltown NSW 21 E11 23 J8 30 A7
Campbelltown SA 59 F6 60 F3
Campbelltown VIC 39 C11
Campbellville QLD 4 E2
Camperdown NSW 19 F5 21 C9
Camperdown VIC 39 H8
Campup WA 73 A13
Campwin Beach QLD 9 D8
Camurra NSW 24 D5
Canaga QLD 7 E9
Canbelego NSW 27 H11
Canberra ACT 30 D3
Canberra CBD ACT 31
Canberra City ACT 31 A3 32 D5
Candelo NSW 30 J4
Cane River Con Park WA 78 F3
Canegrass WA 77 H11
Cangai NSW 25 D11
Cania Gorge Nat Park QLD 7 A9 9 K11
Caniambo VIC 42 D4
Cann River VIC 47 C11
Canna WA 76 F4
Cannawigara SA 63 B10
Cannie VIC 41 G9
Canning Vale WA 71 J5
Cannington WA 71 H5 72 F3
Cannington Mine QLD 12 C5
Cannon Creek QLD 5 H13
Cannon Hill QLD 3 E5 5 E8
Cannon Vale QLD 8 B7
Cannons Creek VIC 37 H10
Cannum VIC 40 K5
Canonba NSW 27 H13
Canowie SA 62 E3 65 F10
Canowindra NSW 22 G3
Canteen Creek (Orwaitilla) NT 89 J11 91 A11
Canterbury NSW 19 G4 21 C9
Canunda Nat Park SA 63 C13
Canungra QLD 5 D13 7 H13
Canyonleigh NSW 22 K6 30 B5
Cap Island Con Park SA 64 G4
Capalaba QLD 3 G7 5 D8 7 G13
Capalaba West QLD 3 F7
Capamauro Nature Res WA 76 G4
Caparra NSW 23 B12
Cape Adieu SA 68 K5
Cape Arid WA 83 J2
Cape Arid Nat Park WA 83 J2
Cape Arnhem NT 87 D13
Cape Barren Island TAS 55 A14
Cape Barrow NT 87 F11
Cape Baskerville WA 79 A8 80 F3
Cape Bauer SA 64 E3
Cape Beatrice NT 87 G13
Cape Bedford QLD 11 A12 16 K7
Cape Bernier WA 81 A12
Cape Borda WA 79 A9 80 F4
Cape Bossut WA 79 C8 80 J2
Cape Bougainville WA 81 A10
Cape Bouvard WA 72 H6 74 E2
Cape Bowling Green QLD 8 A6
Cape Brewster WA 80 C7
Cape Bridgewater VIC 38 J3
Cape Byron NSW 7 J14 25 B14
Cape Carnot SA 64 J5
Cape Clear VIC 39 F10
Cape Cleveland QLD 8 A5
Cape Clinton QLD 9 F11
Cape Cockburn NT 86 B6
Cape Conran Coastal Park VIC 47 D10
Cape Cossigny WA 78 D5 82 B3
Cape Crawford NT 89 C11
Cape Croker NT 86 A6
Cape Cuvier WA 78 H1
Cape De Couedic SA 63 K9
Cape Degerando TAS 55 K14
Cape Direction QLD 16 F4
Cape Dombey NT 86 F2
Cape Don NT 86 B5
Cape Dussejour WA 81 C13
Cape Farewell TAS 54 A6
Cape Farquhar WA 78 H1
Cape Flattery QLD 11 A12 16 J7
Cape Ford NT 86 E2
Cape Fourcroy NT 86 C2
Cape Freycinet WA 73 K13 74 H1
Cape Gambier NT 85 B2 86 C4
Cape Gantheaume SA 63 H9
Cape Gantheaume Con Park SA 63 H9
Cape Grafton QLD 11 D13
Cape Grenville QLD 16 D3
Cape Grey NT 87 E12
Cape Grim TAS 54 B1
Cape Hamelin WA 73 K14
Cape Helvetius NT 86 C2
Cape Hillsborough Nat Park QLD 9 C8
Cape Hotham NT 85 B3 86 C4
Cape Hotham Forestry Res NT 86 C4
Cape Howe NSW VIC 30 K5 47 C14
Cape Jaubert WA 79 C8 80 K2
Cape Jervis SA 61 K1 63 G8 65 K9
Cape Keer-weer QLD 16 G1
Cape Keith NT 85 A3 86 B4
Cape Keraudren TAS 54 A1
Cape Keraudren WA 78 D6 82 A6
Cape Kimberly QLD 11 C12
Cape Knob WA 75 J9
Cape Lambert WA 78 D4 82 C2
Cape Latouche Treville WA 79 B8 80 J2
Cape Le Grand WA 75 H13 83 J1
Cape Le Grand Nat Park WA 75 G14 83 J1
Cape Leeuwin WA 73 J14 74 J2
Cape Leseur WA 76 B1 78 K1
Cape Leveque WA 80 E4
Cape Liptrap VIC 44 H5
Cape Liptrap Coastal Park VIC 44 H5
Cape Londonderry WA 81 A11
Cape Manifold QLD 9 G11
Cape Melville QLD 16 H6
Cape Melville Nat Park QLD 16 H6
Cape Missiessy WA 79 C8 80 K2
Cape Naturaliste TAS 55 C14
Cape Naturaliste WA 73 K10 74 G1
Cape Nelson VIC 38 J3
Cape Nelson State Park VIC 38 J3
Cape Otway VIC 39 K9
Cape Palmerston QLD 9 E9
Cape Palmerston Nat Park QLD 9 E9
Cape Pasley WA 83 J2
Cape Paterson VIC 44 G4
Cape Peron North WA 76 A1 78 J1
Cape Pillar TAS 51 K14 53 H13
Cape Pond WA 81 B8
Cape Portland TAS 55 C13
Cape Range Nat Park WA 78 F1
Cape Richards QLD 11 F13
Cape Riche WA 75 J8
Cape River QLD 8 C3 11 K12
Cape Rodstock SA 64 F3
Cape Ronsard WA 78 J1
Cape Ruthieres WA 81 A12
Cape Schanck VIC 36 K7 39 J13 44 F1
Cape Scott NT 86 F2
Cape Shield NT 87 E12
Cape Sidmouth QLD 16 G4
Cape Sorell TAS 54 K3
Cape St Cricq WA 76 A1 78 J1
Cape St Lambert WA 81 B12
Cape Stewart NT 87 C10
Cape Talbot WA 81 A11
Cape Thouin WA 78 D5 82 B4
Cape Torrens Con Park SA 63 K8
Cape Tribulation QLD 11 B12
Cape Upstart QLD 8 A6
Cape Upstart Nat Park QLD 8 A6
Cape Van Diemen NT 86 B3
Cape Van Diemen QLD 10 C4
Cape Vancouver WA 74 K7
Cape Vanderlin NT 87 J13 89 A13
Cape Voltaire WA 81 B9
Cape Wellington VIC 45 K8 46 K2
Cape Wessel NT 87 A13
Cape Weymouth QLD 16 E4
Cape Wickham TAS 54 A6
Cape Wilberforce NT 87 C12
Cape York QLD 16 B2
Cape York Peninsula QLD 16 F2
Capel WA 73 H10 74 G2
Capella QLD 8 G6
Capels Crossing VIC 41 G11
Capercup WA 73 C10
Capertee NSW 22 F6
Capital Hill ACT 31 D2 32 E5
Capoompeta Nat Park NSW 25 D10
Capricorn Coast Nat Park QLD 9 G11
Capricorn Group QLD 9 H12
Capricorn Roadhouse WA 78 G6 82 H6
Capricornia Cays Nat Park QLD 9 H13
Captain Billy Landing QLD 16 D3
Captains Creek Nature Res NSW 25 B11
Captains Flat NSW 30 E4
Carabost NSW 29 J14
Caragabal NSW 22 H1 29 E14
Caralue SA 64 F6
Caralue Bluff Con Park SA 64 F6
Caramut VIC 38 G6
Caranbirini Con Res NT 87 K11 89 B12
Carapooee VIC 39 B9
Carapook VIC 38 E3
Carappee Hill Con Park SA 64 F6
Caravan Head NSW 19 J4
Carawa SA 64 D3
Carboor VIC 42 E7
Carbrook QLD 5 C9
Carbunup River WA 73 J11
Carcoar NSW 22 G4
Carcuma Con Park SA 63 C8 65 K12
Cardinia VIC 37 G11
Cardross VIC 28 F3 40 B5
Cardwell QLD 11 F13
Careunga Nature Res NSW 24 C5
Carey Gully SA 60 G4
Cargerie VIC 39 F11
Cargo NSW 22 F4
Carina QLD 3 F5
Carina VIC 28 H2 40 F2
Carina Heights QLD 3 F5
Carinda NSW 27 F14
Carindale QLD 3 F6 5 E8
Carine WA 71 D2
Caringbah NSW 19 J4 21 B10
Carisbrook VIC 39 C10
Carlecatup WA 73 A11
Carlingford NSW 19 D3 21 D8
Carlisle WA 71 G5
Carlisle Island Nat Park QLD 9 C8
Carlisle River VIC 39 J9
Carlisle State Park VIC 39 J9
Carlotta WA 73 G13
Carlsruhe VIC 39 D12
Carlton TAS 51 C10 53 F11
Carlton VIC 34 A3 35 D3
Carlyam Nature Res WA 76 H6
Carmila QLD 9 E9
Carmila Beach QLD 9 E9
Carnamah WA 76 G5
Carnarvon WA 76 A2 78 J1
Carnarvon Nat Park QLD 6 A4 8 K6 13 H14
Carnes SA 66 J4
Carnes Hill NSW 21 E10
Carngham VIC 39 E10
Caroda NSW 24 F6
Caroona NSW 22 A7 24 K6
Carpa SA 62 K4 64 G7
Carpendeit VIC 39 H9
Carpenter Rocks SA 63 C14
Carrai Nat Park NSW 25 H10
Carrajung VIC 45 F9 46 G3
Carramar NSW 21 D9
Carranballac VIC 39 F8
Carrara QLD 5 B13
Carrathool NSW 29 F9
Carr-Boyd WA 77 H11 83 E1
Carrick TAS 55 G9 56 H4
Carrickalinga SA 61 G3 63 G8 65 K9
Carrieton SA 62 F1 65 D10
Carroll NSW 24 J6
Carroll Gap NSW 24 H6
Carrolup WA 73 A11
Carrow Brook NSW 23 C9
Carrum VIC 35 J5 37 F8 39 G14 44 D2
Carrum Downs VIC 35 J6 37 F9
Carseldine QLD 3 B4 4 E7
Cartwright NSW 21 E9
Carwarp VIC 28 G3 40 B5
Cascade WA 75 F12
Cascade Nat Park NSW 25 G12
Casey ACT 32 A4
Cashmere QLD 3 A1 4 F6
Cashmore VIC 38 H3
Casino NSW 7 K12 25 C13
Cassilis NSW 22 B6
Cassilis VIC 43 G11 46 B6
Cassini Island WA 81 A9
Castambul SA 60 F4
Castella VIC 37 A11
Casterton VIC 38 E3 63 A13
Castle Forbes Bay TAS 50 H1 53 H9
Castle Hill NSW 19 C2 21 D8
Castle Rock NSW 23 C8
Castle Tower Nat Park QLD 9 J11
Castleburn VIC 43 J9 45 A11 46 C4
Castlecrag NSW 19 D6
Castlemaine VIC 39 C11
Castlereagh NSW 21 G8
Castlereagh Bay NT 87 C10
Castlereagh Nature Res NSW 21 G8 23 G8
Castleton QLD 11 G10
Casuarina NT 84 A3
Casula NSW 21 E10
Cataby WA 74 A2 76 J4
Catamaran TAS 53 K9
Catani VIC 37 G12 44 E4
Cataract Nat Park NSW 25 B11
Cathcart NSW 30 J4
Cathcart VIC 38 D7
Cathedral Beach QLD 7 B13
Cathedral Range State Park VIC 42 H5
Cathedral Rock Nat Park NSW 25 G10
Catherine Field NSW 21 F10
Catherine Hill Bay NSW 20 A1
Cathkin VIC 42 G4
Cathundral NSW 22 B1 27 J14

98 Gordon – Inkerman

Gordon TAS 50 K4 53 H10
Gordon VIC 36 A1 39 E11
Gordon Park QLD 3 D4
Gordon Ruins SA 65 D9
Gordonvale QLD 11 D13
Gormandale VIC 45 E9 46 F3
Gormanston TAS 52 B4 54 J4
Gorokan NSW 20 B2
Goroke VIC 38 B3
Goschen VIC 28 J6 41 F9
Gosford NSW 20 B4 23 G9
Goshen TAS 55 E13
Gosnells WA 71 K6
Gosse Bore SA 66 A1 68 A6 90 K7
Gostwyck NSW 25 H9
Goughs Bay VIC 42 G6
Goulburn NSW 22 K6 30 C5
Goulburn Islands NT 86 B7
Goulburn River Nat Park NSW 22 C7
Goulburn Weir VIC 39 A14 42 E2
Goulds Country TAS 55 E13
Gourock Nat Park NSW 30 F4
Gove Peninsula NT 87 D13
Gowanford VIC 41 F8
Gowar East VIC 39 A9
Gowrie ACT 32 H4
Gowrie Park TAS 54 F6
Goyura VIC 40 H6
Grabben Gullen NSW 22 K5 30 B4
Gracefield WA 73 A13
Gracemere QLD 9 H10
Gracetown WA 73 K12 74 H1
Graceville QLD 3 F3
Gradgery NSW 27 G14
Gradule QLD 6 J5 24 A3
Grafton NSW 25 E12
Graham NSW 22 J4 30 A3
Grahamstown NSW 29 H14 30 D1
Grahamvale VIC 42 C3
Graman NSW 24 D7
Grampians Nat Park VIC 38 C6
Grandchester QLD 5 K10
Grange QLD 3 D3
Grange SA 59 F2 60 F1
Granite Flat VIC 43 D10
Granite Island SA 61 J6
Granite Island VIC 44 H7 46 J2
Granite Point Con Area TAS 55 D11 56 A7
Granite Tor Con Area TAS 52 A5 54 H5
Granny Smith Mine WA 77 F12 83 D1
Grant (site) VIC 43 H9 46 B4
Grant Island NT 86 B7
Granton TAS 50 A4 53 F10
Granton VIC 37 A13
Grantville VIC 37 K11 44 F4
Granville NSW 19 E2 21 D8
Granville Harbour TAS 52 A2 54 H2
Granya VIC 43 B10
Grass Flat VIC 38 A4
Grass Hut NSW 27 D10
Grass Patch WA 75 F13 83 J1
Grass Valley WA 72 C2 74 C4 76 K6
Grassdale VIC 38 F4
Grassmere VIC 38 H6
Grasstree QLD 9 D8
Grassy TAS 54 C6
Grassy Head NSW 25 H12
Grattai NSW 22 D5
Gravelly Beach TAS 55 E9 56 E4
Gravesend NSW 24 E6
Grawin NSW 27 D14
Gray TAS 55 G14
Grays Point NSW 19 K3
Graytown VIC 39 B14 42 E2
Great Australian Bight Marine Park SA 68 K4 83 G7
Great Barrier Reef QLD 9 C11 11 C13 16 F5
Great Basalt Wall Nat Park QLD 8 B2 11 J12
Great Dog Island TAS 55 C9
Great Keppel Island QLD 9 G11
Great Lake TAS 53 A8 55 H8
Great Palm Island QLD 11 G14
Great Sandy Island Nature Res WA 78 E3
Great Sandy Nat Park QLD 7 D13
Great Victoria Desert Nature Res WA 68 F1 83 E6
Great Western VIC 38 C7
Great Western Tiers Con Park TAS 53 B10 55 J10 56 K1
Greater Bendigo Nat Park VIC 39 A12
Gredgwin VIC 41 H10
Green Cape NSW 30 K5 47 B14
Green Fields SA 59 C4
Green Head WA 76 H3
Green Island QLD 4 C7 11 D13
Green Island TAS 50 J5
Green Island Nat Park QLD 11 D13
Green Lake VIC 38 B5
Green Pigeon NSW 25 B13
Green Point NSW 20 B4
Green Valley NSW 21 E9
Greenacre NSW 19 G3 21 C9
Greenacres SA 59 E5
Greenbank QLD 5 F10
Greenbushes WA 73 F12 74 G3
Greendale NSW 21 G10
Greendale VIC 36 A2 39 E12
Greenethorpe NSW 22 H3
Greengrove NSW 20 D4
Greenhill QLD 9 E9
Greenhill SA 59 G6 60 K4
Greenhill Island NT 85 A5 86 B5
Greenhills WA 72 B3 74 C5 76 K6
Greenmount QLD 7 G10
Greenmount VIC 45 G9 46 H3
Greenmount Nat Park WA 72 F3
Greenock SA 60 A6 62 E5 65 H10
Greenough WA 76 F3
Greenpatch SA 64 H5
Greens Beach TAS 55 D8 56 C1
Greens Creek VIC 39 C8
Greensborough VIC 35 B5 37 C8
Greenslopes QLD 3 F4
Greenvale NSW 29 H11
Greenvale QLD 11 G12
Greenvale VIC 35 A2 36 B6
Greenwald VIC 38 G3
Greenway ACT 32 J3
Greenways SA 62 D6 63 C12 65 J11
Greenwell Point NSW 30 C7
Greenwich NSW 21 C8
Greenwich Park NSW 22 K6 30 B5
Greenwith SA 59 B7
Greenwood WA 71 C2
Gregors Creek QLD 4 K3
Gregory WA 76 E2
Gregory Downs QLD 10 G3
Gregory Mine QLD 8 G7
Gregory Nat Park NT 86 K3 88 B3
Greigs Flat NSW 30 J5 47 A14
Grenfell NSW 22 H2 29 E14
Grenville VIC 39 F10
Gresford NSW 23 D10
Greta VIC 42 D6
Greta West VIC 42 D6
Gretna TAS 53 E9
Grevillia NSW 25 A12
Grey Peaks Nat Park QLD 11 D13
Greystanes NSW 19 E1 21 E8
Griffin QLD 4 E6
Griffith ACT 32 F5
Griffith NSW 29 F11
Griffiths Island VIC 38 H6
Griffiths Nature Res WA 75 F12
Grimwade WA 73 F11 74 G3
Gringegalgona VIC 38 E4
Grogan NSW 22 J1 29 F14
Grong Grong NSW 29 G12
Gronos Point NSW 20 F6
Groote Eylandt NT 87 F12
Groper Creek QLD 8 A6
Grose Island NT 86 D3
Grose Vale NSW 20 H7
Grose Wold NSW 20 G7
Grove TAS 50 E3 53 G10
Grove Hill NT 85 F3 86 F4
Grovedale VIC 36 H2
Grovely QLD 3 C2
Gruyere VIC 37 C11
Guanaba QLD 5 C12
Gubbata NSW 29 D11
Gubbata Nature Res NSW 29 D12
Guilderton WA 72 H1 74 B2 76 K4
Guildford NSW 19 F2 21 D9
Guildford TAS 54 F5
Guildford VIC 39 C11
Guildford WA 71 E6
Gulaga Nat Park NSW 30 G5
Gular NSW 24 K1
Gulargambone NSW 24 K1
Gulera QLD 7 F9
Gulf of Carpentaria 10 B3 87 E14
Gulf St Vincent SA 59 G1 60 H1 61 B3 62 G6 65 J9
Gulgong NSW 22 C5
Gulguer Nature Res NSW 21 G10 23 H8
Gull Creek NSW 24 F7
Gulnare SA 62 F3 65 F10
Guluguba QLD 6 D7
Guluwuru Island NT 87 B12
Gum Creek NSW 26 G9
Gum Flat VIC 36 J1
Gum Lagoon Con Park SA 63 C10
Gum Lake NSW 28 B5
Gumble NSW 22 E3
Gumdale QLD 3 F6
Gumeracha SA 60 E5 62 E6 65 J10
Gumlu QLD 8 B6
Gunalda QLD 7 D12
Gunbalanya (Oenpelli) NT 85 C7 86 D7
Gunbar NSW 29 E9
Gunbower VIC 29 K8 41 H12
Gunbower Island VIC 41 H12
Gundabooka Nat Park NSW 27 F10
Gundagai NSW 29 H14 30 D1
Gundaroo NSW 30 C3
Gunderman NSW 20 E5
Gundowring VIC 43 D9
Gundy NSW 23 B9
Gunebang NSW 29 C12
Gungahlin ACT 32 A5
Gungal NSW 23 C8
Gunnary NSW 22 J4 30 A2
Gunnedah NSW 24 J6
Gunner VIC 28 H3 40 E4
Gunnewin QLD 6 C4
Gunning NSW 30 C3
Gunning Grach NSW 30 H3
Gunningbland NSW 22 F1 29 C14
Gunns Plains TAS 54 E6
Gunpowder QLD 10 J3
Gununa QLD 10 D3
Gunyarra QLD 8 C7
Gurley NSW 24 E5
Gurrai SA 28 H1 62 B7 65 J13
Gurrbalgun NSW 79 A9 80 F4
Gurrumuru NT 87 D12
Gurulmundi QLD 6 D7
Gutha WA 76 F4
Guthalungra QLD 8 B6
Guthega NSW 30 G1 43 C14
Guy Fawkes River Nat Park NSW 25 F11
Guy Fawkes River Nature Res NSW 25 G11
Guyra NSW 25 F9
Guys Forest VIC 43 B11
Gwabegar NSW 24 G3
Gwambygine WA 72 C3
Gwandalan NSW 20 A1
Gwandalan TAS 51 F10 53 G12
Gwenneth Lakes WA 79 E11
Gwindinup WA 73 G10
Gymbowen VIC 38 B3
Gymea NSW 21 C10
Gympie QLD 7 D12
Gypsum VIC 28 H4 40 F6

H

H1 Yandicoogina Mine WA 78 G6 82 F5
Hackett ACT 32 C5
Hackham SA 58 B3 59 F5
Hackney SA 58 B3 59 F5
Haddon VIC 39 E10
Haddon Corner QLD SA 12 K6 14 C4 67 A14
Haden QLD 7 F11
Hadleigh NSW 24 D6
Hadspen TAS 55 F9 56 H4
Hagley TAS 55 F9 56 H3
Hahndorf SA 60 H5 62 E7 65 J10
Haig WA 83 F4
Haigslea QLD 5 J9
Haines Junction VIC 39 J10
Halbury SA 62 F5 65 G10
Hale Con Park SA 60 C5
Halekulani NSW 20 A2
Halfway Creek NSW 25 F13
Halidon SA 62 C7 65 J12
Halifax QLD 11 G14
Halifax Bay QLD 11 G14
Halifax Bay Wetlands Nat Park QLD 11 G14
Halinor Lake SA 68 F3
Hall ACT 32 A3
Hall NSW 19 G2 30 D3
Hallett SA 62 E3 65 F10
Hallett Cove SA 60 J1 61 C5
Hallett Cove Con Park SA 60 H1 61 C5
Hallidays Point NSW 23 C12
Hallora VIC 37 H14
Halls Creek WA 79 B13 81 J12
Halls Gap VIC 38 C6
Hallston VIC 44 F6
Halton NSW 23 C10
Hambidge Con Park SA 64 F6
Hamel WA 72 F7
Hamelin Bay WA 73 K13 74 H1
Hamelin Pool Marine Nature Res WA 76 B2 78 K2
Hamersley WA 71 D3 72 C2
Hamilton QLD 3 D4
Hamilton SA 62 E5 65 H10
Hamilton TAS 53 E9
Hamilton VIC 38 F5
Hamilton Downs Youth Camp NT 90 F7
Hamilton Hill WA 71 K2
Hamilton Island QLD 9 C8
Hamley Bridge SA 62 F5 65 H10
Hammond SA 62 F1 65 D9
Hammond Island QLD 16 B2
Hampshire TAS 54 E5
Hampton NSW 22 G6
Hampton QLD 7 G11
Hanging Rock NSW 23 A9 25 K8
Hann River Roadhouse QLD 11 A10 16 K5
Hann Tableland Nat Park QLD 11 D12
Hannahs Bridge NSW 22 B6
Hannan NSW 29 D11
Hannaville QLD 9 D8
Hansborough SA 62 E5 65 H10
Hanson SA 62 E4 65 G10
Hansonville VIC 42 D6
Hanwood NSW 29 F11
Happy Valley QLD 7 B13
Happy Valley SA 60 J2 61 C6
Happy Valley VIC 28 G4 40 C7 43 D8 43 H9 46 B4
Harcourt VIC 39 C11
Harden NSW 22 K3 30 B1
Hardwicke Bay SA 62 H6 65 J8
Harefield NSW 29 H13
Harford TAS 55 E8
Hargraves NSW 22 E5
Harlin QLD 7 F11
Harman ACT 32 F6
Harrietville VIC 43 F9
Harrington NSW 23 B13
Harris Nature Res WA 75 E8
Harrismith WA 74 E6
Harrison ACT 32 B5
Harrisville QLD 5 K12
Harrogate SA 60 G7 62 E7 65 J10
Harrow VIC 38 D3
Hart SA 62 F4 65 G10
Hartley NSW 22 G7
Hartley SA 60 K7
Harts Range NT 91 E10
Hartz Mountains Nat Park TAS 53 H8
Harvey WA 73 G8 74 F3
Harwood NSW 25 D13
Haslam SA 64 D3
Hassell Nat Park WA 74 J7
Hastings TAS 53 J9
Hastings VIC 37 J9 39 H14 44 E2
Hastings Point NSW 25 A14
Hat Head Nat Park NSW 25 J12
Hatfield NSW 28 E6
Hatherleigh SA 63 C13
Hattah VIC 28 G4 40 D5
Hattah-Kulkyne Nat Park VIC 28 G4 40 C5
Hatton Vale QLD 5 K9
Havanna Island QLD 11 G14
Havelock VIC 39 C10
Haven VIC 38 B5
Hawker ACT 32 C2
Hawker SA 65 C10
Hawkesbury Island QLD 16 B2
Hawkesdale VIC 38 G6
Hawkesdale West VIC 38 G5
Hawknest Island NT 87 F12
Hawks Nest NSW 23 E11
Hawley Beach TAS 55 E8
Hawthorn VIC 35 D4
Hawthorndene SA 59 K5
Hawthorne QLD 3 E4
Hay NSW 29 F8 41 B13
Hay Point QLD 9 D8
Haydens Bog VIC 47 A10
Hayes TAS 50 A2 53 F9
Hayes Creek NT 85 F3 86 F4
Hayman Island QLD 9 B8
Haysdale VIC 28 G5 41 D8
Hazelbrook NSW 21 J9
Hazeldean QLD 4 J4
Hazelmere WA 71 E7
Hazelwood VIC 44 E7 46 F1
Hazelwood Island QLD 9 B8
Hazelwood Park SA 59 G5
Healesville VIC 37 B11 42 J4 44 B4
Hearson WA 78 E4 82 C1
Heartlea WA 73 D13
Heath Hill VIC 37 H13
Heathcote NSW 19 K2 21 C11 23 J9
Heathcote VIC 39 B13 42 F1
Heathcote Nat Park NSW 19 K2 21 D11 23 J8
Heathcote-Graytown Nat Park VIC 39 B13 42 E1
Heathfield SA 59 K7 60 H4 61 B7
Heathlands QLD 16 D2
Heathmere VIC 38 H4
Heathwood QLD 3 J3
Hebden NSW 23 D9
Hebel QLD 6 K3 27 B14
Hectorville SA 59 F6
Heggaton Con Res SA 62 K3 64 F7
Heidelberg VIC 35 C4 37 C8
Heirisson Island WA 70 D4
Heka TAS 54 E6
Helensburgh NSW 21 C12 23 J9
Helensvale QLD 5 C12
Helenvale QLD 11 B12 16 K7
Helidon QLD 7 G11
Hell Hole Gorge Nat Park QLD 13 J10 15 B10
Hells Gate Roadhouse QLD 10 E2
Hellyer TAS 54 C4
Hellyer Gorge State Res TAS 54 E4
Hemmant QLD 3 E6
Henbury Meteorite Con Res NT 90 G7
Hendon QLD 7 H11
Henley Beach SA 59 F2 60 F1 61 A5
Henley Brook WA 71 B6
Henrietta TAS 54 E5
Henry Freycinet Harbour WA 76 C2
Hensley Park VIC 38 E5
Henty NSW 29 J12
Henty VIC 38 F3
Hepburn Springs VIC 39 D11
Herbert Wash WA 77 B14 79 K10 83 A3
Herberton QLD 11 E12
Heritage Park QLD 3 K5
Hermannsburg NT 90 F6
Hermidale NSW 27 H12
Hernani NSW 25 G11
Herne Hill WA 71 C7
Heron Island QLD 9 H12
Herons Creek NSW 23 A13
Herrick TAS 55 D12
Hervey Bay QLD 7 A12 7 B13
Hesso SA 65 D8
Hester WA 73 E12
Hewetsons Mill NSW 25 A11
Hewitt NSW 21 F9
Hexham VIC 38 G7
Hexham Island QLD 9 E10
Hexham Swamp Nature Res NSW 23 E10
Heybridge TAS 54 D6
Heyfield VIC 45 C9 46 E3
Heywood VIC 38 H4
Heywood Islands WA 80 C7
Hicks Island QLD 16 D3
Hidden Island WA 80 E5
Hidden Vale QLD 5 K10
Hidden Valley QLD 11 G13
Higgins ACT 32 C2
Higginsville WA 75 C13 77 K11 83 G1
Higginsville Mine WA 75 C13 77 K11 83 G1
High Island QLD 11 D13
High Peak Island QLD 9 E10
High Range NSW 22 J7 30 B6
High Wycombe WA 71 F7
Highbury SA 59 E6 60 F3
Highbury WA 73 A8 74 F5
Highclere TAS 54 E5
Highcroft TAS 51 H11 53 H12
Higher McDonald NSW 20 F3
Highgate WA 71 F4
Highlands VIC 42 G3
Highton VIC 36 G2
Hilgay VIC 38 E3
Hill End NSW 22 E5
Hill End VIC 44 D6 46 E1
Hillarys WA 71 B1
Hillbank SA 59 B6
Hillcrest QLD 3 K4
Hillcrest SA 59 E5
Hillgrove NSW 25 H10
Hillier SA 60 C3
Hillman WA 73 C9
Hillside VIC 43 K11 45 C12 46 D5
Hillston NSW 29 D10
Hilltop NSW 21 G14
Hilltown SA 62 F4 65 G10
Hillview QLD 5 E14
Hillwood TAS 55 E9 56 E4
Hilton WA 71 J2
Hilton Mine QLD 10 K3 12 A3
Hinchinbrook Island QLD 11 F13
Hinchinbrook Island Nat Park QLD 11 F13
Hincks Con Park SA 64 G6
Hincks Con Res SA 64 G5
Hindmarsh SA 59 F3 60 F2
Hindmarsh Island SA 63 E8 65 K10
Hindmarsh Valley SA 61 H6
Hinnomunjie VIC 43 F11 46 A6
Hivesville QLD 7 D10
Hiway Inn NT 86 K7 88 B7
HMAS Cerberus VIC 37 J9
Hobart TAS 49 C2 50 C5 53 F10
Hobart CBD TAS 49
Hobbys Yards NSW 22 G5
Hocking WA 71 A3
Hoddles Creek VIC 37 D12
Hodgson QLD 6 E4
Hoffman WA 73 F8
Hogarth Range Nature Res NSW 25 C12
Holbrook NSW 29 J13
Holden Hill SA 59 E6
Holder ACT 32 F3
Holey Plains State Park VIC 45 E10 46 F3
Holgate NSW 20 B4
Holland Landing VIC 45 D12 46 E5
Holland Park QLD 3 F4
Hollow Tree TAS 53 E9
Holmwood NSW 22 H4
Holsworthy NSW 19 H1 21 D10
Holt ACT 32 C2
Holt Rock WA 75 E9
Holts Flat NSW 30 H3
Holwell TAS 55 E8 56 E2
Home Hill QLD 8 A5
Home Rule NSW 22 D6
Homebush NSW 21 D9
Homebush QLD 9 D8
Homebush Bay NSW 19 E3 21 D8
Homecroft VIC 40 J6
Homerton VIC 38 G4
Homestead QLD 8 B3 11 K13
Homevale Nat Park QLD 8 D7
Homewood VIC 42 G3
Honeymoon Beach WA 81 A10
Hook Island QLD 9 B8
Hookina SA 65 C9
Hope Campbell Lake WA 77 F13 83 E2
Hope Vale QLD 11 A12 16 K7
Hope Valley SA 59 D6 60 E3
Hopefield NSW 29 K11 42 A7
Hopetoun VIC 28 J4 40 G6
Hopetoun WA 75 G10
Hopetoun West VIC 40 G5
Hopevale VIC 28 K4 40 H5
Hoppers Crossing VIC 36 D5
Horfield VIC 41 H11
Horn Island QLD 16 B2
Hornsby NSW 19 B3 20 D7 23 H9
Hornsby Heights NSW 19 B4
Horrocks WA 76 E3
Horsham VIC 38 B5
Horsley Park NSW 21 E9
Horsnell Gully Con Park SA 59 G7 60 G3 61 A7
Hortons Creek Nature Res NSW 25 F12
Hoskinstown NSW 30 E4
Hoskyn Islands QLD 9 H13
Hotham Heights Alpine Village VIC 43 F10
Hotspur VIC 38 G3
Hotspur Island QLD 9 D10
Houtman Abrolhos WA 76 F2
Howard QLD 7 B12
Howard Island NT 87 C10
Howard Springs NT 85 C2 86 D4
Howden TAS 50 F5 53 G10
Howes Valley NSW 23 E8
Howick Group Nat Park QLD 16 H6
Howick Island QLD 16 H6
Howlong NSW 29 K12 43 A8
Howqua VIC 42 G6 46 B1
Howqua Hills VIC 42 G7 46 A1
Howth TAS 54 D6
Hoxton Park NSW 21 E9
Hoyleton SA 62 F4 65 G10
Hugh River NT 91 G8
Hughenden QLD 8 C1 11 K10 13 A10
Hughes ACT 32 F4
Hughes SA 68 H2 83 F7
Hull Heads QLD 11 F13
Humbug Point Con Area TAS 55 E14
Hume ACT 32 H5
Hume Weir NSW 29 K12 43 B9
Humevale VIC 37 A9 39 E14 42 H3 44 A2
Humpty Doo NT 85 C2 86 D4
Humula NSW 29 J14
Hungerford QLD 15 K10 26 B7
Hunter VIC 41 K12
Hunter Island TAS 54 A1
Hunters Hill NSW 19 E5 21 C8
Huntingdale WA 71 K6
Huntly VIC 39 A12
Huonville TAS 50 F2 53 G9
Hurstbridge VIC 35 A6 37 B9 39 E14 42 J3 44 A2
Hurstville NSW 19 H4 21 C9
Huskisson NSW 30 D7
Hyden WA 75 D8
Hyland Bay NT 86 F2
Hynam SA 38 C1 63 B12

I

Iandra NSW 22 H3 30 A1
Ida Bay TAS 53 J9
Idalia Nat Park QLD 8 K2 13 H11 15 A11
Ifould Lake SA 68 H5
Iga Warta SA 65 A11 67 K11
Iguana Creek VIC 43 K10 45 B12 46 D5
Ikuntji (Haasts Bluff) NT 90 E5
Ilbilbie QLD 9 E8
Ilbunga SA 91 K10
Ile du Golfe TAS 52 K7
Ilford NSW 22 E6
Ilfracombe QLD 8 H1 13 F11
Ilfraville TAS 55 E9 56 D2
Ilkurlka WA 83 D6
Illabarook VIC 39 F10
Illabo NSW 29 G14
Illalong Creek NSW 22 K3 30 C2
Illamurta Con Res NT 90 G6
Illawong WA 76 G3
Illili NT 90 E5
Illilliwa NSW 29 F9 41 B14
Illowa VIC 38 H6
Illpurta NT 90 G6
Iltur SA 68 C3
Iluka NSW 25 D13
Ilykuwaratja SA 66 A1 68 A6 90 K7
Imanpa NT 90 H6
Imbil QLD 7 E12
Imintji WA 79 A11 81 G8
Immarna SA 68 H5
Impadna NT 91 H8
Inala QLD 3 H2 5 F9
Inarki SA 68 A2 90 K2
Indented Head VIC 36 G5 39 G13
Indooroopilly QLD 3 F3
Indulkana (Iwantja) SA 66 C1 68 B7
Indwarra Nature Res NSW 25 F8
Ingalba Nature Res NSW 29 F13
Ingebyra NSW 30 H2 43 E14
Ingham QLD 11 G13
Ingle Farm SA 59 D5 60 E3
Ingleburn NSW 21 E10
Inglegar NSW 27 H14
Ingleside NSW 19 B6 20 B6
Inglewood QLD 7 J9 25 A8
Inglewood SA 60 E4
Inglewood VIC 39 A10
Inglewood WA 71 E4
Inglis Island NT 87 C12
Ingliston VIC 36 B2
Ininti NT 79 G14 90 E1
Injarrtnama NT 90 F7
Injinoo QLD 16 B2
Injune QLD 6 C4
Inkerman QLD 8 A6
Inkerman SA 62 G5 65 H9

Lowood – Mongarlowe 101

Lowood QLD 5 J8 7 G12
Loxton SA 62 B6 65 H13
Loxton North SA 28 G1 62 B6 65 H13
Loy Yang VIC 45 E8 46 F2
Loyetea TAS 54 E5
Lubeck VIC 38 B6
Lucas Heights NSW 19 J2 21 D10
Lucaston TAS 50 E2 53 G9
Lucinda QLD 11 G14
Lucindale SA 63 B12
Lucknow NSW 22 F4
Lucknow VIC 43 K11 45 C13 46 D6
Lucky Bay SA 62 J4 64 G7
Lucky Flat NSW 24 G4
Lucyvale VIC 43 C11
Luddenham NSW 21 G10
Ludlow WA 73 H11 74 G2
Ludmilla NT 84 C2
Lue NSW 22 D6
Lugarno NSW 21 C10
Luina TAS 54 F3
Lul-Tju NT 88 E3
Lulworth TAS 55 D9 56 B4
Lumeah WA 73 A12
Lumuku WA 79 A14 81 G13
Lunawanna TAS 53 J10
Lune River TAS 53 J9
Lupton Con Park WA 72 C5 74 D4
Lurg VIC 42 D6
Lurnea NSW 21 E10
Luscombe QLD 5 D11
Lutwyche QLD 3 D4
Lymington TAS 50 J2 53 H9
Lymwood TAS 54 C6
Lynchford TAS 52 C4 54 K4
Lyndbrook QLD 11 E11
Lyndhurst NSW 22 G4
Lyndhurst SA 67 J10
Lyndhurst VIC 35 H7 37 F9 44 D2
Lyndoch SA 60 B5 62 E6 65 H10
Lyneham ACT 32 C5
Lyons ACT 32 F3
Lyons SA 64 A3 66 K3 68 H7
Lyons VIC 38 G3
Lyonville VIC 39 D12
Lyrup SA 28 F1 62 B5 65 H13
Lysterfield Lake Park VIC 37 E10 42 K3
Lytton QLD 3 D6 4 D7

M

Maaroom QLD 7 C13
Maatsuyker Group TAS 52 K7
Maatsuyker Island TAS 52 K7
Mabuiag Island QLD 16 A2
Mac Clark (Acacia Peuce) Con Res NT 91 H10
Macalister QLD 7 F9
Macarthur ACT 32 H5
Macarthur VIC 38 G5
Macclesfield SA 60 K5 62 E7 65 J10
Macclesfield VIC 37 D11
Macedon VIC 39 D13
Macgregor ACT 32 B2
MacGregor QLD 3 G5 5 E9
Mackay QLD 9 D8
MacKenzie QLD 3 G6
Macksville NSW 25 H12
Maclean NSW 25 D13
Macleay Island QLD 5 B9
Macleod VIC 35 B5 37 C8
Macorna VIC 28 K7 41 H11
Macquarie ACT 32 C3
Macquarie Fields NSW 21 E10
Macquarie Marshes Nature Res NSW 27 F13
Macquarie Pass Nat Park NSW 23 K8 30 B7
Macquarie Plains TAS 53 F9
Macrossan QLD 8 B4 11 J14
Macumba Oil Well SA 66 B7
Maddarr WA 79 A9 80 F5
Maddington WA 71 J7
Madora WA 72 G5
Madura WA 83 G5
Mafeking VIC 38 D6
Maffra NSW 30 H3
Maffra VIC 45 C10 46 E4
Maggea SA 62 C6 65 H12
Magill SA 59 F6 60 F3
Magnetic Island QLD 11 G14
Magnetic Island Nat Park QLD 11 G14
Magra TAS 50 A2 53 F9
Magrath Flat SA 63 D9
Maharatta NSW 30 J3 47 A12
Maianbar NSW 21 B10
Maida Vale WA 71 F7
Mailers Flat VIC 38 H6
Maimuru NSW 22 J2 30 A1
Main Beach QLD 5 B12
Main Creek NSW 23 C11
Main Range Nat Park QLD 5 K13 7 H11 25 A11
Maindample VIC 42 F5
Mainoru Store NT 87 F8
Mairjimmy NSW 29 J10
Maitland NSW 23 E10
Maitland SA 62 H5 65 H8
Major Plains VIC 42 C5
Majorca VIC 39 C10
Majors Creek NSW 30 E5
Majura ACT 32 C6
Makiri SA 68 C4
Makowata QLD 9 K12
Makurapiti SA 68 B1 83 B7
Malabar NSW 19 H6
Malaburra WA 79 A9 80 F5
Malaga WA 71 D5
Malanda QLD 11 E13
Malangan WA 79 B14 81 G14
Malbina TAS 50 B3 53 F10
Malbon QLD 12 B5
Malbooma SA 64 A3 66 K3
Malcolm WA 77 F11 83 D1
Maldon NSW 21 F12
Maldon VIC 39 C11
Malebelling WA 72 B3
Malebo NSW 29 H13
Maleny QLD 4 G1 7 E12
Malinong SA 63 D9 65 K11
Mallacoota VIC 47 C13
Mallala SA 62 F5 65 H10
Mallanganee NSW 25 C12
Mallanganee Nat Park NSW 7 K12 25 C12
Mallee Cliffs Nat Park NSW 28 F4 40 A6
Mallison Island NT 87 C12
Malmsbury VIC 39 C12
Malua Bay NSW 30 F6
Malvern SA 59 H4
Malvernton QLD 8 J2 13 G12
Mamboo QLD 8 H5 13 F14
Mambray Creek SA 62 G2 65 E9
Mammoth Mines QLD 10 J3
Manangatang VIC 28 H5 40 E7
Mandagery NSW 22 F3
Mandalong NSW 20 C1
Mandalup WA 73 E12
Mandorah NT 85 C1 86 D3
Mandurah WA 72 G6 74 E2
Mandurama NSW 22 G4
Mangalo SA 62 K3 64 F7
Mangalore QLD 15 E13
Mangalore TAS 53 E10
Mangalore VIC 39 B14 42 F3
Mangana TAS 55 G12
Mangkili Claypan Nature Res WA 77 A14 79 J10 83 A3
Mangoplah NSW 29 H13
Mangrove Creek NSW 20 D4
Mangrove Mountain NSW 20 D3 23 F9
Manguri SA 66 G3
Manildra NSW 22 F3
Manilla NSW 24 H7
Maninga Marley WA 77 E9
Maningrida NT 87 C9
Manjimup WA 73 E13 74 H3
Manly NSW 19 D7 20 B7 23 H9
Manly QLD 3 D7 5 D8
Manly Vale NSW 19 D6 20 B7
Manly West QLD 3 E7
Manmoyi NT 87 D8
Mann River Nature Res NSW 25 E10
Mannahill SA 62 C1 65 D12
Mannanarie SA 62 F2 65 E10
Mannerim VIC 36 H4
Mannering Park NSW 20 B1
Manning WA 71 H4
Manns Beach VIC 45 G9 46 H3
Mannum SA 62 D7 65 J11
Mannus NSW 29 J14 43 A12
Manobalai Nature Res NSW 23 C8
Manoora SA 62 E4 65 G10
Manor VIC 36 E4 39 F13
Manorina VIC 47 D10
Manowar Island QLD 10 C3
Mansfield QLD 3 G5
Mansfield VIC 42 F6 46 A1
Manton Dam Park NT 85 D2 86 E4
Mantung SA 62 C6 65 H12
Manuka ACT 32 F5
Manumbar QLD 7 D11
Many Peaks QLD 9 K11
Manyallaluk (Eva Valley) NT 85 H7 86 G6
Manyirkanga SA 68 A4 90 K4
Manypeaks WA 74 J7
Manyung QLD 7 D11
Mapleton QLD 7 E12
Mapoon QLD 16 D1
Mapurru NT 87 C10
Maralinga SA 68 G4
Marama SA 62 C7 65 K12
Marananga SA 60 A6
Maranboy NT 85 J7 86 G6
Marandoo Mine WA 78 G5 82 F4
Marangaroo WA 71 C3
Marathon QLD 13 A9
Marathon South QLD 13 A9
Maraylya NSW 20 F6
Marayong NSW 21 E8
Marble Bar WA 78 E6 82 D6
Marble Hill SA 60 F4
Marble Island QLD 9 E10
Marburg QLD 5 J9 7 G12
Marchagee WA 76 H5
Marchinbar Island NT 87 B12
Marcus Hill VIC 36 H4 39 H12
Mardan VIC 44 F6 46 G1
Mardella WA 72 F5
Mareeba QLD 11 D12
Marengo VIC 39 K10
Maret Islands WA 81 B8
Margaret River WA 73 K12 74 H1
Margate QLD 4 E6
Margate TAS 50 F5 53 G10
Margooya VIC 28 G5 40 D7
Maria Island NT 87 H11
Maria Island TAS 53 F13
Maria Island Nat Park TAS 53 E13
Maria Nat Park NSW 25 J12
Mariala Nat Park QLD 13 K12 15 C11
Marian QLD 9 D8
Marimo QLD 10 K5 12 A5
Marino SA 59 K2 60 H1 61 B5
Marino Con Park SA 60 H1 61 B5
Marion SA 59 J3 60 H2 61 B6
Marion Bay SA 62 J7 64 K7
Mark Oliphant Con Park SA 60 H3 61 B7
Markwood VIC 42 D7
Marla SA 66 D2 68 C7
Marlborough QLD 9 G9
Marlee NSW 23 B12
Marleston SA 59 G3
Marley Pool WA 72 C3
Marlinja NT 88 D7
Marlo VIC 43 K14 47 D9
Marma VIC 38 B6
Marmion WA 71 C1
Marmion Marine Park WA 76 K4
Marmor QLD 9 H10
Marnoo VIC 38 A7
Marnoo East VIC 39 A8
Marong VIC 39 B11
Maroochydore QLD 4 D1 7 E13
Maroon QLD 5 H14
Maroona VIC 38 E7
Maroota NSW 20 E5
Maroota South NSW 20 E6
Maroubra NSW 19 G6 21 B9
Marp VIC 38 F2
Marraba QLD 12 A4
Marrabel SA 62 E5 65 G10
Marradong WA 72 D7 74 E4
Marramarra Nat Park NSW 20 D5 23 G9
Marrar NSW 29 G13
Marrawah TAS 54 C1
Marraweeny VIC 42 E4
Marree SA 67 H9
Marrickville NSW 21 C9
Marryat SA 66 B2 68 B7 90 K7
Marsden NSW 22 G1 29 E13
Marsden QLD 3 K5 5 E10
Marsden Park NSW 20 F7
Marsfield NSW 19 D4 21 C8
Marshall VIC 36 H3
Marshdale NSW 23 D11
Martin Washpool Con Park SA 63 D10
Martindale NSW 23 D8
Marton QLD 11 A2
Marulan NSW 22 K6 30 C5
Marunbabidi WA 81 D10
Marvel Loch WA 75 B9 77 K9
Mary Kathleen QLD 10 K4 12 A4
Mary River Con Park NT 85 C4
Mary River Con Res NT 86 D5
Mary River Nat Park NT 85 D4 86 D5
Mary River Roadhouse NT 85 F5 86 F5
Mary Seymour Con Park SA 63 B12
Maryborough QLD 7 C12
Maryborough VIC 39 C10
Maryfarms QLD 11 C12
Maryknoll VIC 37 F12
Maryland Nat Park NSW 25 A10
Marysville VIC 37 A13 42 H5 44 A5
Maryvale NSW 22 D4
Mascot NSW 19 G5 21 B9
Maslin Beach SA 61 E5 62 F7 65 K9
Massey VIC 40 J7
Masthead Island QLD 9 H12
Matakana NSW 29 C10
Mataranka NT 85 K7 86 H7
Mataranka Homestead NT 86 H7
Matcham NSW 20 B4
Matheson NSW 25 E9
Mathiesons VIC 39 A14 42 D2
Mathinna TAS 55 F12
Mathoura NSW 29 K8 41 H13 42 A1
Matlock VIC 42 J6 44 A7 46 C1
Matong NSW 29 G12
Matraville NSW 19 H6 21 B9
Maude NSW 28 F7 41 B12
Maude VIC 36 E1 39 G11
Maudsland QLD 5 C12
Mawbanna TAS 54 D3
Mawson ACT 32 G4
Mawson WA 72 A3
Mawson Lakes SA 59 C4
Maxwelton QLD 11 K8 13 A8
Maya WA 76 G5
Mayanup WA 73 D12 74 G4
Mayberry TAS 54 G7
Maybole NSW 25 F9
Maydena TAS 53 F8
Mayfield Bay Con Area TAS 53 C13 55 K13
Maylands WA 71 F5
Maynard Bore SA 68 C5
Mayrung NSW 29 J9
Maytown QLD 11 B10
Mazeppa Nat Park QLD 8 F5
McAlinden WA 73 E10
McCluer Island NT 86 A7
McCoys Bridge VIC 41 J14 42 B2
McCrae VIC 36 J7
McCullys Gap NSW 23 C9
McDowall QLD 3 C3
McGraths Hill NSW 20 F7
McKellar ACT 32 B3
McKenzie Creek VIC 38 B5
McKillops Bridge VIC 43 G14 47 A9
McKinlay QLD 12 B6
McKinnon VIC 35 F4
McLaren Creek NT 89 J9
McLaren Flat SA 60 K2 61 D6
McLaren Vale SA 60 K2 61 E5 62 F7 65 K10
McIntyre VIC 39 A10
McMahons Creek VIC 37 C14 42 J5 44 B5
McMahons Reef NSW 22 K3 30 B2
McMasters Beach NSW 20 B4
McMillans VIC 41 H11
McPhail NSW 22 D2
Mead VIC 41 H11
Meadow Flat NSW 22 G6
Meadows SA 60 K4 62 F7 65 K10
Meandarra QLD 6 F7
Meander TAS 55 G8
Mears WA 72 A5
Meatian VIC 41 G9
Mebbin Nat Park NSW 7 J13 25 A13
Meckering WA 72 B2 74 C5 76 K6
Medina WA 72 G4
Medindie SA 58 A3
Medlow Bath NSW 21 K9
Meeandah QLD 3 D5
Meekatharra WA 76 C7 78 K5
Meelup WA 73 K10
Meenaar WA 72 C2
Meeniyan VIC 44 G6
Meerlieu VIC 45 D12 46 E5
Megan NSW 25 G12
Mekaree QLD 8 K2 13 G11
Melba ACT 32 B3
Melba Gully State Park VIC 39 K9
Melbourne VIC 35 D3 36 C7 39 F14 42 K2 44 B1
Melbourne CBD VIC 34
Meldale QLD 4 E4
Mella TAS 54 C2
Melros WA 72 H6
Melrose NSW 29 B12
Melrose SA 62 F2 65 E9
Melrose TAS 54 E7
Melrose Park SA 59 J4
Melton SA 62 G5 65 G9
Melton VIC 36 B4 39 E13
Melton Mowbray TAS 53 D10
Melton South VIC 36 C4
Melville WA 71 J2
Melville Forest VIC 38 E4
Melville Island NT 85 A1 86 B3
Melville Range Nature Res NSW 24 J6
Melwood VIC 43 K11 45 B12 46 D5
Memana TAS 55 B9
Memerambi QLD 7 D10
Mena Park VIC 39 E9
Menai NSW 19 J2 21 D10
Menangle NSW 21 E12
Menangle Park NSW 21 E11
Mendooran NSW 22 B4
Mengha TAS 54 C3
Menindee NSW 26 K4 28 B4
Meningie SA 63 D9 65 K11
Mentone VIC 35 G5 37 E8 39 G14 44 C2
Menzies WA 77 G10
Menzies Creek VIC 37 E11
Mepunga East VIC 38 J7
Mepunga West VIC 38 J7
Merah North NSW 24 F4
Merbein VIC 28 F3 40 A4
Merbein South VIC 28 F3 40 A4
Merbein West VIC 40 A4
Mercunda SA 62 C6 65 J12
Merebene NSW 24 H3
Meredith VIC 36 D1 39 F11
Meribah SA 28 G1 40 C1 62 A6 65 J13
Merimbula NSW 30 J5
Merinda QLD 8 B7
Meringandan QLD 7 G11
Meringur VIC 28 F2 40 B2 65 H14
Meringur North VIC 28 F2 40 B2
Merino VIC 38 F3
Mermaid Beach QLD 5 B13
Mernda VIC 37 B8 39 E14 42 J2 44 A2
Mernot Nature Res NSW 23 A10
Meroo Nat Park NSW 30 E6
Merredin WA 74 B7 76 K7
Merriang VIC 43 D8
Merriangaah Nature Res NSW 30 H3
Merricks VIC 37 J8 39 H14 44 F2
Merricks Beach VIC 37 K8
Merricks North VIC 37 J8
Merrigum VIC 41 K14 42 C2
Merrijig VIC 42 G6 46 A1
Merrimac QLD 5 B13
Merrinee VIC 28 F3 40 B4
Merrinee North VIC 28 F3 40 B4
Merriton SA 62 G3 65 F9
Merriwa NSW 22 C7
Merriwagga NSW 29 E10
Merrygoen NSW 22 B5
Merrylands NSW 19 E2 21 D8
Merryvale QLD 5 J11
Merrywinebone NSW 24 E2
Merseylea TAS 54 F7
Merton NSW 29 K11 42 A6
Merton VIC 42 F4
Messent Con Park SA 63 D9
Messines QLD 25 B10
Metcalfe VIC 39 C12
Methul NSW 29 G13
Metricup WA 73 J11
Metung VIC 43 K12 45 C14 46 E7
Meunna TAS 54 D4
Mia Mia VIC 39 C13
Miallo QLD 11 C12
Miami QLD 5 B13
Miandetta NSW 27 H12
Miara QLD 7 A11 9 K12
Michaelmas and Upolu Cays Nat Park QLD 11 C13
Michelago NSW 30 E3
Mickleham VIC 36 A7
Middingbank NSW 30 G2
Middle Beach SA 62 F6 65 H9
Middle Brother Nat Park NSW 23 B13
Middle Camp NSW 20 A1
Middle Dural NSW 19 A2
Middle Island QLD 9 E10
Middle Island WA 83 J2
Middle Lagoon WA 79 A9 80 F4
Middle Park QLD 5 F9
Middle Point NT 85 C3 86 D4
Middle Swan WA 71 D7
Middlecamp Hills Con Park SA 62 K4 64 F7
Middlemount QLD 8 G7
Middleton QLD 12 D6
Middleton SA 61 H7 63 F8 65 K10
Middleton TAS 50 K5 53 H10
Midge Point QLD 9 C8
Midkin Nature Res NSW 24 D5
Midland WA 71 D7 72 F3 74 C3 76 K5
Midway Point TAS 51 B8 53 F11
Miena TAS 53 B8 55 J8
Miepoll VIC 42 D4
Miga Lake VIC 38 C3
Mike O/P Mine WA 79 F8
Mil Lel SA 38 F1 63 B14
Mila NSW 30 J3 47 A11
Milabena TAS 54 D4
Milang SA 63 E8 65 K10
Milawa VIC 42 D7
Milbrulong NSW 29 H12
Milchomi NSW 24 G2
Mildura VIC 28 F3 40 A5
Mile End SA 58 C1 59 G3
Miles QLD 6 E7
Milford QLD 5 H13
Milguy NSW 24 D6
Milikapiti NT 86 B3
Miling WA 76 H5
Milingimbi NT 87 C10
Mill Park VIC 35 A4
Millaa Millaa QLD 11 E13
Millaroo QLD 8 B5
Millbank NSW 25 H11
Millchester QLD 8 B4 11 J14
Miller NSW 21 E10
Millers Point NSW 18 A1
Millfield NSW 23 E9
Millgrove VIC 37 C12 42 K4 44 B4
Millicent SA 63 C13
Millie NSW 24 E4
Millmerran QLD 7 H9
Millner NT 84 B2
Milloo VIC 41 K12
Millstream Chichester Nat Park WA 78 E4 82 D2
Millstream Falls Nat Park QLD 11 E12
Millswood SA 59 H4
Millthorpe NSW 22 G4
Milltown VIC 38 G4
Millwood NSW 29 H13
Milparinka NSW 26 D2
Milperra NSW 19 G2 21 D9
Milton NSW 30 D6
Milton QLD 5 F8
Milvale NSW 22 J2 29 F14
Milyakburra NT 87 F12
Milyu Nature Res WA 70 D1
Mimili (Everard Park) SA 68 C6
Mimosa Rocks Nat Park NSW 30 H5
Mincha VIC 41 H11
Mindarie SA 62 C6 65 J12
Minden QLD 5 J8
Miners Rest VIC 39 E10
Minerva QLD 8 J6
Minerva Hills Nat Park QLD 8 J6
Mingary SA 65 D13
Mingay VIC 39 F9
Mingela QLD 8 B4 11 J14
Mingenew WA 76 G4
Mingoola QLD 25 C9
Minhamite VIC 38 G6
Minilya Roadhouse WA 78 H1
Minimay VIC 38 B2
Mininera VIC 39 E8
Miniyeri NT 87 H8
Minjah VIC 38 G6
Minjary Nat Park NSW 29 H14 30 D1
Minjilang NT 86 B6
Minlaton SA 62 H6 65 J8
Minnamurra NSW 23 K8
Minnie Water NSW 25 E13
Minnipa SA 64 E4
Minore NSW 22 C3
Mintabie SA 66 D1 68 C6
Mintaro SA 62 F4 65 G10
Minto NSW 21 E10
Minyip VIC 38 A6 40 K6
Miralie VIC 28 H5 41 E9
Miram VIC 40 K2
Miram South VIC 38 A3 40 K3
Miranda NSW 19 J4 21 C10
Mirani QLD 9 D8
Mirannie NSW 23 D10
Mirboo VIC 44 F7 46 G1
Mirboo North VIC 44 F7 46 G1
Miriam Vale QLD 9 J12
Mirikata SA 66 H5
Mirima (Hidden Valley) Nat Park WA 81 D14
Mirimbah VIC 42 G7 46 A2
Miririnyunga (Duck Ponds) NT 88 F4
Miriwinni QLD 11 E13
Mirrabooka QLD 15 F13
Mirrabooka WA 71 D4
Mirranatwa VIC 38 D6
Mirrindi NT 88 F4
Mirrnatja NT 87 D10
Mirrool NSW 29 F12
Missabotti NSW 25 H12
Mission Beach QLD 11 E13
Missouri Mine WA 77 H10
Mistake Creek NT 79 A14 81 G14 88 C1
Mitakooki QLD 12 A4
Mitcham SA 59 J4 60 G2 61 A6
Mitcham VIC 35 D7
Mitchell ACT 32 C5
Mitchell QLD 6 D3
Mitchell - Alice Rivers Nat Park QLD 10 A7 16 K2
Mitchell River Nat Park VIC 43 J10 45 A12 46 C5
Mitchell River Nat Park WA 81 C9
Mitchells (site) VIC 42 H7 46 B1
Mitchellville SA 62 J3 65 F8
Mitchelton QLD 3 D2
Mitiamo VIC 41 J12
Mitre VIC 38 B4
Mitta Mitta VIC 43 D10
Mittagong NSW 22 K7 30 B6
Mittyack VIC 28 H4 40 E6
Moa Island QLD 16 A2
Moama NSW 29 K8 41 J13 42 B1
Moana SA 60 K1 61 D5
Moana Sands Con Park SA 60 K1 61 D5
Mobrup WA 73 B13
Mockinya VIC 38 C5
Modbury SA 59 D6 60 E3
Modbury Heights SA 59 C6
Modbury North SA 59 D6
Modella VIC 37 G13 44 E5
Modewarre VIC 36 H1
Moe VIC 44 D7 46 F1
Moganemby VIC 42 D4
Moggill QLD 3 H1 5 F9
Mogo NSW 30 F6
Mogriguy NSW 22 C3
Mogumber WA 74 A3 76 J5
Moil NT 84 B3
Moina TAS 54 F6
Mokepilly VIC 38 C7
Mokola Con Park SA 62 E3 65 F10
Mole Creek TAS 54 G7
Mole Creek Karst Nat Park TAS 54 G7
Mole River NSW 7 K10 25 C9
Molesworth TAS 50 B3 53 F10
Molesworth VIC 42 G4
Moliagul VIC 39 B10
Molka VIC 42 E3
Molle Islands Nat Park QLD 9 B8
Mollerin Nature Res WA 76 H6
Mollymook NSW 30 D6
Molong NSW 22 F4
Moltema TAS 55 F8
Molyullah VIC 42 D6
Mona Vale NSW 19 B7 20 B6 23 G9
Mona Vale TAS 53 B11 55 J11
Monadnocks Con Res WA 72 E5 74 D3
Monak NSW 28 F4 40 A5
Monarto Con Park SA 60 K7
Monash ACT 32 H4
Monash SA 62 B5 65 H13
Monbulk VIC 37 D11 42 K3 44 C3
Moncrieff ACT 32 A4
Mondrain Island WA 75 H14
Monduran Dam QLD 7 A11 9 K12
Monea VIC 42 E3
Monegeetta VIC 39 D13 42 H1
Monga NSW 30 E5
Monga Nat Park NSW 30 E5
Mongarlowe NSW 30 E5

Tyagarah Nature Res – Whitemark 107

Tyagarah Nature Res NSW 25 B14
Tyagong NSW 22 H2 30 A1
Tyalgum NSW 7 J13 25 A13
Tyalla VIC 28 H2 40 E3
Tycannah NSW 24 E5
Tyenna TAS 53 F8
Tyers VIC 45 D8 46 F2
Tylden VIC 39 D12
Tyndale NSW 25 E13
Tynong VIC 37 F12 44 D4
Tynong North VIC 37 F12
Tyntynder Central VIC 28 H6 41 E9
Tyntynder South VIC 28 H6 41 F9
Tyrendarra VIC 38 H4
Tyrendarra East VIC 38 H4
Tyringham NSW 25 G11
Tyrrell Downs VIC 28 J5 40 F7

U

Uarbry NSW 22 B6
Ubobo QLD 9 J11
Ukatjupa NT 79 K14 90 K1
Uki NSW 7 J13 25 A13
Ulamambri NSW 24 J4
Ulan NSW 22 C6
Ulandra Nature Res NSW 22 K2 29 G14
Ulaypai SA 68 A4 90 K5
Uleybury SA 60 C4
Ulidarra Nat Park NSW 25 G13
Ulidia NSW 25 B12
Ulinda NSW 22 A5 24 K4
Ulkiya SA 68 B3 90 K4
Ulladulla NSW 30 E6
Ullina VIC 39 D10
Ullswater VIC 38 C3
Ulmarra NSW 25 E13
Ulong NSW 25 G12
Ultima VIC 28 J6 41 F8
Ultimo NSW 18 D1
Uluru - Kata Tjuta Nat Park NT 90 J4
Ulverstone TAS 54 E6
Umagico QLD 16 B2
Umbakumba NT 87 F13
Umerina SA 66 C1 68 B6
Umina NSW 20 B5
Umpukula SA 68 A3
Umpukulunga SA 90 K3
Umuwa SA 68 B5
Unanderra NSW 21 D14
Undara Volcanic Nat Park QLD 11 F11
Undera VIC 42 C3
Underbool VIC 28 H3 40 E4
Underwood QLD 3 H5
Underwood TAS 55 E10 56 E6
Undina QLD 10 K6 12 A5
Ungarie NSW 29 D12
Ungarra SA 64 G6
Ungo QLD 8 K1 13 H10
Unicup Nature Res WA 73 C14 74 H4
Unley SA 58 D2 59 G4 60 D2 61 A6
Unnamed Con Park SA 68 E2 83 E7
Upper Bingara NSW 24 F7
Upper Blessington TAS 55 F11
Upper Bowman NSW 23 B11
Upper Caboolture QLD 4 F5
Upper Castra TAS 54 F6
Upper Colo NSW 20 G5
Upper Coomera QLD 5 C11
Upper Esk TAS 55 F12
Upper Ferntree Gully VIC 37 E10 42 K3 44 C3
Upper Hermitage SA 60 E4
Upper Horton NSW 24 F6
Upper Kedron QLD 3 D1
Upper Manilla NSW 24 H7
Upper McDonald NSW 20 F3
Upper Mount Gravatt QLD 3 G5
Upper Mount Hicks TAS 54 D5
Upper Myall NSW 23 C12
Upper Nariel VIC 43 D12
Upper Natone TAS 54 E5
Upper Orara NSW 25 G12
Upper Plenty VIC 39 D14 42 H2
Upper Rollands Plains NSW 25 K11
Upper Scamander TAS 55 F14
Upper Stone QLD 11 G13
Upper Stowport TAS 54 E5
Upper Sturt SA 59 K6
Upper Swan WA 72 F2 74 C3 76 K5
Upper Tallebudgera QLD 5 C14
Upper Yarra Dam VIC 37 B14 42 J5 44 B5
Uraidla SA 59 H7 60 G4 62 F7 65 J10
Uralla NSW 25 H9
Urana NSW 29 H11
Urandangi QLD 12 C2
Urangeline NSW 29 J12
Urangeline East NSW 29 J12
Urania SA 62 H6 65 H8
Uranquinty NSW 29 H13
Urapunga NT 87 G9
Urapuntja (Utopia) NT 91 C9
Urawa Nature Res WA 76 E4
Urbenville NSW 7 J12 25 A12
Urilpila NT 90 J3
Urlampe NT 12 D1 91 D14
Urrbrae SA 59 H5
Urunga NSW 25 G12
Useless Loop WA 76 B1 78 K1
Utah Lake NSW 27 E8
Uxbridge TAS 53 F9

V

Vacy NSW 23 D10
Valencia Island NT 86 B6
Valley Heights NSW 21 H8
Valley View SA 59 D5
Van Diemen Gulf NT 85 A4 86 C5
Vanderlin Island NT 87 J13 89 A13
Vandyke Creek Con Park QLD 8 J6
Vansittart Bay WA 81 A10
Vansittart Island TAS 55 C10
Varley WA 75 E9
Vasey VIC 38 D4
Vasse WA 73 J11
Vaucluse NSW 19 F7 21 B8
Vectus VIC 38 B5
Veitch SA 62 B6 65 J13
Venman Bushland Nat Park QLD 3 J7 5 D9
Ventnor VIC 37 K9 39 J14 44 F2
Venus Bay SA 64 F4
Venus Bay VIC 44 G5
Venus Bay Con Park SA 64 F3
Venus Bay Con Res SA 64 E3
Verdun SA 60 H4
Veresdale QLD 5 F12
Vermont VIC 37 D9
Verona NSW 30 H5
Verona Sands TAS 53 H10
Verran SA 64 G6
Vervale VIC 37 G12
Victor Harbor SA 61 J6 63 F8 65 K10
Victoria Park WA 71 G4
Victoria Point QLD 5 C9
Victoria River NT 86 J4 88 A4
Victoria Rock Nature Res WA 75 B11 77 J10
Victoria Valley TAS 53 D8 55 K8
Victoria Valley VIC 38 E6
Victory Well SA 68 C5
Villawood NSW 19 F2
Villeneuve QLD 4 H3
Vincentia NSW 30 D7
Vineyard NSW 20 F7
Vinifera VIC 28 H6 41 E9
Violet Town VIC 42 D4
Virginia QLD 3 C5
Virginia SA 60 C2 62 F6 65 H10
Vista SA 59 D7
Vite Vite VIC 39 F8
Vite Vite North VIC 39 F9
Vivonne SA 63 J9
Vivonne Bay Con Park SA 63 J9
Vokes Hill Corner SA 68 E3
Vulkathuna-Gammon Ranges Nat Park SA 65 A11 67 K11

W

Waaia VIC 42 B3
Waarre VIC 39 J8
Wabba Wilderness Park VIC 43 C11
Wabma Kadarbu Mound Springs Con Park SA 66 H7
Wacol QLD 3 H1 5 F9
Wadbilliga NSW 30 G4
Waddamana TAS 53 C8 55 K8
Waddi NSW 29 G10
Waddikee SA 64 F6
Wadeye NT 86 G1
Waeel WA 72 B2
Wagaman NT 84 B3
Wagant VIC 28 H4 40 E6
Wagerup WA 72 F7
Wagga Wagga NSW 29 H13
Waggabundi QLD 10 H3
Waggarandall VIC 42 C5
Wagin WA 73 A9 74 F5
Wagonga NSW 30 G5
Wahgunyah VIC 42 B7
Wahgunyah Con Res SA 68 K5
Wahroonga NSW 19 C4 20 C7
Waikerie SA 62 C5 65 H12
Wail VIC 38 A5
Wairewa VIC 43 K13 47 D8
Waitchie VIC 28 J5 41 F8
Waite Creek Settlement NT 90 D3
Waitpinga SA 61 J5 63 F8 65 K10
Waitpinga Con Park SA 61 J3
Wakool NSW 29 J8 41 F12
Walalkarra SA 68 C4
Walang NSW 22 G6
Walbundrie NSW 29 J12
Walcha NSW 25 J9
Walcha Road NSW 25 J8
Waldegrave Island Con Park SA 64 F4
Walebing WA 74 A3 76 J5
Walga Gunya WA 77 C8
Walgett NSW 24 F1 27 E14
Walgoolan WA 74 B7 77 J8
Walhalla VIC 45 C8 46 E2
Walitjara SA 68 A3 90 K3
Walka NT 79 J14 83 A7 90 H1
Walkamin QLD 11 D12
Walkaway WA 76 F3
Walker VIC 37 A14
Walker Flat SA 62 D6 65 J11
Walker Island TAS 52 K7 54 B2
Walkers Crossing SA 67 D12
Walkerston QLD 9 D8
Walkerville SA 59 F4 60 F2
Walkerville North VIC 44 H6
Walkerville South VIC 44 J6
Wall SA 62 D7 65 J11
Walla Walla NSW 29 J12
Wallabadah NSW 23 A8 24 K7
Wallabadah Nature Res NSW 23 A9 24 K7
Wallabi Group WA 76 F2
Wallabrook SA 38 B1 63 B11
Wallaby Island QLD 10 A6 16 G1
Wallace VIC 39 E11
Wallace Rockhole NT 90 G7
Wallacedale North VIC 38 G4
Wallacia NSW 21 G9 23 H8
Wallaga Lake Heights NSW 30 G5
Wallaga Lake Nat Park NSW 30 G5
Wallal QLD 15 E13
Wallaloo VIC 38 B7
Wallaloo East VIC 38 B7
Wallamba Nature Res NSW 23 C12
Wallan VIC 39 D14 42 H2
Wallan East VIC 39 D14 42 H2
Wallangarra NSW 7 K10 25 C10
Wallangra NSW 24 D7
Wallany SA 68 B4 90 K4
Wallarah Nat Park NSW 23 F10
Wallaroo NSW 32 A2
Wallaroo SA 62 H4 65 G8
Wallaroo Nature Res NSW 23 D11
Wallatinna SA 66 D2 68 C7
Wallaville QLD 7 A11
Wallendbeen NSW 22 K2 29 G14 30 B1
Wallerawang NSW 22 F7
Walleroobie NSW 29 F12
Walli NSW 22 G4
Wallinduc VIC 39 F9
Wallingat Nat Park NSW 23 C12
Wallington VIC 36 H4
Wallon QLD 5 H9
Walloway SA 62 F1 65 E10
Wallpolla Island VIC 40 A3
Walls of Jerusalem Nat Park TAS 52 A6 54 H6
Wallsend NSW 23 E10
Wallumbilla QLD 6 E6
Wallundry NSW 22 J1 29 F14
Wallup VIC 40 K5
Walmer NSW 22 D3
Walpa VIC 43 K10 45 B12 46 D5
Walpeup VIC 28 H3 40 E5
Walpole WA 74 K4
Walpole-Nornalup Nat Park WA 74 K4
Waltara NSW 20 D7
Walu NT 79 J14 90 H2
Walungurru (Kintore) NT 79 G14 90 E1
Walwa VIC 29 K14 43 A11
Walyahmoning Nature Res WA 77 H8
Walyinynga SA 68 A4 90 K4
Walytjatjata NT 68 A1 79 K14 90 K2
Walyunga Nat Park WA 72 F2
Wamberal NSW 20 B4
Wamberal Lagoon Nature Res NSW 23 G10
Wambool Nature Res NSW 22 G6
Wamboyne NSW 29 D13
Wammuta QLD 12 B4
Wamoon NSW 29 F11
Wamuran QLD 4 G4 7 F12
Wamuran Basin QLD 4 G4
Wanaaring NSW 26 D7
Wanagarren Nature Res WA 74 A1 76 J4
Wanbi SA 62 B6 65 J12
Wandana Nature Res WA 76 E4
Wandandian NSW 30 D6
Wandearah East SA 62 G3 65 F9
Wandearah West SA 62 G3 65 F9
Wandella NSW 30 G5
Wandering WA 72 C6 74 E4
Wandiligong VIC 43 E9
Wandilo SA 63 B13
Wandin North VIC 37 C11
Wando Bridge VIC 38 E3
Wando Vale VIC 38 E3
Wandoan QLD 6 D7
Wandong VIC 39 D14 42 H2
Wandoo Con Park WA 72 D4 74 D4 76 K5
Wandsworth NSW 25 F9
Wanganella NSW 29 H8 41 E13
Wangara WA 71 B3
Wangarabell VIC 47 C12
Wangaratta VIC 42 C6
Wangary SA 64 H5
Wangerrip VIC 39 K9
Wangetti QLD 11 C12
Wangkatjungka (Christmas Creek) WA 79 C12 81 K9
Wangoom VIC 38 H7
Wanguri NT 84 A3
Wanilla SA 64 H5
Wanjarri Nature Res WA 77 D10
Wankari NT 79 J14 83 A7 90 H1
Wanko QLD 15 E13
Wanna Lakes WA 83 D6
Wannamal WA 74 B3 76 J5
Wannarn WA 79 J13 83 A6
Wanneroo WA 71 A3 72 G2 74 C2 76 K4
Wanniassa ACT 32 H4
Wannon VIC 38 F4
Wannoo Billabong Roadhouse WA 76 C3
Wanora QLD 5 H8
Wantabadgery NSW 29 H14
Wanwin VIC 38 G2
Wapengo NSW 30 H5
Wapet Camp WA 78 E3
Wappinguy NSW 22 C7
Waragai Creek Nature Res NSW 25 E13
Warakurna WA 79 J13 83 A7
Warakurna Roadhouse WA 79 J13 83 A7
Waramanga ACT 32 G3
Warana QLD 4 D1
Waranga VIC 39 A14 42 D2
Waratah TAS 54 F4
Waratah Bay VIC 44 H6
Waratah North VIC 44 H6
Warburn NSW 29 F10
Warburton VIC 37 C13 42 K4 44 B5
Warburton WA 79 K12 83 B5
Warburton East VIC 37 C13
Warby Range State Park VIC 42 C6
Ward Island SA 64 G3
Wardang Island SA 62 H6 65 H8
Wardell NSW 25 C14
Wards Mistake NSW 25 F10
Wards River NSW 23 C11
Warialda NSW 24 D7
Warianna QLD 13 B10
Warilla NSW 23 K8 30 B7
Warkton NSW 22 A5 24 K3
Warkworth NSW 23 D9
Warmun WA 81 G13
Warmun (Turkey Creek) WA 79 A14
Warncoort VIC 39 H10
Warneet VIC 37 H10 44 E3
Warnertown SA 62 G3 65 F9
Warnervale NSW 20 A2
Warooka SA 62 H7 65 J8
Waroona WA 72 F7 74 E3
Warra QLD 7 E9
Warra Nat Park NSW 25 F10
Warrabah Nat Park NSW 24 G7
Warrabillinna SA 68 B5 90 K6
Warrabkook VIC 38 G5
Warracknabeal VIC 40 K6
Warradale SA 59 J2
Warraderry NSW 22 G2
Warragamba NSW 21 G10 23 H8
Warragamba VIC 41 K12
Warragoon NSW 29 K11 42 A6
Warragul VIC 37 G14 44 D6
Warrah Creek NSW 23 B8
Warrak VIC 39 D8
Warrakoo VIC 28 F2
Warrambine VIC 39 G10
Warramboo SA 64 F5
Warrandyte VIC 35 C7 37 C9 42 K3 44 B2
Warrandyte State Park VIC 35 B7 37 C9 42 K3 44 B2
Warranmang VIC 39 C9
Warranulla NSW 23 C11
Warrapura WA 83 A7
Warrawee NSW 20 C7
Warrawenia Lake NSW 28 D3
Warrayure VIC 38 F5
Warreah QLD 8 C2 11 K11 13 A11
Warrego Mine NT 89 G8
Warrell Creek NSW 25 H12
Warren NSW 22 A1 27 J14
Warren Con Park SA 60 D5
Warren Nat Park WA 73 F14 74 J3
Warrenbayne VIC 42 E5
Warrenben Con Park SA 62 J7 64 J7
Warrentinna TAS 55 D12
Warriewood NSW 20 B6
Warrigal QLD 8 C2 11 K12 13 A12
Warrill View QLD 5 J11
Warrimoo NSW 21 H8
Warrina SA 66 E6
Warringa TAS 54 E6
Warrion VIC 39 H10
Warrnambool VIC 38 H6
Warrong VIC 38 H6
Warroo NSW 22 F1 29 D13
Warrow SA 64 H5
Warrumbungle NSW 24 J2
Warrumbungle Nat Park NSW 24 J3
Warrupura WA 79 J14 90 H1
Warruwi NT 86 B7
Wartburg QLD 9 K12
Wartook VIC 38 C6
Warup WA 73 A9
Warwick QLD 7 H11 25 A10
Warwick WA 71 C2
Warwick Farm NSW 19 G1
WA-SA Border Village SA 68 K1 83 G7
Wasaga QLD 16 B2
Washpool Nat Park NSW 25 D11
Wasleys SA 60 A3 62 F6 65 H10
Watagan NSW 20 E1
Watagans Nat Park NSW 23 E9 23 E9
Watalgan QLD 9 K12
Watanobbi NSW 20 B2
Watarrka Nat Park NT 90 G5
Watarru SA 68 C2
Watchem VIC 40 J7
Watchupga VIC 28 K4 40 H7
Waterfall NSW 21 C11 23 J8
Waterfall Gully SA 59 H6
Waterford VIC 43 J9 45 A11 46 C4
Waterford WA 71 H4
Waterhouse TAS 55 D12
Waterhouse Con Area TAS 55 C11
Waterhouse Island TAS 55 C11
Waterloo SA 62 E4 65 G10
Waterloo TAS 50 J1 53 H9
Waterloo VIC 39 D9
Waterloo WA 73 G9
Waterloo Corner SA 59 A3
Waterman WA 71 C1
Watervale SA 62 F4 65 G10
Watgania VIC 38 E7
Watheroo WA 76 H5
Watheroo Nat Park WA 76 H4
Watinuna SA 68 B5
Watson ACT 32 C5
Watson SA 68 H4
Watson Island NT 87 J13 89 A13
Watson Oil Field QLD 14 H6
Watsonia VIC 35 B5 37 C8
Watsons Bay NSW 19 E7 21 B8
Watsons Creek NSW 25 H8
Watsons Creek VIC 37 B9
Watsons Creek Nature Res NSW 25 H8
Wattamolla NSW 21 B11
Wattamondara NSW 22 H3
Wattle Creek VIC 39 C8
Wattle Flat NSW 22 F6
Wattle Glen VIC 37 B9
Wattle Grove NSW 21 D10
Wattle Grove TAS 50 J2 53 H9
Wattle Grove WA 71 H7
Wattle Hill TAS 51 A10 53 F11
Wattle Island VIC 44 K7 46 K1
Wattle Park SA 59 G6
Wattle Park VIC 46 E6
Wattle Point VIC 45 C13
Wattle Range SA 63 B13
Wattle Vale VIC 39 B14 42 E2
Waubra VIC 39 D10
Wauchope NSW 23 A13 25 K12
Wauchope NT 89 J9 91 A9
Waukaringa SA 62 D1 65 D11
Wauraltee SA 62 H6 65 H8
Waurn Ponds VIC 36 H2 39 H12
Wavell Heights QLD 3 C4
Waverley NSW 19 F7 21 B8
Wayatinah TAS 52 D7
Waychinicup Nat Park WA 74 J7
Waygara VIC 43 K13 47 D8
Wayville SA 58 D2 59 G4
Weabonga NSW 25 J8
Weavers SA 62 H7 65 J8
Webbs NSW 22 C2
Webbs Creek NSW 20 F4
Wedderburn NSW 21 E12
Wedderburn VIC 41 K10
Wedderburn Junction VIC 41 K10
Weddin Mountains Nat Park NSW 22 H2 29 E14
Wedge Island SA 62 K7 64 J6
Wedge Island TAS 51 H10
Wedge Island WA 74 A1 76 J4
Wedge Islands TAS 53 H11
Wednesday Island QLD 16 B2
Wee Jasper NSW 30 D2
Wee Jasper Nature Res NSW 30 D2
Wee Waa NSW 24 F4
Weegena TAS 54 F7
Weelhamby Lake WA 76 G5
Weemelah NSW 24 C3
Weemol NT 87 F9
Weerangourt VIC 38 G4
Weerite VIC 39 H9
Weetah TAS 55 F8
Weetaliba NSW 22 A5 24 K4
Weetalibah Nature Res NSW 22 B5
Weetangera ACT 32 C3
Weethalle NSW 29 E12
Weetulta SA 62 H5 65 H8
Wee-Wee-Rup VIC 41 H12
Wehla VIC 39 A10
Weilmoringle NSW 6 K1 27 C12
Weimby NSW 28 G5 41 C8
Weipa QLD 16 E1
Weismantels NSW 23 C11
Weitalaba QLD 9 J11
Weja NSW 29 D12
Welaregang NSW 29 K14 43 B12
Weldborough TAS 55 E12
Welford Lagoon QLD 13 H10 15 A9
Welford Nat Park QLD 13 H9 15 A8
Wellesley Islands QLD 10 C4
Wellingrove NSW 25 E9
Wellington NSW 22 D4
Wellington SA 63 D8 65 K11
Wellington Nat Park WA 73 F9 74 F3
Wellington Point QLD 5 C8
Wellsford VIC 39 A12
Wellstead WA 74 J7
Welshmans Reef VIC 39 C11
Welshpool VIC 45 G8 46 H2
Welshpool WA 71 G6
Wembley WA 71 F3
Wembley Downs WA 71 E2
Wemen VIC 28 G4 40 D6
Wentworth NSW 28 F3 40 A4
Wentworth Falls NSW 21 K9 22 G7
Werakata Nat Park NSW 23 E10
Weranga QLD 7 F8
Werneth VIC 39 G10
Werombi NSW 21 G11 23 H8
Werrap VIC 40 H4
Werribee VIC 36 E5 39 F13 42 K1
Werribee Gorge State Park VIC 36 B3 39 E12
Werribee South VIC 36 E5 39 G13
Werrikimbe Nat Park NSW 25 J10
Werrimull VIC 28 F2 40 B3
Werrington NSW 21 G8
Werris Creek NSW 24 K7
Wesburn VIC 37 C12
Wesley Vale TAS 54 E7
Wessel Islands NT 87 B12
West Beach SA 59 G2 60 G1 61 A5
West Bore No. 2 SA 68 B5
West Cape Howe Nat Park WA 74 K6
West End QLD 2 D1 3 E3 5 E8
West Frankford TAS 55 E8 56 F1
West Gosford NSW 20 C4
West Group WA 75 H12 83 J1
West Hill QLD 9 E8
West Hill Island QLD 9 E9
West Hill Nat Park QLD 9 E9
West Hobart TAS 49 C1
West Hoxton NSW 21 E10
West Island NT 87 J12 89 A12
West Island QLD 16 B1
West Island SA 61 K6
West Island Con Park SA 61 J7 61 K6
West Kentish TAS 54 F7
West Killara NSW 21 C8
West Lakes SA 59 E1 60 F1
West MacDonnell Nat Park NT 90 F7
West Pennant Hills NSW 19 C2
West Perth WA 70 A1 71 F3
West Pine TAS 54 E6
West Pymble NSW 19 D4 20 C7
West Ridgley TAS 54 E5
West Ryde NSW 19 E4
West Scottsdale TAS 55 E11
West Swan WA 71 C6
West Wyalong NSW 29 E13
Westbourne Park SA 59 H4
Westbury TAS 55 G9 56 H2
Westby NSW 29 J13
Westby VIC 28 J7 41 G11
Westdale WA 72 D5
Western Creek TAS 54 G7
Western Flat SA 38 A1 63 B11
Western Junction TAS 55 G10 56 J6
Western Port VIC 37 H10
Western River SA 63 J8 64 K7
Western River Con Park SA 63 J8 64 K7
Westerway TAS 53 E8
Westfield WA 71 K7
Westgate QLD 15 D14
Westmar QLD 6 H6
Westmead NSW 19 E2
Westmeadows VIC 35 A2
Westmere VIC 39 F8
Westminster WA 71 D3
Weston ACT 32 F3
Weston Creek ACT 32 F2
Westonia WA 74 B7 77 J8
Westwood QLD 9 H9
Westwood TAS 55 F9 56 H4
Wetherill Park NSW 21 E9
Weymouth TAS 55 D10 56 B5
Whale Beach NSW 20 B6
Wharminda SA 64 G6
Wharparilla VIC 41 J13 42 B1
Whealbah NSW 29 E9
Wheelers Hill VIC 35 F6
Wheeo NSW 22 K5 30 B4
Wherrol Flat NSW 23 B12
Whetstone QLD 7 J9 25 A8
Whidbey Isles Con Park SA 64 J4
Whim Creek WA 78 E5 82 C3
Whiporie NSW 25 D13
Whirily VIC 41 H8
White Beach TAS 51 H11 53 H12
White Cliffs NSW 26 G5
White Dam Con Park SA 62 D4 65 G11
White Flag Lake WA 77 H11
White Flat SA 64 H6
White Gum Valley WA 71 J2
White Hills TAS 55 F10 56 H6
White Hut SA 62 J7 64 J7
White Lake WA 79 J8
White Mountains Nat Park QLD 8 C2 11 K12 13 A11
Whitefoord TAS 53 D11
Whiteheads Creek VIC 42 F3
Whiteman WA 71 C5
Whitemark TAS 55 C9

List of abbreviations

CBD	– Central Business District
Con Area	– Conservation Area
Con Park	– Conservation Park
Nat Park	– National Park
Nature Res	– Nature Reserve
Rec Park	– Recreation Park
Reg Res	– Regional Reserve
Res	– Reserve

4WD Maps

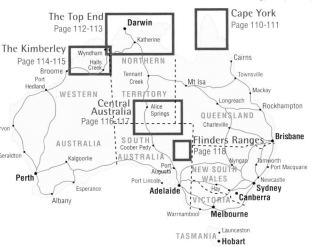

Pentecost River crossing, WA (81 E12)

The Top End
Page 112-113

Darwin
Katherine

Cape York
Page 110-111

The Kimberley
Page 114-115

Wyndham
Halls Creek
Broome
Port Hedland

Cairns
Townsville

NORTHERN

WESTERN   TERRITORY

Central
Australia
Page 116-117

Alice Springs

Tennant Creek

Mt Isa

Mackay

Longreach

Rockhampton

QUEENSLAND

Charleville

AUSTRALIA

Geraldton

Kalgoorlie

SOUTH
AUSTRALIA

Coober Pedy

Flinders Ranges
Page 118

Brisbane

Perth

Esperance

Port Augusta
Port Lincoln

NEW SOUTH
WALES

Nyngan

Tamworth
Port Macquarie

Newcastle

Albany

Adelaide

Hay

VICTORIA

Sydney
Canberra

Warrnambool

Melbourne

TASMANIA

Launceston
Hobart

Legend

Road Classifications
The following road and track classifications are based on a general assumption that map users are familiar with the often-rough condition of outback roads and tracks. Any unsealed road or track can be hazardous due to washouts, sand, mud or bull-dust patches and extreme corrugations. Use classifications as a general guide and always seek local advice.

GPS-Plotted Roads & Tracks—Purple
These roads and tracks were accurately plotted with a GPS and laptop computer during field work. Distances were also checked and have been rounded to the nearest kilometre (variations may occur due to wheel-slip and/or tyre pressure).

Other Roads and Tracks—Red
This road and track information has been compiled from 1:250,000 Geodata and other sources. The exact location and/or condition of these roads and tracks must therefore be treated with caution. (All highway information has been verified.)

Major Highway	*sealed*
Major Road	*sealed unsealed*
Minor Road	*sealed unsealed*
Track - 4WD only	----------
Rough Track- Very rough, becoming overgrown or difficult to follow.	··········
Major Road	*sealed unsealed*
Minor Road	*sealed unsealed*
Track - 4WD only	----------
Rough Track- Very rough, becoming overgrown or difficult to follow.	··········
National Hwy/Route Number	1 96
State Route Number	4 A32
Kilometres	★ 100 ★ ·50· 50·
Railway with Siding or Station	disused
Major Township	**Broome**
Major Aboriginal Community	● Beagle Bay
Minor Township	● Coen
Minor Aboriginal Community	● Bulgin
Homestead	■ 'Waterbank'
Point of Interest	● Memorial
Tower	☡
Waterhole/Rockhole/Pool	● East WH
National Park	
Aboriginal Land	
Saline Coastal Flat	
Reef/Cay	
Subject to Inundation	
Marine Park	
Lake, Mainly Dry Lake/Salt	
Lake Swamp	
Mangrove	
Sandridges	

i	Information Centre
▲	Camping Area with facilities
▲	Bush Camping
☖	Roadside Rest Area
☖	Rest Area with Overnight Camping
⚎	Outback Rest Area (no facilities)
⥌	Lookout
▣	Caravan Park/Sites
⌂	General Store
✉	Post Office or Agency
✕	Operating Mine Site/Area
✕	Abandoned Mining Area
⛑	Ranger Station/Parks Office
✚	Hospital/Medical Facility/Clinic
✈	Airport
✦	Airstrip/Airfield
✦	Royal Flying Doctor Base
✦	Abandoned Airstrip/Airfield
⛽	Leaded, Unleaded and Diesel
⛽	Leaded
⛽	Unleaded
⛽	Diesel
⛟	LPG Autogas
⛽	Bottled Gas Refills
🔧	Mechanical Repairs
◎	Tyre Repairs
🛏	Accommodation
☎	Public Telephone (remote areas only)
🍴	Meals
⚐	Drinking Water (remote areas only use at own risk)
⚑	Police Station
E	Eftpos
●	All Facilities (includes camping area with facilities, accommodation, caravan park/sites, general store, meals, fuel, LPG Autogas, bottled gas refills, mechanical repairs, tyre repairs)

GPS Guide

	Latitude (DMS)	Longitude (DMS)	Latitude (Dec)	Longitude (Dec)
Cape York				
Archer River Roadhouse	13°26'13"S	142°56'27"E	-13.43704	142.94070
Bamaga	10°53'36"S	142°23'10"E	-10.89323	142.38604
Cape York	10°41'15"S	142°31'51"E	-10.68758	142.53091
Captain Billy Landing	11°37'43"S	142°51'16"E	-11.62871	142.85457
Chili Beach	12°37'57"S	143°25'36"E	-12.63242	143.42660
Coen	13°56'44"S	143°11'56"E	-13.94558	143.19896
Eliot Falls	11°23'03"S	142°24'48"E	-11.38423	142.41335
Jardine River Ferry Crossing	11°06'14"S	142°17'04"E	-11.10393	142.28432
Telegraph Road T/O (from Peninsula Development Road)	13°04'50"S	142°46'07"E	-13.08042	142.76862
Telegraph Road T/O (from southern bypass road intersection)	12°05'39"S	142°33'32"E	-12.09415	142.55897
Telegraph Road T/O (from northern bypass road intersection)	11°27'15"S	142°25'04"E	-11.45413	142.41791
Ussher Point	11°09'19"S	142°47'50"E	-11.15529	142.79728
Weipa	12°37'24"S	141°52'44"E	-12.62346	141.87883
Wenlock River Crossing	12°27'21"S	142°38'28"E	-12.45579	142.64120
Top End				
Borroloola	16°04'15"S	136°18'26"E	-16.07078	136.30722
Darwin	12°27'26"S	130°50'12"E	-12.45722	130.83664
Jabiru	12°40'32"S	132°49'53"E	-12.67558	132.83141
Katherine	14°27'55"S	132°15'48"E	-14.46517	132.26347
Mataranka	14°55'17"S	133°03'54"E	-14.92127	133.06500
Nhulunbuy	12°11'11"S	136°46'55"E	-12.18652	136.78201
Pine Creek	13°49'15"S	131°49'59"E	-13.82077	131.83295
Roper Bar Store	14°44'23"S	134°31'39"E	-14.73970	134.52750
Timber Creek	15°38'53"S	130°28'36"E	-15.64816	130.47679
Kimberley				
Bell Gorge T/O (from Gibb River Road)	17°09'02"S	125°23'09"E	-17.15053	125.38575
Broome	17°57'19"S	122°14'21"E	-17.95538	122.23922
Bungle Bungle Ranger Station	17°25'13"S	128°17'59"E	-17.42024	128.29962
Bungle Bungle T/O (from Great Northern Hwy)	17°25'49"S	127°59'34"E	-17.43025	127.99276
Derby	17°18'34"S	123°38'25"E	-17.30933	123.64032
Fitzroy Crossing	18°11'50"S	125°34'00"E	-18.19714	125.56663
Halls Creek	18°13'29"S	127°39'59"E	-18.22485	127.66647
Kalumburu Road T/O (from Gibb River Road)	16°07'08"S	126°31'12"E	-16.11892	126.52008
Kununurra	15°46'41"S	128°44'39"E	-15.77813	128.74414
Mitchell Falls	14°49'14"S	125°41'33"E	-14.82055	125.69254
Mornington	17°30'38"S	126°06'38"E	-17.51048	126.11057
Mt Barnett Roadhouse	16°42'59"S	125°55'32"E	-16.71652	125.92567
Pentecost River Crossing	15°47'49"S	127°52'53"E	-15.79690	127.88137
Tunnel Creek	17°36'24"S	125°08'44"E	-17.60661	125.14549
Windjana Gorge	17°24'29"S	124°57'38"E	-17.40795	124.96051
Wyndham	15°29'13"S	128°07'27"E	-15.48690	128.12429
Central Australia				
Alice Springs	23°41'51"S	133°53'01"E	-23.69748	133.88362
Ayers Rock (Uluru)	25°20'39"S	131°01'56"E	-25.34421	131.03222
Birdsville	25°53'56"S	139°21'12"E	-25.89901	139.35342
Boulia	22°54'41"S	139°54'34"E	-22.91139	139.90935
Chambers Pillar	24°52'00"S	133°49'00"E	-24.86655	133.81659
Dalhousie Springs	26°25'21"S	135°30'11"E	-26.42248	135.50307
Finke	25°34'58"S	134°34'35"E	-25.58272	134.57642
Gosses Bluff	23°49'10"S	132°18'14"E	-23.81951	132.30377
Henbury Meteorite Craters	24°34'14"S	133°08'43"E	-24.57067	133.14538
Kings Canyon	24°15'00"S	131°34'00"E	-24.24996	131.56670
Mount Dare	26°04'09"S	135°15'04"E	-26.06926	135.25104
Old Andado	25°22'45"S	135°26'26"E	-25.37928	135.44046
Oodnadatta	27°32'58"S	135°26'58"E	-27.54957	135.44946
Ormiston Gorge	23°37'32"S	132°43'45"E	-23.62559	132.72930
Palm Valley	24°03'28"S	132°44'46"E	-24.05771	132.74620
Poeppel Corner	25°59'49"S	137°59'57"E	-25.99687	137.99906
Rainbow Valley	24°19'50"S	133°38'00"E	-24.33069	133.63322
Ross River Tourist Camp	23°35'36"S	134°29'29"E	-23.59334	134.49143
The Lambert Centre	25°36'31"S	134°21'43"E	-25.60861	134.36181
The Olgas - Kata Tjuta	25°18'08"S	130°44'19"E	-25.30226	130.73871
Warburton Crossing	27°03'46"S	138°46'37"E	-27.06265	138.77681
Warburton Crossing T/O (from Birdsville Track)	27°06'29"S	138°49'21"E	-27.10800	138.82262
Yulara Tourist Village	25°14'43"S	130°58'50"E	-25.24529	130.98055
Flinders Ranges				
Arkaroola Village	30°18'43"S	139°20'10"E	-30.31186	139.33615
Artimore	30°59'42"S	138°42'40"E	-30.99502	138.71114
Balcanoona	30°31'58"S	139°18'20"E	-30.53271	139.30564
Blinman	31°06'56"S	138°41'20"E	-31.11566	138.68879
Brachina Gorge	31°20'16"S	138°33'06"E	-31.33783	138.55153
Hawker	31°53'21"S	138°25'12"E	-31.88915	138.42003
Leigh Creek	30°35'35"S	138°24'17"E	-30.59312	138.40486
Lyndhurst	30°17'16"S	138°20'57"E	-30.28787	138.34930
Marree	29°38'42"S	138°03'42"E	-29.64512	138.06175
Parachilna	31°07'58"S	138°23'39"E	-31.13277	138.39409
Wilpena	31°31'45"S	138°36'12"E	-31.52909	138.60341

4WD

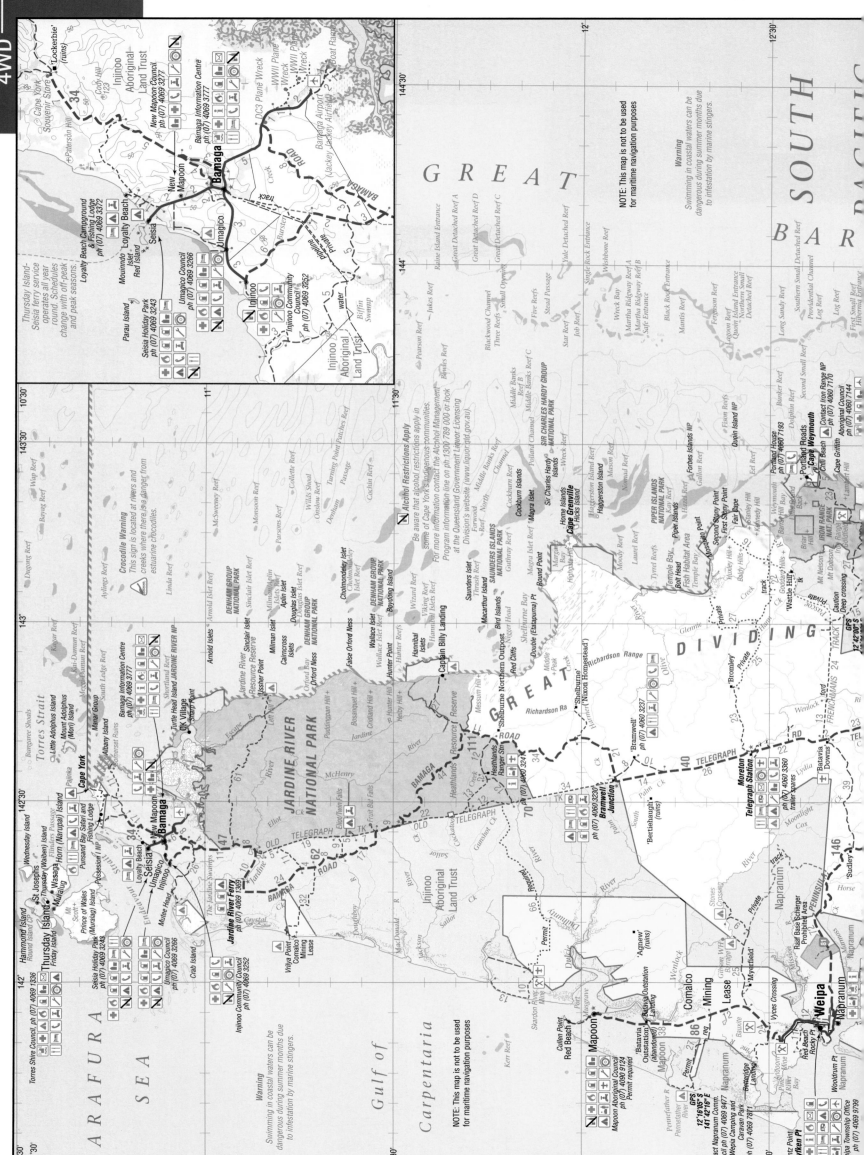

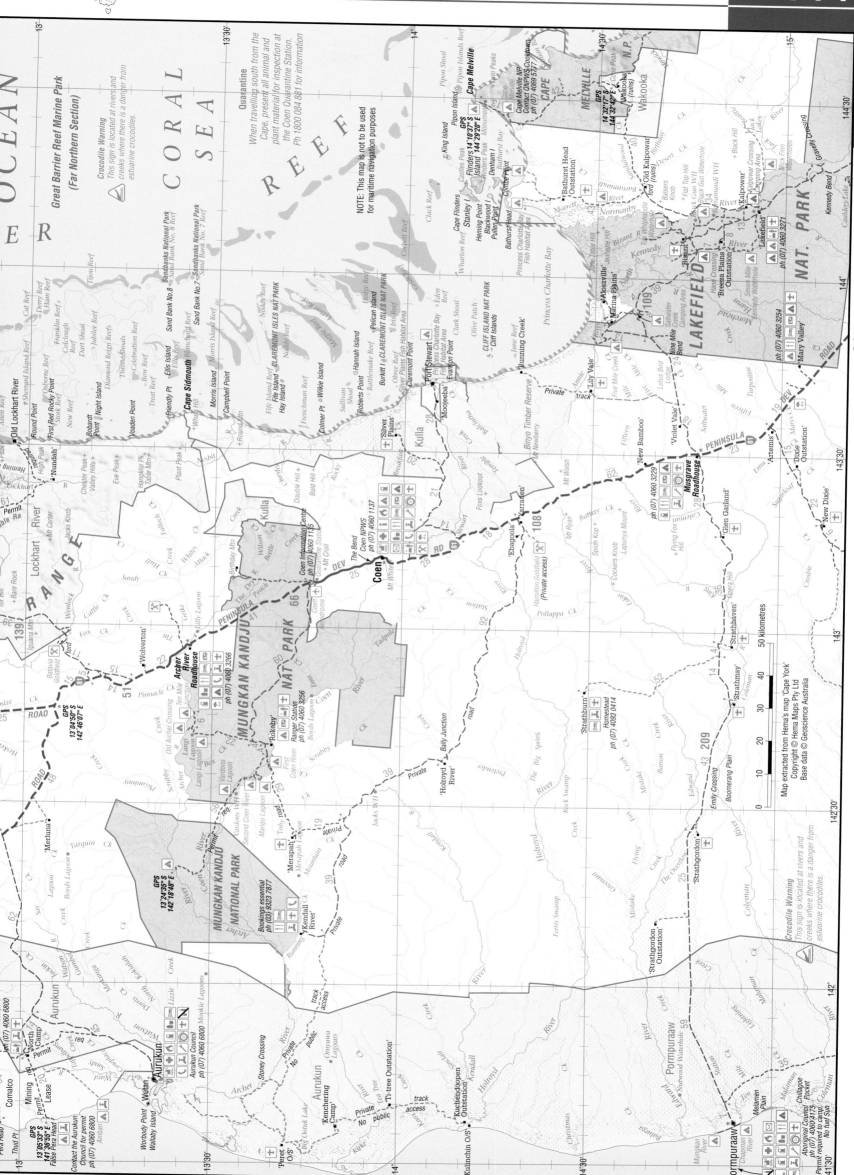

OCEAN

CORAL SEA

REEF

Great Barrier Reef Marine Park
(Far Northern Section)

Crocodile Warning
This sign is located at rivers and creeks where there is a danger from estuarine crocodiles.

Quarantine
When travelling south from the Cape, present all animal and plant material for inspection at the Coen Quarantine Station.
Ph 1800 084 881 for information

NOTE: This map is not to be used for maritime navigation purposes

CAPE MELVILLE N.P.
Cape Melville NP
Contact QNPWS/Cooktown
ph (07) 4069 5777
GPS
14 32'17" S
144 32'42" E

LAKEFIELD NAT. PARK

ph (07) 4060 3271

ph (07) 4060 3254

CLAREMONT ISLES NAT PARK

CLIFF ISLAND NAT PARK

Coen Information Centre
ph (07) 4060 1135

Coen NPWS
ph (07) 4060 1137

Coen

PENINSULA DEV RD

MUNGKAN KANDJU NAT PARK

Archer River Roadhouse
ph (07) 4060 3266

Ranger Station
ph (07) 4060 3256

Musgrave Roadhouse
ph (07) 4060 3229

MUNGKAN KANDJU NATIONAL PARK

Bookings essential
ph (03) 9323 7877

GPS
13 24'35" S
142 18'48" E

GPS
13 04'50" S
142 46'07" E

ROAD

Contact the Aurukun Council for permit
ph (07) 4060 6800
GPS
13 05'33" S
141 36'55" E

Aurukun Council
ph (07) 4060 6800

Aurukun

Mining road
Lease
Permit req

Aboriginal Council
ph (07) 4060 4175
Permit required to camp.
No fuel Sun

Pormpuraaw

Crocodile Warning
This sign is located at rivers and creeks where there is a danger from estuarine crocodiles.

50 kilometres
0 10 20 30 40

Map extracted from Hema's map 'Cape York'
Copyright © Hema Maps Pty Ltd
Base data © Geoscience Australia

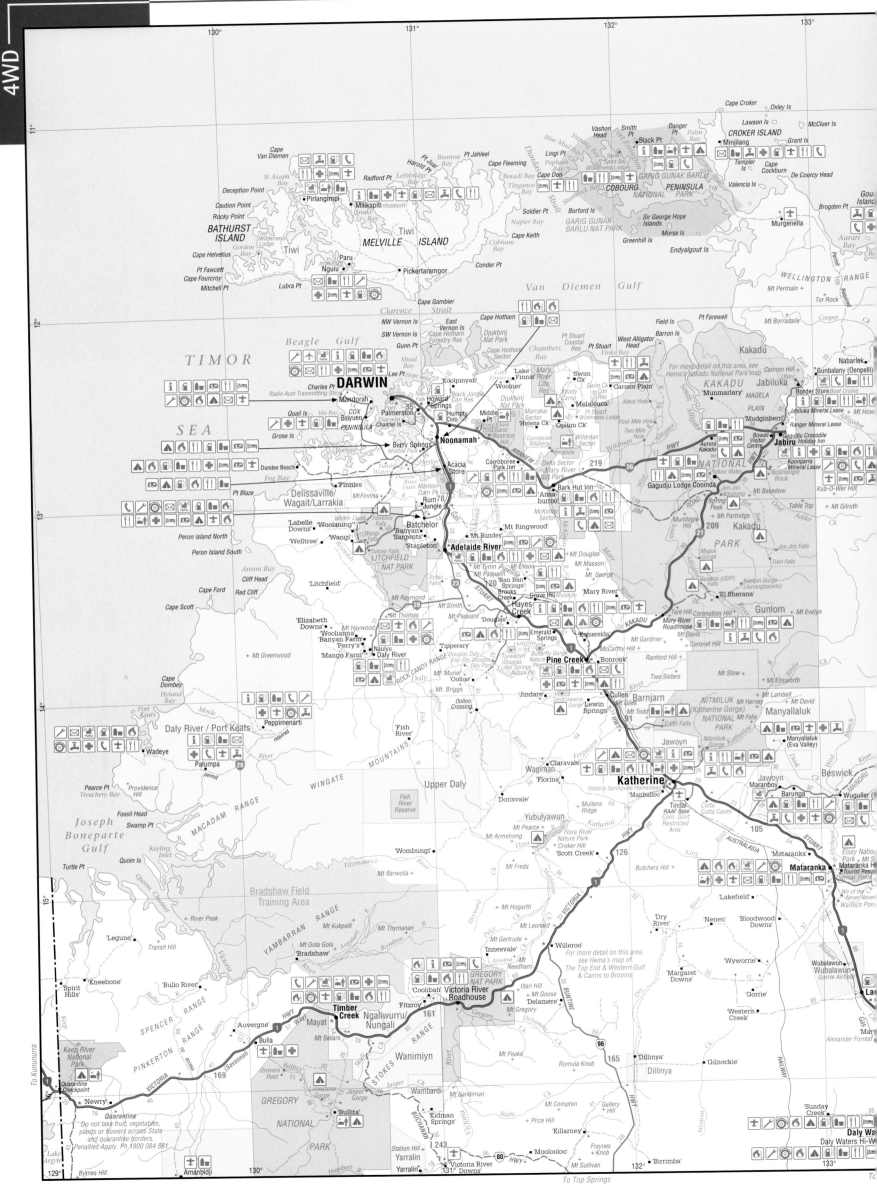

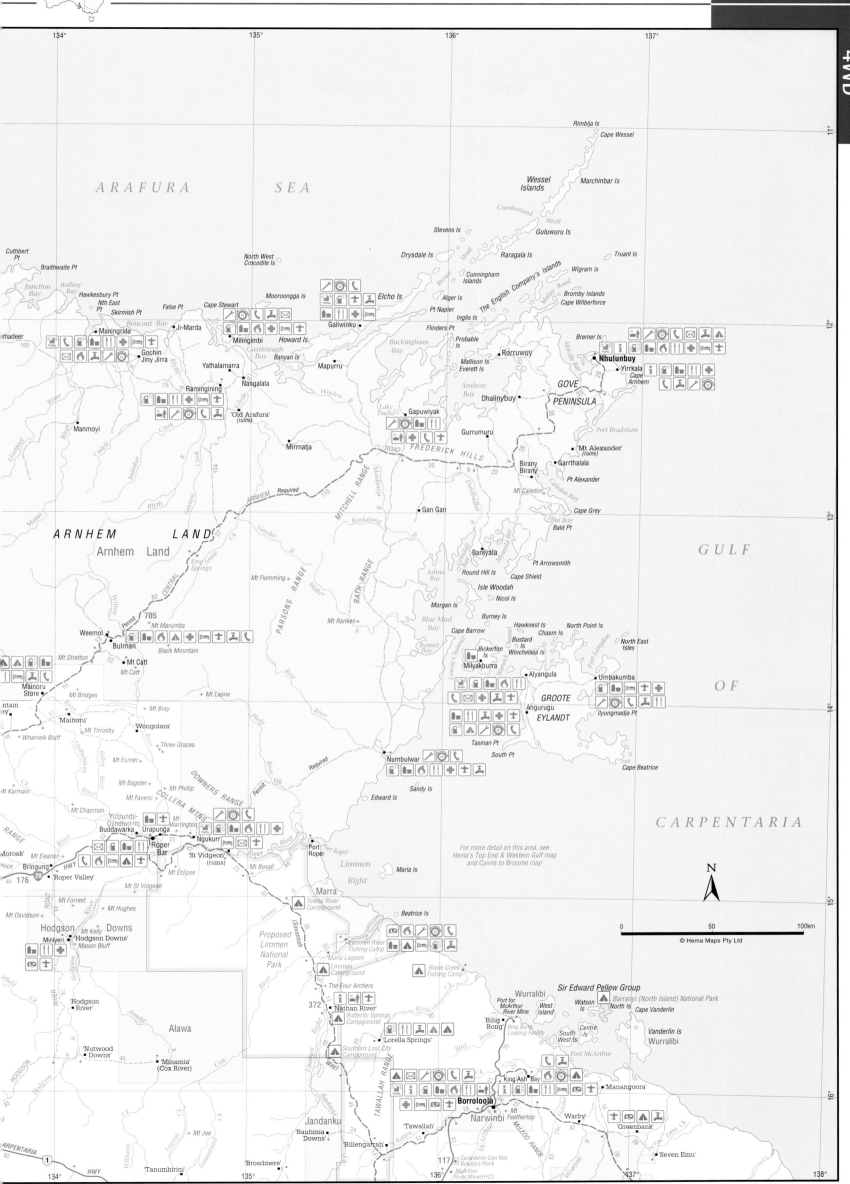

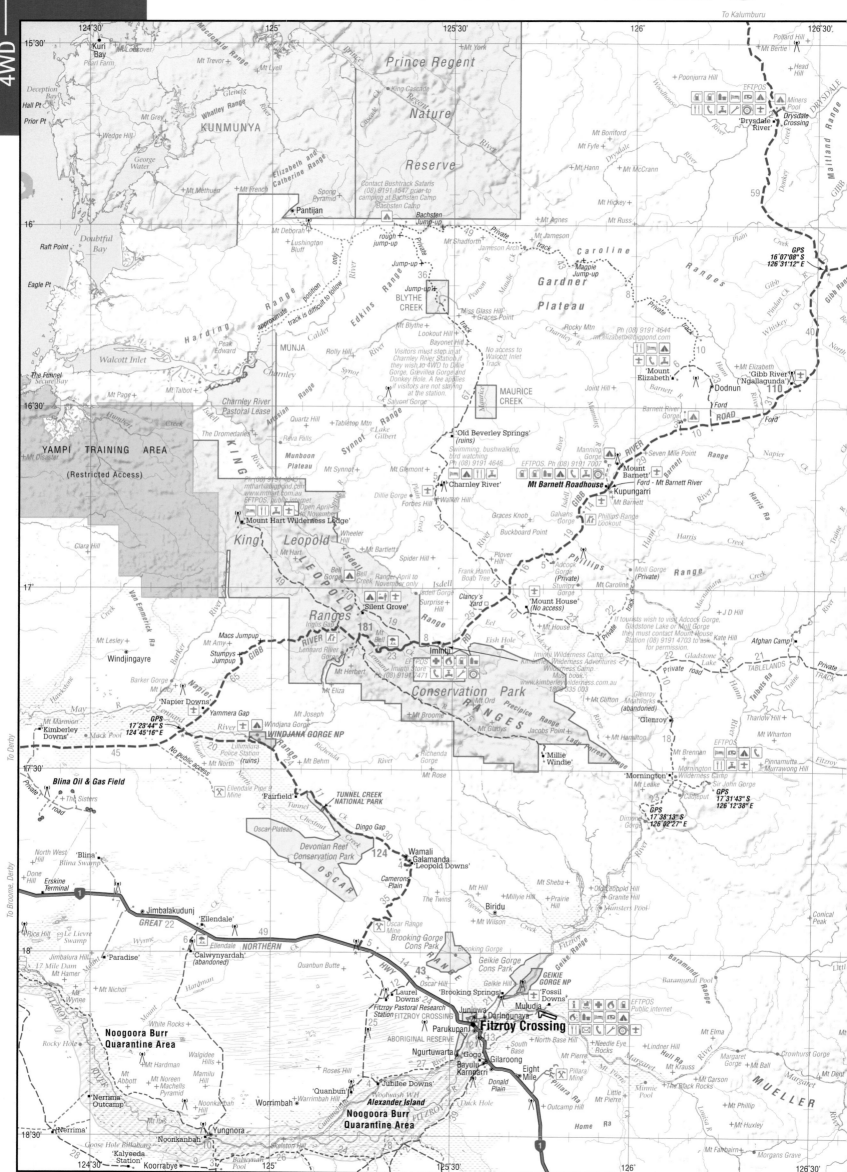

4WD

Map extracted from Hema's map "The Kimberley"
Copyright © Hema Maps Pty Ltd
Base data © Geoscience Australia

0 10 20 30 40 50 kilometres

Wyndham
Kununurra
Halls Creek

Noogoora Burr Quarantine Area

Nulla Nulla
Nine Mile
Parry
Goolime
Lagoons Nat Res
'The Diggers Rest'
'Home Valley'
Bindoola Creek and Jump Up (Ford)
Mt Cockburn North
Boab Prison Tree
The Grotto
Gap Point
Ph (08) 9169 4322

Durack River homestead was destroyed by floods in February 2002, and Jacks Waterhole is no longer accessible to the public.
'Durack River' (abandoned)
Ph (08) 9161 4321
Rollies Jump Up
Gregories Jump Up
New York Jump Ups
Mosquito Hills
Mt Dorophy
Mt Lawley
Wades Bluff
'Ellenbrae'
Bald Hill
Oomaloo Falls
Mt Edith
Bluey O'Malley's Crossing

GIBB
ROAD
252
59
23
26
Durack River
Pentecost Range
PENTECOST RIVER

r Plateau
Chapman Range
Private Overgrown track
'Pentecost Downs' 'Karunjie' (abandoned)
Gemini Hills
Bluff Face Range
Neal Knob
Salmond Gorge
Mt Throssell

El Questro Station Resort
Ph (08) 9169 1777
www.elquestro.com.au
'El Questro' Gorge
Emma Gorge Resort
Amalia Gorge
Zebedee Springs
Chamberlain Gorge

Fish Hole
Matteo Rock
Tier Gorge
Mt Rob
Optic Hill
Wuggubun
Wooloah
'Dunham River'
Doon Doon Roadhouse
Ph (08) 9167 8004
doondoonroadhouse@bigpond.com
153
39
62

Dunham Pilot Dam
Saw Ranges
CARR BOYD RANGES
Deception Ra
VICTORIA HWY 1
35
45
8

Kununurra
Mirima Village
HIDDEN VALLEY (MIRIMA) NAT PARK
Yuna Springs
Frank Wise Institute of Tropical Agricultural Research
Mt Septimus
'Ivanhoe'
Bell Springs
Four Mile
KEEP RIVER N.P.
Policemans Hole
Gurrandalng
Mirima
Dingo Springs
Quarantine Checkpoint
Barlton Gorge
Lake Argyle Tourist Village
Argyle Historic Homestead
Dam Wall
Spillway
Mt Brooking
Shangri La Mine
'Carlton Hill'
Point Spring Nat Res
'Kheebone'
'Spirit Hill'
Pincombe Range
Martin Bluff
Black Rock Falls
Middle Springs
Crocodile Farm
Ord River Nat Res

Lake Argyle
Behn Gorge
'Rosewood'
Byrnes Hill
The Twins
'Argyle Downs'
Mt Quirk
Reflex Hill
Mt Misery

'Kachana Station'
Air access only
Ph (08) 9168 2576
Crocodile Hole
Mt Lookout
Pompeys Pillar
Glen Hill
Mt Evelyn
Bow River Mine (abandoned)
Argyle Mine
Argyle Village
'Lissadell'
Mt Pitt
Mt Nyulasy
No public access
'Spring Creek'
Spring Hill
Mt Close
Darlu Darlu
DARLU
MALNGIN 2
'Bamboo Springs'

DURACK RANGE
Wilson River
Gordons Gorge
Devils Elbow
Chamberlain River
Patterson Gorge
Bow Hill
BOW RIVER

Turkey Creek Roadhouse
Ph (08) 9168 7882, EFTPOS
Gija Visitor Centre
Ph (08) 9168 7882
(holiday season only)
Warmun (Turkey Creek)
TURKEY CREEK
'Bow River'
Fig Tree Hole
'Texas Downs'
Mt Jarrad
GREAT NORTHERN HWY
Turkey Hill
Mt Button
Mt Deception
Boundary Knob
'Mistake Creek'
Mt Elder
View Hill
MALNGIN

VIOLET VALLEY
'Mabel Downs'
Kalungkurriji
Mt Remarkable
Wurrenranginy
Violet Hill
Lumuku
'Osmond Valley'
Mt Parker
Mt John
Purnululu Cons Reserve
Osmond Ra
Glass Hill
Mt Buchanan
PURNULULU NATIONAL PARK
Malangan
'New Ord River'
'Old Ord River'

Barangya
Mt King
'Bedford Downs'
Teronis Gorge
Yulumbu
Mt Bedford
Mt Wells
Dave Hill
GPS 17°25'49" S 127°59'34" E
Leycesters Rest
Spring Creek
Nicks Bite
Black Point
Kurrajong Camp
Echidna Chasm
Mini Palms Gorge
Piccaninny Gorge
Cathedral Gorge
Doughboy Hill
Ord Hill
Headley Knob
Mt Napier
DUNCAN ROAD

Tungarary Gorge
Springvale Hill
'Springvale'
Mabel Hill
Little Panton River
'Alice Downs'
Grant Peak
Alice Hill
Waardi Camp
Bellburn Airstrip
Bungle Bungle Wilderness Camp
Kimberley Wilderness Adventures
Wilderness Camp
Must book
www.kimberleywilderness.com.au
1800 335 009
No access to Purnululu National Park
The Island
'Turner'
'Turner' Hill
Kartang Rija
Mt Forster
Mt Coghlan
Crocodile Gorge
The Bluff
'Nicholson'
(Permission required)
Marella Gorge
Marella Hole
GPS 18°02'43" S 128°53'34" E
BUNTINE HWY

O'Donnell River Gorge
Three Sisters Hill
Fig Tree Pool
Neville Gorge
Mt Amhurst
One Palm Tree Gorge
'Moola Bulla'
Mardiwah Loop
Milba
China Wall
Halls Creek Mine
'Sophie Downs'
Old Halls Creek
Caroline Pool
Golden Crown
Mt Kinahan
Elvire Gorge
'Flora Valley'
'Great Antrim Plateau'
EFTPOS Public internet
Halls Creek
Ph (08) 9168 8999
Halls Creek Lodge
Nicholson Camp
Edward Ra
Antrim Plateau
Ant Hill
Addie Creek
Oaks Mtn
'Flora Valley'
Top Lily Pool

Nicholson Plains
'Koongie Park'
'Rockhole'
Mt Angelo
'Lamboo'
'Old Lamboo'
McAlly Hills
Eagle Hawk Crossing Gorge
Matheson Bluffs
Mount Amhurst
Scott's Dam
Ruby Queen Mine
White Elvire River Mine
'Old Elvire'
Wungu
Leedawooloo
Palm Springs
Sawpit Gorge
The Lily WH
Windoo Hill
Eva
Shut
GREAT NORTHERN HWY
TANAMI RD
DUNCAN ROAD
174

To Darwin
To Top Springs
To Fitzroy Crossing
To Billiluna

127° 127°30' 128° 128°30' 129°
15°30'
16°
16°30'
17°
17°30'
18°
18°30'

WESTERN AUSTRALIA
NORTHERN TERRITORY

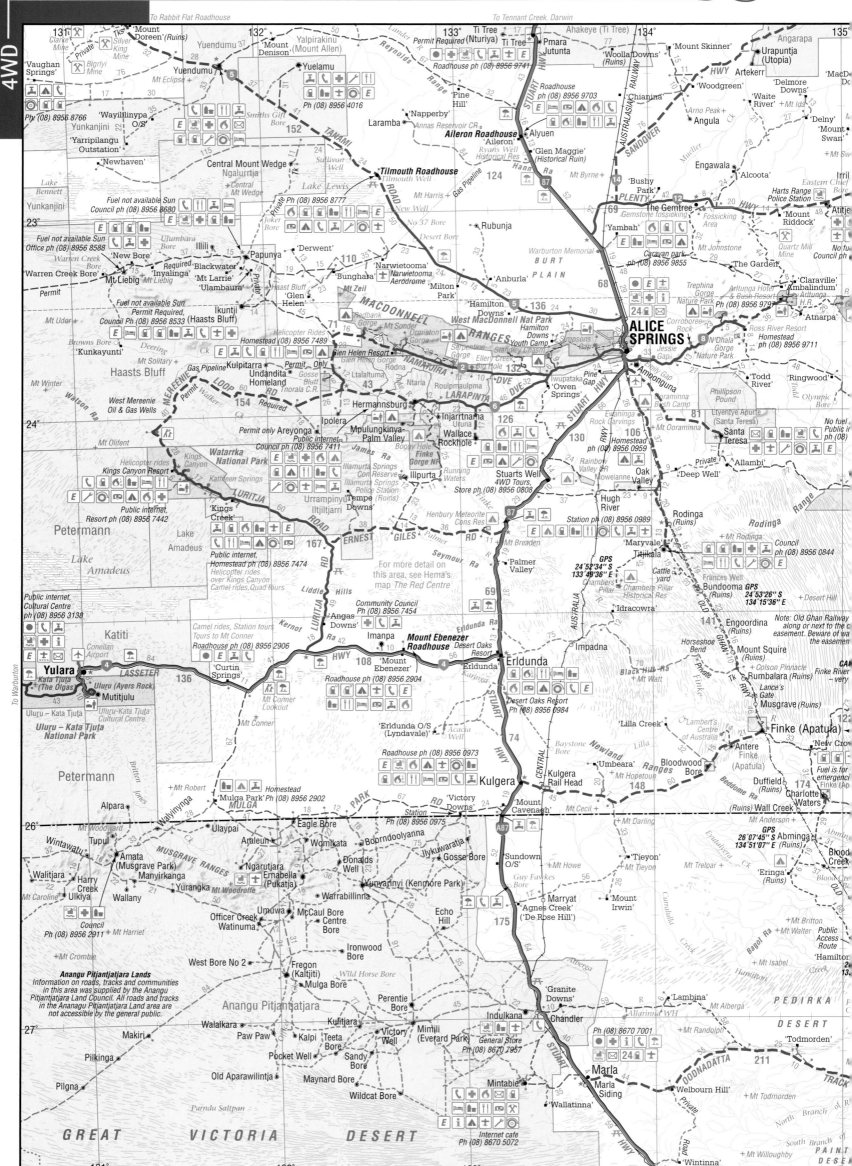

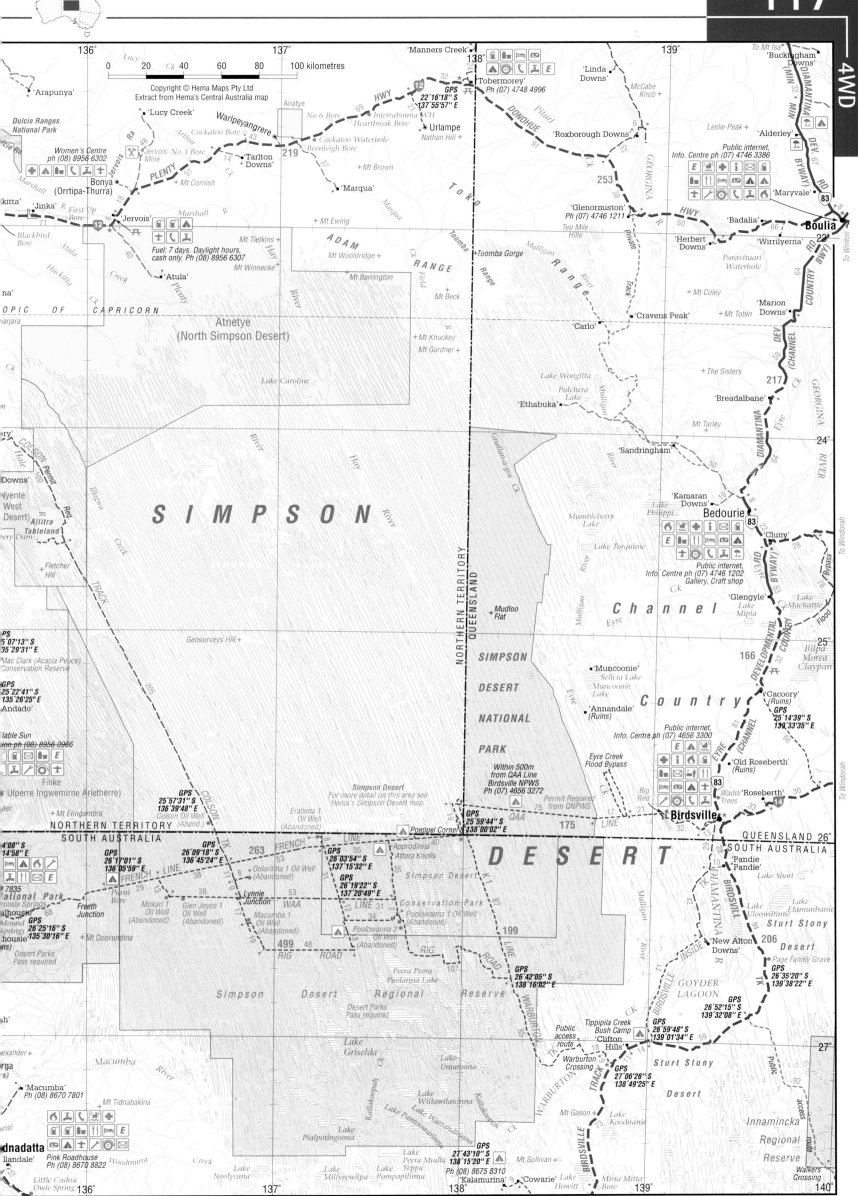

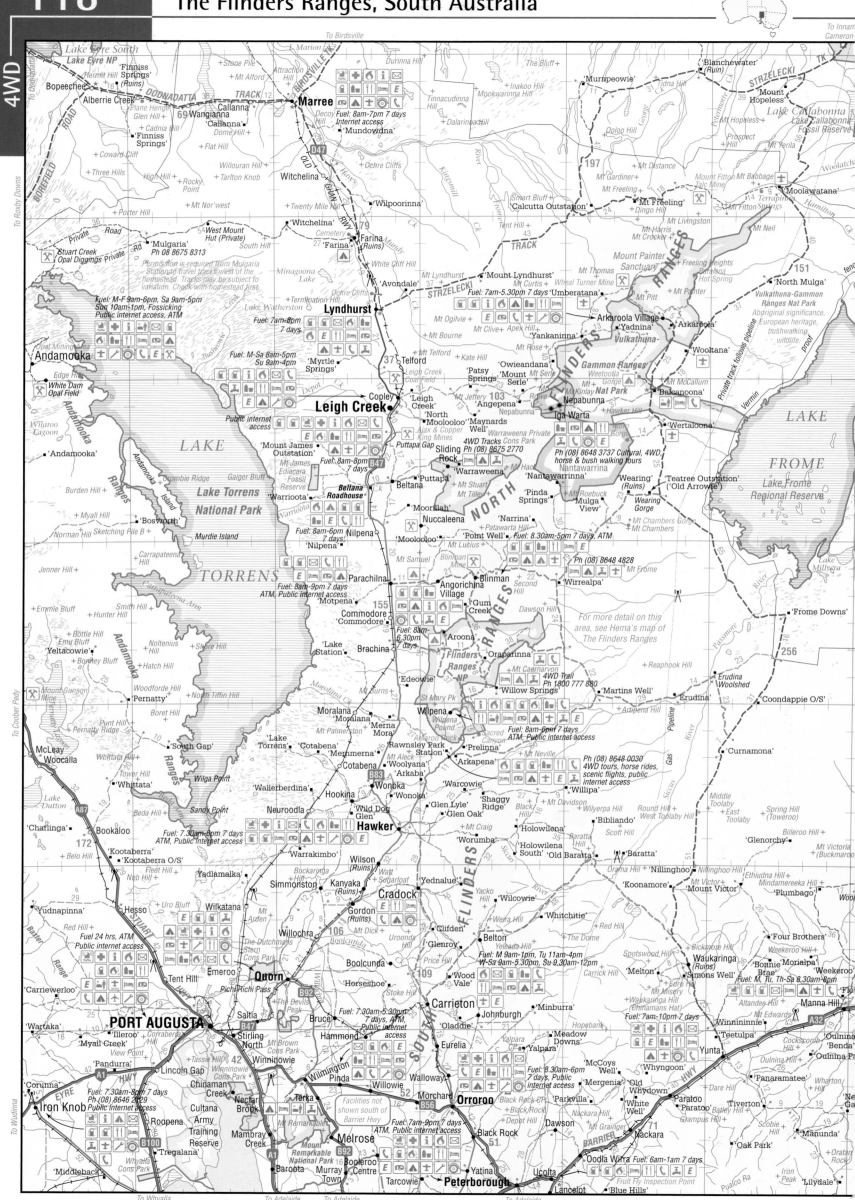